Hitler, the Allies, and the Jews

This book offers a new analysis of the Holocaust as a multiple trap, its origins, and its final stages, in which rescue seemed to be possible. With the Holocaust developing like a sort of doomsday machine set in motion from all sides, the Jews found themselves between the hammer and various anvils, each of which worked according to the logic created by the Nazis that dictated the behavior of other parties and the relations between them before and during the Holocaust. The interplay between the various parties contributed to the victims' doom first by preventing help and later by preventing rescue. These help and rescue efforts proved mainly self-defeating, and various legacies about them emerged during the Holocaust and are heatedly debated even today. Their real nature is uncovered here on the basis of newly opened archives worldwide.

Shlomo Aronson is a professor of Political Science at the Hebrew University of Jerusalem. He has written and edited numerous books on the Holocaust and Middle Eastern politics, including *David Ben-Gurion: The Renaissance Leader and the Waning of an Age* (1999) and *New Records – New Perspectives* (2002). Dr. Aronson has also been the organizer of conferences in the field, including the International Conference on Intelligence and the Holocaust, held at the Graduate Center, City University of New York, in June 2003, and "New Records – New Horizons," held in Israeli universities in December 1998, pertaining to new records opened worldwide on World War II, the Holocaust, and the birth of Israel.

Praise continued from back cover . . .

"*Hitler, the Allies, and the Jews* is an ambitious attempt to trace the interactions of a number of different parties before and during World War II and the Holocaust. It argues convincingly that the behavior of each party can best be understood as a partial reaction to its assessment of the others. A real contribution to the field of Jewish, Nazi, and World War II studies."

Richard Breitman, American University

"Shlomo Aronson's book presents a new way of looking at the history of the Holocaust. Aronson perceives the fate of the Jews as the result of a "trap," formed through the interaction of the German perpetrators, Jewish victims, and the Allied governments. The actions of each of these three groups have already been documented in numerous studies, but never have the interaction of all three been analyzed in one work. Aronson's book is a major contribution to Holocaust historiography."

Henry Friedlander, Emeritus, Brooklyn College

"Aronson's book is a triumph in profundity. A rich and original analysis, it provides extensive research into the entrapment and impotence of the Jewish people before and during the Holocaust. Shlomo Aronson has artfully incorporated significant and recently declassified intelligence records from a range of archives. The result is a fascinating suspense story that sometimes reads like fiction. Deftly navigating between the "big picture" and the telling detail, Shlomo Aronson provides us with answers to the question of how great democratic peoples and great democratic leaders could have failed to provide help to the trapped Jews at the beginning of the war and to rescue them at the end of the war. This study of the past raises disturbing questions about the present and the future."

Dr. Tuvia Friling, State Archivist of Israel

Hitler, the Allies, and the Jews

SHLOMO ARONSON

The Hebrew University of Jerusalem

CAMBRIDGE
UNIVERSITY PRESS

CAMBRIDGE UNIVERSITY PRESS
Cambridge, New York, Melbourne, Madrid, Cape Town, Singapore, São Paulo, Delhi

Cambridge University Press
32 Avenue of the Americas, New York, NY 10013-2473, USA

www.cambridge.org
Information on this title: www.cambridge.org/9780521838771

First published 2004
First paperback edition 2006
Reprinted 2007

Printed in the United States of America

A catalog record for this publication is available from the British Library.

Library of Congress Cataloging in Publication Data

Aronson, Shlomo, 1936 –
Hitler, the Allies, and the Jews / Shlomo Aronson.
    p.   cm.
Includes bibliographical references and index.
ISBN 0-521-83877-0
1. Hitler, Adolf, 1889–1945.   2. National socialism.   3. Holocaust, Jewish (1939–1945).
4. Jews – Persecutions – Germany.   5. World War, 1933–1945 – Diplomatic history.
6. United States – Foreign relations – 1933–1945.
D810.J4A76   2004
940.53/1822   2004040797

ISBN   978-0-521-83877-1 hardback
ISBN   978-0-521-68979-3 paperback

This book is dedicated to the memory of my mother's family, the Klenieczs, all of whom perished in Poland during 1942–1943, and to the memory of Shlomo Hacohen Aharonson, Rabbi of Kiev and Tel Aviv.

Contents

Acknowledgments

This book could not have been written without the help and knowledge of others. Professor Gerhard L. Weinberg of the University of North Carolina, Chapel Hill, was the foremost helper. He read various drafts of this manuscript, challenged various conclusions that I had adopted at earlier stages, and even corrected my Hebrew-German-English as far as this was possible. He certainly is not responsible for the final version in any way, but his patience, sense of humor, and especially knowledge of the sources and broad approach to World War II as a global drama were essential to making this book a contribution to an enormous existing scholarly literature.

Professor Henry Friedlander of CUNY read a previous draft of this book, and his wise corrections, critique, and knowledge produced a "road map" for me to rectify its shortcomings as best I could. Both Weinberg's and Friedlander's kind and warm personalities transformed my acquaintance with them into a lasting friendship.

Dr. Peter Longerich of the University of London and I worked together on the entry "The Final Solution" in the Yale *Encyclopedia of the Holocaust*. I have learned much from his year-long work in German and former Soviet archives. Much of his description of the phases of the Final Solution was incorporated with due credit into the chapters dealing with this topic, but he is not responsible in any way for my own interpretation of the decision leading to it.

Professor Yehuda Bauer of Hebrew University has read various early drafts of this book, and his pioneering work was a constant inspiration and a major source that I have quoted extensively, although my findings brought me finally to conclusions that differ from his.

Professor Richard Breitman of American University, now serving as historian, Inter Agency Working Group (IWG), Nazi War Crimes Disclosure Act, whose support and collaboration I gained years ago, was as helpful as before. Dr. Timothy Naftali of the University of Virginia, also serving as IWG historian, extended a helping hand as well. The interested reader is referred to the combined report of the IWG historians, *United States Intelligence and the Nazis*, published by NARA in 2004.

My archival research greatly profited from several generations of archivists at the U.S. National Archives and Records Administration (NARA), starting with the late John Mendelsohn and the very much alive Robert Wolfe, to the indispensable John Taylor and Lawrence MacDonald of the Military Branch, and to Dr. Greg Bradsher, the Director of the Holocaust-Era Assets Records Project at NARA, all of them walking mines of knowledge and immense personal support, which culminated in Dr. Bradsher's help in making me a NARA Fellow in 2001–2002 and in transforming my fellowship into a very fruitful one. This fellowship, made possible thanks to Dr. Michael Kurtz, Assistant Archivist, Office of Record Services, and to Mr. John W. Carlin, the Archivist of the United States, was combined with a consultancy to the Inter Agency Working Group, Nazi War Crimes Disclosure Act, whose work was conducted at NARA under Mr. David van Tassel, Staff Director of the IWG, and Mr. Larry Taylor, its Executive Director, whose help each in his own way made my final visit to the National Archives an experience in enjoyable support. Mr. R. Kirk Lubbes, whose company runs the organization and financing of the IWG, made my work as easy as possible. Mr. William Cunliffe, Special Assistant to NARA Staff, was discovered to be a most knowledgeable (but behind the scenes rather shy) expert, whose support in identifying newly released records proved vital.

Mr. Ralph Erskine and the BBC team, of which I was a consultant under Mr. David List and Mr. Detlef Siebert, were of great help in regard to the British Public Record Office at Kew, Surrey.

The other source of hereto unknown records was the Hagana Archive in Tel-Aviv, whose directors, Dr. Irit Keynan and Mr. Neri Ereli, were eager to help and placed their own personnel at my disposal. Dr. Yaakov Lazovik, the Director of Yad-Vashem Archive, provided me with immense technical help.

I am also indebted to the UCLA 1939 Club Holocaust Chair, which I held upon commencing this research. This endowment allowed me to start traveling to the U.S. National Archives and to the Franklin Delano Roosevelt Memorial Library in Hyde Park, New York. The United States Holocaust Memorial Museum, Center for Advanced Holocaust Studies, Mr. Paul A. Shapiro, Director, and the Visiting Scholars Program of the Library of Congress, directed by Dr. Lester I. Vogel, made the continuation of my research in the American archives possible by generously extending fellowships and office facilities. My ongoing research endowment attached to my position at Hebrew University, Jerusalem, was as essential as the other contributions in making this work possible. Hebrew University also contributed directly to the publication of this book. While in Los Angeles, I was treated almost as a member of the family of Stanley and Barbara Zax, and while in Washington I enjoyed the hospitality over years of Rabbi Samuel Z.

Fishman and his wife, Tamar, whose house in Bethesda, Maryland, became my second home.

Several "generations" of research assistants stood by me, and their hard work was matched only by their kindness and loyalty. I thank Ms. Rena Feiler of New York City, Ms. Margie Pinski of Bethesda, Maryland, Dr. Oded Brosh and Dr. Oded Heilbronner of Jerusalem, Mr. Eldad Haruvi of Kibbutz Alonim, and Mr. Greg Murphy of Colesville, Maryland.

Irit, my friend, was a spiritual source of strength and an invaluable helping hand during the struggle with the records of the darkest age in modern history.

Finally, I am indebted to Mr. Lewis Bateman, my Cambridge Senior Editor, whose patience, endurance, optimism and wise advice, and sense of humor guided me from the beginning through various stages of refining this manuscript until it met his sharp sense of required maturity.

Hebrew University, Jerusalem, January 2004

Abbreviations

Abwehr	German Military Intelligence
AFHQ	Allied Forces Headquarters
AJC	American Jewish Committee
AJDC	American Joint Distribution Committee
ASCI	Assistant Chief of Staff, U.S.
Ast	Abwehrstelle, German Army Intelligence station
AUS	U.S. Army
BA	Bundesarchiv, German Federal Archive
BBC	British Broadcasting Corporation
BDC	Berlin Document Center, copies at NARA
BdS	Befehlshaber der Sicherheitspolizei – regional head of the Nazi Security Police
CIA	Central Intelligence Agency, U.S.
CIC	Counter Intelligence Corps, U.S. Army
C in C	Commander-in-Chief
CID	Criminal Investigation Department, British
CIG	Counter Intelligence, "C" Group (Foreign Propaganda), CIC, U.S.
COI	Coordinator of Information – predecessor of OSS
CSDIC	Combined Services Detailed Interrogation Center(s), British
CZA	Central Zionist Archive
DSO	Defense Security Office, British MI5 (regional)
DDMI	Deputy Director of Military Intelligence, British
DMI	Director of Military Intelligence, British
EH	*Encyclopedia Hebraica*
FDR	Franklin Delano Roosevelt
FDR Library	Franklin Delano Roosevelt Memorial Library
FEA	Foreign Economic Administration, U.S.
FIS	Foreign Information Service – section of COI – U.S.

FO	Foreign Office, British
G-2	U.S. Army Intelligence
GC & CS	Government Code and Cypher School, British
Gestapo	Geheime Staatspolizei, Nazi Germany's Secret Police
GHQ	General Headquarters
GOC	General Officer Commanding
GOC in C	General Officer Commanding-in-Chief
Gruf.	SS Gruppenführer – SS Lieutenant General
GSA	German Studies Association
HCC	Historic Cryptographic Collection, U.S.
HGS	CID information received from JA
HIAS	Hebrew Immigrant Aid Society
HICEM	Jewish Refugee Society
HMSO	His or Her Majesty's Stationary Office
HQ	Headquarters
ICRC	International Committee of the Red Cross
IGCR	Intergovernmental Committee on Refugees
IMT	International Military Tribunal (Nuremberg)
ISK	Illicit Services, Knox
ISLD	Inter-Service Liaison Department – British MI6 in Middle East
ISOS	Intelligence Service Oliver Strachey – decrypts of German radio messages, British
ISOSICLE	subsection of ISOS, decrypts of German SD messages
ISSU6	Inter-Service Signal Unit 6 – SOE in Mediterranean, British
IZL	Irgun Zvai Leumi – National Military Organization, Zionist military underground
JA	Jewish Agency
JAG	Judge Advocate General, U.S.
JHGS	*Journal of Holocaust and Genocide Studies*
JIC	Joint Intelligence subcommittee, British Chiefs of Staff (COS)
JICAME	Joint Intelligence Collection Agency Middle East, U.S.
JIS	Joint Intelligence Staff, British
KL – KZ	Konzentrationslager, concentration camp(s)
LEHI	Lohami Herut Yisrael – Stern Group, radical Zionist
LRB	*London Review of Books*
MEIC	Middle East Intelligence Center, British
MEW	Ministry of Economic Warfare, British
MGFA	Militärgeschichtliches Forschungsamt, Potsdam

MID	Military Intelligence Division, War Department – U.S.
Mapai	Mifleget Poalei Eretz Yisrael – Zionist Labor Party
MI5	Home Intelligence, British
MI6	Secret Intelligence Service, British (also SIS)
MI9	British Intelligence Organization in charge of rescuing servicemen from behind enemy lines
MOI	Ministry of Information, British
MO4	SOE in Balkans, also Force 133, British
NARA	National Archives and Records Administration, U.S. (also NA)
NG documents	Nuremberg Government, U.S.
NKVD	Soviet Secret Police
NSA	National Security Agency, U.S.
NSDAP	National Socialist German Workers Party – The German Nazi Party
NYRB	*New York Review of Books*
NZO	New Zionist Organization, Jabotinsky's political party
Ogr.	SS Obergruppenführer – SS General
OKW	Oberkommando der Wehrmacht, Supreme HQ of the German Armed Forces
OKW/Chi VN	Chifrierabteilung of the OKW, verlässliche Nachrichten, reliable news read by the code breakers of the OKW
ONI	Office of Naval Intelligence, U.S.
ORT	Russian abbreviation of Organization for Rehabilitation and Professional Training among Jews
OSS	Office of Strategic Services, U.S. Intelligence Agency
OSS-FNB	OSS bureau in charge of information gathering on foreign nationals in the United States
OSS-R&A	OSS division in charge of research and analysis
OSS-SI	OSS division in charge of secret intelligence
OSS-SO	OSS division in charge of subversive and guerilla operations behind enemy lines
OSS-CID	Central Information Division
OSS-MO	Moral Operation, OSS branch in charge of "black propaganda"
OSUSCC	Office of U.S. Chief of Counsel, War Crimes (Nuremberg)
OWI	Office of War Information, U.S.
PICME	Political Intelligence, Middle East, British
PKP	Communist Party of Palestine
POW(s)	prisoner(s) of war
PPR	Polish Workers Party
PWE	Political Warfare Executive, British
PRO	Public Record Office, British

PS documents	Paris Storey records, assembled for IMT in Paris, France, in office commanded by Colonel Robert G. Storey, U.S.
PSF	President's Secretary Files (FDR Library)
RAF	Royal Air Force
RFSS	Reichsführer SS – head of the SS – Heinrich Himmler
RG	Record Group, U.S. National Archives
RSHA	Reichssicherheitshauptamt – Reich Main Security Office, combined Gestapo, Criminal Police, and SD organization of the SS and the Nazi state
RSS	Radio Security Service, British
SA	Sturm Abteilung, Nazi storm troopers
SD	Sicherheitsdienst of the Reichsführer SS – Nazi Party Intelligence Office and later Home and Foreign Intelligence Office of the Third Reich
SD Ausland	Amt (office) VI of the RSHA, in charge of foreign espionage
SHAEF	Supreme HQ, Allied Expeditionary Force, Europe
Shai	Sherut Yediot, Hagana's Home Intelligence
SIGINT	Signal Intelligence
SIM	Italian Secret Service
SIME	Security Intelligence, Middle East, British
SIPO	Sicherheitspolizei, Security Police – combined Gestapo and Criminal Police organization of the SS and the Nazi state
SIS	Signal Intelligence Service, U.S. – later SSS, SSA
SO	Special operations branch of the OSS
SOE	Special Operation Executive, organization in charge of subversion and guerilla warfare behind enemy lines, British
SPD	Sozial Demokratische Partei Deutschlands
SPOC	Special Projects Operations Center, British
SS	Schutzstaffel, Nazi Party and Third Reich's race and security order
SSO	Special Service Office, RAF
SSU	Strategic Service Unit(s), successor organization of OSS, U.S.
TAJB	*Tel Aviver Jahrbuch für deutsche Geschichte* – TA annual for German history
TICOM	Target Intelligence Committee, British and U.S.
U.K.	United Kingdom
U.S.	United States
USAFIME	United States Forces in the Middle East
VfZ	*Vierteljahreshefte für Zeitgeschichte*

VOA	Voice of America
WRB	War Refugee Board, U.S.
WVHA	Wirtschafts – und Verwaltungshauptamt, SS main office in charge of the concentration and death camps
X-2	Counterintelligence branch, OSS
ZOA	Zionist Organization of America

PART I

THE MAKING OF THE MULTIPLE TRAP

The Phases 1933–1939
The Initial and the Double Trap

The Nazi regime's treatment of Jews between 1933 and 1939 was gradually radicalized.[1] Each new phase was preceded by public acts of violence instigated by party radicals and then finally transformed into anti-Jewish legislation. The process could be described as a dialectical relationship between organized actions coming from below and legal–administrative measures undertaken from above. The forces at work (e.g., storm troopers and local party bosses) usually brought about Hitler's own intervention, which assumed the form of a state act and created thereby a new, temporary anti-Semitic consensus that provided a basis for the next, more radical wave of activities from below and intervention from above.

Each wave of more radical behavior was related to developments in domestic political and economic affairs in Germany itself and in its relations with foreign powers. Between each wave, however, there were periods of relative calm and stabilization. Yet the very nature of the Nazi phenomenon was dictated by its dynamism. It could not accept a status quo for a long time but perceived in it a return to the past, which it wanted to prevent. Hence, a policy aimed at retention of the status quo would have been an inadmissible gain for existing pre-Nazi forces and values in society such as Christianity, liberalism, and leftist ideologies. Therefore, from a Nazi point of view, such a development would have been a triumph for "Jewish-inspired" forces. At the same time, each wave of anti-Semitic radicalization incorporated the expansion of Nazi power at the expense of the traditional elites and created new institutions to deal with the issue and/or directed the

---

[1] Parts of this section were taken from the entry "The Final Solution: Preparations and Implementation" in *The Encyclopedia of the Holocaust* (Walter Laqueur, General Editor), (New Haven and London: Yale University Press, 2001, pp. 184–198), written by Dr. Peter Longerich and myself.

existing bureaucratic machineries toward the anti-Semitic schemes of the regime.[2]

The first wave of Nazi radicalism started in March 1933 with acts of violence against Jews as individuals and Jewish property. It was transformed into a general "boycott" organized by the new regime and culminated in the anti-Jewish legislation of spring 1933. With this wave, the Jews were completely removed from German public life. This phase brought about the rebirth of autonomous Jewish life in Germany, including a central representative body, and at the same time a large wave of emigration abroad. Nazi fears of a counterboycott by Jewish organizations abroad and the Nazis' interest in enhanced Jewish emigration led to an agreement with the Zionist organizations toward a limited transfer of Jewish assets to Palestine.

The second phase started with a wave of mob activities against Jews in several German cities in spring and summer 1935. It culminated in the Nuremberg anti-Jewish legislation, which implemented the biological separation of Jews and transformed them into second-class citizens, or rather subjects, of the Third Reich. Anti-Jewish economic legislation, demanded by the party radicals, was not yet adopted. However, massive pressure was brought to bear on Jewish businesses toward their "aryanization."

Here the significance of the "Four Year Plan" of 1936 must be emphasized. The Four Year Plan was geared toward mobilizing the German economy for war and making the German armed forces "ready for combat" by 1940. Inspired by the Soviet "Five Year Plans" and their success in at least creating an industrial base for the Soviet Union and in helping modernize the Red Army, Hitler – and Hermann Göring, his newly appointed economic czar – did not hide their intention to copy the Soviet example and outdo it. In the current scholarly literature, 1935 is understood to have been the point in time in which "the growth in Soviet military power was real, and the aims of their extensive rearmament were unmistakable," at least in terms of defending the USSR all around.[3] Yet the Nazi Four Year Plan had the target of "liberating" the German economy from the "Jewish yoke." In this connection, Hitler declared in a secret memo to Göring that "Judaism as a whole" should be made responsible for any damage done to German industry and hence to the German nation by (Jewish) individuals. The extremely violent nature of Hitler's anti-Semitic view combined with his future policy of expansion and global ambition was reflected here in two laws that he intended to enact. One would threaten industrial saboteurs with death, and the other would make the entire "criminal race" responsible for acts of sabotage committed

[2] Peter Longerich formulated the general description of the Nazi anti-Jewish policy before the Final Solution for our entry in *The Encyclopedia of the Holocaust*.

[3] See David M. Glanz, *Stumbling Colossus: The Red Army on the Eve of World War* (Lawrence: University of Kansas Press, 1998, p. 258).

by individuals.[4] This latter law proved to be unnecessary at the time since Jewish acts of sabotage inside Germany never took place, and on top of this continued Jewish deliberations about boycotting German exports did not materialize, obviously because of the fear that the Jews in Germany could suffer as a result of the foreign boycott. For his part, Hitler might have learned to use Jews as hostages – a point to which we shall return. Yet already at this stage, the foundation for the machinery of destruction of the Jews and others was being laid. First, in 1935, Himmler unified the German police forces under his command and started to amalgamate them with the SS while recruiting key persons in other state agencies as "Verbindungsführer," or those who served him on top of their loyalty to their civilian agencies. The fear – and contempt – toward the traditional German-Prussian bureaucracies and their exponents required such measures in Nazi eyes plus the recruitment of trustworthy people whose whole career would be tied to the regime's future. The Four Year Plan, with its anti-Semitic connotations, gave Göring extra powers in the sense that he (later also the highest-ranking military officer in the German armed forces) could overrule the regular government agencies and issue orders directly to ministers or subordinates of ministers or heads of other agencies.[5]

Much less known than Göring is Herbert Backe. Backe was Secretary of State in Richard Walter Darré's Ministry of Food Supply and Agriculture but also Göring's Commissioner of Food in the Four Year Plan and Himmler's Chief of Settlement in the SS's own Race and Settlement Main Office under Darré as nominal head. Born in Batumi, Georgia, Backe was a "border German" of unique background. According to his SS personal file, the Russian authorities arrested him upon the outbreak of World War I. He fled to Germany after the Bolshevik Revolution, was appalled by the conditions imposed on his old motherland by the British blockade (ascribed to Jews and their war against Germany), worked as a miner and studied agriculture, joined the Sturm Abteilung (SA, Nazi storm troopers) in 1922, and became a Nazi Ortsgruppenleiter in 1925.[6] A Diplom Landwirt (agronomist), Backe served as an expert at the NSDAP's Reichsleitung (i.e., in the Nazi Party's national headquarters in Munich), but in December 1933 he was recruited to the SS by Himmler and became both a "Führer" in the SS's own Race and Settlement Office and Secretary of State in the Food and Agriculture Ministry. In 1936, he also became Göring's Food Commissioner. In this capacity,

---

[4] See *Trials of War Criminals before the Nuremberg Military Tribunals under Control Council Law No. 10, Nuremberg, October 1946–April 1949*, Volume XII (Ministries Case), Doc. NI-4955, pp. 430–439.

[5] See Consolidated file of Interrogations of Hermann Göring, ED/288 – John Toland Papers – Container 12, U.S. Library of Congress. It should be noted that Göring, who was interviewed at length by American interrogators after his capture, was never asked about his direct role in the Final Solution.

[6] BDC personal file, NA microfilm, Roll 03343 SCO-025.

he could issue orders to his own minister and thus neutralize the somewhat incalculable Darré later on. Backe, like Hitler himself, was very much motivated by the lessons of the British blockade, which had significantly contributed to the collapse of the German home front and to the revolution of November 1918, while at the same time he was regarded as an expert on Russia. His role in both areas, related to his key positions as Food Commissioner and Himmler's key aid, will be elaborated further when we discuss 1940 and the "Final Solution" decision itself.

The third phase of the Nazis' persecution of the Jews started with a series of anti-Jewish acts of violence immediately following the Austrian "Anschluss" in March 1938 and culminating in the pogroms of November 9–11, 1938, known as "Kristallnacht." This previously unprecedented violence was crowned by collective punitive measures and the most radical legislation to that point, which was aimed at total expropriation of Jewish property and forced emigration. The policy of forced emigration was institutionalized in January 1939 when a Central Office for Emigration was created within the Geheime Staatspolizei (Gestapo) following the establishment of a similar office in Vienna in summer 1938. This meant that the handling of the "Jewish Problem" rested more and more with the SS, while, at the same time, the forced emigration policy could be seen in Nazi eyes as not only allowing them to be rid of unwanted Jews but as exporting anti-Semitism abroad.

Before the outbreak of the war, Hitler was ready to allow Jewish emigration to Palestine, declared by the British and by the League of Nations to be a "Jewish Homeland" and later harboring an option of Jewish sovereignty.[7] Yet Palestine proved to be the scene of the Arab rebellion of 1936–1939, which developed into a major revolt against the British (and the Jews) in 1937. Thus, Arab actions enter our picture in the sense that the Nazis might have seen in the difficulties that emerged for the British in the Middle East due to Jewish emigration, and the Arab responses to it, yet another double gain to themselves as a result of the forced exodus of Jews to Palestine. Yet the same calculation led the British to curb Jewish emigration into Palestine once

---

[7] See Michael Wildt, *Die Judenpolitik des SD 1935 bis 1938* (Stuttgart: Schriftenreihe für Zeitgeschichte, Deutsche Verlags-Anstalt, 1995, pp. 40–45), regarding the "Palestine oriented" policy of the SD and its ups and downs and limits, dictated among other reasons by the Arab rebellion of 1936–1939; see further "The SD and Palestine: New Evidence from Captured German Documents in Moscow," Dr. Wildt's contribution to *New Records – New Perspectives*, ed. Shlomo Aronson (Sede Boker: Ben-Gurion Research Institute, 2002, pp. 64–77) and see Yehuda Bauer, *Jews for Sale? Nazi–Jewish Negotiations, 1933–1945* (New Haven and London: Yale University Press, 1994, pp. 44–54), Dalia Ofer, *Illegal Immigration during the Holocaust* (Jerusalem: Yad Izhak Ben-Zvi, 1988) (in Hebrew), especially Chapter 1: "The Illegal Immigration before WWII" and part 1: "The Illegal Immigration 1939–1941," and Francis R. Nicosia, "Ein nützlicher Feind. Zionismus im nationalsozialistischen Deutschland 1933–1939, *Vierteljahreshefte für Zeitgeschichte (VfZ)*, 37(1989): 367–400.

they were preparing for war with Nazi Germany, which was a concession to Arabs and Muslims.

The timing of the enhanced stage of forced emigration by the Nazis may be explained by a combined sense of success and failure, as expressed in typical Sicherheitsdienst (SD) reports,[8] according to which the regime had been stalled since the Olympic games of 1936. The Jews were still a part of the German economy, although removed from the political sphere, and emigration grew slowly.

Thus, we can follow the unwinding of the initial trap when the government of a modern, hereto civilized nation degraded its own citizens to the level of persecuted subjects and sought to deport them to foreign lands by force. Having lost their previous civil rights, their identity, and large parts of their property, if not all of it, these trapped people found themselves totally at the mercy of foreign powers.

The related double trap can be described as follows. For Hitler, the transformation of Central Europe and parts of Eastern Europe into a German-inhabited racial superpower was a conditio sine qua non; that continental Lebensraum (the racial "living space") was to be "judenrein" (Free of Jews) at any rate. However, the forced emigration of the Jews from at least a part of that territory to begin with could be doubly beneficial: If spread all over the West, or in Western spheres of influence, the West being the only possible shelter for Jews due to its liberal traditions and Jewish influence therein, Germany would not only be rid of the Jews but Jewish refugees – through their admittance in large numbers, the public attention given to them in times of ongoing economic stress, social tensions, and limited rearmament – would fan anti-Semitism in the host countries and thereby serve the German interest in the relevant countries and possibly weaken their ability to resist Germany. If admitted to the Western world, anti-Semitism could thus help create a popular common base with Nazism, threatening the popular base of Western elites. This could force them to be more susceptible to German demands or risk trouble at home, not only with the resurrected Germany and its genial leader but thanks to the pressure of "International Jewry" and local Jews who would do their best to help their brethren. If this was the Nazi aim (and here lies the double trap), the relevant host nations were destined to refuse to play the Nazi game because of their domestic conditions and their growing sensitivity to the Nazi challenge to their interests and

---

[8] See Wildt, *Die Judenpolitik*, pp. 84–105, Einleitung, and the relevant SD reports published by him starting in 1934 and my own discussion of the early Jewish politics of Gestapo and SD on the basis of several SD reports quoted therein, in Shlomo Aronson, *Reinhard Heydrich und die Frühgeschichte von Gestapo und SD* (Stuttgart: Deutsche Verlags-Anstalt, 1971) in which I have underlined the role of the SD as a factor contributing to the "race for the worst" among the Nazi agencies dealing with Jews. See also Otto D. Kulka, *The Jewish Question in the Third Reich: Its Significance in National Socialist Ideology and Politics* (Jerusalem: Hebrew University, 1975), Vol. II, Dok. 28, SD Lagebericht of January 1938.

values, which would require a national consensus to resist the Nazis in due course. For Hitler, however, any resistance to his schemes as a whole would assume Jewish connotations – not just because of expedient, propaganda-oriented, "functional" reasons but because the West was indeed perceived by the Nazis as if it was "Jewish ridden," and also could be portrayed as "Jewish influenced" when it opposed Nazi Germany due to its traditions and system of government.[9] Actual Jewish political influence in the Western countries was nil, and any Nazi arrangement with the Bolshevik and hence Jewish-inspired Soviet Union was to be temporary, pending Stalin's own behavior and that of the West.

If Herman Rauschning – the former Nazi Gauleiter of Danzig – can be trusted, in spite of some doubts about his truthfulness,[10] he was told by Hitler that the Jews were his – the Führer's – most important trump card against "the democracies" and that Jewish refugees were "a valuable hostage to me." The Jewish "asset" in Hitler's hands against the democracies could be interpreted (according to Rauschning's book, which was available in English in 1939) in the sense that Hitler would use the Jews in the West to work against Western interests and expose the West as being influenced by Jews in due course. Hitler could blame Western elites for being Jewish-ridden or Jewish-influenced if they opposed him, and he hoped to involve the Jews themselves and their alleged tools in a process that could discredit the elites in the eyes of the masses by pushing them to accept the unwanted refugees or face an unwanted war. The behavior of foreign Jews and foreign governments combined would decide the fate of the hostages when it came to war: a limited war, securing Nazi goals step-by-step, or a global one, which could entail the hostages' total doom. Foreign governments did not necessarily accept the linkage created by Hitler between Jews and his hegemonic plans in Europe, which he then transformed into an open threat to kill the Jews altogether should it come to a second world war in his "prophecy speech" of January 30, 1939.

In fact, this speech marked the first time that Hitler publicly addressed the Jewish question in Europe as an issue of life or death in a continental context and in the context of a possible second world war. He proclaimed that if "international finance Jewry *in and outside Europe* (italics added) should succeed in thrusting the nations once more again into a world war, then the result will not be the Bolshevization of the earth and with it the victory of Jewry, but the elimination of the Jewish race in Europe."[11] This statement

---

[9] See Adolf Hitler, *Monologe im Führerhauptquartier, 1941–1944. Die Aufzeichnungen Heinrich Heims*, Werner Jochmann, ed. (Hamburg: Albrecht Knaus Verlag, 1980, pp. 93, 383–384).

[10] Hermann Rauschning's *Hitler Speaks* was first published in English in London (London: T. Butterworth, 1939, p. 233).

[11] Text in Max Domarus (ed.), *Hitler: Reden und Proklamationen 1932–1945* (Würzburg: Edition Schmidt, 1962–1963, Bd. II, pp. 1056–1058).

could be understood as an open declaration of Hitler's basic intention to eliminate the Jews anyway, especially because he was the one who was thrusting the nations into war. The same speech could, however, be seen as a threat aimed at the West, allegedly influenced by Jews, to refrain from opposing Hitler's hegemonic plans in Europe by force, which would allow him to deal separately with Poland, then with France and Britain (depending on London's own behavior), then with the Jews under his control, possibly by exiling them into some godforsaken place, and then, when the circumstances allowed it, with the USSR, culminating finally in a grand reckoning with the United States.

2

Western Responses

Let us now examine several Western reactions to Hitler's forced emigration policy, which followed the pogroms of 1938. I shall repeat only briefly the more recent research results of those qualified historians who have studied British and American refugee policies at the time of Hitler's rise to power and since that time, not because they are not important but because they are, and the reader may consult them separately.[1] Indeed, after his reelection campaign of 1936, President, Franklin D. Roosevelt (FDR) became more open to Jewish pleas to help their compatriots. Yet this generated angry reactions in the U.S. Congress,[2] which threatened to cut even the existing immigration quotas, and from 1937, FDR was caught in the pendulum of rising conservative reaction to his policies in general. Public opinion polls carried out in 1938 yielded an enormous vote against allowing a large number of Jewish exiles from Germany to immigrate to the United States. Hence, another aspect of the double trap was the growing wave of anti-Semitism in the United States, in some collusion with the persecution of the Jews by the Nazis instead of a growing sympathy with their plight, as officials, politicians, and ordinary people feared more Jewish refugees and Jewish interest at home would drive them to war abroad.

The president considered settling the Jews elsewhere rather than in his country. Like many other members of his class, FDR was not free of various

---

[1] See Richard Breitman and Alan M. Kraut, *American Refugee Policy and European Jewry, 1933–1945* (Bloomington and Indianapolis: Indiana University Press, 1987); Tommie Sjöberg, *The Powers and the Persecuted: The Refugee Problem and the Intergovernmental Committee on Refugees* (Lund: Lund University Press, 1991, Part IV, pp. 126–165).

[2] Sjöberg, *The Powers and the Persecuted*, pp. 105–108, especially p. 107, also quoting Charles Stember's not uncontested research: "Of more serious concern is the hostile attitude towards Jews held by the ordinary American." After analyzing a number of polls taken in the years 1938–1940, Stember concluded that "as many as 60 per cent of Americans perceived Jews as a group possessing objectionable traits, such as greed, dishonesty, and aggressiveness." (Charles E. Stember, *Jews in the Mind of America*. New York, London: Basic Books, 1966.)

anti-Semitic perceptions of foreign Jews, and therefore he might have considered them as a political burden whose admittance in large numbers, if allowed by Congress at all, would complicate and overshadow his real priorities.[3] In fact, FDR adopted a verbal strategy of condemnation against Nazi Germany, culminating in the Evian Refugee Conference of 1938, which created a framework of Western international cooperation in the so-called Intergovernmental Committee on Refugees (IGCR) that was aimed at the very beginning against the prevailing isolationist mood while avoiding any far-reaching commitment toward the refugees themselves. More German-Austrian refugees were allowed to enter the United States between March 1938 and September 1939 than ever before, but the numbers were small in comparison to the dire need.[4] However, the impression was created that FDR's growing anti-Fascist and especially anti-Nazi rhetoric and the plight of the Jews were intertwined, the latter being the source of the former, and indeed this would become a major Nazi argument. Hence, the President tried to keep this impression from taking dangerous routes and also considered views dictating caution that were expressed by isolationists and defeatists (such as his own ambassador to St. James's Court in the late 1930s in conversation with Neville Chamberlain) without necessarily accepting all of them.[5]

The American ambassador was obviously Joseph P. Kennedy, who is quoted by Arthur M. Schlesinger, Jr., as having told Herbert Hoover, following the British guarantee given to Poland, that Neville Chamberlain, the British Prime Minister, had said to him that "he hoped the Americans and the Jews would now be satisfied but that he [Chamberlain] felt that he had signed the doom of civilization."[6] In fact, Chamberlain's reluctance to oppose Hitler before 1939 was very much anchored in economic motives and realpolitik. Like others, he believed that the Versailles treaty ending World War I humiliated Germany, and yet he recognized the German Reich, once its restrictions melted away, as the most important Central European power; he was ready to give Hitler that status, he recognized that a new war might ruin the British Empire, and he might have expected the United States to assume the role of a new superpower at British expense after the war, a prospect he disliked. He

---

[3] Anti-Semitic comments from Roosevelt and even Harry Truman are quoted in Michael Beschloss, *The Conquerors: Roosevelt, Truman and the Destruction of Nazi Germany 1941–1945* (Waterville, MA: Thorndike Press, 2002), much later against the background of the Holocaust.

[4] Breitman and Kraut, *American Refugee Policy and European Jewry*, p. 74. About Evian and the American initiative toward the creation of the Intergovernmental Committee on Refugees (IGCR) see Sjöberg, *The Powers and the Persecuted*, pp. 99–105, and Bauer, *Jews for Sale?* pp. 30–43.

[5] See Arthur M. Schlesinger, Jr., *Robert Kennedy and His Times* (Boston: Houghton Mifflin, 1978, p. 34), and William W. Kaufman, "Two American Ambassadors: Bullitt and Kennedy," in *The Diplomats 1919–1939*, eds. Gordon Craig and Felix Gilbert (Princeton, NJ: Princeton University Press, 1953).

[6] Schlesinger, *Robert Kennedy and His Times*, p. 84.

thus might have preferred to talk to the American ambassador about Jews and civilization, not about his real concerns. But in fact Chamberlain was an ordinary insular politician, who might have shared Lord Beaverbrook's fear that the Jews were dragging Britain into war.[7] Winston Churchill, and to a growing degree Franklin Roosevelt, understood by now that Adolf Hitler and his "new" Germany were the utmost danger to civilization, even more than communism, but FDR had no mandate to act under the rigid rules of the U.S. Constitution and the nation's political tradition. The British did, if one forgets the domestic consensus necessary to fight another general war. Yet the question remained whether this war would become a "Jew's war." Lord Beaverbrook is quoted by Tony Kushner[8] as having written as late as 1938: "They [the Jews] do not mean to do it. But unconsciously they are drawing us into war. Their political influence is moving us in that direction." Certainly there were "influential Jews" in Britain and in the United States, but at that time all of them combined had much less influence than the Prime Minister himself, Lord Beaverbrook himself, and press magnates such as Lord Rothermere, whose papers were sometimes virulently anti-Semitic. Perhaps Lord Beaverbrook meant the most outspoken members of the Jewish Board of Deputies in England, radical individuals such as the publisher Victor Golancz, whose interests were usually non-Jewish and antiestablishment, Professor Felix Frankfurter in America, whose ties with FDR loosened greatly after 1939, or the writer and columnist Walter Lippmann, who did not want to know about Jews then or later.[9] Hitler, however, saw Jewish money and power behind them all, which allegedly silenced Rothermere's press or was at least argued to have done so as a matter of common wisdom. In fact, Rothermere's press were "silenced" regarding Nazi Germany because of Hitler's own behavior and outright mistakes in understanding British – no less so American – behavior, values, and politics, which would have been his supreme duty to learn about before he found himself at war with them[10] but which were divorced totally from specific Jewish interests.

Joe Kennedy is quoted by Schlesinger as having written in a draft autobiography that "a number of Jewish publishers and writers" assailed him

7 See Tony Kushner, *The Persistence of Prejudice: Antisemitism in British Society during the Second World War* (Manchester and New York: Manchester University Press, 1989, p. 12).

8 Ibid.

9 See Ronald Steel, *Walter Lippmann and the American Century* (New York: Vintage Books, Random House, 1981), especially pp. 186–196. Lippmann had endorsed in a *New Republic* article in 1915 the view that "Jew-baiting produced the ghetto and is compelling Zionism. The bad economic habits of the Jew, his exploiting of simple people, had caused his victims to assert their own nationality." (Steel, *Walter Lippmann and the American Century*, p. 189.) Since then he usually preferred silence in regard to Jewish matters altogether.

10 In his *Monologe*, Hitler spoke on August 31, 1942, in a less definite fashion, mixing up British upper-middle-class "interests in rearmament" as a factor per se and Jewish influence. Such a qualification could be found in Hitler's views of Stalin's anti-Semitism (Hitler, *Monologe*, pp. 378ff.).

after he made his opinion publicly known against war with Nazi Germany. They wanted war, he thought: "They should not be condemned for such an objective. After all, Hitler was destroying the lives and the fortunes of their compatriots. Compromise could hardly cure that situation; only the destruction of Nazism could do so." Joe Kennedy did not identify with the plight of the Jews under Hitler's control enough to risk the destruction of "civilization"[11] by opposing Hitler by force, even if he well understood that from a certain viewpoint, which he tainted as "Jewish," no compromise with Hitler was possible; in fact, it was Churchill's view that saw for Western civilization no way to avoid destroying Nazism, whereas Kennedy was talking of saving civilization by not risking war with Nazism. Civilization was for him Western and Christian – anti-Bolshevist, not Jewish–Christian as it is called today. Jewish efforts to underline their own contribution to Western culture and humanity at the time could not dissuade Kennedy from his conviction that his brand of "civilization" could coexist with Hitler. The trouble was that, in Hitler's view Western civilization was Jewish–Christian, a fact corroborated by British rejection of his hegemonic plans in Europe and Roosevelt's open rejection of Nazism. Churchill, the aristocratic liberal, the democratic Tory, the half-modern traditionalist, the anti-socialist agitator, rather than Joe Kennedy, understood enough of Hitler's challenge to Western civilization and to British interests, traditions, and values once a 200 or 300 million strong SS empire stretched from the Rhine eastward. He perceived in Hitler the German gutter running berserk, under the most primitive hater, who allowed instincts, forces, and values that Western civilization has fought and tried to control for at least a millennium to assume a modern political form and take roots in the soil of a great power.[12] In this context, Judaism did contribute significantly to Western civilization, in Churchill's eyes, and this was also diametrically true in Hitler's eyes. For Chamberlain, the offshoot of upper middle-class interests and fears mixed with aristocratic Tory obligations and pride, the issue seems to have remained for a long time the problem of elites and masses. Hitler had indeed mobilized the German masses by now, so why and when should Chamberlain oppose them and pay the expected disastrous price rather than arrange a deal with them, and did he have a mandate from the British masses to oppose him by force? Obviously, the more Chamberlain conceded to Hitler, the more the latter asked for and grasped for afterward, and Churchill's minority view of Nazi Germany proved to be right and finally destroyed both Chamberlain and Hitler.

In fact, Hitler went after Jews, Judaism, and Christianity by invoking Jews and Judaism as the main issue, aspiring at the same time to create a dominant German superpower, whereas Chamberlain and Kennedy did not

---

[11] Schlesinger, *Robert Kennedy and His Times*.
[12] See Churchill's *The Second World War*: Volume I, *The Gathering Storm*, Hebrew translation (Tel-Aviv: Am-Hasefer Publishers, 1957, p. 92).

necessarily accept the connection between Jews, Judaism, and Christianity and Western values in general. Although once they decided to resist Hitler, even if truly shocked by Kristallnacht and other Nazi atrocities accompanied by repeated German bids to agree on mass Jewish emigration, as proposed by Hjalmar Schacht and his successors in this capacity in Hitler's name as late as 1939 and mentioned later by Hitler's adjutant as the "incredible bid" he made to the British in 1937,[13] people like Chamberlain tended to treat the two issues of the Nazi strategic–political challenge and the Jewish Question separately, although combined by Hitler into one. Hitler's bid for hegemony in Central and Eastern Europe was unacceptable, as was his anti-Semitic postulate, which made the Americans and British seem to be Jewish tools. Yet – following the atrocities of Kristallnacht – at least the entry of various "Kindertransporte" (transport of children) into Britain was allowed, while the entry of Jews into Palestine was radically restricted, and its future as an Arab country was promised. Then the British Isles were closed when war broke out. The British elite was up to convince themselves and then the masses that Hitler should be destroyed for the sake of their own interests and their British values. This must not have been done mainly because of the "persecution" of the Jews, because the Jews were not the issue at stake whereas for the Arabs they were, and hence Arab demands regarding the curbing of entry of Jews into Palestine had to be taken into consideration. Jews should not become a political commodity at Hitler's hands that would allow him to maintain that the British and the French, by guaranteeing Polish sovereignty and then adhering to it, declared war against him and German "rights" in Eastern Europe were Jewish tools, which they of course were not. They were also determined to avoid the impression that they were in order to assemble the support of the masses at home to fight Hitler and neutralize Arab and possibly Muslim wrath as best they could. Whether this was politically the only course open to them is a historical question that we will look at when we study Churchill's behavior as prime minister. Churchill seems to have had both the interest and the power to change this attitude and impose his will on the many "anti-Semites," as he himself called several highly placed officials dealing with the Middle East, among other things.[14] But the very nature of the trap situation was not caused by British anti-Semites. For Hitler, the Jews

---

[13] See Gerhard Engl, *Heeresadjutant bei Hitler 1938–1943: Aufzeichnungen des Major Engel*, edited by and with commentary by Hildegard von Kotze; *Schriftenreihe der Vierteljahreshefte für Zeitgeschichte* 29 (Stuttgart: Deutsche Verlags-Anstalt, 1974). Engel was Hitler's Army adjutant at the time, and his diary, published twenty years after the war ended, should be used rather critically, but it does reflect Hitler's way of putting things in real time, such as the entry dated October 8, 1939, and the one dated February 2, 1941.

[14] For Churchill and the Jewish Problem, see Bernard Wasserstein, *Britain and the Jews of Europe 1939–1945* (London, Oxford: Institute of Jewish Affairs and Clarendon Press, 1979, pp. 207, 227, 305, 345).

finally trapped themselves when he became their Haman, Chamberlain caused the rest when he declared war on Nazi Germany, as did Churchill when he continued it, and as did Roosevelt when he supported the British as best he could, all of which opened the road to the end of the forced emigration policy and to the Final Solution.

The Middle East situation was dictated among other reasons by the small size of the regular British Army combined with Arab military action and threats. Since regular British Army units had been committed to put down the Arab rebellion in Palestine (which had commenced in earnest in 1937), they would be badly needed at home if a long war with Hitler's Germany was planned, although hopes were maintained that the war might be short due to Germany's economic vulnerability. The Arabs had to be appeased, obviously at Jewish cost, if the British wanted to raise the huge armies deemed necessary to fight the Jews' worst enemy and maintain calm in the vital Arab–Muslim region. But since Hitler was pushing Jews out at that stage and not yet killing them en masse, the impression could have been created among the Zionists and Jews abroad, as it was and still is, that the closure of Palestine's gates to Jewish refugees under Arab pressure, when they still could find a haven in the British mandate territory designated as the only "Jewish homeland," provided that the rights of the Arabs were not to be impaired, meant in fact their death sentence, imposed by the British (and Arabs). This decision was made before Hitler's Final Solution decision and Hitler's own decision to close the gates of Europe upon the trapped Jews were made.

Yet even the limited transports of children that were allowed entry into Britain were not simple to undertake when a hesitant cabinet yielded to the pressure of public opinion – a public it did not trust because of possible anti-Semitic repercussions later on.[15] When Kushner quotes anti-Semitic expressions made even during the war by no lesser people than H. G. Wells, George Bernard Shaw, and George Orwell, "the former remarking on several occasions in the war that Nazi anti-Semitism was a natural development from Mosaic Law," one can perhaps better follow the calculations of British politicians in this regard.[16]

Politicians of the caliber of Chamberlain and Kennedy, as quoted earlier, had expressed doubts about another war with Germany, yet the destruction of Nazism had become under Chamberlain the main war aim. Chamberlain went as far as making the war a "crusade," even if he might have had his doubts about it for a long period of time. This was the result of Hitler's own behavior after Munich, which made him a legitimate target for a moral campaign requiring mass support at home and no trouble in the Muslim parts of the Empire. Following a long battle to avoid war, such a crusade seemed

---

[15] See Wasserstein, *Britain and the Jews of Europe*, p. 346, and Kushner, *The Persistence of Prejudice*, pp. 115–119.

[16] Kushner, *The Persistence of Prejudice*, p. 93.

justified both in terms of Hitler's behavior and the mass support necessary to oppose Hitler's own brand of mass mobilization and overtures toward the British masses in anti-Semitic and other terms. This crusade had to be coined in simple, rather noncontroversial terms, whereas Jews were controversial. British public opinion was very sensitive to Jewish affairs in the late 1930s, due to the refugee question, among other things. Blamed by Hitler for the alleged exploitation of the German people since time immemorial, for World War I and the November 1918 Revolution, for Versailles and for the 1923 hyperinflation, and for the destruction of Germany's culture and values, including the robbery of "a million cows," thus denying German children their milk, Jews were subjected to a curious "character assassination" in both abstract and concrete terms.[17] But these extreme arguments were not fully alien to British observers of years before. Sir Horace Rumbold, the British ambassador in Germany from the late 1920s and after Hitler's rise to power, wrote home that since the revolution of 1918, Jews had been given fair play in every walk of life.[18] The result was that "Jewish racial superiority . . . at any rate in German eyes" asserted itself alarmingly. Jewish achievements and advances were entirely out of proportion, and this provoked bitter resentment in some German circles (one may be reminded that the British themselves closed their own gates to Jewish emigration in 1905–1919). In addition, Jews were closely associated with the political left – with democracy and pacifism. Some were involved in financial scandals during periods of economic upheaval, so the best elements of the Jewish community would suffer for the sins of the worst, according to Sir Horace.

When this typical British view of alien Jews was combined with Hitler's demand that if the West was so humanitarian, why didn't it absorb them when he was determined to push them out, it did not make them more welcome in the West.

Soon Chamberlain would remove his own Minister of War, Leslie Hore-Belisha, one of the best minds in that outfit, but also "so impatient, ebullient – so Jewish," as Chamberlain is quoted to have said[19] about him, and refuse to appoint him to the sensitive post of Minister of Information.

---

[17] The robbery of the cows and the other ironical statements regarding the Jews and the West were made by Hitler in his January 1939 "prophecy" speech; see Wildt, *Die Judenpolitik*, pp. 52–61.

[18] See Richard Breitman, *Official Secrets: What the Nazis Planned, What the British and Americans Knew* (New York: Hill and Wang 1998, pp. 21–22).

[19] Kushner, *The Persistence of Prejudice*, p. 4.

3

A Flashback on the Palestine Question

The role of Palestine and Zionism, of Arab reaction to the latter, and Allied behavior in this regard should now be outlined in a historical perspective that goes back to the origins of the British official statement of policy known as the "White Paper" on Palestine of May 1939, which in fact reversed British obligations toward the Jews in favor of the Arabs; in order to understand this reversal, a look back to the mid-1930s and to the Arab rebellion in British Palestine between 1936 and 1939 is required.

The rebellion was not only the result of the growing Jewish immigration to British Palestine caused by Hitler and by the rise of Fascism elsewhere in Europe but also the result of a German–Italian challenge to the supremacy of the Anglo-French in the Middle East, which seemed to some Arab nationalists to be an alternative to British direct or indirect rule.[1]

According to Bernard Lewis, the German model of unification and transformation of separate entities into a mighty Reich had earlier been a source of inspiration to Arab nationalists, who could not adopt the British or the French forms of domestic liberalism and democracy and resented their imperial rule.[2] Another option would have been American support for the Arab cause, the Americans having no colonial or imperialist interests in the region. This was pursued by the Palestinian scholar and statesman George Antonius and his Catholic mentor Charles Crane. Yet Crane's efforts, and the support given to him by the American Consuls in Jerusalem and by U.S. State Department officials, were hampered by his support of the Grand Mufti of

---

[1] For the most updated research on the Palestinian uprising, based primarily on British records, see Yigal Eyal, *The First Intifada: The Suppression of the Arab Revolt by the British Army 1936–1939* (Tel-Aviv: Ma'arachot Publishing House, second printing 1999) (in Hebrew).

[2] See Bernard Lewis, *Semites and Anti-Semites: An Inquiry into Conflict and Prejudice* (New York: W. W. Norton, 1986, pp. 146–147), and Lewis' sources, pertaining to the initiative of Hajj Amin el Husseini in creating a Nazi–Muslim alliance since Hitler's ascendance in 1933, even if his sources seem to be secondary.

Jerusalem, who leaned toward Nazi Germany and finally became its open ally.[3]

With Hitler having brought Germany to a new glory, Western models were even less attractive to Arab nationalists, who at the same time felt threatened in their very homeland by "masses" of invading Jews, thanks to British control over the country. In neighboring Arab countries such as Egypt and Iraq, the British were ready in the mid-1930s to make growing concessions to the Arab population toward independence. In Palestine, the Arab leadership calculated that it could achieve independence without any compromise with the Zionists. The Labor Zionist leader David Ben-Gurion tried at the time to convince Arab leaders that Jewish support for their own independence, contingent upon Arab recognition of the Jewish right to return to Palestine and an Arab–Jewish federation, would be important enough in Arab eyes for them to accept such terms, especially with the help of Zionist influence in the West.[4] How serious these federative plans were for an inherently national movement such as the Zionists is a matter of debate, but the question proved to be irrelevant at the time since the Arab leaders rejected the proposal. At the same time, Jewish influence in general, let alone Zionist power, was in decline since Hitler's ascendance and the Fascist threat to Western interests in the Middle East.

In stages, Palestinian leaders assumed an increasingly noncompromising attitude in response to the growing power and prestige of the German–Italian Axis and exposed its rivals at home as "compromisers" or as traitors to the cause. This formula worked well among some Arabs of British Palestine, if not all of them, when combined with the actual use of violence against dissidents.[5]

The Palestinian leadership was now to a growing extent in the hands of Jerusalem's Husseini family and mainly in the hands of one of its sons, Amin,

---

[3] See Menachem Kaufman, "George Antonius and the United States, the Offspring of Palestinian Arab Relations with the United States," in *Contemporary Jewry, Studies in Honor of Moshe Davis*, edited by Geoffrey Wigoder, The Institute of Contemporary Jewry (Jerusalem: Hebrew University 1984, pp. 21–51) (in Hebrew).

[4] See Meir Avizohar, "Fighting Zionism," Introduction to the academic publication of David Ben-Gurion, *Left Behind (Post-Mortem) Memoirs, Volume VI, January–August 1939* edited and annotated by Meir Avizohar (Tel-Aviv: Am-Oved, 1987, pp. 18–21) (in Hebrew). See also Avizohar's full-scale work, *National and Social Ideals as Reflected in Mapai – The Israeli Labour Party – 1930–1942* (Tel-Aviv: Am-Ovrd 1990), (in Hebrew), and Yosef Gorny's *Policy and Fantasy: Federal Plans in the Zionist Political Thought 1917–1948* (Jerusalem: Yad Ben-Zvi, 1993) (in Hebrew).

[5] For a balanced research of the development of Palestinian nationalism, see Yehoshua Porath, *The Palestinian-Arab National Movement, 1918–1929* (London: Frank Cass 1974), and Volume II, *The Palestinion-Arab National Movement, 1929–1939: From Riots to Rebellion* (London: Frank Cass 1977). See further Daniel Karpy, "The Mufti's Plan to Poison the Waters of Tel-Aviv," in *HA-UMMA* (The Nation), No. 152 (Summer 2003), 37–41 (in Hebrew), and Daniel Karpy "The Mufti of Jerusalem, Amin el Husseini, and his Political Activities during WWII" (October 1941–July 1943), *Hazionut (Zionism)* 9 (1971), 285–316 (in Hebrew).

who held the religious title of Mufti of Jerusalem by virtue of an early British move toward co-opting him. The leadership adopted the most radical approach and demanded that the British immediately stop Jewish immigration and land purchases by Jews in the wake of Arab independence, possibly in conjunction with Syria and Iraq. In 1936, an Arab general strike followed these demands, which lasted 175 days and was followed by widespread acts of violence against Jewish and British property and attempts on Jewish and British lives. This in turn became an open rebellion against the British mandatory power and against Jews at large.

The Zionist leadership, comprised of Chaim Weizmann, the acknowledged spokesman of the British-oriented wing of the World Zionist movement, the main Labor Zionist leaders Berl Katzenelson, David Ben-Gurion, Moshe Shertok-Sharett, and the leaders of the Labor Zionist Left, Yitzhak Tabenkin, Meir Ya'ari, and others, in spite of the serious differences among them on other issues, agreed on a policy of self-restraint (Havlaga) in response to the Arab rebellion, codenamed the "Events" or "Incidents" (Me'oraot in Hebrew) of 1936–1939. This response was calculated to avoid strong British countermeasures if the Yishuv (the Jewish community in Palestine) resorted to counterterrorism, to reduce the Jewish community to a similar but less numerous and threatening status than that of the Arab rebels in British and Western eyes, and to enhance cooperation with the British military authorities. The unavoidable strategy was to maintain cooperation as far as possible with the British, who had to maintain order in the country under their control, while developing the autonomous Jewish self-defense organization already existent since the Arab riots of 1920. Indeed, the result of the 1936–1939 Arab "riots" was the influx of Jewish youth into the illegal defense organization "Hagana," the adoption of new tactics and offensive measures by special units created by an unusually motivated British officer, Captain Orde Charles Wingate, who was soon removed due to his close relations with the Yishuv, and the mobilization of thousands into the British-equipped special police.

Thus, the Arab rebellion stimulated a partial militarization of the Yishuv and helped create a consciousness of military power that was adopted and cultivated by its leaders to face a forthcoming, if unavoidable, open war with the Arabs should the British renounce their Palestine mandate as a result of a general world crisis.

This was, however, only one side of the picture. In fact, the Jewish community in Palestine remained rather small (about half a million), retained a rather voluntary character, lacked a united enforcing authority in various areas associated with a regular state such as security, and had no clear-cut concept of how to organize its illegal military branch Hagana – whether on a local basis for mainly defensive purposes or as a national territorial army for a long time. Its regular (in the sense of being a sort of standing force ready for immediate action) spearhead, the "Palmach," was in fact born during the first years of World War II. The command of the Hagana was in the hands of a coalition representing the main political parties of the Yishuv and lacked a unified structure and a clear military concept in spite of the Arab challenge.[6]

For many Zionists,[7] the Lord Peel Commission's partition plan for Palestine, as recommended to the Imperial Government in 1937, was an interim stage in which the basic British tendency to drop the Jewish "homeland" promised in the Balfour Declaration of November 1917 and cemented in the League of Nations' Mandate over Palestine given to the British in favor of the Arabs, whose rights were mentioned in both documents as well, was interrupted for awhile. The Peel Commission plan contained, however, two important recommendations – to partition Western Palestine between Arabs and Jews along the lines of their relative strength and to transfer the Arab population, by force if necessary, from the Jewish state.

The Zionists debated the partition of their dreamland, having already lost its Eastern part in the 1920s to the Hashemite Emir Abdullah,[8] while the British dropped it altogether later on due to Arab rejection thereof and Britain's own grand European strategy.

These fateful cleavages within the Yishuv, when previous clashes between the radical–liberal leader Vladimir Jabotinsky and the Socialist parties following Hitler's rise to power combined with the partition debate, divided the Socialist camp itself. Partition was anathema not only to Jabotinsky. Among the main Labor leaders, Ben-Gurion was the only major figure to endorse it, together with Chaim Weizmann, the moderate leader of the World Zionist Organization. Jabotinsky's arguments were based among other reasons upon the assumption that the British must be brought to accept the Jews as their real allies and supporters in the entire region. Yet Middle East oil was among the few assets monopolized by the British in comparison to the Axis' oil supplies, and the Middle East in general was an imperial strategic juncture of the highest importance if Japan had to be taken into account on top of the Italian Fascist menace. Thus, the more the British were preparing to fight Hitler and his allies, the less ready they were to allow the immigration of his principal victims, the Jews, into Palestine. They introduced in May 1939 the above-mentioned White Paper on Palestine, which indeed reduced Jewish immigration to small annual quotas, to be stopped altogether in five years;

---

[6] See Avizohar, *National and Social Ideals as reflected in Mapai*, pp. 247–249.

[7] Avizohar, "Fighting Zionism," pp. 20–21.

[8] For a comprehensive history of the period, see Moshe Lissak, Anita Shapiro, and Gavriel Cohen (eds.), *The History of the Jewish Yishuv in Palestine since the First Alya: The British Mandate Period*, Volume II (Jerusalem: The Israel Academy of Sciences and Humanities, 1995) (The First Alya refers to the first modern immigration wave in the 1880s) and specifically Shmuel Dotan, *The Partition Controversy during the Mandate Period* (Jerusalem: Yad-Izhak Ben-Zvi Publications, 1980), and Shmuel Dotan, *Reds: About Domestic Communist Rejections of Different Kinds of Zionism during the '30s, '40s, and '50s* (Kefar Sava: Shevna Hasofer Publications, 1993). (All three works are in Hebrew.)

the Paper restricted the purchase of land by Jews to almost nothing (the legislation itself was to be introduced a little later) and promised the election of executive bodies in which the Arab majority would be determinant.

The British suspended the last clause once Winston Churchill, a declared "Zionist," was appointed prime minister of a national coalition in Britain in 1940. Churchill even supported the arming of the Yishuv[9] against the pro-German Arabs and as a local asset in the struggle with the Axis, but this must have been seen by several members of his own cabinet and by the British Middle Eastern authorities as one of Winston's "follies," which he then had to drop. It would finally surface again in a different form by late 1943.

[9] See Ronald W. Zweig, *Britain and Palestine during the Second World War* (Woodbridge, Suffolk: The Boydell Press for the Royal Historical Society, 1986, pp. 4, 17–19, 20–23).

4

1939 to "Barbarossa" – The Foundation of the Multiple Trap

The occupation of Poland added two dimensions to the previous "Jewish politics" of Nazi Germany. More than two million Polish Jews were now under German control, and the war atmosphere allowed atrocities, which upon the German invasion were carried out on a large scale against the Polish elite and Jews.[1] At the outset of World War II, Hitler ordered a full-scale euthanasia program aimed at the murder of tens of thousands of people defined as mentally ill, handicapped, or retarded. In this, the war combined with yet another devaluation of human lives, and experience was gathered in executing mass murder in gas chambers.[2]

On September 21, 1939, the chief of the Nazi "Security Police" (Gestapo and Criminal Police) and the SD, Reinhard Heydrich, discussed with his aides the Jewish Question as a whole, including the German Jewish issue, the evacuation of Jews into Poland, and a possible evacuation of Polish Jews into Soviet-occupied Poland. Finally, Heydrich issued an express letter to his subordinates in Poland with regard to the shorter-range solution of the Jewish question and longer-range plans.[3] He ordered the concentration of Polish Jews in such a way that they could later be moved as quickly as possible. The final stop for the evacuees was not clearly specified, but it is clear that Heydrich was aiming at a "Reservat," a specific territory in the eastern part of occupied Poland. This Reservat was planned also to absorb all Jews from Greater Germany. Adolf Eichmann, the "resettling" expert of the combined Gestapo and SD authority, the Reich Main Security Office of the SS (Reichssicherheitshauptamt, or RSHA), decided to set up a transit

---

[1] This chapter is also based largely on the Longerich–Aronson entry in the *Yale Encyclopedia of the Holocaust*.

[2] See Henry Friedlander, *The Origins of Nazi Genocide, from Euthanasia to the Final Solution* (Chapel Hill: University of North Carolina Press, 1995).

[3] Nuremberg document PS-3363, quoted in all the major scholarly discussions of the origins of the Final Solution.

camp for the deportees in Nisko on the San River in the eastern part of the Nazi-occupied General Gouvernement in Poland. Following the arrival of the first transports of the deportees from Upper Silesia, from the German-occupied Czech "Protektorat," and from Vienna in Nisko in October 1939, this experiment, obviously improvised, was abandoned after a short period of time. This was partially due to military concerns about mass concentrations of Jews not far from the Soviet–German demarcation line. The experiment also proved that improvised mass deportations in wintertime would result in immediate mass death – which at that time was not intended, at least in terms of assigning direct German responsibility to it. The role of the SS in these matters should be further clarified in the sense that Heinrich Himmler was appointed at that time to pursue the "Germanization" of occupied territory, while Hermann Göring remained the Head of the Four Year Plan – initially conceived in terms of preparing the economy and the armed forces for war while making "Jewry in its entirety" responsible for "acts of sabotage" against the German nation. Hence, anything that could be perceived as such acts, say Western proclamation of war against Germany or early British efforts, undertaken in 1940, to mount a bombing campaign against Germany, justified "countermeasures" against Jews.[4] Moreover, under Göring, Herbert Backe, Secretary of State in the Reich Food Ministry, formally under Richard Darré, served as Göring's man in charge of food supplies rather than his nominal chief Darré. According to his Nuremberg interrogation, Darré was perceived by Himmler at the time, in spite of his ranks as Reichsminister and Reichsamtsleiter, as a subordinate SS General.

Darré refused to accept Himmler's control and as a result was prohibited from entering occupied Polish territory – Himmler's territory to a growing extent.[5] Backe became more and more a link between Göring, who would later issue several major orders regarding the Jewish Question, Himmler, and Hitler himself. At Nuremberg, Backe (who had committed suicide beforehand) was described by Darré as a member of Hitler's inner circle and thus as a racial fanatic who later played a role in the Final Solution decision.[6]

---

[4] See *Die Tagebücher von Joseph Goebbels*: Sämtliche Fragmente, Elke Fröhlich (ed.) (München: Sauer Verlag, 1987, Teil 1, Aufzeichnungen 1924–1941, Band 4, 1.1.1940–8.7.1941, pp. 252, 486–487, 488–489, 704–705).

[5] See Darré's letter of complaint to Göring (no date) and Backe's response dated June 27, 1941, Darré's SS personal file, and Records of the United States Nuremberg War Crimes Trials Interrogations, 1946–1949, Washington, NARA, Richard Darré, Roll 12.

[6] Zionist rescue operative Rezső Kasztner, about whose roles during and after the war we shall learn a lot more, interrogated several Nazi officials at Nuremberg; here I refer to a protocol given to me courtesy of Mr. Dov Dinur, Haifa: Vernehmung des SS-Obergruppenführer Erich von dem BACH-ZELEWSKI am 30 Maerz 1948 von 15,30 Uhr bis 17,00 Uhr durch Mr. Herbert MEYER und Dr. Kestner fuer. . . . (There are no details of the interrogation's framework. The grammar and spelling errors are as in the original – S.A.).

After the collapse of the Nisko Plan, leading Nazis did not give up the idea of deporting all Jews under German control to the Polish-occupied General Gouvernement or, under certain circumstances, to a special Reservat in the Lublin area. From expressions made by leading authorities in occupied Poland during the winter of 1939–1940, we learn that such a Reservat was also supposed to serve the purpose of pushing Jews over the demarcation line into Soviet-occupied territory in Poland or to remove and to "decimate" them by means that remained unclear to the Nazis themselves. From these expressions, we may gather the intention to treat the deportees brutally and bring about a serious loss of life among them, but not yet to kill them all.

At the same time, such plans were also connected with plans for large resettlements from territories annexed by the Germans in western Poland. In fact, the deportations of Poles and Jews from these areas began at the end of 1939, but the growing resistance of the "General Governor" of Poland, Hans Frank, who was supposed to absorb the deportees, brought about the temporary cessation of these deportations until Himmler asserted his authority thereon.

The Jews living in the General Gouvernement itself were subjected in the meantime to especially harsh treatment: they were marked by yellow stars from November 1939, their freedom of movement was limited from December 1939, and immediately afterward they were hurled into closed ghettos and later subjected to slave labor. Then came Germany's swift victory over France in summer 1940, which must have had various major ramifications for the Jews. On the one hand, it enhanced Hitler's prestige to unprecedented heights among Germans and Germany's continental allies or potential ones. It became the source of his unlimited authority within the armed forces and initially allowed him to pursue his ideological goals with a sense of omnipotence.[7]

At first, the victory over France and Britain's isolated position generated an expectation that London would come around (indeed it was Churchill's "Finest Hour" in avoiding it) when the British had to create a consensus among themselves to fight Hitler, who had created a consensus among the Germans and many continental Europeans around his leadership and needed only to maintain it.[8]

---

[7] See Jürgen Förster, "Hitler's Decision in Favor of war against the Soviet Union," *Germany and the Second World War: The Attack on the Soviet Union*, Part I of Volume IV, edited by the Militärgeschichtliches Forschungsamt (henceforth referred to as MGFA), Potsdam, Germany (Oxford: Clarendon Press, 1998, pp. iv, 14–15). Note Förster's emphasis on Britain's decision and American aid rendered to it in the context of Hitler's view of the "Jewish-capitalist warmongers."

[8] See John Lukacs, *Five Days in London, May 1940* (New Haven and London: Yale University Press, 1999, pp. 6–33), especially his discussion of defeatism among members of Chamberlain's and Churchill's governments after the fall of France.

For his part, Hitler did hope after the fall of France to force an "understanding" with the British on his terms.[9] He even seemed to have perceived his conquered land in Poland as being quite big enough in pure territorial terms in a meeting with Mussolini in March 1940[10] and seemed prepared to delay the issue of the "East" (i.e., that of Soviet Russia) for "ten years" to come or even leave it to his successor.[11] No issues related to the Jews were "solved" during that time between 1938 and 1941. Obviously, these pronouncements could have been empty assertions covering up Hitler's real intentions – securing a "Lebensraum" at Soviet expense. Yet Hitler's actual behavior was an admixture of long-range, global-ideological thinking and decisions influenced by his adversaries' real and imagined behavior. Ongoing British resistance, American aid rendered to the British, and Stalin's behavior may have combined to yield "Barbarossa" sooner rather than later.

After the war, several of the Nazis interrogated at Nuremberg claimed that the continued British resistance, which entailed the quest to eliminate the Soviet Union as a future ally of the British and possibly of the Americans as well, contributed heavily to deciding the fate of Jews. As the initial decision to physically destroy them was made in this context – and in the context of the American aid that at least kept the British afloat – even if there was no written order as one might have expected to have been issued, a series of such decisions were made in a general framework already existent and issued to a variety of executioners in various areas.[12]

But before the British position became evident and final and the Americans were mobilized by FDR to assist the British, the German victory over France seems to have created the opportunity to "solve" the whole Jewish Question in Europe outside of Europe in cooperation with France and Great Britain. The idea, which became known as the "Madagascar Plan," was to ship four million Jews to an island off the east coast of Africa. Such a solution should, of course, have been combined in Hitler's eyes with his other hegemonic plans in Europe and the acceptance by the West of Nazi Germany as the creator of a "new order" on the European continent. It further entailed

[9] See Bernd Stegemann, "Hitler's Ziele in ersten Kriegsjahr 1939/1940," *Militärgeschichtliche Mitteilungen* No. 1 (1980), 92–103, based among other things on General Halder's note, "Wir suchen Fühlung mit England auf der Basis der Teilung der Welt" ("we are seeking an understanding with England on the basis of the division of the world"), which appears on p. 97 of the article.

[10] Meeting with Mussolini on March 8, 1940, *Documents on German Foreign Policy*, Series D, Vol. 8, No. 663, pp. 871 ff.

[11] For more sources and a discussion, see Shlomo Aronson, "Die Dreifache Falle, Hitler's Judenpolitik, die Aliierten und die Juden," *VfZ* No. 1 (1984), 42–44, and the connection created by Hitler between Britain's decision to continue to fight, Soviet behavior in 1940 allegedly encouraging the British, and his decision to attack Russia.

[12] Kasztner's interrogations at Nuremberg, especially of German Foreign Office officials Horst Wagner and Eberhard von Thadden, seem to lend weight to this argument. Protocols given to me by courtesy of Mr. Dov Dinur, Haifa.

a "hostage-taking" dimension against the Americans, according to Adolf Eichmann, the director of the forced emigration project, and to a German Foreign Ministry official in the sense that the deportees would remain under SS control to guarantee "the good behavior of their brethren in America."[13] What motivated the British in the first place was not only their resolute resistance to Hitler's hegemonic plans for Europe but that they were mobilized to destroy his regime altogether. Yet while the Germans were firmly behind Hitler (a consensus was created in the Third Reich about his genial qualities and opposition was brutally repressed), in Great Britain the consensus about fighting him at all costs was created to a large extent by Hitler and Churchill, each in their own way, following a series of blunders and defeats of disastrous magnitudes. These factors required sensitivity and political attention to home opinion in the face of the prevailing odds, which pushed everything Jewish aside or made it even a cumbersome, annoying matter.

The Middle East situation especially seemed to dictate the ongoing restrictions on Jewish immigration, more so when the fighting was raging also with Italy and later with German forces sent to help Mussolini. As quoted by his army adjutant, Hitler said on October 8, 1939, that he used to ask himself again and again why he had treated the Jews "so humanely" between 1935 and 1937. By 1939, the Jewish Question had quite seriously popped into Hitler's eyes once again when he visited Poland, demonstrating to him that it must be solved not only in Germany but in the countries under German influence. But at that time, Hitler said, he had endorsed the idea of getting rid of the 600,000 German Jews in a "businesslike fashion." His plan, which he allegedly had offered to the British in 1937, was to take the German Jews as a "working force" to Palestine, and he did mean it seriously, he said. But this idea failed with the British, and others too were hardly enthusiastic. The British told him bluntly by means of a diplomatic message that the Jewish Question in Palestine troubled them enough, and they did not need any more trouble. Hitler thus did not hesitate to tell his audience a series of sheer lies since no such diplomatic exchange ever existed. But Hitler did create the impression that he had tried some positive solution and was rebuffed by the others. Hence, he developed at that stage, according to his adjutant, another plan, which was to concentrate the Jews in huge ghettos in Poland, in Lodz and in Lublin, in deserted barracks and the like, where he would let them run their business on their own, even by invoking their own police force, and fight among themselves. It would be possible, he said, to send there also the Jews of the Czech "Protektorat." At this point, the general idea of some territorial

---

[13] The official was Karl Rademacher of the German Foreign Office – also interrogated by Kasztner at Nuremberg. See further Eichmann's Interrogation, Eichmann Trial, Jerusalem, Prosecution Collection T/37, Volume II, p. 18.

solution seems to have been prevailing in his mind, where the conditions of life in these areas would have decimated the Jews in stages.[14]

Still, forced emigration of sorts remained in force – no Final Solution was ordered for at least a year and a half after September 1939. The nature of a Final Solution could thus vary, but the essence would assume a more and more violent character to those who believed that Hitler would have left millions of Jews to live in peace in his Polish ghettos.

On February 2, 1941, Hitler's army adjutant, Major Engel, quoted Hitler as he was speaking to a mixed group of army and party men on the solution of the Jewish Question that on one hand the war would enhance a speedy solution to the problem but on the other hand it would create many difficulties. At first, Hitler could only break the power of the Jews in Germany, but now the target could be the elimination of Jewish influence in all the Axis countries. In Poland and Slovakia, Hitler could do it alone, but in France it would be much more difficult and there it would be especially important. If Hitler only knew where to put these several million Jews – they were not that many. He would approach France and ask the French to make Madagascar available for this purpose. In response to Martin Bormann's question of how Madagascar could be reached in wartime, Hitler responded that he must think about it. He would have loved to put a whole fleet at the disposal of such an endeavor, but in wartime this would be a problem indeed, and he would not put the lives of German naval crews at the mercy of enemy submarines. Now, as Britain went on fighting, Hitler was thinking differently about many things and not with any degree of greater sympathy toward the Jews. Here Hitler repeated his alleged offer to the British in 1937, and he told his audience that he had combined Egypt and Palestine as a possible "solution" at this time.

The fantastic aspirations, the numbers mentioned in the Madagascar plan, and Madagascar's possible use for a variety of purposes, including as a hostage camp to influence American behavior toward Germany, may have been an interim measure toward the physical elimination of the Jewish presence in Europe plus some imagined gains against Washington, but as such it was a rather important development toward the "Europeanization" of the Jewish Question and some kind of far-reaching solution thereof. The territorial plans of that period, Madagascar included, and the plans to concentrate the Jews in the Reservat in the Lublin area already at this early stage entailed clear-cut murderous dimensions since the living conditions of the deportees would have been insufferable.[15]

---

[14] See Engel, *Heeresadjutant bei Hitler.*

[15] About the internal Nazi deliberations and differing opinions pertaining to emigration of Polish Jews before the invasion of Russia, see Richard Breitman, *The Architect of Genocide: Himmler and the Final Solution* (New York: Alfred A. Knopf 1991, pp. 142–144).

Thus, when the British continued the fight and won the battle over their skies, the Americans not only made it possible for them to survive but took direct measures against the German submarine warfare after having frozen all the German assets in the United States in 1940. Hitler's hegemony in Europe seemed challenged from two sides – the Western, including the American, and the Soviet.

The radicalization of Hitler's treatment of Jews would adopt the extreme measure of wholesale killings when Hitler attacked Russia after he got himself into growing trouble with America, meaning that he would see in the United States a factor restraining his final "account" with the Jews at least for the time being, pending America's own behavior. The Engel diaries substantiate this linkage when we read Hitler's response therein in March 1941 to the American Lend-Lease legislation. Accordingly, this legislation was a casus belli, and indeed in due course there would be no way out of it because Roosevelt and the big Jewish finances behind him wanted it and must want it, since Germany's victory in Europe would mean terrible financial losses for American Jews in Europe. Having thus politicized the motives of the President of the United States without any connection to their reality and to his own threat to America once he created his hegemony in Europe, Hitler added a typical violent remark by saying that it was a pity that Germany did not possess along-range bomber as yet to attack American cities. This lesson he would have loved to teach the American Jews. In the meantime, the British went on fighting. They destroyed Mussolini's fleet at Taranto and at Cape Metaphan and his land forces in the Western Desert, driving the rest of them into Libya, and were in the process of liberating Somalia and Ethiopia. At the same time, they were mounting their own bombing campaign against Germany proper, which, however, proved to be much less menacing than the Germans were expecting it to be. The British landed in Greece, including Crete, but were forced out. The Americans drew closer and closer toward the British, even if not close enough to join them with all their potential might. All these multidimensional developments, in terms of various parties and various related strategic–political and ideological motives, most of which were not related to Jews, could be understood by the Nazis not just as they were. Aimed against the vary survival of the Nazi regime, the British and their American helpers were allegedly tools at the hands of the Jews. But in fact Hitler was the one who made the British resist him and the Americans come to aid the British, while Jews under Hitler's own control fell between him and his enemies. Since we have here three forces at work – the Nazis, the British, and the Americans – we can describe this as a sort of a triple trap. This triple trap, however, was just the beginning. The double trap described earlier became larger, when Hitler decided to invade the Soviet Union in order to destroy a potential British ally and exploit its vast resources for "defensive" measures related to the impact of the British blockade and to Soviet demands and for offensive measures in the sense of broadening Germany's Lebensraum once and for all. At the same time, he hoped that the Japanese would engage the Americans elsewhere. If the Jews of Europe had any hostage value with the Americans until then, by now they had lost it. Thus, decisions made by other parties (e.g., the British and Americans, who were separated from the fate of the enemy's main victim – the Jews under Hitler's control) in response to the enemy's behavior, defending themselves against the enemy's challenges or enhancing their own interests as the Japanese did, resulted in deciding the fate of the victims caught between them all. The dialectics of this multidimensional situation – the German–British, the German–British–American, the German–British–American–Soviet, and the Japanese–American–German – created here the basis for the Final Solution of the Jewish Question, whose roots were obviously anchored in the Nazis' ideology and sense of omnipotence at that stage but also in their sense of disillusionment and revenge against the British, Americans, and Soviets. Stalin's Soviet Union had to be crushed first before the British–American threat could be successfully averted.

The story of the German–Soviet relations that preceded "Operation Barbarossa" is told in the most comprehensive fashion by the German team of the Research Institute for Military History in Potsdam. The authors painted a rather complex picture based on German records heretofore less known and hardly used in previous research.[16] According to these records, the undecided outcome of the war and the effect of the Western blockade required a high degree of Soviet economic support, which may have meant the unlikely subordination of Stalin's own economic needs to those of Germany. At any rate, it would have made Germany dependent on the USSR and prompt unacceptable political and strategic demands by Stalin pertaining to Soviet influence in Eastern and Southeastern Europe and "in the long term, would make use of Germany's increasing dependence in order to steer the 'brown revolution' into Bolshevik channels,"[17] as the Nazis saw it.

Hence, a process was set in motion that inevitably would lead to "Barbarossa" and to the ensuing transformation of the war into a global conflict, thus revealing the unfolding of the trap for the Jews as a sort of unstoppable doomsday machine. In fact, one could have differentiated among Soviet Jews and especially between Stalin and Soviet Jews. After all, Stalin had dismissed his Foreign Minister, Maxim Litvinov (who was Jewish), before he entered into negotiating his pact with Hitler. Many victims of Stalin's 1936–1938 purges were Jewish, among them the best-known leaders of the original Bolshevik Revolution, who made so many Westerners worry about the Soviet Revolution as being a Jewish-led threat in the late 1910s and in the 1920s. In the Baltic States and eastern Poland, annexed by the USSR in

---

[16] See Rolf-Dieter Müller, "From Economic Alliance to a War of Colonial Exploitation," in *Germany and the Second World War: The Attack on the Soviet Union*, pp. 118 ff.

[17] Müller, *Germany and the Second World War: The Attack on the Soviet Union*, p. 121.

1939–1940, many Jews, especially Zionists such as Menachem Begin, were arrested by the NKVD (the Soviet Secret Police) and sent to Siberia – a fact that did not escape Hitler's eyes.[18] Thus, a knowledgeable German officer, Colonel Ritter von Niedermayer, could publish an enthusiastic article in favor of German–Soviet cooperation "after a further suppression of 'Jewry' in the Soviet Union that would render the 'Eurasian military front' unassailable."[19] Although it expressed a sort of consensus in the German military that "Jewry" must be "suppressed," Niedermayer's opinion did not prevail, however.

Indeed, Stalin might have been perceived a bit differently by Hitler if we were to invoke anti-Semitism as a master variable explaining "Barbarossa"; Stalin was immune to democratic pressures and Western elite habits and upper-class deals and machinations as perceived by Hitler, and he at least displayed, especially since the annexation of the Baltic States and eastern Poland in 1939–1940, interesting anti-Semitic traits, which Hitler was very sensitive in grasping. He was not able to make Stalin personally – in private – just a "Bolshevik-Jewish" tool.[20] Hitler's Soviet policy was certainly ideologically motivated but also dependent on what he perceived to be Soviet behavior and intentions, intimately connected with British and American behavior. A major test of sorts was Soviet expansion westward starting with the winter campaign against Finland, the annexation of the Baltic States, and the proximity of Soviet air bases to German vital centers such as Berlin or the Rumanian oil fields at Ploesti. Further Soviet demands in Europe in 1940 combined with Hitler's hate and understanding of communism as a "Jewish-inspired" ideology that may serve the interest of the huge, threatening, but inherently weak prey in the east.

All this and more had finally led to "Barbarossa" and to the Final Solution. Yet our argument at this phase remains that the Jews were the victims of these developments, having no influence over them as a "race," a "nation," or even as separately organized groups, as they were perceived to be by the enemy and many other parties.

The domestic and regional contexts leading Hitler to "Barbarossa" are illuminated in detail by the German military historians quoted earlier. According to these sources, during the Polish campaign and until the victory over France, Germany went out of its way to cooperate with the Soviet Union since the German armament industry performed rather poorly and a total mobilization of the economy had to be avoided for political reasons pertaining to the lessons derived from World War I. On top of this, the exceptionally harsh winter of 1939–1940 and setbacks in the German campaign for control of the neutral continental markets "further increased tensions within

[18] See Hitler, *Monologe*, p. 363.
[19] Müller, *Germany and the Second World War: The Attack on the Soviet Union*, p. 121.
[20] Hitler, *Monologe*, p. 336.

the German war economy, with finally the prospect of a 'collapse of food supplies in the course of the second year of the war, as in 1918'" expected by Herbert Backe.[21] Backe, the Secretary of State and SS General, would play a central role as an "expert on Russia" and as a source of food and a solution for Germany's economic problems related to his – and Hitler's own – trauma of 1918 and the "Jewish blockade" that preceded it. (In fact, the economic czar of the imperial regime at this stage of World War I, who had contributed much to its sustained war effort until the November Revolution, was Walter Rathenau, the Jewish industrialist who later became Weimar's Foreign Minister and was assassinated soon after the Rapallo Conference, which created the base for Soviet–German cooperation at the time.) When arrested by the Allies after the war, Backe was regarded as one of the "most political SS activists among the (service) ministries" and as a member of a racist "order" around Hitler himself.[22] In fact, his role as a food commissioner at home and as a "Russian expert" as well was a combination that helped lead to "Barbarossa" with its genocidal aims.[23]

By the winter of 1939–1940, both sides were interested in a compromise, which led to the German–Soviet economic agreement of February 11, 1940. Stalin agreed to move closer to his German ally following his Finnish campaign and due to his fears that Hitler might switch sides and find a common denominator with the West. Hitler agreed to supply the Soviet armament industry with modern sensitive technologies, having decided to "employ all reserves for his planned campaign against France, without any regard to the future," in his typical win-or-bust modus operandi.[24] Stalin for his part was interested in a prolonged war of attrition between Nazi Germany and the Western powers and delivered his part of the deal – delayed until then due to problems with German coal deliveries – upon the opening of the German offensive in the West.

The enormous victory in the western campaign transformed Germany's role in its own eyes into that of continental superpower in the making, extending its sphere of interest to Southeastern and Eastern Europe, even to the "Siberian region and across the Mediterranean into Africa,"[25] while trying to secure its rear "on the assumption of an early compromise peace with Britain... right up to the end of 1940." Such a "compromise peace"

---

[21] Müller, *Germany and the Second World War: The Attack on the Soviet Union*, p. 124, note 33.

[22] See Robert M. W. Kempner, *SS im Kreuzverhör* (München: Rütten + Loening Verlog 1965, pp. 227ff). Deputy prosecutor Kempner briefly interrogated Backe at Nuremberg before the latter committed suicide.

[23] See also Dwork papers in NA RG 200 pertaining to Backe's alleged role as a member of "an inner circle around Hitler," as conveyed to OSS by Gerhart Riegner in Switzerland. Riegner was the source of the "Schulte Report," the first conclusive evidence on the Final Solution decision. In a second report, Riegner referred to Backe as one of the initiators of that decision.

[24] Müller, *Germany and the Second World War: The Attack on the Soviet Union*, p. 126.

[25] Ibid., 129.

would have allowed Nazi Germany to turn against the Soviet Union and at least occupy its "economically valuable western territories."[26] The German Army High Command was now ready to prepare for this since the Third Reich had extended its hegemonic role much farther east and southeast.[27] Independently of his General Staff and German business circles aiming at least at the occupation of the Ukraine and parts of the Soviet Union, Hitler informed the military on July 31, 1940, of his "firm resolve 'to eliminate Russia.'"[28] Thus, Hitler went far beyond the "dimensions ... [envisioned by the] General Staff: Hitler, in view of the by then obvious necessity to continue the war against Britain for an uncertain period of time and to prepare for an American entry into the war," did not aim "merely at 'gaining space' but at smashing the Russian state at a single blow."[29] However, his rage against the West, which in fact remained divided to a large extent until his own declaration of war against the United States, had transformed Germany's eastern campaign into a genocide against Soviet Jews to begin now that the war had become global, and it entailed the elimination of Jews and commissars as a matter of course and the starvation of millions of others. When this campaign continued, the genocide was broadened to all the Jews of Europe, notwithstanding the ongoing conflict in the Soviet Union but very possibly related to the growing American support of the British since early 1941.

The invasion of Russia created the framework of the multiple trap because Soviet territory was from the beginning an object of a radical Nazi policy toward its inhabitants, with Jews on top as an ideological issue and as a "security problem" when millions of Jews in the Nazi rear seemed to be a threat to their military occupation and future plans for these territories. Yet the decision to invade the USSR and hence to kill the Jews therein was prompted by the behavior of Britain and America, who could hardly have acted otherwise to protect their own interests and values.

The British, of course, calculated in 1940 and most of 1941 – when they were left alone – that help might come from America, and this obviously did not escape Hitler's attention. In Churchill's own words, American involvement, as he described the transfer of the fifty old American destroyers to the British in September 1940 in exchange for leasing rights granted by the British to the Americans to bases in the West Indies and in Newfoundland, was "a decidedly unneutral act by the United States."[30] According to common historical tradition, wrote Churchill in his World War II memoirs, this act would have justified "a declaration of war against the [Americans – S.A.]

---

[26] Ibid., 134, and note 80.
[27] Ibid., 134.
[28] Ibid., 135 and note 84.
[29] Ibid., 135.
[30] Churchill, *The Second World War*, Volume II, p. 322 (Hebrew translation).

by the German government." In fact, this was wishful thinking at this point. Churchill further described this act as the first in a long row of more and more unneutral acts in the Atlantic, which immensely – but not decisively – served the British war effort. Yet Churchill concluded this chapter by saying that Hitler could not afford to react to this American involvement before he subdued the British. About this and the crowning American contribution to the survival of the British by means of the Lend-Lease Act of March 1941, which made the United States the "arsenal of democracy," and then President Roosevelt's order to the U.S. Navy to escort convoys bound for Britain more than halfway into the Atlantic, Churchill might have been wrong. Hitler did respond, in my view, but not directly against the British only, nor against the Americans. The March 1941 date, according to the logic of Hitler's 1939 "prophecy," was the beginning of the drawing of plans for the "Final Solution of the Jewish Question in Europe," coupled with the invasion of Russia first.

Growing American aid to the British was prompted in fact by American fears that the British might succumb to German might, and hence all of Europe, including the British Isles and the British Navy, could fall into German hands and thus threaten the United States directly. Churchill cleverly played upon American fears that Britain might fall after all, promising the Americans that in that case the British Navy would not be surrendered to the Germans – an act that a "Quisling Government" in Britain would certainly undertake; hence, the Roosevelt administration should at least give him the destroyers, "Lend-Lease," and naval protection, acts that indeed brought the United States closer to the British than Hitler was willing to tolerate in some respect. If Hitler declared war against America, this would have been the "simplest solution to many difficulties."[31] Hitler did not yet do so directly, deciding first to knock out the Soviets and start paying the bill to "the Jews."

We have no room here to discuss the Lend-Lease Act itself, in which FDR's Jewish Secretary of the Treasury, Henry Morgenthau, Jr., was deeply involved, Roosevelt's "Arsenal of Democracy" speech, and the active role played in this regard – against a strong and influential domestic opposition silenced only by the Japanese at Pearl Harbor – of Associate Supreme Court Justice Felix Frankfurter.[32]

Frankfurter was a symbolic figure of a Jewish "gray eminence" in FDR's court, as Bernard Baruch was to an extent among Wall Street tycoons. Baruch was a close friend of Churchill and had his ties with the president. Judge Samuel Rosenman, another close friend, was made speechwriter and counsel of the White House after Pearl Harbor. Such people, Morgenthau included,

---

[31] Churchill, *The Second World War*, Volume II.
[32] See *Roosevelt and Frankfurter: Their Correspondence 1928–1945*, annotated by Max Freedman, (Boston: Little Brown 1967).

must have fed Hitler's wrath. Frankfurter worked hard indeed to involve the president as soon as possible in the battle with Fascism, but he was one Democrat among many liberal and anti-isolationist Republican non-Jews who did not succeed until the Japanese finally and fully involved the United States in the war – with Hitler declaring war on the United States first. However, Frankfurter's close relations with FDR dwindled to a much less significant exchange after the declaration of war. Frankfurter, Baruch, Governor Herbert Lehman of New York, Secretary Morgenthau, and Judge Rosenman, whose job was to assist the President loyally in accord with FDR's own priorities, let alone Walter Lippmann, were not motivated primarily by Jewish interests nor associated with Jewish organizations, except for Frankfurter's ties with the Zionists. On the contrary, all of them were liberal Democrats and anti-Fascists first, and this no historian can change ex post facto by demanding them to be what they were not. Only liberal democracy could have allowed them, as members of a minority, the rights in which they were interested and that they had sincerely adopted as true Americans. As true Americans, they were intimately conscious of isolationism, nativism, and anti-Semitism in America itself but much less capable of fathoming Hitler's mind. Immediately after Pearl Harbor, and during the mostly bleak 1942, the first peak year of the Holocaust, people like them were fully absorbed with the mobilization of the huge, individualistic, less organized, peaceful America to fight Germany first and then Japan while maintaining the general national consensus about the war, which was achieved after Pearl Harbor and Hitler's declaration of war against the United States.

In the meantime, Stalin became an ally of the British and later of the Americans, carrying the heaviest burden of the war. Hence, this alliance, unnatural as it was, was a doomsday machine for the Jews when they became the prey of the enemy, first when Hitler destroyed the Jews in Soviet areas and then when he broadened this murderous campaign to the rest of the continent due to various reasons such as the Allied bombing campaign against Germany and the very feasibility of a "Final Solution" of gigantic dimensions, which indeed proved possible in practical terms (to be discussed in later chapters), among them in response to the challenge of the West, now Stalin's ally. In fact, the West responded to Hitler's initial challenge without any attention being paid to the fate of the victims as a matter of necessity to win over the same enemy.

The maintenance of this grand, unnatural alliance quadrupled the trap from a Jewish point of view because alliance politics assumed supreme significance. If the rescue of Jews – Hitler's dying enemies, whom be blamed for Allied behavior – threatened alliance politics, they became a source of trouble for the Allies in their war imposed on them by Hitler. They refused to let it be tainted as a "Jew's war" by their own deeds and even by too much attention paid to the victims – by direct or indirect negotiations with the Nazis or by dealing with Hitler's allies, if at all feasible – which seemed not only to threaten the domestic consensus about the war but also to endanger the alliance if not specifically aimed by the Nazis at driving a wedge between the Allies. Indeed, this could have been the case when we study the rescue deals that seemed to have been offered by the SS to Jewish intermediaries, who – along with their dying brethren – became German tools in Allied eyes, thus transforming rescue endeavors into self-defeating mechanisms in most cases, quadrupling the trap in connection with fears of fourth parties under possible Nazi influence – the Arabs.

5

The "Final Solution" Decision and Its Initial Implementation

The decision to kill the Jews could have been made by Hitler regardless of the war and its development. In other words, the decision was to be made, and the war allowed it to be implemented in various stages. Yet there is a problem with this assertion, and this must be seen in the light of the forced emigration policy beforehand, which obviously did not entail the physical annihilation of the deportees. Nor can we prove on the basis of Hitler's moves before late 1940 that he had envisioned a multifront war, which would allow him to implement a decision to kill the Jews wherever he found them. Such a decision was made in October or November 1941, following the initial decision to destroy the Jews in occupied Soviet territory. Before that, various territorial "solutions," including the Madagascar Plan, were considered within the overall framework of the war as it had developed until then, including dubious American neutrality, British policies and actions, including bombing raids on Germany, and Nazi–Soviet relations. Hence, my argument is that the Final Solution decision was the result of a radicalized German policy toward the Jews in the context of the behavior of third parties toward the Third Reich as it affected Hitler after the "Battle of Britain." Yet one may ask immediately how Soviet Jews became the first victims of Hitler's wrath against the British and the Americans while Polish Jews were under Germany's control since fall 1939. Indeed, the very fact that the Polish Jews in other territories occupied by Germany since 1939–1940 were not liquidated until later, following the initial decision to kill the Soviet Jews, requires explanation.

The initial decision to destroy the Soviet Jews evolved as a matter of course to those already in Nazi hands and to all others in connection with the broadening and the prolongation of the war and in response to third parties' behavior. The experience gained allowed the few to kill the very many, and the initial decision evolved by a combined drive from above and from among the executioners while the German home front and others in the Nazi sphere of influence either remained passive or even helped them in various ways. Thus, the initial secrecy in regard to the Final Solution was gradually lifted, at least by Hitler himself and some others, while the failure of the forced emigration policy was used to blame the third parties for the Final Solution itself.[1]

In fact, the forced emigration policy continued for some time after the outbreak of World War II. Then came the Madagascar plan, which depended on British and French cooperation within the larger framework of Hitler's "new order" in Europe, which the British rejected offhand, and the related challenges to the German war economy and to the dependence on Soviet good will and the Soviets' growing demands. At the same time came the growing American aid to the British, ascribed to the Jews, and finally Hitler's related decision to invade Stalin's USSR and the initial decision to kill the Jews therein.

On the basis of various documented evidence,[2] it could be concluded which role was played by whom in regard to written orders pertaining to the Final Solution, who issued them, and why. Hitler announced the initial decision regarding "Barbarossa" in July 1940, aiming at May 1941 as the target date.[3] Along these lines, as we are told by the newest research on the Russian campaign, Göring a few days later issued instructions to the effect that the "new order" plans were to be based on the assumption that Germany would extend her economic sphere of power "in Europe and in the rest of the world as far as possible."[4] As in the case of the 1936 Four Year Plan, any Jewish threat to this German claim should have been punished by death. The role of Göring and possibly Herbert Backe is important here because Backe was the one who painted the negative picture at home resulting from the British blockade while promising economic salvation if the Soviet Union were attacked,[5] and Göring remained the highest-ranking German officer, in charge of the survival of the German people and Germany's future world status.

By the end of 1940, Heydrich – the chief operator in things Jewish at this stage – was ordered to prepare a new plan for the disposition of the

---

[1] See "Wannsee Protocol," Nuremberg document NG-2586-G, in which Heydrich justified the Final Solution by invoking the failure of the forced emigration policy, obviously in order to convince the representatives of the civilian bureaucracies that the third parties were to be blamed for the Final Solution by refusing to absorb the Jews.

[2] The whole description of the early stages of the Final Solution here is taken from the entry "The Final Solution," in the *Yale Holocaust Encyclopedia*, by Peter Longerich and myself. Since the entry did not quote our documentary sources, I have introduced here only the most important among them.

[3] Horst-Dieter Müller, in *Germany and the Second World War: The Attack on the Soviet Union*, p. 135.

[4] Ibid., note 85.

[5] Ibid., p. 124, note 23.

Jews from German-controlled Europe (except for the Soviet areas).[6] At this stage, it was not clear in which direction this deportation was to be carried out, following the failure of the Madagascar Plan. Yet once Hitler started the planning for "Barbarossa," one can believe that the Jews were to be deported en masse to the territories of the Soviet Union, which were supposed to be occupied in the summer of 1941. This background should explain Heydrich's order of January 1941 to resume the deportations from the Polish General Gouvernement. The destinations were perceived as a transition area only, but the transports, which started in February and also included Jews from Vienna, collided in March 1941 with the military transports of Operation "Barbarossa" and stopped as a result of them.

Heydrich's preparations for a general disposition of the European Jews were continued, however. In the same month of March 1941, Heydrich submitted to Göring a draft plan for the "Final Solution of the Jewish Question."[7] The final order was signed by Göring on July 31, 1941, following an agreement that had been reached in regard to the role of Alfred Rosenberg's new Ministry in the Occupied Eastern Territories. The July document gave Heydrich the authority, " ... to act in order to carry out all the necessary substantive and material preparations for an overall [Gesamtlösung] solution of the Jewish question in the German area of influence in Europe."

At the same time as the Russian campaign was conceived in terms of solving the "Jewish Problem" in Europe in occupied Soviet territory, the Nazi authorities also planned a campaign of annihilation against the elites of the occupied peoples, especially Jews and Bolsheviks. The military planning and the actual developments on the ground (i.e., the serious problem of supplying the troops along the enormous Soviet front) and the ensuing setbacks in carrying out a short campaign contributed to the radicalization of the initial campaign against the Jews in which all the components of the invading forces were involved. The view that the Jews were an enemy that should be annihilated or at least brutally neutralized prevailed among all of them as a matter of course and was related to the conquest of the vast Soviet territory as a must if Germany were to prevail and secure its Lebensraum.[8] Yet it was a period of some probing and experimenting since the henchmen were counting on local pogroms that might have decimated the Jews and did not know in advance how the German Army would behave in front of an organized killing of unarmed civilians by the Germans, as local pogroms did

[6] See Theodor Dannecker to Eichmann on January 21, 1941, *Vichy–Auschwitz: Die Zusammenarbeit zwischen den Deutschen und Französischen Behörden bei der Endlösung der Judenfrage* (Reinbeck bei Hamburg: Serge Klarsfeld, 1989), p. 371.

[7] See Götz Aly, *"Endlösung," Völkerverschiebung und der Mord an den europäischen Juden* (Frankfurt: S. Fischer Verlag, 1995, pp. 227ff).

[8] See Jürgen Förster, "Securing 'Living Space,'" in *Germany and the Second World War: The Attack on the Soviet Union*, part VII, pp. 1188–1244.

not assume the character of a wholesale massacre. Having resorted to mass shootings on their own, the Germans created later on local auxiliary police units to carry out such actions. The motives behind this ever-growing carnage seem to be clear. First, there was an initial or basic order given by Hitler and further broadened in the context that I have ascribed to his reply to the Allied (mainly British–American) response to his challenge. Second, there was a so–called "security" motive – which explained Heydrich's growing role – in terms of doing away with a potential enemy behind the back of the German armies, which was combined with ideological and racial motives requiring no further elaboration here.

Thus, the German policy in occupied Russia developed into three waves of anti–Jewish action. The first one had begun at the very outbreak of the Russian war by means of pogroms and improvised executions. The definition of the target population was broad enough to allow mass executions in various areas. Sometimes, the entire male population of military service age was destroyed at that stage.

The second wave, which started in August 1941, was much wider in scope and aimed also at whole families, including women and children. It is estimated that during the first two months about 50,000 people were shot, while between August and year's end about half a million were put to death.

The third wave started following the initial conquest by the Germans of given areas and the creation of local, permanent occupation organs. It consisted of ghettoization, compulsory work, and continued mass shootings.

This third phase began in the western parts of the occupied territories in August 1941 and in the eastern parts thereof in the fall of that year. The policy pertaining to the destruction of the Jews in the Soviet Union had now a long-range, systematic character. In addition to the growing interest in the temporary use of Jewish slave labor for the war industry, the Nazi Security Police apparatus and the local occupation authorities realized that the destruction of Soviet Jews by shooting them was difficult to carry out fully. The reasons for this view were several: first, the very large number of potential victims whose threatened murder by mass shootings became known; second, the coming winter, which made digging pits by the victims themselves more difficult; and third, the strain felt by the killers themselves. In August 1941, there began therefore the search for alternative modes of mass murder.

In the September–October period, there were several preparations made toward the establishment of killing centers in Poland, operated by euthanasia experts transferred to the East, which exposes the fact that the mass murder of Jews was also taking place outside of the Soviet Union. Thus, the planned Final Solution of the whole European Jewish Question in Soviet territory following a short campaign there had already begun in another form during the initial fighting there and was broadened in steps to an overall program to destroy all the Jews of Europe. The detailed implementations of decisions made in this regard were issued separately by Hitler, Himmler, Göring, Heydrich, and a variety of SS officers in regional charge, culminating in spring and summer 1942 in an overall pattern mainly carried out in that year and in 1943, except in the special cases of the ghetto of Lodz, which survived almost until the end of the war, and of some Polish Jews used as slave laborers. By 1944, only one large Jewish community remained intact, the Hungarian one, while Rumanian Jewry suffered tremendous losses at the beginning of the Russian campaign. Yet later the Antonescu regime waited for the Germans to win that campaign and in the meantime stopped the deportations to Transnistria. One-third of the Slovak Jewry also survived until 1944. The small communities of Bulgaria, Albania, and Denmark survived until the end of the war, as did a larger number of French Jews under Vichy's regime due to local specific circumstances.

The Slovak, Hungarian, and Rumanian cases will be discussed in some detail later on because they seem to have entailed various rescue options.

The process of radicalization of the Final Solution in general could be explained by invoking a number of factors within the larger framework of a limited war that was in the process of being transformed by the Nazis themselves into a world war.[9]

First, the very creation and use of a multistaged killing machine as described above generated an inner logic of destruction that was related to the prolongation and brutalization of the war in Russia itself. This brutalization was preconceived, and the orders were given to the killing units ahead of the campaign itself, but it assumed a life of its own on the ground.

Second, given the inner structure of the Nazi regime and the permanent competition and rivalry among its leading representatives, any act of radical anti-Semitism was encouraged, welcomed, and served the personal ambition of individuals. This institutionalized a cumulative radicalization of anti-Semitism, a process that I have called elsewhere a "competition towards the worst."[10]

Third, the proclamations of the top Nazis that the "Judenproblem" would be solved during a war drove the radical elements in the party to develop various murderous expectations in this regard. Yet the fact that the war was not over soon but assumed a new and more threatening character – including British air raids, which started at the end of 1940, and losses at the front – strengthened these existing expectations and were combined with sharp emotions of revenge. During the second half of 1941, a sort of competition emerged among various Gauleiter as to who among them would be the first to make his region literally "judenfrei." The deportation of the Jews was perceived to be a sort of relevant reward for the war effort, both

---

[9] I quote here Peter Longerich's contribution to our entry in the *Yale Holocaust Encyclopedia*.
[10] See my work *Reinhard Heydrich und die Frühgeschichte von Gestapo und SD*, pp. 252–254.

in an ideological–political sense and in a practical sense, especially in terms of housing.[11]

Fourth, it could be argued that the prospect of a unique giant military victory beyond one's fantasy, which seemed to be achievable in the Soviet Union, could have given the Nazis the sense of omnipotence necessary to go beyond their previous modes of operation.[12]

Fifth, there existed further a theory about the Final Solution that perceived the destruction of the European Jews as just the first step toward more universal Nazi goals. The so-called "spearhead theory," formulated by the neo-Marxist scholar Franz Neumann, at the time head of the Research and Analysis Section of the Office of Strategic Services (OSS-R&A) specializing in German affairs,[13] took for granted that the destruction of the Jews was acceptable to Germans, and thus it legitimized (by creating the precedent for the disposal of the Jews) far-reaching plans of destruction aimed at other nations. Another theory could be seen as a more recent version of the same and argued that the destruction of the Jews was an instrumental part of a Nazi plan to invoke ethnic cleansing measures against other nations and create a "pure German" area of settlement and economic modernization.[14] Missing here is Hitler's assertion to the former Mufti of Jerusalem already in November 1941[15] that the Jews of the Middle East would be exterminated as well even though Germany had no direct ambition in that region but would have turned most of it over to Fascist Italy and/or to the Arabs. Both theories try to "universalize" the Final Solution and therefore minimize the centrality of anti-Semitism in the Nazi doctrine and actual behavior by making the Jews "functional" tools aimed at other targets. Both theories may explain the historical reality in the sense that during the Holocaust the mass murder of Jews seemed "justified" and popular, at least in the eyes of the killers and many in other nations, and was explained by neo-Marxist scholars in "functionalist" terms as an economic, imperialist war aimed at others, whose destruction would be legitimized by killing Jews first. As we shall see, both theories would be refuted by the continuation of the Holocaust by Hitler and several other executioners until the very end of the Third Reich,

---

[11] For specifics about the impact that a British bombing raid on Hamburg as early as September 1941 had on Karl Kaufman, the Gauleiter of Hamburg, who asked Göring to " have the Jews evacuated" as a result of the British attack, see Frank Bajohr, "Karl Kaufman – Gauleiter in Hamburg," *Vierteljahreshefte für Zeitgeschichte*, 43/2 (1995): 267–296.

[12] See Christopher Browning, *Initiating the Final Solution – The Fateful Months of September–October 1941* (Washington, D.C.: United States Holocaust Memorial Museum, March 13, 2003).

[13] On Neumann's "Spearhead Theory," see Petra Marquardt-Bigman, "Amerikanische Geheimdienstanalysen des nationalsozialistischen Deutschlands, *Tel Aviver Jahrbuch für deutsche Geschichte (TAJB)* (1994): 325–344.

[14] See Götz Aly, "*Endlösung.*"

[15] See Weinberg, *A world at Arms*, p. 302, note 144 for his sources.

when no such gains against others could be expected. The Nazis had at least won the lost war on one major front – the war against the Jews – as formulated by Hitler in his "political testament," and made no concessions on this central issue as a legacy left for the future to be pursued later by the neo-Nazi movement.

Yet the reaction abroad to the Holocaust may have been a bonus calculated by Hitler himself when he said on October 25, 1941, in the presence of his henchmen Himmler and Heydrich:[16]

"I have prophesied upon the Jewry, that the Jew would disappear from Europe, *when the war wouldn't be avoided* (italics added). This criminal race has two million dead of the World War [I–S.A.] on their conscience, now hundreds of thousands again. No one should tell me: we cannot simply push them into the morass! Who cares then about our own people! *It is fine, that the scare [Schreck], that we exterminate the Jews is spreading ahead of us.*" (Hitler, Monologe, p. 44)

This is, in my view, a rather important statement, accompanied later by several similar public statements made by Hitler himself with regard to his January 1939 "prophecy" and by Joseph Goebbels in "Das Reich" following the Warsaw ghetto uprising. These statements all tell us that the Final Solution was not at all the secret that we might have thought. That Hitler was personally involved as the initiator and the one who finally brushed aside previous partial alternatives that might have contained murderous tendencies and actual options for mass murder as early as late 1940 seems for some to remain an open issue due to the failure thus far to find a written order signed by him. When Hitler finally became an ideological mass murderer, blaming Jews for his world war and the previous one, he remained a politician, calculating a possible bonus from the mass murder: "It is fine, that the scare that we exterminate the Jews is spreading ahead of us." As I interpret it, it might have driven the West to "do something," which Western leaders would not in terms of making political mistakes by rendering the Jews utmost importance in public and thereby falling into the trap of a "Jew's war," which could have driven a wedge between Western elites and anti-Semites in their own countries. Hitler possibly aimed also at creating an atmosphere of fear and awe – and of understanding and support – among others, both the Allies and occupied peoples, "thanks to the scare that we exterminate the Jews." Perhaps he even thought that the Jews themselves would put pressure to bear on the Allies to do something about it, thus exposing the Allies governments as fighting a "Jew's war." Hitler could then have exploited this for his own purposes, and it was in fact all his propaganda agencies were talking about later on even when Allied governments were usually silent.

One could add to this a possible calculated domestic political advantage for Hitler in terms of creating a sense of collective guilt, binding the German

---

[16] Hitler, *Monologe*, p. 44.

people to the regime as at least passive participants in an unprecedented crime, at least in their own eyes and in the eyes of the belligerent third parties. That is to say that any domestic activity against the Nazi regime would have been seen as unacceptable to a third party government once such a crime was already, and irreversibly, in progress. At the same time, the third parties did very little actually to rescue the Jews because, among other reasons, this crime was a German crime and for them to take a side was a politically dangerous, irritating issue. This demonstrates the depth of the trap.

6

The "Final Solution" in Some Detail and More on Its Justification

The ongoing debate between those who are called "intentionalists" and those called "functionalists" among the scholars who deal with the origins of the "Final Solution of the Jewish Question"[1] should be mentioned here briefly. In my view, the debate represents two artificially separated aspects of Hitler's motives and actions while missing a most important mixture in him of what he believed to be his political genius and political action in response to the challenge, which he offered to others. This was combined with a sense of victimization and threat, of taking revenge and making his point in spite of and because of others' refusal to respond positively to his shorter-range overtures, plus rationalization mechanisms that legitimized his longer-range aims and basic convictions.

What we have here is the multidimensional behavior of a man who was capable of living in several combined spheres: those of his ideology, his political and strategic calculations, and his reaction to his enemies' actions and their reactions for his own actions, which always made them responsible for his own actions against them. His previous successes, fears, and contempt toward his enemies should be added to the adopted and probably fragile perception of himself as a genial phenomenon, the redeemer of his own people and the incarnation of their best traits, previously in a state of decay. The best traditions of his people were being revived thanks to his political intervention, which was saving them from the fearsome threats of modern life, but this required an ongoing effort as long as he was alive. His qualities as a politician included bluffing and gambling, acting and hostage taking, divide-and-rule methods and open threats, and a unique blend of contempt toward the weak and respect mixed with a sense of challenge toward the strong. All this was mixed with the refusal to accept established elites at home and abroad and with the drive to challenge the strong and prove that

---

[1] The short description of the "Final Solution" herein was mostly Peter Longerich's contribution to our entry in this regard in the *Yale Holocaust Encyclopedia*.

his own power was earned and "natural," not obsolete and degenerated as he perceived the old German elite and to an extent the British elite to be,[2] resulting from unique historical circumstances as he understood the American multiracial democracy[3] to be, or weak and contemptuous as he perceived the East European ocean of inferior races to be, which thus would allow Germany to create its own continental superpower of racially pure Aryans in Eastern Europe when circumstances would allow and dictate it.[4]

The intentionalists miss Hitler's tactics at the same time possibly combined with his sincere belief, once the West declined to play his forced emigration game and resorted to war, of making the Jews responsible for Allied actions, as Jews were indeed among his most active opponents from the beginning, and Judaism as such contributed immensely to the decline in values that he intended to save and revive. Yet the Jews and their alleged tools, such as Churchill, Eden, and even Chamberlain at the time, were in Hitler's eyes "too egoistic" to take care of their own interests by seriously listening to him and understanding that the very lives of their brethren under his control were at stake, as well as the very survival of the British Empire itself. Hence Hitler's expectation was that the more the Jews tried to get their brethren out, the more they would serve his interests of spreading anti-Semitism or tainting the war as Jewish. At the same time, he perceived the Allies as being susceptible to alleged Jewish influence and actions, against their own interests, in addition to their personal egotistical interest in war profits.[5]

The functionalists seem to have paid too much attention to the bureaucratic zeal and cooperation between the Gestapo and SD, to the power game played between the SS and other centers of power in the Third Reich, to Eichmann's zeal as deportation expert, and to Heydrich's preparations and actual difficulties in pushing Jews into the West, to Madagascar, and into occupied Poland, and later his zeal as a driving force behind the Final Solution itself. The decision maker, however, was and remained Adolf Hitler, and he may have been surprised to find that industrial genocide proved to be rather easy, at least in the German-occupied territories.

The general policy aimed at the destruction of the European Jewry as a whole was adopted a little later, once the initial policy was implemented in Soviet territory. Among functionalist reasons it was due to the German sense of omnipotence at that time coupled with an enormous sense of revenge. But this sense of revenge was combined with self-pity as Hitler rationalized many other atrocities. Indeed, he said in his "Table Talks" that under the

---

[2] See Hitler, *Monologe*, p. 333 and also pp. 93, 110, for example.

[3] Hitler, *Monologe*, p. 187.

[4] For initial reading, see Adolf Hitler, *Mein Kampf*, 1934 edition (München: Eher Verlag 1934, pp. 669–705, 721, 723), and Wolfgang Horn, "Ein unbekannter Aufsatz Hitlers aus dem Frühjahr 1924," *VfZ* 16 (1968), 280–294.

[5] Hitler, *Monologe*.

circumstances of a struggle in which his own people were dying because of the Jews, he had no reason to keep the Jews under his control alive, and he might have been assisted in this regard by Herbert Backe, the old, trusted crony whose early support of the Nazi cause was said to have been a result of the impact of the British blockade over Germany during World War I, which the Germans perceived as a sort of genocidal campaign. Once the decision was made, the killing of the Jews became an object in itself, quite openly proclaimed by Hitler as such.[6] The utmost secrecy in which the actual murder was executed was thus a matter of the operational efficiency by various German agencies as far as the victims, and possibly also as far as Germans who could not be trusted, were concerned. Still, something political remained in the decision's continued execution from Hitler's own point of view.

In the initial stages, in the mind of the German people, the enormous crime was executed by all branches of the German government, and as such was rather visible to the non-Jewish environment. German and Austrian Jews disappeared and their property and homes were "Aryanized." In the occupied territories, Wehrmacht and Order Police units joined the SS in the killing missions. Soon enough, Hitler publicly declared the victims to be "the prey of concentration camps" according to his "prophecy" of January 30, 1939. Thus, the policy of genocide became a proclaimed, widely seen, obvious, and acceptable policy. Yet as such this policy made the bystanders sort of accomplices, at least in Hitler's eyes and possibly their own eyes.[7]

The systematic deportations from Germany proper to the death centers established in Poland began in early spring 1942. In fact, Auschwitz emerged as one of them only around summer 1942. Yet the execution of the Final Solution decision did not mean that a detailed, preconceived blueprint was simply carried out, but the Final Solution was a general framework for genocide, executed in various ways, requiring many decisions to be made and executed by many people under different circumstances. In my view, Hitler made the initial decision to destroy all the Jews late in 1941. The rest of the time involved implementation, requiring the "proper" means, even some concessions in given circumstances, lessons learned, and the use

---

[6] Hitler's September 30, 1942, public assertion at the Sportpalast in Berlin that his January 30, 1939, "prophecy" about the destruction of the Jews was being implemented now; see Franklin Watts (ed.), *Voices of History 1942–1943* (New York: Gramercy Publications, 1943, p. 121), text as monitored and translated by Foreign Broadcast Monitoring Service, FCC, and see further Domarus (ed.), *Hitler: Reden und Proklamationen*, Volume II, pp. 1828 ff. Hitler had referred to the "prophecy" as a threat that others might have laughed at but which would become true like many other "prophecies" he had already made before in January 1942 in a speech held also at the Sportpalast.

[7] See Hans-Heinrich Wilhelm, "Wie geheim war die 'Endlösung'?" *Miscellanea: Festschrift für Helmut Krausnick*, edited by Wolfgang Benz (Stuttgart: Deutsche Verlag-Anstalt, 1980, pp. 131–148) in addition to Domarus, *Hitler: Reden und Proklamationen*.

of the victims for domestic and foreign political purposes. Yet the staged implementation of the Final Solution may also explain the hopes and the efforts of those who vainly tried to save those who temporarily escaped death. The transports from the West, Germany itself included, were organized by the SS Reich Main Security Office's (RSHA) Jewish Section under Adolf Eichmann. The Order Police supplied the guards, and the transportation was supplied by the German Ministry of Transportation and/or directly by the German-controlled European railway system. Many other civil authorities played an active part in preparing, organizing, and benefiting from the deportations, such as the judiciary, the finance administration, the Ministry of Propaganda, and the local authorities. In order to deport thousands from a German or Austrian city or town, the whole local police apparatus was mobilized; a large shipping area, such as the local freight depot, was taken over and guarded. A variety of other agencies were actively involved: Internal Revenue agents produced lists of property and confiscated it, agents of the Labor Office revoked labor certificates, and officials of the Housing Office assembled the keys and decided on the transfer of the emptied apartments to the new dwellers. In Poland, units of the regular police and personnel from the SS training camp at Travniki were regularly used to carry out the deportations.

The German Foreign Ministry was actively involved in the rather complicated implementation of the Final Solution in German-allied nations. Its representatives, working together at home with the RSHA and even in competition with the SS in some cases, were actively involved in the legal, administrative, and political setup in various German-allied countries. They maintained contact with local ethnic German groups and put pressure to bear in cooperation with them or directly upon reluctant allies to carry out the Final Solution in various ways, including the transfer of the victims to German hands.

This proved to be the case on the ground, but Hitler himself might have had his doubts about his own people early on. He might have considered early British, and later Allied, bombing as a serious threat to his regime, which proved in fact either to be irrelevant to German civilian morale or actually to boost it.[8] Yet the fear of another November 1918, which was a major experience transforming Hitler into a "Politiker" and considered to have been a Jewish stab in the back, which of course it was not, still haunted him.

The big difference this time was to be sought in his Nazi Revolution and in his way of "educating" his people – especially the young – to adopt Nazi values. Hitler certainly did not trust the older generation – generals included – or the members of the higher middle classes or the old proletariat. The crimes committed in their names and by members of such classes, however, were

---

[8] Albert Speer interview with the author.

yet another chain binding them to his regime. The irony was that most of
the military collaborated with him directly or indirectly in implementing
the Final Solution, and only a small minority tried to rebel against him
later on. The irony for the future would be that Hitler's final defeat helped
counter the argument that he might have won the war after all if not stopped
by treacherous domestic intervention. At least Allied deliberations did not
miss this point.

The discussion of Jews continued even when they were being murdered
en masse. Hitler used to argue among his cronies[9] that "Judaism" had destroyed Rome, the "fighting empire," which Hitler tried to imitate by using
Roman methods of acquiring and maintaining power, not without growing
support from the Germanic tribes. Rome was for Hitler the incarnation of
the exercise of power that was essential to keep a pagan civilization alive,
and Judaism supposedly had decisively contributed to the decay of Rome's
creative paganism by injecting into the veins of the Romans values and be-
liefs that destroyed their "natural" behavior and transformed them more
and more into humble servants of unnatural, Jewish values. The Jews used
those values, which they allegedly never followed themselves, to subdue the
ancient world and destroy it from within. The characteristic heroism, form
of government, and creativity of the cultures involved, including those of
the ancient Germans when Christianized, were weakened and destroyed to
a serious extent while directly serving the Jews who invented those values
for their cynical purposes. This is how the nonfighting, commercial, racially
conscious, separate "Jewish state" took root among the peoples of Europe
and had sustained itself since time immemorial.

While the Final Solution was implemented, Hitler repeated again and
again, speaking freely to his cronies,[10] that Pauline Christianity – by itself
a dreaded enemy of Jews for almost two millennia – brought havoc upon
"Aryan" Europe in the sense that it bound it to the values and rules of behavior of the Jewish God. Yet the Jews themselves worshiped and still worship
their real God, the one and only golden calf. This they supposedly did while
amusing themselves about the gentiles, trapped by Jewish religious commitments that strangled their vitality, their natural instincts, and their creative
will. Sure enough, Hitler pretended to have carried Schopenhauer's philosophy on the role of the human will in his bag during the previous war and
referred to Nietzsche as well in this connection and also to Kant[11] possibly

---

  [9] Hitler, *Monologe*, p. 65, and see English translation of earlier publication of the same, Hitler's
    Secret Conversations (New York: Farrar, Straus and Young, 1953, pp. 72–73).
 [10] Hitler, *Secret Conversations*, pp. 63–64: "On the road to Damascus, St. Paul discovered that
    he could succeed in ruining the Roman state by causing the principle to triumph of the
    equality of all men before a single God – and by putting beyond the reach of the laws his
    private notions, which he alleged to be divinely inspired." October 21, 1941, midday.
 [11] Hitler, *Secret Conversations*, pp. 583–584, May 16, 1944.

because of the latter's sharp criticism of the Jewish political tradition,[12] which he picked up in some anti-Semitic writings.

Thus, he said in the Table Talks[13] that "The end of the war would bring with it the final destruction of the Jew. The Jew is the incorporation of egoism... he has no ability to deeply deal with spiritual matters... if he pretended to deal with literature or art, he did it because of snobbery and speculation... *their egoism reaches such a degree, that they can not even risk their lives to defend their own interests*..." (italics added). This statement could support both sides of an argument that Hitler expected – or did not expect – the Jews abroad to understand that their interest was to do everything to save their brethren under his control, and even risk their lives to do so, but instead they made others, the Western Allies, fight him, even when he added at the same time that Churchill did it because of an outdated British policy of a European balance of power. Still, the result would be the inevitable doom of the Jews: "The policy represented by Churchill is to nobody's interest, in short, but that of the Jews. But *that* [italics in original] people was chosen by Jehovah because of its stupidity. *The last thing that their interest should have told the Jews to do was to enter into this war*" (italics added). Indeed, Hitler never expected the Jews to rise and fight. The Warsaw ghetto uprising was quite a surprise to him.[14]

[12] See Fania Oz-Salzberger, "Jewish Sources of the Modern Republic," in *Tcheleth, a Periodical for Israeli Thought* 13 (2002), 89–130.

[13] Hitler, *Secret Conversations*, pp. 96–97, November 5, 1941, evening.

[14] Albert Speer interview with author.

7

The Zionists' Dilemmas

During the forced emigration phase, Jews expelled by Eichmann, many after a period of internment at Dachau and other concentration camps and having been released provided they immediately left German-controlled territory, sought a refuge anywhere. This included Palestine, and they tried to enter that country "illegally" with the help of the Jewish Agency, which at this stage was ready to do its best to support their effort and set aside previous considerations of securing "legal" entry quotas from the British.

The British restrictions on emigration to Palestine forced the Zionist parties involved to use "conspiratorial" measures. They camouflaged their activities and sometimes used the services of dubious persons, conditions typically imposed by the British themselves, who then became suspicious of them and the methods of illegal immigration that they themselves forced the Jews to undertake.[1] The Zionists had to hide their immigration operations from British Intelligence agents and try to defy the Imperial networks, which grew enormously after the outbreak of the war and kept many eyes on the half million Jews then living in Palestine. The Jewish Agency was thus engaged in "illegal" emigration as long as the Nazis allowed it, and they turned their attention to the neighboring Arab countries as well, seeking a common denominator with the British in fighting the Germans while at the same time offering their own services to them in order to make themselves useful to the war effort as best they could in order to gain politically and morally from such assistance.

Seeking at least to mobilize support among the regional branches of the British Intelligence services toward Zionism and Jews, the Jewish Agency was ready to risk a sabotage operation against German oil shipping on the Danube by sending Zionist operatives to Rumania in 1940 and later by supporting Allied Intelligence questioning centers for Jewish refugees to identify

[1] For the story of illegal Jewish immigration into Palestine, see Dalia Ofer, *Illegal Immigration during the Holocaust* (Jerusalem: Yad Izhak Ben-Zvi, 1988, pp. 21–54) (in Hebrew).

military targets in enemy territory and by rendering other intelligence information in German allied nations such as Rumania.

Sometime in 1941, the Nazis forbade Jewish emigration, but many Jews in Palestine and abroad perceived the British to be the main obstacle to letting Jews escape from Europe into Palestine, especially when the few refugees who managed to arrive were sent by the British authorities to Mauritius, an island in the Indian Ocean several hundred miles east of Madagascar. The rescue debate, which would go on for decades after in various forms, seemed from then on to be concentrated on the British refusal to allow refugee Jews to disturb their relations with Arabs, and hence Arabs would be blamed for preventing rescue. In fact, the British went on with their previous anti-immigration policy once they decided to defeat Hitler (and cultivate their imperial interests in the area), who had pushed Jews out in the first place. This was a terrible vicious circle, which was dominated now by Nazi refusal to let Jews out rather than by British refusal to let them in. Still, in Arab eyes, the Jews would seem to be the operators and agents of British imperialism, an argument that had been spread widely the 1930s by the pro-American scholar and diplomat George Antonius, by Fascist and Nazi propaganda organs, and later by Hajj Amin el Husseini, the former Mufti of Jerusalem, who was then in Berlin.

Thus, one may say that the Arab rebellion of the late 1930s was a political success in spite of its military failure. It stopped a growing wave of Jewish refugees from entering the country legally and mobilized British power to curb illegal immigration during the first two years of World War II.[2] The White Paper of May 1939 forced the Yishuv's leadership to confront seemingly unsolvable dilemmas – whether to declare a rebellion of their own against Britain, the only power after a while that stood against Hitler, the arch enemy, while trying to advance their own case and rise up against the only ones who were fighting him and offering hope that he would finally be defeated, while Hitler, not the British, went particularly after Jews. A few among the Yishuv were ready and willing to support such a unilateral Jewish action, which would have taken place in a country essential to the Imperial troops fighting nearby and surrounded by an Arab ocean. Most of the followers of Vladimir Jabotinsky, who died in 1940 (e.g., the nationalist Zionists), accepted this logic. A splinter group among them, the Stern group, did not and resorted to a terror campaign against the British mandatory power while seeking an understanding with Fascist Italy and Nazi Germany since the Axis powers seemed to be willing to follow a policy of Jewish migration out of Europe. Thus, a common interest was to bind the Axis powers and the Sternists in making Palestine such a haven while getting rid of the British and the

---

[2] See Dalia Ofer's English version of the work cited in note 1, *Escaping the Holocaust: Illegal Immigration to the Land of Israel, 1939–1944* (New York: Oxford University Press, 1990, pp. 128–174).

"collaborating" Zionist leadership.[3] This must have been seen, and was so understood by the British, as a direct terrorist campaign not just against law and order in a country under their control but as a threat to their war effort.[4] The Labor Zionist leaders believed that the Stern terror campaign against the British was morally and politically absurd, aimed as it was toward possible cooperation at least with Fascist Italy and even with Nazi Germany due to the latter's (in the meantime given up) interest in mass Jewish emigration, which was not free of radical anti-Jewish intentions and was supported by acts of extreme violence that rendered any real Jewish–Nazi common denominator absolutely impossible. The other choice for the Yishuv was to join the British in fighting the Germans as best they could while trying to abolish the White Paper due to the new circumstances imposed by the war. The repercussions on the German side were not considered, I believe, because of a degree of inexperience and naiveté among the Zionists at the time with regard to the Third Reich, while they tried to present themselves to the Western Allies as if they could indeed use their networks in Europe to gather information and otherwise help the Allied cause.

The gradual outcome was the emergence of an "activist" school among the Yishuv's leaders, David Ben-Gurion and Yitzhak Tabenkin among them, which tended during the "Phony War" (i.e., the period between the outbreak of the war and the German offensive in the West in 1940) to demonstrate the Yishuv's own frustration and rejection of the White Paper by invoking a variety of political, rather than military, means to make the country "less safe for the British," whose primary interest at that time was domestic quiet and acceptance of their restrictions. Ben-Gurion named this policy in early 1940 as the double-edged strategy of fighting the Nazis as if there was no White Paper and opposing the British as if there were no Nazis.[5] Soon enough, Hitler's armies invaded the Low Countries and France, and that "activist" approach had to be replaced by any possible cooperation with the British to fight the Axis menace while seeking to maintain some ways of getting Jews to Palestine during the hostilities, which by intervals grew into a global war. Once the Final Solution gradually became known, the Yishuv leadership

---

[3] For scholarly studies of the Stern group, see Ya'akov Shavit, *The Myths of the Right* (Tel-Aviv, Zofit: Beit Berl and Moshe Sharett Institute, 1986) (in Hebrew), and Yosef Heller's *LEHI: Ideology and Politics, 1940–1949*, Volumes I and II (Jerusalem: Zalman Shazar Center and Ketter Publications, 1989) (in Hebrew).

[4] Sources: British police intelligence (CID) reports of late 1940, Hagana Archive, Rep. 47, and see Eldad Haruvi, "The Criminal Investigation Department of the Palestine Police Force 1920–1948," Ph.D. thesis, Haifa University, November 2002.

[5] See Tuvia Friling, "David Ben Gurion and the Catastrophe of European Jewry 1939–1945," Ph.D. thesis, Hebrew University, Jerusalem, 1990 (in Hebrew). Friling later published a two-volume work based on this thesis and more, entitled *Arrow in the Dark: David Ben-Gurion, the Yishuv's Leadership and Rescue Efforts during the Holocaust* (Sede Boker, Jerusalem, and Tel-Aviv: Hebrew University and Ben-Gurion University Press, 1998) (in Hebrew).

resorted to overt actions, such as rallies, demonstrations, demands for the Allies to exert pressure on the perpetrators, the exchange of Germans in Allied hands with Jews, and for the Allies to make public threats against the executioners. They realized after a while that the Allies would not undertake any significant overt action due to their fear of a "Jew's war." Several among the Yishuv went on with overt actions, but others – mainly David Ben-Gurion, as we shall see – tried various covert options, which explains the significance of intelligence records and the related action and inaction of the bureaucracies involved in this narrative later on.

The former Mufti of Jerusalem in the meantime was not satisfied with the White Paper even when strictly implemented, and he drew closer and closer to the Axis, having approached the Nazi Consul-General in Jerusalem for Arab–Muslim cooperation as early as 1933 to offer him Muslim – not just Arab – support of the Nazi cause. He was involved in anti-Allied activities throughout the Arab world from the outbreak of World War II, helped a pro-German regime become established for a short time in Iraq until the British crushed it,[6] then left for the pro-German Iran, and finally was given refuge in Berlin. Still, even when Vichy-ruled Syria was occupied by British Imperial troops with some Jewish aid (the future General Moshe Dayan served the invading Australian troops in Syria as a scout and lost his eye – winning much political clout in the future thereby) and Iraq cleared of its pro-Nazi government, the British Middle East HQ, British diplomats and intelligence officers, and their colleagues in London were very worried about a violent Arab reaction should Jews be allowed to enter Palestine in numbers and harbored their own negative view of the Zionists. For their part, the Zionists would ask for a Jewish army to be created within Allied ranks to no avail until November 1944, when both FDR and Churchill agreed on the creation of a "Jewish Brigade Group" within the British Army.

Amin Husseini likewise would recruit Muslim volunteers in Bosnia for the SS, and in the meantime he was involved at least in political efforts to discredit the Western war effort as "Jewish," connecting it with the Palestine question, in preventing any future emigration of Jews to Palestine, and with propaganda efforts among the Arabs of the Middle East and Muslims in general against the Allies and Jews alike, calling for an open campaign to slaughter the latter "wherever you find them,"[7] a strategy that benefited the Arab cause rather than damaging it during most of World War II, as we shall see.[8]

---

[6] For the development of British–Arab relations at the political level, see Yehoshua Porath, *The Test of Political Reality: Palestine, Arab Unity and British Policy*, 1930–1945 (Jerusalem: Yad Izhak Ben-Zvi, 1985) (in Hebrew); see especially pp. 257–260. (The English translation of the title is my own.)

[7] See note 22 in Chapter 8.

[8] See notes 2 and 22 in Chapter 8.

8

Dimensions of the Allied Response to Hitler's "Jewish Politics" and the Deepening of the Trap

Divided into several stages and issues, the response of the British – and the neutral Americans until December 1941 – to Hitler's Jewish policies was partially based upon incomplete information on Nazi actions and intentions, supported by different interests and prejudices, to be described as partially inertial and partially political. Churchill alone was the exception when he publicly referred to the mass shootings in the Soviet Union as early as August 24, 1941, without, however, mentioning Jews by name: "Since the Mongol invasions of Europe in the sixteenth century, there has never been methodical, merciless butchery on such a scale, or approaching such a scale. We are in the presence of a crime without a name."[1] At first, the fear of "masses" of Jewish refugees invading their shores or sensitive areas such as the Middle East dominated British minds, among other things due to the success, in their eyes, of German propaganda beamed into the Arab Middle East from Berlin, from the Fascist Italian radio station at Bari, and later from Vichy France's stations and even from occupied Athens.[2]

As far as British executive officials were concerned, their fears were coupled with the vision of a common Zionist–Nazi interest to move Jews out of Europe to Palestine and related to the Nazi threat to their values and their civilization, which was also accompanied by an optimistic evaluation of Western European power and Hitler's own weaknesses once they resorted

---

[1] See the discussion of the source of this speech in Breitman, *Official Secrets*, pp. 88–109.

[2] Radio Berlin played a role already during the 1936–1939 Arab rebellion in Palestine by trying to drive a wedge between the British mandatory authorities and the Arabs of Palestine and the neighboring countries. Radio Bari, which joined Berlin in this regard, later split into a variety of Arabic-speaking stations, "The Arab Nation," "Free Egypt," and "Young Africa," which were silenced in 1943. Berlin broadcasted in Arabic until the end of the war as "The Voice of Free Arabism," and Athens broadcasted in Arabic until its liberation as "The Station of the Free Arabs." See Weekly Review of Foreign Broadcasts, FCC no. 118, 3-4-1944, NA, G-2 Regional files, Palestine, box 3029.

to fighting him. Yet it required time to mobilize the British nation and create a huge field army following the first draft proclaimed by a British government in peacetime.

To this the traditional belief was added that the Western European powers would prevail due to Germany's meager resources, while Germany's economy was believed to have been already mobilized fully after years of slave labor imposed by the regime on the masses. If so, Germany should have been led, through leaflets and other propaganda measures, to concentrate on its own sufferings. Getting ready for a long war and preparing to mobilize an army of forty to fifty divisions was not the only measure taken by the Chamberlain cabinet, but it required that the Allies steer away from the controversial Jewish Question and dictated continued mass support of the fighting elites at home and across the British Empire, especially in its strategic, oil-rich regions. Recognizing Hitler's popularity, the British still kept hoping that a German domestic collapse would occur. Hitler's popularity dictated that there could be no "Jew's war" at this early stage. The war aims for the Germans also should be formulated in terms of liberating them from the yoke of a dictatorship whose aim was to subdue other nations by force and exploitation.

An important point made by Tony Kushner regards the attitude of the security forces, which we shall encounter on our own. According to Kushner, "It must be suggested that in the conspiratorial world of the security forces, being Jewish and anti-Nazi was no proof of loyalty to the British cause." The officer in charge of counterespionage at British Home Intelligence (MI5), Maxwell Knight, whom we shall meet again, "could distrust an agent simply because she had a Jewish lover,"[3] while "the security forces had been in the forefront to link Jews with international Bolshevism in the post-war world, and it does not seem that their views had totally changed in the Hitlerite period."[4] This is what I call "historical inertia," which was typical not just of anti-Semites but of so many Jews at the time.

Kushner added to the previous research the relationship between the government and public opinion in this regard and first counted the number of

[3] Kushner, *The Persistence of Prejudice*, pp. 143 and 143n. There is an ongoing discussion about Knight's role in regard to the British Fascist movement (i.e., when he was recruited by the MI5, which has not yet been settled), as the MI5 archives remain inaccessible. See also a letter to the editor by David Turner, "Fascism in the Archives," *London Review of Books*, March 5, 1998.

[4] Kushner, *The Persistence of Prejudice*. Knight's paranoia and methods of fighting his alleged traitors and enemy agents finally discredited him to such an extent that his future warnings against Soviet spies in Britain remained unnoticed, while those "moles" were very real indeed. For further background on his career, see Bernard Porter, *Plots and Paranoia: A History of Political Espionage in Britain 1790–1988* (London and New York: Routledge, 1992, pp. 165, 171–173).

Jewish refugees allowed to enter the British Isles after September 1, 1939.[5] These numbered several thousand among the total of 70,000 Jews who had been allowed entry since 1933. The policy was primarily based on security grounds, as the government believed that any refugee arriving after the start of the war would have needed the approval of the Germans, and specifically of the Gestapo, since the latter was in charge of all Jewish affairs at that time and in direct control over the border police under Gestapo Chief Heinrich Müller. Müller's boss, Reinhard Heydrich, was also the chief of the SD, the Nazi Party's and the SS's intelligence organization. Both the Gestapo (the criminal police, merged under Heydrich into the so-called "Security Police," SIPO or Sipo) and SD were combined to a large extent into one operation in 1939 within the framework of the Reich Security Main Office (RSHA) of the SS.[6]

Thus refugees, whom Hitler had tried to push out, could have been perceived as his agents. Yet in the background loomed the larger and not baseless conspiracy theory that Hitler used the Jews to create anti-Semitism in Britain, as Foreign Office officials agreed that "National Socialism had 'gained many supporters merely by exploiting Antisemitism.'"[7] When Herbert Morrison became the Labor Home Secretary in October 1940, "the domestic Antisemitism argument became even more powerful against the entry of Jewish refugees in the war."[8]

The Colonial Office produced its own version of the conspiracy theory; the head of its Middle East Department, H. F. Downie, went further, believing that Jewish illegal (beyond the restricted quotas allowed by the British White Paper of May 1939) immigration into Palestine was "a conspiracy," "facilitated by the Gestapo and the Jewish Agency."[9] Indeed, an eager SD operative, Adolf Eichmann, had been pushing Jews out since the Anschluss of Austria early in 1938, and later he, the hardworking Chief Emigration Officer, continued his deportations from occupied Czech regions and Germany proper in the framework of a newly created "Central Authority for Jewish Emigration" under Gestapo Chief Heinrich Müller and Reinhard Heydrich, the head of the Security Police and SD. But in fact this was the more ruthless, and more efficient, implementation of what had been declared German policy since 1933, carried out by the more ruthless arm of the Nazi government, not an espionage affair and not even a "conspiracy" conceived by the SD and

---

5 Kushner, *The Persistence of Prejudice*, p. 152.
6 For the structure and field units of the RSHA during 1941–1943, see Raul Hilberg, *The Destruction of the European Jews* (London: W. E. Ellen, 1961 edition, pp. 184–186). This description remains largely relevant, albeit Hilberg's seminal work has been expanded since and published in a multivolume edition.
7 Kushner, *The Persistence of Prejudice*, p. 153n.
8 Ibid.
9 Ibid., 152.

the Jewish Agency. Thus, several Western officials could have shared Hitler's opinion that the absorption of Jewish refugees anywhere was serving Nazi Germany's aims.[10]

The Colonial Office's Downie wrote that he regretted "that the Jews are not on the other side in this war"[11] and was described by a Foreign Office colleague, R. T. Latham, as though he regarded "the Jews as no less our enemies than the Germans" and that he tried to link the two by "secret and evil bonds," one example of which I noted earlier when I argued that a proximity was created in Western minds between the Jews and the Nazis.

Another argument regarding some "evil bonds" allegedly existing between the Gestapo and the Zionists was later taken for granted by intelligent and relatively knowledgeable British Intelligence officers such as Christopher Sykes (Sir Mark Sykes' son), not only when on active duty in Cairo during World War II, but in the 1960s as a historian of Israel's birth, which we will discuss in Chapter 12. Since security in the Middle East became a military responsibility with the outbreak of World War II, the autonomy of the Security Section of the staff of GHQ Middle East, which later became known as Security Intelligence Middle East (SIME, which we will encounter later) under Brigadier Raymond Maunsell, did not immunize it from prevailing images and legends common in London and repeated by Sykes years later regarding a sort of common denominator existing between the Zionists and the Gestapo.[12] This, however, may have been related to various rescue endeavors that seemed to have combined Jewish and Nazi interests, while in London people such as V. F. W. Cavendish-Bentinck, the future Duke of Portland and the chairman of the British Joint Intelligence Committee, simply reacted coolly to a report about the use of gas chambers to kill Jews because

---

[10] Regarding the priority given by the SD itself to Palestine as a possible haven for German Jews at first, and Eichmann's trip with his superior, Herbert Hagen, to Palestine in 1937 to meet among others not mentioned in that study (a possible Arab connection) a Zionist activist named Feibl Polkes, see Wildt, *Die Judenpolitik*, pp. 43–45. The British refused their entry, and the missions' failure might have, as Wildt maintains, dampened SD expectations from Palestine and the Zionists. This may have been partially true also thanks to the Arab rebellion and Lord Peel's partition plan of the same year, which foresaw a sovereign Jewish state in Palestine. But according to Wildt, Hitler early in 1938 "underlined again his decision of spring 1937, to continue the emigration policy, paying no attention to the host country," *Die Judenpolitik*, p. 44. See Major Engel's diary cited elsewhere, quoting Hitler's twisted description of his 1937 decision.

[11] Kushner, *The Persistence of Prejudice*, p. 152.

[12] For an introductory brief history of SIME, see Nigel West, *MI6* (London: Widenfeld and Nicolson, 1983) and also Michael Howard, *British Intelligence in the Second World War: Volume 5, Strategic Deception* (New York: Cambridge University Press, 1990, pp. 31–32, 36), and H.O. Dovey, "Security in Syria, 1941–1945," *Intelligence and National Security* 6, No. 2 (April 1991), 418–446.

"The Poles and to greater extent the Jews, tend to exaggerate German atrocities in order to stoke us up."[13]

A similar argument was used by General J. F. C. Fuller, the British tank pioneer and war historian, a decade after the war.[14] "Stoking us up" referred to the fear that the "Jews and Poles" were dragging the British to fight their wars for them against Germany. Hence the guarantee to Poland given by Chamberlain after the occupation of Prague by Hitler was foolish, and making the war an anti-German, and in fact anti-Nazi, ideological crusade was even worse because the "crusade" served the values and interests of others, not the British, and finally played into Stalin's hands. Hitler indeed hoped sometimes for such a British opinion to prevail during World War II itself.

Kushner's quotes from Downie and others remind us of one more aspect of the multiple trap: the role of bureaucracies. Especially in times of war, bureaucracies already had enormous power in Great Britain. The majority at the cabinet level, in the various ministries, in the military, and in intelligence agencies who had harbored since World War I anti-Semitic and anti-Zionist perceptions or had developed them since then because of Hitler's rise to power and the need to fight him and his allies, influenced their American counterparts a great deal.

In the American bureaucracy dealing with refugees and foreign Jews (i.e., the Department of State), people such as Breckenridge Long soon took over and oversaw refugee matters with a large degree of discretion, in cooperation with their British counterparts.[15] From 1941, however, the issue largely was no longer a "refugee" issue and a visa matter. The Germans were the ones who now prevented the Jews from leaving Europe. Still, allowing Jews to enter their domains in some significant numbers was a matter of Allied policy, which continued to be determined by fear of domestic anti-Semitism, by other priorities, by the Palestine policy of the British, followed by the Americans, and by the existing legislation by the U.S. Congress. Yet the working of the doomsday machine mentioned earlier could be demonstrated here by a document pertaining to a late period during the war that was found in the papers of the Acting Secretary of State, Edward R. Stettinius, Jr., once the full dimensions of the Holocaust had become known and publicly pressing, which outlined the views of its authors. I do not know who they were, but they offered operational suggestions for the State Department's action – recommending negotiations with Germany, which indeed were endorsed as desirable and made public as such in a massive rally in Madison Square

---

[13] Kushner, *The Persistence of Prejudice*, p. 159.

[14] See J. F. C. Fuller, *A Military History of the Western World*, Volume Three (New York: Funk and Wagnalls, 1956, pp. 372–375), among other anti-Semitic remarks.

[15] See Breitman and Kraut, *American Refugee Policy and European Jewry*, pp. 3–4, 125–145, 238–246.

Garden on March 1, 1943, under the exhortation "Stop Hitler Now."[16] This rally was very much the result of the efforts of Jabotinsky's National Military Organization (or IZL) mission to the United States, which under the leadership of Hillel Kook (also known as Peter Bergson) followed up on Jabotinsky's own efforts, before he died in New York in 1940, to enlist the United States in the Jewish–Zionist cause.[17] Later on, supported by screenwriter Ben Hecht and other PR-oriented American Jews and non-Jews, the Bergson group adopted a purely rescue-oriented strategy, divorced from Zionist interests, and hence could be the originator of the following statement:

"If initial negotiations on humanitarian grounds fail, *consideration should be given to further appeals offering a quid pro quo to the Germans such as hope of less severe peace terms or the possibility of reduced bombing of certain cities or areas*" (italics added). One could immediately argue that Hitler might have achieved here what he might have toyed with in the first place by putting the Jews to death: that the survival of any of them still alive could be linked to Western concessions to him, or rather to other advantages gained in relation to Jews in terms of Allied public opinion and Soviet reaction to active rescue efforts entailing negotiations with the Germans on Jews. Hence, the Allied leadership could not accept this logic of the Final Solution, and Jewish leaders in the West could not make them negotiate with Hitler for "less severe peace terms" or accept "reduced bombing," since Nazi Germany was killing only Jews. The trap situation is emphasized here again when we realize that the Jews became a burden to third parties because they were being murdered, and hence their fate seemed to become a tool in the hands of the killers in their relations with third parties (i.e., the Western Allies) that undermined the consensus needed to fight Hitler. These third parties were preoccupied with the conditions necessary in their eyes to guarantee their ultimate military–political crusade against Hitler. Kushner quoted Sir Alexander Cadogan, Permanent Under-Secretary of State in the Foreign Office, who had refused to publish a White Paper on conditions in the concentration camps[18] at first due to his doubts about the Jewish sources who supplied them but also due to the argument that "the Germans will only say that this is further proof that the British Empire is run by international Jewry." The British White Paper was finally published, due to German atrocity propaganda about concentration camps in South Africa, but Jews were played down in favor of "perfectly good Aryans such as (pastor Martin) Niemöller," as it was "necessary, at all

---

[16] *Edward R. Stettinius Papers*, University of Virginia, unsigned memo dated January 7, 1944, courtesy of Richard Breitman.

[17] See for the most recent research on the "Bergson group" Judith Tydor Baumel, *Between Ideology and Propaganda: The "Irgun" Delegation and the Origins of American-Jewish Right-Wing Militancy* (Jerusalem: Magnes Press, Hebrew University, 1999).

[18] Kushner, *The Persistence of Prejudice*, p. 157.

costs, to avoid anything that would give strength to the Jews' War accusation."[19] The White Paper sold well but was generally regarded as a failure; thus, the Ministry of Information instructed its wartime affiliates in July 1941 that atrocity propaganda "must deal with indisputably innocent people. Not with violent political opponents. And not with Jews."[20] Since this was just about the time when the Final Solution in Soviet-controlled areas was ordered, the question is why this policy was maintained long afterward by the British Ministry of Information (MOI) and its American counterparts and by the BBC for many, and sometimes contradictory, reasons. One of the answers was the British refusal to engage in what seemed to be "atrocity propaganda," described as a monopoly of the Nazis, and its appreciation of the British public as being too civilized, fighting and enduring as a matter of controlled pride, and not to be seen as cheaply manipulated by "atrocity stories," true as they were, accepted by the BBC chiefs.[21] The other reasons, on the contrary, seemed to be related to the fear of the effectiveness of Nazi propaganda, based on the lessons the Germans had learned from the success of British propaganda during World War I, which now were related to the "Jew's war" issue.

A similar logic dictated both Allies impression regarding the very effective German propaganda among Arabs. In a typical Nazi broadcast to the region in April 1943, taken very seriously by U.S. Army Intelligence (G-2), the Germans claimed that[22] "The wicked American intentions toward the Arabs are now clear . . . they are endeavoring to establish a Jewish empire in the Arab world. More than 400,000,000 oppose this criminal American (just 140,000,000) movement. Arabs! . . . Kill the Jews wherever you find them." This appeal, made by the former Mufti of Jerusalem, Hajj Amin el Husseini, triggered the following statement by the U.S. Intelligence commentator:

The Arab propagandists in charge of Berlin propaganda have staged the present show with great cunning. The anti-Jewish theme has in the past constituted a good half of the German propaganda directed to the Near East. Constant vilification of Jews in terms calculated to make them repugnant to the Arab mind have included alleged attempts by the Jews on the life of Mohammed and their imputed domination of the Allied policies in the Near East ("Allied Jewish nations") reached new peaks calling for violence in Palestine. (Weekly Review of Foreign Broadcasts, FCC No. 118)[23]

---

[19] Ibid.
[20] Ibid., 158.
[21] See Jean Seaton, "Reporting Atrocities: The BBC and the Holocaust," in Jean Seaton and Ben Pimlott (eds.), *The Media in British Politics* (Aldershot: Hants, 1987), pp. 163–164.
[22] See Weekly Review of Foreign Broadcasts, FCC No. 118, and see also MID 350.092 ME, prepared by EV Branch CIG (Counter Intelligence "G" Group), Subject: Axis Broadcasts to the Middle East through June 1943, G-2 Palestine box 3029.
[23] Ibid.

The catch situation may be clear enough when we read in the same file a directive to Voice of America (VOA) to treat the peoples of Palestine in its own broadcasts accordingly. Zionist aspirations should be avoided by all means. The Jews were "our ardent supporters," but not the Arabs. Therefore, the Arabs should be approached rather than Jews, especially due to the "effectiveness of enemy propaganda." The American Consul-General in Jerusalem, Lowell C. Pinkerton, was quoted in the same file to the effect that Axis propaganda in Palestine was effective indeed. The Zionists were described as if they were promised a state of their own in Palestine in the secret clauses of the "Atlantic Charter" (no such clause was hidden therein) and due to Zionist activities in America. An anti-American sentiment emerged among the Palestinian Arabs, especially because Arabs heard "what they wanted to" from the few who listened to the enemy's radio.

By the end of 1942, the British addressed themselves (however, one time only) to the Final Solution and openly condemned Hitler's murder of the Jews. Several practical actions were considered regarding the possible entry of refugees into Britain, and bodies were created to deal with them, but nothing came out of this, as was described first by Bernard Wasserstein.[24]

Foreign Secretary Eden's statement in the House of Commons in this regard "was regarded as a mistake by the Foreign Office, for it raised public expectations of government action in aiding the Jews of Europe, when no such policy was intended." Thus, British officials of that kind, reflecting the "establishment's" opinion, were doubly afraid of their own people in this respect: they were conscious of domestic anti-Semitism and of domestic sympathy to Jews later during the war as well, and they had to maneuver between both – and the Zionists – in order not to help Jews and to avoid domestic repercussions and trouble with Arabs, and possibly with the Soviets, once they did. For officials such as Foreign Secretary Eden this may have meant either real concessions to Hitler or even the impression that Jewish matters assumed top priority for the British government and thus tainted the war as "Jewish," which in fact it was because Jews were its main victims. Avoiding such traps from their point of view, including possible repercussions in the sensitive Middle East, was a rather skillful game that various British personalities and agencies played almost to the end of the war, sometimes against Churchill's own efforts, at least in regard to Palestine, and carried America's counterparts with them most of the time.

Several British politicians made their own calculations in this regard clear not only to American colleagues (speaking in terms of "growing domestic anti-Semitism" in mid-1942[25] and gaining their basic support, which

[24] *Britain and the Jews of Europe*, pp. 183–221.
[25] Wasserstein, Sir John Hope-Simpson to Speaker Sam Rayburn.

was reflected in the almost zero outcome of the 1943 Bermuda Refugee Conference[26]) but to Zionist leaders as well.

In a letter to Dr. Chaim Weizmann, the President of the World Zionist Organization, dated March 4, 1943, the British Minister in Washington, Ronald I. Campbell, responded in the name of the ambassador, Lord Halifax, and Foreign Secretary Eden to Weizmann's bid to allow 70,000 Rumanian Jews to emigrate immediately, an idea that seemed, in Zionist eyes, to have been endorsed by the Rumanian government itself. Campbell wrote:[27]

His Majesty's Government has no evidence to show whether the Rumanian proposal was meant to be taken seriously. *But if it was, it was already a piece of blackmail which if successful would open up the endless prospect on the part of Germany and her satellites in Southeastern Europe of unloading at a given price all their unwanted nationals on overseas countries* (italics added). (CZA file S25/7570)

Campbell went on to say that his government "in conjunction with the governments of the United Nations will continue to give earnest study" to all "practical means" of "alleviating the refugee position," which, however, and this was his main point, "were consistent with the fullest war effort," "*but to admit the method of blackmail and slave purchase would be a serious prejudice to the successful prosecution of the war*" (italics added). He further stated that "as they see it [i.e., his political superiors], the blunt truth is that the whole complex of humanitarian problems raised by the present German domination of Europe, of which the Jewish question is an important but by no means the only aspect, can only be dealt with completely by an Allied victory." The trap is clear: The Jews may become an obstacle on the road to destroying the machine, which in fact was destroying them, more than others while being blamed by the engineers of that machine for the efforts undertaken by third parties to destroy the German state altogether. The British minister repeated the cunning argument that "any step calculated to prejudice this is not in the real interest of the Jews of Europe" – if any of them would survive to have any "interests" at all.

Weizmann's answer to Campbell's letter, if any, is not known. As a British-oriented Zionist, enjoying high esteem among them, Weizmann was treated by the British as one of their own. Both Weizmann, the President of the World Zionist Organization, based in Britain, and David Ben-Gurion, the Chairman of the Jewish Agency, based in Jerusalem, might have even understood the cruel logic of Campbell's argument. Yet for Ben-Gurion this would mean that the Jews should take care of their own interests – the sooner the better – and the place to pursue it, in a grand Zionist scale, was in the United States. Enough experience had been gained with the British by now, even though

---

[26] For Bermuda, see Breitman, *Official Secrets*, pp. 181–187; Breitman and Kraut, *American Refugee Policy and European Jewry*, pp. 139–143. 176–180; and see discussion in text.
[27] Central Zionist Archive (CZA), Jerusalem, file S25/7570.

Ben-Gurion was still ready to argue with them and try to persuade them. But he left most of that to Weizmann and to Moshe Shertok, the head of the Jewish Agency's Political Department, though he never broke with the British completely. After all, they fought Nazi Germany, controlled Palestine, and were accessible to democratic pressure at home – and maybe to American overtures as well. In his way, Weizmann tried the Americans, too, using his old, behind the scenes personal diplomacy, but to no avail.[28]

The Palestine question and Arab reactions to the opening of Palestine to large-scale Jewish immigration deepened the trap from 1941, while at the same time the very survival of the Palestine Jews depended on British efforts to retain the Middle East under their control. This in turn required in their view concessions to Arabs on account of the Jews. This seemed to be the case in 1942 as well, but in 1943 the threat to Allied control in the area seemed to be over, if we discount the next stage – the transfer of the huge Allied armies present in the Middle East to fight in Europe, leaving behind a sort of military vacuum.

The ensuing process seemed to guarantee the defeat of the Axis, finally, but it took time, and at least in the land warfare in Burma – the Japanese bridgehead toward India – it was a very difficult endeavor indeed. China's fate was here a major complex, as was FDR's goal to be a future partner in a new world order.

India was not just Churchill's "pearl in the Imperial crown," but it was a vast, major, potentially independent whole subcontinent in which some pro-Japanese and semi-Fascist elements had been at work. Japan did adopt its own concept of an Asian "New Order," which contained anti-Western elements and pretended to liberate other Asian nations from the Western European, and possibly the American, direct and indirect yoke.

Japan, which was free of any anti-Semitic intentions, contributed thus to the extension of the Jewish trap. If the Jews had any real influence over FDR, and understood Hitler's wrath over American aid to the isolated British before Pearl Harbor and Hitler's possible interest in a Japanese attack upon the United States, which finally transformed the war into a "world war" in which the Jews would be "this time annihilated" according to Hitler's prophecy, they should have pressed Roosevelt to leave the British alone and not drive the Japanese up against a possible wall. This absurd proposition was not only impossible to execute but shows at the same time that Hitler made the Jews responsible for policies that in fact did not serve their "particularistic" interests and yet they still were perceived as "egotistic" and "particularistic," and not just by Hitler.

[28] For a recent study, see David H. Shapiro, *From Philanthropy to Activism: The Political Transformation of American Zionism in the Holocaust Years 1933–1945* (Jerusalem: Bialik Foundation, 2001, pp. 142–177) (in Hebrew), and see the text.

The Soviet dimension of the trap was divided into two parts. One was Stalin's refusal to allow the specific Jewish aspect of the Nazi atrocities committed in his territories to be recognized as such, which was combined with the need to maintain the coalition that Hitler created between East and West until the complete eradication of the Nazi regime. The other aspect, raised by the representative of the American War Refugee Board (WRB) and which will be dealt with later when we discuss of official American rescue efforts undertaken from early 1944, was the mobilization of Soviet influence in a country such as Bulgaria to protect its Jewish citizens and later possibly to use the Soviet policy of deporting Germans from territories occupied by the Red Army as a tool to stop the deportation of the remaining Jews to their death by the Germans. The first option included the appointment of an official representative of the WRB in Moscow, and the second one was supposed to involve Pope Pius XII as well, as a party interested in preventing the deportation of Germans. I shall return to the related intelligence decrypts in due course, but it should be noted in advance of this that nothing much emerged out of either option. While Soviet intentions with regard to the future of Eastern Europe, primarily Poland, and the fate of the remaining Jews therein may have included the Zionist option in order to consolidate Soviet rule in what became the Eastern bloc outside of the Soviet Union itself (as historian Matitiahu Minz is trying to follow in Soviet archives), this entailed no active help in rescuing Jews specifically.

9

The War Priorities of the Western Allies and Rules of Economic Warfare Related to the Holocaust, 1941–1944

From the Allied point of view, 1941 and most of 1942 were the worst war years, while the Jewish Yishuv in Palestine was threatened directly by the tide of Erwin Rommel's victories in the North African desert war and the German advance toward the Caucasus. The landings in North Africa in November 1942, preceded by the British offensive at el-Alamein, aimed at the realistic and important drive to push the German and Italian armies out of a strategically important global crossroads containing the future reserve of the world's oil, and the growing role of Muslims and Arabs in this connection and in connection with strategic calculations regarding future Allied activities in Europe and in the Indian–Burmese theater were related to Allied domestic political considerations. The ensuing Tunisian campaign proved to be rather long – about seven months – and was crowned with the capitulation of the German and Italian armies in May 1943. But later, the battle over Sicily and the landings in southern Italy proved to be a bloody, long, and extremely difficult campaign along the Italian peninsula, which ended practically with the war's end two years later.

The Allies did not overcome the U-boat menace until May 1943 and at that time started to plan the landing in France, while in the meantime the bombing campaign against Germany was a substitute for operations on the European mainland.

Thus, before the turning of the tide in North Africa, and even afterward, the bombing campaign against German cities and German strategic targets, undertaken first by the British at night and then by the Americans at daylight, became for the British War Cabinet a growing substitute for a premature invasion of the continent, inpired at first by inexperienced Americans aiming at "Sledgehammer" – a landing in Europe as early as 1942. For air-power strategists, the bombing campaign became a war-winning idée fixe because of its popularity at home, which was helped by the British government itself, despite its growing awareness of the campaign's limits.

However inaccurate, costly, and many times ineffective it was, in Germany the bombing of the cities was described as a Jewish war against civilians, as I was told by Albert Speer and still heard from common people in Germany in the early 1960s as an established fact, on top of published sources such as the Nazi-controlled press, that required and explained the violent fate of other Jews.[1]

This, in turn, could have been added to Allied doubts whether any mentioning of the Holocaust would enhance their propaganda against the Nazis if Jews were to be publicly mentioned, also an issue requiring a deeper look. Indeed, a general statement regarding the punishment of Axis war crimes was issued in December 1943, known as the Moscow Declaration, but it was never repeated afterward by all Allies.

In fact, the British obtained some information on the mass shootings in Russia by decoding German police messages in real time but did not share the information with the Americans. About a year later, Washington had its own sources and was conscious of the overall Final Solution in summer 1942[2] and finally convinced itself that Hitler was indeed fulfilling his threats and prophecies after reviewing the Riegner–Schulte report and other sources in 1942.[3]

In my view, politicians in both Britain and the United States had tried at first not to make the issue of the systematic murder of the Jews public for a number of reasons. One of them must have been the fear that once they did they would have to do something about them and thus transfer the onus of the blame from Nazi shoulders to their own in the sense that inaction would make them seem to be collaborators with the perpetrators. On the other hand, action seemed to them to be irrelevant to their actual war-fighting problems if not endangering them in the sense that making the Jewish issue a major challenge to themselves would just play into Hitler's

---

[1] The popular connection between German Jews and the bombing offensive against Germany in 1943 was described to me by my landlady in Arolsen/Landkreis Waldeck, a small town in North Hesse in 1962, where I learned the German language in a Goethe Institute, as if German Jews who allegedly had emigrated from the neighborhood to Britain following the November 1938 pogroms marked their own villages of origin for the Bomber Command's attacks. Since I could immediately locate the names and ascertain the fate of those migrants, thanks to the Red Cross' International Search Service of WWII Victims Head Office located in that very town, I told my landlady, who could have done it herself, that they were not able to reach England, got stuck in Holland, and finally perished in Auschwitz.

[2] See Breitman *Official Secrets*, Chapter 8, American Assessments, and see also David S. Wyman, *The Abandonment of the Jews: America and the Holocaust 1941–1945* (New York: Pantheon Press, 1984, Part II, Chapter 3), whose facts in this regard and others were checked by me using the relevant FDR Library files at Hyde Park, New York, and see Walter Laqueur, *The Terrible Secret: The Suppression of the Truth about Hitler's "Final Solution"* (Jerusalem and Tel-Aviv: Schocken Publishing House, 1981) (Hebrew translation).

[3] See Walter Laqueur and Richard Breitman, *Breaking the Silence* (New York: Simon and Schuster, 1986).

hands. At the same time, the Allies were exposed to the Nazis' use of Jews against them while the Nazis were killing Jews en masse. According to FCC daily reports in mid-1943, "anti-Semitism continued to be the main subject in German political propaganda."[4] The Jews were blamed for the Allied aerial bombing of defenseless civilians, and hence the Germans were warned that they were fighting against an "implacable enemy," while the West was described as if it was undergoing growing anti-Semitic sentiments. Western peoples began "to realize that the cause for which they are suffering is not their own."

The impact of such Nazi arguments on the Allies was exactly the opposite of what the Nazis were aiming at. The Allies refused to be drawn into Jewish matters in terms of active rescue efforts or anti-Nazi propaganda of their own, possibly in order not to follow Hitler's logic in this regard when public opinion had to remain mobilized to fight Hitler rather than a "Jew's war." Finally, the United States, and less so the British, became more involved and open in regard to the Holocaust, triggering hopes among the Germans that this would mean anti-Semitic repercussions in the West and no relaxation of their own murder campaign but what seemed to the Allies to be the use of Jews as hostages or tools to drive a wedge between them. Thus, the rescue efforts contributed to the deepening of the trap.

The very facts about the Holocaust became publicly known in the democratic West during late 1942. An Allied, Western refusal to recognize and condemn these acts was neither possible nor morally acceptable. The horrible news was made public and the genocide of the Jews condemned by the British later in 1942, but no action followed because "action" for them meant again making the Jews a central issue in a war fought for Western survival, even some kind of negotiations with Hitler or gestures toward his satellites, the resumption of the "flooding" of the West by millions of "unwanted aliens" as expressed by the high British minister in Washington quoted earlier, or immediate reprisals against Allied prisoners of war (POWs) following threats of postwar judgment, as we shall see later in some detail in the chapter discussing the preparations for the Nuremberg War Crimes Trial.

The "hot potato" syndrome was quoted by British Ministry of War Information officials, who expected their own public would suspect that people who were singled out as victims – even by Hitler – would be perceived as having earned such treatment.[5]

Elmer Davis, the director of the American Office of War Information (OWI), was afraid that Allied World War I propaganda against the Germans, which proved later to have been quite exaggerated, had created a continuing

---

[4] See, for example, FCC Daily Report, 5-13-1943: German propaganda, NA, G-2 Palestine Files, box 3027.
[5] See Laqueur, *The Terrible Secret*, pp. 92–93.

aversion to horror stories of that kind. Yet according to the MOI historian[6] the main reason might have been the anti-Jewish prejudice in the British Commonwealth and sustained anti-Semitism reported by British Intelligence at home in 1940 and 1941.[7] In the first half of 1942, such reports dwindled, and the decision on both sides of the Atlantic later in 1942 to go public after all in regard to the Final Solution did cause strong feelings against Hitler and his henchmen. However, at the same time, people "became more conscious of Jews whom they did not like here" as a result of the massacre of their brethren abroad.

In 1943, the Allies were in better shape but had publicly adopted the formula of "unconditional surrender," by itself a British conviction as a result of British experience gained in the peace soundings of 1939–1940, which, as we are told by Gerhard Weinberg, "had left a residue of very strong doubts about any and all Germans who claimed to be moderate and wanted assurances of some sort as to the future of Germany as preliminary to overthrowing the Nazi regime. When finally given some such assurances, they had proceeded to lead the invasions of a series of neutral countries."[8]

In the case of the Americans, the issue was related not only to the famous precedent created by General Ulysses S. Grant following the Vicksburg Campaign – which Grant himself did not implement – but in Gerhard Weinberg's view "unconditional surrender" was intimately connected to President Wilson's insistence on an armistice rather than a German surrender in 1918, which had very serious domestic, foreign, and German ramifications well remembered by FDR – a former member of Wilson's administration. Further, the public assurances in this regard were aimed at the hard-pressed Soviets in order to calm possible doubts in Moscow that the capitalist West would align itself with an undefeated Germany. It might, however, also have been the result of the domestic outcry following the administration's decision to make a deal with Vichy's admiral Darlan following "Torch," the Allied landings in North Africa.

Even before it was proclaimed as official policy, "unconditional surrender" officially forbade any negotiations between the Allies and the German government on anything but surrender without conditions. Legislation was invoked and regulations issued within the general rules of economic warfare on both sides of the Atlantic that forbade ransom deals with the enemy. The official history of the British economic blockade and its interpretation by Bernard Wasserstein[9] do not need to be repeated here except for what

---

[6] Ibid., 93.
[7] Ibid.
[8] Ibid., 438–439.
[9] See Wasserstein, *Britain and the Jews of Europe*, pp. 246–247, 322–323, 352–355, and also W. N. Medlicott, *The Economic Blockade*, Volume II (London: Kraus International Publications, 1959).

Wasserstein described as a rigid and inflexible attitude toward Jews in occupied Europe compared to others such as Greeks (and compared to the more flexible and less rigid attitude of the American authorities toward their own commercial ties with Axis firms, I might add). On the face of it, both nations enforced their blockade on Germany separately, with the British complaining that the Americans were sloppy and less serious about it. Yet the net result of both nations' efforts, culminating in "Operation Safehaven" aimed at preventing Germany from using neutrals for foreign currency deals and purchases,[10] was a growing if not a complete shortage of the currency needed to buy foreign raw materials and goods. This may explain Nazi interest in obtaining them by all means, using experts in smuggling and embarking upon individual human trade, and also the Allied sensitivity toward such deals.[11] We can add to Wasserstein's scholarship on the British blockade a number of documents that shed some light on ransom deals pertaining to the Holocaust in cooperation between both Western nations. Accordingly, Paul Dreyfus, a well-known head of a private bank in Basel, was in serious trouble with the British and the American authorities late in 1942 for having been involved in buying, from Germans, exit permits to allow Dutch Jews to depart from Nazi-occupied Holland.

"When confronted with the possibility of being placed on the British Black List and the American Proclaimed List (thereby not being able to conduct business with Allied individuals or companies)," so we are told by archivist and historian Greg Bradsher, "he signed a statement for the British diplomatic authorities in Basel indicating he would refrain from the Jewish ransom traffic. To follow up on this statement, he provided the British with a related statement, who supplied it to the Americans."[12] The British Black lists (there were two of them – one of suspects and one of proven enemy or enemy-controlled firms or individuals trading with the enemy) and the American Proclaimed List were among the tools of Allied economic warfare. Another tool was the direct seizure of a firm's board by the relevant American agencies. In this case, the records we have start with a confidential cable dated October 30, 1942, signed by Leland Harrison, the American Minister in Switzerland, and sent to the American Embassy in London with regard to the Proclaimed Listing of two persons, one of them named

---

[10] See Greg Bradsher, *Holocaust-Era Assets* (College Park, MD: NARA), for Safehaven reports.

[11] The Gestapo/SD embarked upon a now rather well-known operation forging foreign currency as well. For the shortages in vital raw materials that had to be imported, and the general picture of the German war economy and its rather late mobilization to fight a sustained, multifront war, see Alan S. Milward's classic (which I read in German) *The German War Economy 1939–1945* (Stuttgart: Deutsche Verlags-Anstalt, 1966). (German translation as *Schriftenreihe der Vierteljahreshefte für Zeitgeschichte*).

[12] See Greg Bradsher, "A Time to Act: The Beginning of the Fritz Kolbe Story, 1900–1943," *Prologue*, 34, No. 1 (Spring 2002), 7–24. (*Prologue* is NARA's quarterly publications.)

Anna Hochberg.[13] The second document related to this, dated December 4, 1942, is a summary of Dreyfus's statement in which he denied any dealings with Hochberg, obviously a German or a German-connected agent. Another German agent, Walter Buechi, approached him concerning an exit permit for Dreyfus's sister-in-law and family (in occupied Holland). "When D. stated that the price was excessive, B. replied that the price would be reduced for larger parties and made the 5 million franc proposition," whereupon Dreyfus was pressed by others to go ahead with the deal, which involved the Dutch Consulate General in Zurich as well and a former Dutch diplomat. Indeed, the Dutch Consul General informed Sam E. Woods, his American colleague, that although he did not know Dreyfus personally, "when conversing on a possible arrangement for exit permits, et cetera [meaning ransom – S.A.], that it became a common practice to refer to such cases as Dreyfus affair cases."[14] For his part, Dreyfus stated that he reluctantly submitted a 5 million franc proposition to the Dutch Legation in Bern, "and there was no question that his bank should finance the deal or that he should get commission." The Dutch Minister (representing the Dutch government in exile, located in London) confirmed this to his British colleague,[15] who went on to report that Dreyfus denied any dealing with other German agents named but stated that agent Buechi asked him to "purchase exit permits for Hugo Kaufmann, a banker in Amsterdam, since deported. D. refused on grounds that K. was not a relation." Thus, since Kaufman was already dead and "not a relation," the British Minister asked the Ministry of Economic Warfare (MEW) whether it could exclude the possibility that agent Buechi or some third party took Dreyfus's name in vain in Kaufmann's case. This sad story continued when the British Minister told the MEW the story of B.A. de Vries, Dreyfus's brother-in-law and family. "D. asks whether we would penalise him for purchasing exit permit for him, his wife, child and father at price ranging from 1–200,000 Swiss francs." The matter was referred to the MEW in view of their previous "formulae" concerning trading with the enemy, but the Minister added that "D. is willing to give us written undertaking to abstain from this traffic and will not act in case of his family without your sanction. Unless your evidence of collaboration with HOCHBERG (capital letters in the original) and approach to KAUFMAN [sic] is conclusive, we do not recommend luke A DREYFUS. We recommend luke A Buechi at present Hotel St. Gothhard, Zurich." The Commercial Secretariat of the British Legation informed His Britannic Majesty's Consulate General in Basel that the MEW was now ready to accept Dreyfus's statements. "We

[13] RG 84, Entry 3220 – US Legation Bern, box 3, file 840.1, repeated to State Department as number 4902.
[14] Woods to Harrison, January 25, 1943, same file as in note 13.
[15] H. M. Minister, Bern, to M.E.W. London, Arfar no. 4510, same file as in note 13 (American copy), dated December 4, 1942.

are, however, instructed to obtain a written assurance that he and his bank will abstain from any further dealings connected with the sale of exit permits to Jews. *This assurance should relate only to the Jewish traffic* (italics added). Dreyfus should understand that our acceptance is without prejudice to the negotiations for a comprehensive undertaking, when the form of such an undertaking has been agreed and if it is then decided to ask for one."[16] No such "undertaking," say to regulate the issue of ransoming in direct negotiations with the Germans, was ever agreed upon. On the contrary, ransoming involving relatively large sums of foreign currency such as in this case remained strictly forbidden until the very end of the war by both Allies. What we learn from this and from the related exchange between the British Commercial Secretariat in Bern and its American counterpart was that an undertaking has been obtained from Paul Dreyfus "that he will have no further dealings regarding the Jewish ransom traffic."[17] Thus Dreyfus was rehabilitated, at least in American eyes, and later was asked by Allen Dulles, head of the Office of Strategic Services (OSS), Bern, to help create the connection with Fritz Kolbe, the German who betrayed Nazi Foreign Minister Ribbentrop's secrets to the Americans.

If Jews were to be rescued, seemingly the only real option for the Yishuv and the Jewish leadership abroad would have been to bring pressure to bear on Allied governments to relax the ransom rules and even negotiate with the Nazis against their own declared policy.

The Americans did not contest the original British view, which abhorred any direct "deals" with the Third Reich in regard to Jews, as we have seen with regard to the "Dreyfus Affair." Indirect deals, however, involving money transfers to neutral countries in order to save the Jews of Transnistria or help the Jews in Vichy France survive, caused a huge British–American controversy (as David Wyman told us), and finally some money was licensed for such purposes.[18] For Wyman, the viability of the whole scheme was a secondary issue compared with the missing morality on the part of the British and the U.S. State Department officials. However, the issue was more complicated than that – denying the Third Reich the foreign currency badly needed for its war machine was a legitimate goal. Doing it mainly at the expense of the dying Jews was a morally shameful matter.

Yet "Torch" – the American–British landing in North Africa – added another dimension related to rescue, which was now important to the Americans as well, and this was the issue of Arabs and Muslims and Jews, combined into one package once American forces landed in Arab lands, and the military bureaucracy related to this was created in cooperation with the British.

---

[16] Same file as in note 13, dated January 11, 1943.
[17] Same file as in note 13, letter dated February 19, 1943.
[18] Wyman, *The Abandonment of the Jews*, pp. 178–191.

Reports and recommendations of U.S. Army Forces in the Middle East (USAFIME) and related agencies (G-2, OSS, CIC) in this regard will be quoted further. Many were political reports pertaining among other things to Palestine as a problematic haven for Jews and as such a Zionist, "particularistic," dangerous business that would jeopardize the war effort. This opinion was not far from early impressions by the future head of OSS, General William Donovan, that were gathered for the president and officially endorsed by the head of G-2, General George V. Strong, later in the war. Bargaining with Hitler was, however, not only forbidden by the official policy of "unconditional surrender" but also perceived by the Allies as a dangerous and self-defeating matter due to its possible exploitation by the Germans for their own purposes, such as giving them direct evidence that the war was indeed a "Jew's war," which they could use at will in any given moment such as the forthcoming assault against Hitler's "Fortress Europe." While the issue of a great power such as Germany murdering children, women, and unarmed men at its will until its ultimate defeat remained a matter of debate among British officials, the big worry remained that too many Jewish refugees might flood Britain itself, Palestine, or other British possessions. The question, which we will answer later, is whether the Allies had legitimate reasons to suspect Nazi moves in this regard on top of their own domestic and Arab-related calculations.

At any rate, "unconditional surrender" was a euphemism, a tool, to address Allied fears and had a variety of motives such as maintaining the grand alliance with the Soviets while formulating a clear-cut war goal instead of repeating Woodrow Wilson's mistakes.

PART II

THE RESCUE DEBATE, THE MACRO PICTURE, AND THE INTELLIGENCE SERVICES

IO

Missed Opportunities?

The so-called "rescue debate" (e.g., the accusations leveled against the Jewish leadership in Palestine and in the United States, as well as against the British, with the American administration being added to the list a little later) could be divided into contemporary concerns, some motivated by politics and some by morality, and to ongoing serious and less serious historiographic inquiries. None, however, has invoked the trap theorem to explain the actual multidimensional aspects of the tragedy. Some have even invoked rescue options as if they really existed and hence golden opportunities were missed, or at least the reader may be led to such conclusions.

The problem here with regard to the Zionists, blamed by various politically motivated persons but also by historians for "Palestinocentrism" (e.g., for focusing on their own narrow community's interests while abandoning the Jews of Europe to their fate), does not only relate to the archival sources but to the reconstruction of the "spirit of the time," which must be based on a "kaleidoscopic" overall study of the realities of that period from German, Allied, and Jewish points of view combined. Allied and Jewish behavior must be reconstructed on the basis of more sources and interviews. In some research, the "spirit of the time" is hidden or simplified to Allied adherence to the Casablanca Conference decree of "unconditional surrender," while the behavior of the mainstream Zionists is possibly taken for granted in the sense that they indeed were primarily interested in their narrow, nationalistic socialist dream. I shall try to explain this, and more, in this chapter.

The Labor Zionist leadership belonged to a generation of pioneers who were rather critical of Diaspora Jews as a part of their Zionist philosophies; they resented Jewish habits and ways of life abroad. Hence, they accepted arguments not only about Jewish images but also about actual Jewish reputations, which combined egotistical pursuit of one's own benefit, inability to defer satisfaction, pushiness, greed in some cases, inflated egos, habitual infighting and the search for status, lack of loyalty to the common cause, envy, hate, and competition typical of relatives of a problematic family. The leadership explained this as having resulted from life in exile, and although they foresaw a catastrophe awaiting these Jews, they expected nothing like the Holocaust.

At the same time, the Zionists vehemently rejected anti-Semitic allegations and speculations about Jews, were proud of Jewish civilization and – with reservations – of its contributions to Christianity, science, the arts, and the various literary and philosophical achievements in the various countries in which Jews lived, arguing that these would not be recognized and honored in the present hostile environment, and at the same time they sought a real (in their mind), secular meaning for Jewish "chosenness." Adopting a critical view of the Jewish pretension to be "chosen" in the sense that traditional Judaism seemed to them to have become a mechanical, if not an empty, backward, and sometimes primitive quest to be better than others, they sought to become better by giving their society new social humanist contents, partially based on ancient teachings, primarily of the prophets and partially based upon various modern socialist teachings. They observed with dismay the results of the crisis of traditional Judaism in the sense that many secularized Jews became "Luftmenschen" – alienated, detached losers in a world totally changed during and after World War I, but yet they also observed enormous energies being released by the very transformation of 2,000 years of traditional life now being secularized, which they had sought and indeed represented themselves as they mobilized for their various goals.

The Zionist vision of revival and regeneration entailed universal values, and in some areas, such as the creation of the kibbutzim and other cooperative endeavors and socialist projects, Zionists even partially succeeded in getting Jews to radically change their previous ways of life, and thus their differences with Jabotinsky's right-wing followers and radical antagonists such as Avraham "Yair" Stern were genuine. At the same time, the Laborites were linked in many ways to the Diaspora communities from which they had come and of which they pretended to be the spearhead and savior alike. Due to these elements in their various ideologies, they sought to cultivate a "new Jew" in Palestine, although they had differing views of how this should be done. At the same time, as socialists, they had their sense of superiority over the Western, liberal conservative democracies, especially during the appeasement period, and later perceived the West's behavior with a mixture of hope and doubt when they realized how sensitive the Jewish issue had become in the West. They certainly understood that sensitivity, whose only remedy for them was Zionism or a terrible disaster awaiting the Jews. This in turn dictated their view of Arabs as those whose fate was not endangered but on the contrary whose influence may have made the danger facing Jews even more perilous.

From its inception, Labor Zionism adopted a "catastrophic" view of the Jewish Diaspora. Hence their own solution gave the Labor Zionists a sense of pride over the Diaspora Jews, who were facing now the most terrible catastrophe, which even the Zionists never envisioned. Yet the Zionists always perceived themselves a part of the "Greater Jewish People," Diaspora Jews included, and in fact remained very much in touch with the Diaspora, especially working among Zionists abroad, but arguing with and against the non-Zionists as if all Jews were still one greater, if loose, family. Now the Zionists found themselves right about an impending doom awaiting the European and possibly Middle Eastern, Arab Diaspora, in the most horrible way, requiring action, but totally dependent on others – the democracies at war. The Laborites were caught between their sense of being a sort of a torch, the light leading to Jewish salvation, informing their dying brethren abroad about their collective enterprises, about their defense organizations and immigration efforts at home, and all kinds of rescue endeavors, which either would be rejected by the Allies or even get the Zionists in serious trouble with them. This did not mean that the Laborites neglected open political campaigning: Ben-Gurion's postulate was given to Jewish moral claims that once Pearl Harbor destroyed American isolationism they would impose a Jewish state on the Arabs during the war and allow it to serve as a haven for the dying European Jews.

At the same time, the sense of Jews being slaughtered because of their image and real reputation was not new in principle for Labor Zionists and required efforts to create the "new Jew" in terms of social equality and pioneering enterprises, while at the same time seeking the creation of a Jewish Army in Allied ranks and later immediate independence while working toward a variety of rescue efforts.

Yet the grand political and strategic picture of the war, the proximity between major developments in the battlefields, and the unfolding of the murderous scheme against the European Jews were not of interest to historians focusing on the Jews alone when combined with the logic and the styles of Allied leaders and the enormous Allied bureaucracies, preoccupied with their own priorities and their own internal controversies such as that related to the air war. Therefore, focusing on the Labor Zionists alone, without penetrating their mind and psyche, may produce a "Palestinocentric" image of them and the resulting argument that they missed opportunities of rescue. Yet one needs the "kaleidoscopic" tool to analyze the realities of the elites and bureaucracies among which the Laborites were trying to maneuver.

A "Kaleidoscopic" view of the democracies at war required a good understanding of the strategic situation: the fact that the British were alone until "Barbarossa," which seemed at first to be an enormous Nazi success. The Americans joined the British and the Soviets fully not before Pearl Harbor and only then began to mobilize 12 million civilians to fight the Axis powers. The Nazis had been very successful at exploiting the spirit and the enormous capabilities hidden in the German nation and in the German youth. Most or all of the Nazi activists were pretty young and indeed succeeded in using the generation gap and sense of a youth liberating itself from 19th century

German Victorians while retaining, if not enhancing, the qualities of one of the best war machines in the world.

The mobilized "masses" in the West were comprised of three generations. Most of the elite had been born and educated before World War I. This was true also with regard to most professional Army officers and Intelligence brass in both Britain and the United States. The second, younger generation was groomed during and after World War I and was partially traditional but partially exposed to the interwar processes and related ideas in a way that its political behavior could undergo ups and downs in the eyes of the political elites. The young, however, who would be doing most of the actual fighting, could be seen by the elites as the least known and as the most vulnerable to the horrors of war, to enemy propaganda, and to the challenges of modern life as the elites understood them in a world whose foundations had changed so rapidly since their own years of traditional life. This may indeed have been the case when we look at the old and new bureaucracies dealt with here and could have been tested in the most demanding fashion had Hitler not broken the bulk of the Wehrmacht on the chests of the soldiers of the Red Army.

11

The Intelligence Services and Rescue Options

The discussion of intelligence services on the Allied and the German sides (after all, the Gestapo and SD were among other things intelligence-gathering agencies) in this book assumed its central role due to the covert nature of hoped-for cooperation between the Zionists and other Jewish organizations working for rescue once experienced Jewish leaders such as David Ben-Gurion had realized that overt action by the Allies had many limits due to the menace of a "Jew's war," which the Allies intended to avoid by all means at their disposal unless domestic opinion imposed such an action upon them. At the same time, Nazi and Allied intelligence gathered information on the Holocaust, on rescue efforts, and on the Zionists and other Jewish organizations that were supposed to cooperate with them. This information led also to various actions that contributed their share to the workings of the doomsday machine.

In comparison to the regular bureaucracies, such as the British Foreign and Colonial Offices, which had adopted a rather anti-Zionist policy since the late 1930s that was followed by the politicians heading them on cabinet level but not Churchill himself,[1] and in comparison to the General Officer Commanding in Chief (GOC in C) Middle East, who always feared an Arab revolt in his back yard, MI6, or the Secret Intelligence Service (SIS) (i.e., the British Foreign Intelligence Service), was a little more open to the rescue of Jews and to Zionist overtures as far as activities planned against the Axis powers were concerned. According to Christopher Andrew, SIS Berlin agent Frank Foley, who "has been a Zionist sympathizer since the First World War," built up an intelligence network of well-placed Jewish businessmen, among them Wilfried Israel, the British-born heir of a famous

---

[1] See also, in addition to works already mentioned, Gavriel Cohen, "Churchill and the Genesis of the Cabinet Committee on Palestine (April–June 1943)," *Hazionuth* 4 (1976) (in Hebrew), and Michael J. Cohen, "The British White Paper on Palestine, May 1939, Part 2: The Testing of a Policy, 1942–1945," in *Historical Journal* 19 (1976), 727–758.

business dynasty, who maintained "clandestine contacts with a number of Nazi administrators during the early years of the Third Reich." Foley, like the SIS Station Chief in Prague and later in Istanbul during World War II, Harold Gibson, was also able to sympathize with the plight of Jewish refugees and helped Jews to emigrate.[2] Foley's espionage activities among German Jews, and the later use of refugees by the Allies to obtain military information on the Axis powers, officially supported in this by the Jewish Agency, might have added a shadow of security risk, from a German point of view, to the Nazi policy of forced emigration.[3] Still, among other MI6 officers, which came to be known as the ISLD (Inter-Service Liaison Department) in the Middle East, there were other opinions about Jews, refugees, and Zionists.

Section V, the counterespionage section of MI6 under Felix Cowgill and later under Tim Milne, was an ultrasecret operation because it handled the so-called ISOS, the decrypts of Abwehr (German Military Intelligence) and SD cables, among other top-secret communications exchanged by German agencies but also the Jewish Agency's cables. Thus, Section V at first did not distribute its ISOS decrypts between MI6's own sections and hardly made them available to ISLD. Later on, however, we find a distribution list contained in ISOS decrypts that included practically every interested agency: the various sections of MI6, the Director of Military Intelligence (DMI), the Director of Naval Intelligence, and the various sections of MI5. Thus, Section V was working in cooperation with representatives of the Foreign Office and was active in Cairo under the umbrella of ISLD.[4]

Later, the British established an interrogation center mainly for Jewish refugees in Atlit, near Haifa, and in Homs, Syria. The Syrian center became a combined British–American effort, as did another center of that kind on Cyprus.[5] Thus, Jewish refugees, if allowed to enter Allied-controlled territory, could become a source of intelligence, and hence the Zionist rescue workers would try to work with Allied intelligence services, which, at the

---

[2] See Christopher Andrew, *Her Majesty's Secret Service: The Making of the British Intelligence Community* (New York: Viking, 1986, p. 379), and see Michael Smith, *Foley, The Spy Who Saved 10,000 Jews* (London: Coronet Books, Hodder and Stoughton, 1999). SIS' "Z" Organization's (the SIS operation against Germany) Chief, Claude Dansey, recruited the retired Royal Navy Commander Kenneth Cohen as his assistant in 1937. Wilfried Israel was a Zionist and operated a rescue network in Portugal later during World War II. For the Z Organization and its demise later during the war in favor of other operations, see Nigel West, *MI6*, pp. 8–73, 79, 83, 95, 115–129.

[3] See also remarks in this regard in R. V. Jones, *Most Secret War* (Tel-Aviv: Ma'arachot Publishing House, 1984, p. 76) (Hebrew translation); see Andrew, *Her Majesty's Secret Service*, p. 382.

[4] See Robert Cecil, "Five of Six at War: Section V of MI6," *Intelligence and National Security* 9, No. 2 (April 1994), 345–353. The author was one of the wartime representatives of the FO in Section V. Kim Philby, the Soviet agent, also became a senior member of Section V, having first served at SOE See Cecil, "Five of Six at War," p. 349.

[5] See Report on British Allied Interrogation Organization dated January 9, 1943, NA, RG 226, Entry 210, box 100, folder 414.

same time, were gathering information on Jews and Zionists as a part of their own tasks. Thus, intelligence gathered by OSS-Secret Intelligence (OSS-SI), including reports related to rescue efforts of Jews and other matters reported by Jewish OSS agents, would be sent by OSS for evaluation by "Broadway" (a general code name for MI6) and influence decisions made by them.

MI6 was in charge of breaking the German military, police, SD, and Gestapo wireless traffic known as ISOS and ISOSICLE produced by "Enigma" machines of various kinds. Its Section V chief and later MI6 Director, Colonel (later made Major General Sir) Stewart Menzies, cultivated special relations with Colonel (later Brigadier and then Major General) William J. Donovan, the future OSS Director. In November 1942, Donovan sent a trusted aide to MI6, including to its ISOS code-breaking operation, and later on a team of Donovan's own X-2 (Counterintelligence) people arrived at MI6 headquarters in St. Albans and in the now famous code-breaking center at Bletchley Park, "and lasting friendship resulted," according to historian Robert Cecil.[6] Thus we should seek German Police, SD, and Gestapo decrypts made by the British in OSS archives, but nothing meaningful has been found as yet except specific SD and Gestapo (also other SS main offices) radio transmissions among other things telling the sad story of the deportation of the Jews of occupied Italy (specifically Rome), which was decrypted by the British and found in 2000 in the U.S. National Archives. Also some decrypts of Abwehr radio transmissions are available at the National Archives, specifically those of the "Klatt Organization" (a German Intelligence unit located in Sofia, Bulgaria, whose head was half-Jewish and thus had to be replaced). Both of these decrypts will be discussed later. The related vast British decrypts are not yet fully available to research.

As we have seen, the British did break the relatively primitive code used by the German Order Police for several months upon the inception and the initial phases of the Final Solution in occupied Soviet territories. Thus, the role of the large number of German Order Police units involved in carrying out the Final Solution in addition to the special SS squads that were supposed to have been solely responsible for the carnage has made its dimensions and the decision to liquidate as many Jews as possible in occupied Russia from the start clearer to historians.[7] More information on the early stages of the Holocaust, including the early history of Auschwitz, was available to British code breakers, but rather than informing the Americans about it late in 1941 and during 1942, they supplied intelligence information to the Soviets.[8] The reason for this could have been a rather unclear picture of German intentions at first: Whether the slaughter was systematic, aimed at

[6] Cecil, "Five of Six at War," pp. 350–351.
[7] Breitman, *Official Secrets*, pp. 88–121.
[8] Ibid., 109.

the Jewish population as a whole, at other population groups as well, at using Jews and others for slave labor, and the like.[9]

OSS records tell us more on British – American cooperation in regard to the Abwehr, SD, and Gestapo ISOS decrypted by the British. Donovan's man in England, OSS operative George K. Bowden, wrote to the OSS Director on March 23, 1943, under the header "British ISOS,"[10] that Colonel Cowgill of SIS was against OSS having access in England to British SIS material known as ISOS, which gave the British an "extraordinary knowledge of personalities and activities of the German Abwehr and Gestapo." Bowden, a Chicago lawyer and the number two man at the OSS New York office in its infancy under Allen Dulles, and who recruited Arthur Goldberg and other key members of OSS later on, complained that the British protest was "merely a conduit in conveying to England a protest by General George Strong," U.S. Army Intelligence Chief, who suddenly realized that the "civilian" OSS had access to signal intelligence that the U.S. Army tried to keep to itself.[11] Strong indeed failed in torpedoing the OSS–MI6 cooperation that had emerged before and continued after his above quoted intervention, but the British insisted on having a decisive role played by the OSS branch or division known as X-2, which received decrypts or information derived from ISOS decrypts. Thus, X-2 became an organization within an organization, according to historian Timothy Naftali,[12] receiving OSS-SI reports but not supplying its own reports to SI – a typical rivalry like that which emerged between General Strong and General Donovan. All of this will become relevant to us when we study the implication of these relations and the role of X-2 in regard to what was or seemed to be one of the most important rescue options during the Hungarian Holocaust.

British influence over their American Army colleagues was considerable and may explain U.S. Army Counter Intelligence Corps (CIC) and G-2 reports on Jews and Zionists, some of which were copied verbatim from the original British source.

MI5, the counterintelligence organization whose main activity was concentrated within the British Isles and Empire, already known for decades as being rather suspicious of alien Jews, expanded rapidly after the outbreak

---

[9] See Nicholas Terry, "Conflicting Signals: British Intelligence on the 'Final Solution' Through Radio Intercepts and Other Sources, 1941–1942," *Yad-Vashem Studies* (32), Spring 2004 (forthcoming).

[10] NA, RG 226, Entry 210, box 83, folder 340.

[11] The U.S. Army's Signal Corps, or Signal Intelligence Agency, which became the existing National Security Agency (NSA), decrypted cable traffic of Japan and many other nations. Decrypts pertaining to the Holocaust require an enormous search in the files of the so-called HCC library of the wartime agency, which I tried to launch at NARA during late 2001 and early 2002, but I gained the impression that most of these decrypts were irrelevant to the study of the Holocaust, except those stored in RG 457.

[12] In conversation with the present writer, December 2001.

of the war. However, one should distinguish between MI5's activities within the British Isles and its operation in various regions of the Empire in which MI5 "stations" known as Defense Security Offices (DSOs) may have developed a rather autonomous character due to their distance from Britain, the wartime strain, and the local and regional nature of their operations.[13] The head of DSO Jerusalem, Colonel John Teague, was objective, fair, and ready to cooperate with the Jewish Agency whenever this proved to be useful for his own purposes. But this reflected the typical view and experience of field officers against the values, aims, and character of their superiors in London and possibly also at the MI5 regional center known as Security Intelligence Middle East (SIME). In London, the intervening authorities could be Foreign Office officials and MI6 officers such as Group Captain Frederick Wintebotham and others who were firmly against any collaboration with Jews or Zionists.[14]

In addition to the MI5 stations and SIME, which necessarily dealt with counterespionage and any possible rescue "deals" with Nazi Germany, the Palestine Police Force was an important intelligence producer.[15]

The Political Branch of the Criminal Investigation Department (CID) operated under Sir Harold MacMichael, the British High Commissioner for Palestine, a veteran of the Colonial Service, in cooperation with MI5 and MI6 local stations and with their regional networks. On top of those, two specific British regional intelligence bodies for the Middle East as a whole, with Palestine given a top priority among them, were set up during 1939, with headquarters in Cairo: the Middle East Intelligence Center (MEIC) and SIME.[16] Later on, a third body, Political Intelligence, Middle East (PICME), was set up under the GOC in C, Middle East.[17] All of them dealt in various ways with Jews (i.e., Jews suspected of being enemy agents), with Palestine, with the Zionists, with rescue efforts as interpreted by them, obviously with the Arabs elites, masses, and enemy activities, and direct and indirect issues such as the former Jerusalem Mufti's propaganda broadcasts beamed

---

[13] About the DSOs, see West, *MI6*, pp. xxii, 126, and David A. Charters, "British Intelligence in the Palestine Campaign, 1945–47," *Intelligence and National Security* No. 1 (January 1991): 115–140.

[14] I shall return to this issue when discussing British and Hagana cooperation in sending Zionist operatives recruited to "A-Force" to the Balkans later in 1944.

[15] The main archival source in this regard, which became available to historians only recently, is repository 47, CID, at the Hagana Archive in Tel-Aviv.

[16] For an introductory brief history of SIME, see West, *MI6*, Howard, *British Intelligence in the Second World War: Volume 5, Strategic Deception*, pp. 31–32, 36, and Dovey, "Security in Syria, 1941–1945."

[17] For dates and details, see H. O. Dovey, "The Middle East Intelligence Center," *Intelligence and National Security* 4 (October 1989), 800–812, H. F. Hinsley et al., *British Intelligence in the Second World War*, Volume I (London: Her Majesty's Stationery Office, 1979), especially pp. 26–30, and West, *MI6*, pp. 125–130.

from Berlin to the Middle East,[18] Menachem Begin's "rebellion,"[19] declared against the British early in 1944, and the Sternists on a weekly, ad hoc, or sometimes daily and immediate basis. The topics are reflected very well in the U.S. Army G-2 and OSS reports and messages that I have used.

In the early 1940s, a British Minister of State, Middle East, was sent to Cairo to provide for the political aspects of military planning in cooperation with the "Middle East War Council." The "Council" was comprised of the key British diplomats and Arab experts in the area such as Sir Miles Lampson, the British envoy in Egypt, his colleague in Baghdad, Sir Kinahan Cornwallis, Bill Smart, an important Arab expert, and the British High Commissioner for Palestine, Sir Harold MacMichael. The Minister Resident was usually the chairman.

MEIC proved to be short-lived, and in fact it was replaced by SIME under Colonel (later Brigadier) Raymond Maunsell, who had served with the Transjordanian Frontier Force and later at GHQ in Cairo.[20]

SIME was also an important source of political information on Arabs and Jews, which found its way also to the American military authorities during the peak years of the Holocaust. According to Dovey, "the volume of information in the periodical summaries – from M.E.I.C. and S.I.M.E. – shows that S.I.M.E. had a large network of informants throughout the region." Next to or above SIME's offices in the same General Headquarters (GHQ) building in Cairo, yet another intelligence operation, dealing with counterespionage and double agents, the above-mentioned MI6 operation known as ISLD, was established during 1940[21] and soon supplied pretty good information, as reflected in American reports fed by SIME or by ISLD. As far as MEIC was concerned, its December 1942 diary shows that Brigadier I. N. (later Sir Iltyd) Clayton was then commanding the Center and that it had a Syrian detachment. Clayton, whose elder brother Gilbert was the key figure in the British Arab Bureau established by Sir Mark Sykes during World War I[22] among many other activities he pursued later in British Palestine and in the Arab world, had spent seven years on attachment to the Iraqi Army during the 1920s and later was appointed head of the British Middle East Office and finally the political aide to the GOC in C, Middle East. Both Claytons were not exactly friends of the Zionists. The April 1943 diary, according to Dovey, shows that Iltyd Clayton was posted to the office of the Minister of State as Arab Adviser. The bulk of the staff, twelve officers,

[18] See for an American sample thereof NA, RG 165, Entry 77, Director of Intelligence, War Department, G-2 Regional File 1933–1944, Palestine, box 3027.

[19] Ibid.

[20] See West, *MI6*, p. 125; and Dovey, "The Middle East Intelligence Center," p. 803.

[21] For details on the early history of ISLD, see West, *MI6*, pp. 127–128.

[22] See David Fromkin, *A Peace to End All Peace: The Fall of the Ottoman Empire and the Creation of the Modern Middle East* (New York: Owl, 1989), pp. 170–172, 194, 219–223, 329, 335, 419, 467–470.

went to a new organization, PICME, which practically replaced MEIC following a decision made by the Political Committee of the Middle East War Council on March 31, 1943.[23] Brigadier C. D. Quilliam was in command. We shall encounter Quilliam directly and in close cooperation with his OSS counterpart in Cairo.

SIME, the British regional military equivalent of MI5, was from 1940 under the GOC in C, Middle East in Cairo.[24] Several SIME officials were old hands at the Special Service Office (SSO, a unit attached to the Royal Air Force (RAF) and in charge of counterintelligence in the 1930s), some of whom knew the Zionists well and were ready to cooperate with them to expose Nazi spies and prepare for a possible Axis occupation. Royal Air Force intelligence officers were also active in creating ties between Zionists and the SIS and its hybrid organizations in the region and outside of it, but others were more suspicious.

The fear of a renewed Arab rebellion in Palestine, if not of a general Arab revolt across the Middle East if the White Paper policy were to be abandoned, in which event a jihad would be followed as declared by the former Mufti of Jerusalem in 1941, or when British Army units stationed in Palestine would be sent to subdue the pro-Nazi regime in Iraq (an endeavor that would prove to be very successful) prevailed among the British top military. General (later Field Marshal) Sir Archibald P. Wavell, the GOC in C, was especially opposed to the Iraqi venture, fearing an Arab rebellion in Palestine and trouble in Egypt.[25] In fact, Churchill had to compel him to restore British control over Iraq in 1941. But the seemingly almighty Prime Minister had to abandon his own idea, to arm the Jews of Palestine and hence free the British troops stationed in the rear of the desert front to be engaged in real fighting elsewhere, due to strong opposition at home and in the region.[26] The fear of trouble with the Arabs and Muslims in general remained very much in the mind of Wavell's successors, Sir Claude Auchinleck, Sir Harold Alexander, and Sir Henry Maitland "Jumbo" Wilson, who inherited this traditional view with the officials who had adopted it.

Several other reasons explain this fear on top of an elitist fear of primitive masses, which may go back to the Mehdi's rebellion in the Sudan. Wavell's own experience in fighting the rebelling Palestinians in the late 1930s and the Muslim question in India, including the problem of Muslim soldiers in the British Indian Army, must be borne in mind. Yet the Foreign and the Colonial Offices in London shared what Churchill called a "pro-Arab and an anti-Jewish" view, which may be explained by the mixture of prejudices,

[23] Dovey, "The Middle East Intelligence Center."

[24] See also Howard, *British Intelligence in the Second World War*, Volume 5, pp. 31–32.

[25] See Churchill, *The Second World War*, Volume III, pp. 222–223.

[26] See Zweig, *Britain and Palestine during the Second World War*, pp. 20–30.

images, and reputations of Jews, combined with Imperial interests and security considerations, some of them of typical conspiratorial nature.

A distinguished contemporary historian, Sir Michael Howard, described British fears, writing in 1990 as follows:[27]

The British were based on countries whose populations were elements in a Levantine society extending around the shores and throughout the islands of the eastern Mediterranean, bound together by commercial and family links dating back over millennia; a society whose complexity foreign security authorities could barely comprehend... the region might be described as an intelligence officer's paradise and a security officer's hell. (Howard, *British Intelligence in the Second World War*, p. 31)

Sir Michael's wit of the 1990s is of course just a reminiscence of British security officers' fears regarding a possible Nazi–Zionist collaboration that could explode in the region.

Such calculations were fed by a basic perception of Jews as if they – and especially Zionists – were rather close to the hypernationalistic, egotistical, unfair, and inhuman characteristics of Fascism itself entertained by Herbert Downie of the Colonial Office as quoted in Chapter 8. Sir John Shackburgh of the Foreign Office, who was in charge of the Palestine section, had supported the Zionist endeavor, but later in the 1930s he seemed to have changed his attitude, as historian Arnold Toynbee has done.[28] Downie, however, had been transferred in 1942, and Shackburgh retired about that time. The politicians who had formulated the Palestine policy of the late 1930s were replaced as well, as historian Ron Zweig tells us. But in fact old and new officials maintained the basic principles of the 1939 White Paper as it became the official policy of His Majesty's Government in order to win Arab support for Britain in its battle with the Axis and prevent an injustice to the Arabs, "and any second thoughts on it [such as emanated from Churchill – S.A.] would only renew the difficult and heated controversy which had absorbed so much 'official' energy during the years following the Arab revolt in 1936."[29] Hence, the British officials involved would at least use intelligence and arguments among themselves and especially in dealing with the Americans, and some would associate the Zionists with the Nazis, in Downie's tradition.

These British services and individuals fed the American intelligence branches when established in the area as late as 1943. G-2, CIC[30] and OSS, the Navy's Office of Naval Intelligence (ONI), and the regular diplomatic

---

[27] Howard, *British Intelligence in the Second World War*, Volume 5, p. 31.
[28] See Zweig, *Britain and Palestine during the Second World War*, pp. 133, 180.
[29] Ibid., 180.
[30] For a short history of CIC, see Ian Sayer and Douglas Botting, *America's Secret Army: The Untold Story of the Counter Intelligence Corps* (London: Grafton Books, 1989). Regarding CIC's activities in the Middle East from September 1942 until V-E Day, see pp. 60–61. The information contained therein is correct but incomplete.

system of reporting and evaluating the Middle East situation were largely British-fed. We can find further influence by the British in reports disseminated by the American theater Joint (i.e., interservice) Middle East Intelligence Collection Agency (JMEIC).

The few American diplomats serving in the area since the 1930s cooperated informally with their British colleagues before the entry of the United States into the Middle East picture. The U.S. State Department had never endorsed Woodrow Wilson's positive view of the Zionist idea, and since the mid-1920s it had developed a growing interest in, and sympathy toward, Arabs, even as the United States itself sank into complete isolationism.[31]

The OSS Director, William J. Donovan, a retired World War I Colonel and later General, was personally known to President Roosevelt, who had sent him overseas after the fall of France to ascertain the chances of the British. The Departments of State and War, like Joseph Kennedy, the American ambassador in London, were pessimistic about Britain's chances of survival – so Christopher Andrew tells us.[32] Donovan, on the other hand, came and left as a strong supporter of Britain's chances and interests wherever he went, including in the Balkans and in the Middle East, which he toured from Cairo to Baghdad, as we are told by Bradley F. Smith.[33] According to Andrew, Donovan's SIS friend in New York, the wealthy Canadian industrialist William (later Sir William) Stephenson,[34] who helped arrange Donovan's tour and the red carpet reception for him from Churchill downward, cabled SIS headquarters that Donovan helped bring about the American destroyer deal that preceded the Lend-Lease Act of March 1941.

The punishment of the Jews in this context was not far from Hitler's own mind, but members of MI5 and ISLD suspected at least a Zionist–Nazi common denominator to get the Jews into Palestine even during the war, and hence Zionist cooperation with these two important bureaucracies was always limited.

According to Christopher Andrew,[35] Whitehall's initial interest in sabotage and subversion operations against Germany harbored in SIS "stemmed chiefly from an exaggerated belief in Germany's economic vulnerability." In fact, Germany was vulnerable economically at that time, as we have seen,

---

[31] See in this regard Amitzur Ilan, *America, Britain and Palestine, 1939–1945: The Inception and the Development of American Involvement in the British Palestine Policy* (Jerusalem: Yad Izhak Ben-Zvi, 1979) (in Hebrew), to be quoted later in some detail.

[32] Andrew, *Her Majesty's Secret Service*, pp. 466–467; for Donovan's trip in 1940, see Bradley F. Smith, *The Shadow Warriors: O.S.S. and the Origins of the C.I.A.* (New York: Basic Books, 1983), pp. 46–53.

[33] Bradley F. Smith, *The Shadow Warriors*, pp. 123–139.

[34] Stephenson previously served SIS in Europe, not very successfully, as West tells us, but Churchill insisted upon appointing him as SIS Chief in New York, and this proved to be a major success, at least regarding Donovan.

[35] Andrew, *Her Majesty's Secret Service*, pp. 472–476.

but this would drive it to the attack against the Soviet Union and to the Final Solution.

Once the Germans won the six-week Blitzkrieg in the West, which began on May 10, 1940, the British developed high hopes in regard to guerrilla warfare behind the Germans' back. As Christopher Andrew puts it: "the failure of regular warfare was now to be redeemed by irregular warfare." As a result of this, Andrew tells us, the adoption of the guerrilla warfare strategy led to the removal of its execution from SIS control, while the emerging new Special Operation Executive (SOE – first under Hugh Dalton and later under Lord Selborn) developed into a rather impressive operation, scoring success years later mainly in Norway and in France and much less so if at all in Central Europe and the Balkans.

The Joint Chiefs reported to the War Cabinet on May 25, 1940, that, if France fell, "Germany might still be defeated by economic pressure, by a combination of air attack on economic objectives in Germany and on German morale and the creation of widespread revolt in her conquered territories."[36] None of these options could have harbored special attention being given to Jews. On the contrary, "German morale" could hardly be undermined if Germans were to perceive the attacks against German targets as serving Jewish interests. The occupied European nations would rise against the Nazi yoke only for the sake of their own interests and values, supported by the British. At the same time, the British could hardly support Zionist minority claims in Palestine and appear as an occupying power subduing Arab majority resistance to both Jews and the British if the country were opened to Jews escaping from occupied Europe as long as they were coming in large numbers.

Later, however, when some of the guerilla war illusions were swept aside in favor of the defense of the British Isles proper (and the Middle East), the support of the British masses, which took most of the burden, and the maintenance of domestic morale became an utmost priority. In turn, this priority, combined with immediate and intense troubles caused by the war situation itself, excluded alien Jews. Yet the idea of enticing sabotage warfare behind German backs, thanks to the expected overwhelming mass resistance in the occupied countries, was adopted by Hugh Dalton. This ambitious Labor politician became Minister of Economic Warfare in Churchill's cabinet. He was confident that

by the end of the year 'the slave lands, which Germany had overrun,' would rise in revolt, and that Nazism might then 'dissolve like the snow in the spring.' 'Regular soldiers, he complained, are not the men to stir up revolution, to create social chaos or to use all those ungentlemanly means of winning the war which come so easily to the Nazis.' (Christopher Andrew, *Her Majesty's Secret Service*, p. 476)

[36] Ibid., 475–476.

The Zionists, in turn, were also infested with the guerrilla warfare mania and tried later in the war to mobilize, train, and parachute hundreds of Hagana commandos into occupied Europe, for which they needed British – and American – tools and political support. The British agency in charge of such action, the SOE, seemed to the Zionists to be the obvious partner in this regard, but the actual dropping of the Zionist commando mission later on into Yugoslavia on its way to Hungary was executed in fact by "Force A," a part of MI9, a British Army organization responsible for assisting escapees from POW camps or evaders of captivity, while SOE helped resistance and partisan movements, in which the Zionists were primarily interested but hardly able to find their way between the various British agencies acting behind enemy lines and sometimes at odds with each other.

The embryo of the future Israeli "Mossad," the Intelligence Service of the Jewish Agency, under Reuven Zaslani (later Zaslani's name was changed to Shiloah) was in charge of such commando operations, trying to develop ties with the related British services and OSS. For this they finally found allies even among otherwise not very friendly British officials such as Brigadier I. N. Clayton, who preferred to have the Jews fight the Germans outside Palestine.[37] Very little came out of this, due among other things to other priorities among the British and Americans, security checks required on the Zionist candidates, and involvements on the ground due to countermeasures by Germany and its allies. In fact, the whole idea was detached from the realities on the ground, to be examined in some detail with regard to the Hungarian case. But real heroes, such as poet Hannah Szenes, and myths were born, which would in turn explode in the face of their originators during the "Kasztner trial" in independent Israel when Labor Zionist efforts to deal with the Gestapo seemed to have been exposed as though they had torpedoed the efforts of Zionist commandos sent by the Laborites themselves to entice the Hungarian Jews to fight the Germans.

Traditional suspicions of Jews and Zionists at SIS and SOE were not necessarily as negative as those typical of SIME, PICME, and even MI9's higher command in London, but all carried political preferences with regard to wartime dilemmas and priorities that were also related to the postwar future of the region.

The web of British intelligence in the Middle East also included the theater branch of the "Imperial Censorship" – the mail, radio, and telegraph censorship – reporting to Whitehall and to a variety of interested offices across the Empire, such as in India (due to the Muslim element in the Subcontinent), and also to American censorship. British censors, several dozen of them working in Jerusalem under the future Viscount Samuel, the son of the liberal politician and first British High Commissioner in Palestine,

---

[37] See Yehuda Bauer, *Diplomacy and Underground in Zionism, 1939–1945* (Jerusalem: Sifriat Poalim, 1966), p. 239 (in Hebrew).

opened all relevant foreign letters from and to Palestine. The censors monitored cables and finally submitted regular reports plus samples to the Allied joint censorship board in Bermuda. An American censor by the name of Nicholas Andronovich, actually a G-2 Captain and a White Russian by origin, who hardly spoke accent-free English, joined the British censorship office in Jerusalem later during the war.[38]

American Army officers, such as General Russell A. Osmun, "brought with them a distrust of Jews and hostility toward Zionism" when they joined the Joint Intelligence Collection Agency, Middle East (JICAME) in Cairo, a branch of G-2 charged with coordinated intelligence activity in the region.[39] Operating under heavy British influence, both Osmun and Andronovich, plus Major Edwin M. Wright, an Arabist connected with the American University in Cairo and a G-2 "authority" on Palestine, fed their superiors with their views and evaluations during the peak years of the Holocaust, arguing among other things that the Soviets were behind the exodus of Holocaust survivors from Poland into Palestine.[40]

The Yishuv's leadership was thus under a sort of siege, of which it became very conscious. Hence official records of the leadership meetings are a poor source for studying their real actions. Yet the British Palestine authorities and their counterparts in Whitehall perceived themselves to be under a sort of Jewish siege due to Zionist influence "in high places" (e.g., due to Churchill's own traditional Zionist inclinations and Dr. Weizmann's personal relations with the prime minister and a few cabinet ministers). This connection, however, did not suffice even to prevent measures undertaken from time to time by the Palestine authorities against the Yishuv because of its illegal immigration schemes and against its illegal military preparedness, which were enhanced when the British seemed to get ready to evacuate Palestine in the face of Erwin Rommel's onslaught.[41]

At the same time, the Yishuv's mainstream leadership searched for common denominators with the Allies wherever they could find them. The general Jewish public was torn between its views of hostile British policy toward Jewish refugees from Europe. Public opinion was focused also on the

---

[38] See for details on Palestine censorship NA, Entry 190, General OSS Correspondence, Cairo-SI-OP-15. On Andronovich and his ties with Arabs and the anti-Zionist British, see Joseph W. Bendersky, *The "Jewish Threat": Anti-Semitic Politics of the U.S. Army* (New York: Basic Books, 2000), p. 320.

[39] Bendersky, *The "Jewish Threat."*

[40] Ibid., 377. G-2 agent Mordechai Allen disagreed, but senior American officers believed in 1945 that the Soviets were "seeking a sphere of influence" in the Middle East by pushing Jews into Palestine.

[41] See Ronald Zweig, "The Political Use of Military Intelligence: Evaluating the Threat of a Jewish Revolt against Britain during the Second World War," in *Diplomacy and Intelligence During the Second World War: Essays in Honor of H. F. Hinsley* (Cambridge: Cambridge University Press, 1985), pp. 109–125, 286–293.

sometimes harsh and open measures invoked against the Hagana and its illegal arms hideouts and on the leadership's call upon them to mobilize to the British Army to help fight the Nazis. This call was at first followed with great enthusiasm, to the dismay of the British authorities in the area, who saw in the Jewish volunteers Zionist political recruits aspiring for an autonomous Jewish army within their ranks, and thus made them serve in auxiliary units raised among Arabs and Jews. Thus, the initial drive vanished after a while and had to be pursued by the Yishuv's leadership again and again later on, with limited success.

Thus, the Zionists' problem was to impose themselves on a rather reserved network of foreign political, military, and intelligence bodies to help Jews and support the Zionist idea in spite of themselves. A special case was the Political Warfare, or "black propaganda," agency under the Ministry of Information, which was active in the Middle East and other theaters and later worked together with Elmer Davies's American foreign propaganda machine Office of War Information (OWI) and with OSS' own "black propaganda" outfit, all of which steered away from Jews as best they could. Sometimes, to discredit high-ranking Nazis, such agencies even used anti-Semitic-related fabrications that might have returned to the Allied camp as intelligence.[42]

Mostly, the Special Operation Executive (SOE, also called MO4), the fresh and unconventional British foreign sabotage and guerrilla organization in the Middle East working under the Ministry of Economic Warfare in the Middle East under several names, such as Inter-Service Signal Unit 6 (ISSU6), the Special Projects Operations Center (SPOC), and the like, were ready to mobilize the Zionists for their war with Germany and cooperate with official Zionist bodies, but the actual job was done by MI9. Here the Zionists regarded commander Wolfson, stationed in Istanbul, and Force A commander Lieutenant Colonel Simonds as the "friends" who did indeed appreciate their devotion and abilities.[43] Several years after the outbreak of the war, SOE transmitted Jewish Agency cables from London to the Head Office in Jerusalem behind the censor's back, possibly also in order to read them on its own, but was ordered to stop the cable traffic late in 1942. Yet SOE–Zionist schemes to use large numbers of Jewish commandos in occupied Europe were always blocked by London,[44] while SOE was instructed

---

[42] See, for example, NA, RG 226, Entry 190, Director's Office and Field Stations, box 31, Bern, MO ("black propaganda").

[43] See Central Zionist Archive doc. S25/7902, Shertok's farewell speech in honor of Reuven Zaslani, when the latter was supposed to conclude his tour of duty as head of the Jewish Agency's embryonic Secret Service, and see Zaslani's own report on his activities in the same file, both made on November 27, 1944.

[44] See Zaslani's report cited in note 42, and Yoav Gelber, *The History of Voluntary Mobilization of the Yishuv*, Volume III (Jerusalem: Yad Izhak Ben-Zvi, 1983). The translation of the Hebrew title of this monumental three-volume history is mine.

to report on Zionist political ambitions in Palestine and while the common guerilla endeavors in occupied Europe under the auspices of MI9 proved to be haphazard and mostly futile.

The Jewish Agency had by 1941 already developed some kind of illegal radio traffic with its representatives in London and in the United States but had no similar radio contact with continental Europe.[45]

A story by itself was the recruitment of Irgun Zvai Leumi (a Zionist military underground, translated as National Military Organization and abbreviated from the Hebrew as IZL) activists by SIS to run an espionage network in the Balkans. The organization was established under Jabotinsky's auspices late in the 1930s as a separate Jewish underground in Palestine mainly as a result of the Arab revolt and following the ruling Labor Party's decision not to respond to it by force.[46] Jabotinsky was worried about the radical tendencies among IZL leaders, but he retained his traditional British orientation and thus irritated the radicals, who opted for an open anti-British and anti-Arab terror campaign in response to Arab terrorism. In the meantime, war broke out, and IZL split upon Jabotinsky's call to his followers to join the British to fight Nazi Germany, reviving thereby his World War I precedent of creating a "Jewish Legion" in its rank toward assuming military control over Palestine after the war upon his sudden death in 1940. All of the other Zionist groups independently made this claim for a fighting Jewish army in the ranks of the British Army.

IZL commander David Raziel decided on cooperation with the British against the Axis, the main enemy. Under Avraham "Yair" Stern, a minority group of radicals openly endorsed a quasi-Fascist ideology,[47] continuing to see in the British the main enemy. In 1940, an "Italian connection" was pursued, and Stern argued that Hitler – and by now Mussolini, too – were disseminating some kind of verbal rather than operational anti-Semitism. Stern then decided to become a "belligerent" against the British, ignored the Yishuv's elected leadership, and tried to negotiate a formal agreement with the Italians, spellbound by their initial advances in North Africa and bombing raids against Tel-Aviv and Haifa, based on the alleged common interest of Zionists and Fascists in removing the Jews from Europe and in working together against the British at the same time. The final goal was to create a Jewish entity in Palestine with Italy's help, to be backed up by Nazi Germany, that might adopt a semi-Fascist regime.[48]

---

45 Testimonies of Shlomo Lavi and Menachem Yitzhaki, the pioneers of the Hagana's illegal communication service, which first operated from Kibbutz G'vat and then had an operator in London as well, in private communications to the Hagana Archive and in "Yoman G'vat," no. 1553, courtesy of Hagana historian Gershon Rivlin.

46 On the birth of the independent IZL and the emergence of the Stern group later on, see Heller, *LEHI*, pp. 39–110.

47 See Stern's quotes in Heller, *LEHI*, pp. 77, 111.

48 See draft of 1940 agreement, published by Heller, *LEHI*, between pp. 128 and 129.

IZL cooperated with the Hagana in swallowing Stern's bids for negotiations with Fascist Italy by pretending to represent Mussolini.[49] In other words, IZL–Hagana representatives lured Stern into believing that they were Mussolini's emissaries in order to prevent him from pursuing real negotiations with the Fascist Italians. Later Stern tried to contact the Germans, having read published press stories on German plans for a territorial solution of the Jewish question in Poland, which failed (e.g., Eichmann's "Nisco Plan"), and about the Madagascar Plan.[50] Stern indeed succeeded in at least creating the impression that some Zionists and the Nazis had a far-reaching common interest and thus became an outlaw, a pariah, not only for the Labor Zionists but also for leading members of Jabotinsky's political party, the New Zionist Organization (NZO), and IZL, who rejected this bid for cooperation with the Axis.

Under David Raziel, Jabotinsky's followers split, as we have already seen, and the majority were ready to cooperate with the British to fight pro-Axis elements abroad such as the Iraqi nationalists under Rashid Ali el-Qeillani, who managed to assume power in Iraq for a short while in 1941 in cooperation with Amin el-Husseini, the former Mufti of Jerusalem. At that time, as Bauer tells us[51] and the Hagana's Home Intelligence records substantiate, a high degree of cooperation existed between Jabotinsky's disciples in the IZL–NMO and the British Palestine Police and the CID (the police intelligence of the Palestine British government), which colored their reports on the Labor Zionists in terms close to the anti-socialist credo of Jabotinsky's followers – equating Mapai's civilian militia with the "Gestapo," deliberately mixing it up with the Nazi SA.[52] (Mapai was the mainstream Labor political party at the time.)

Stern and his small group of followers continued to perceive the British as the main enemy.[53] British CID files contain information on Stern's continued

---

[49] See Heller, *LEHI*, pp. 113–114. The operation was conducted by one Moshe Rotstein, a former IZL operative, according to Yitzhak Berman's testimony to me.

[50] Heller, *LEHI*, pp. 127–128.

[51] Bauer, *Diplomacy and Underground in Zionism*, pp. 112–113.

[52] See Hagana Archive, Repository 112 Shai/Porshim (Hagana Home Intelligence, records pertaining to IZL and the Sternists), file 1502 b, dated January 31, 1947, in which the poisoned relations between the Revisionist Party under Dr. Arie Altman, the IZL, and the Stern group are described, including a degree of collaboration between Altman and the British authorities back in the early 1940s in this regard. A rather detailed chapter on this topic is called "The Pritzker Crossroad" and is offered by Shabtai Teveth in his book *The Vanished Years and the Black Hole* (Tel-Aviv: Dvir Publishing House, 1999) (in Hebrew), pp. 245ff.

[53] See Inspector General (Palestine Police) Allen Saunders to Chief Secretary, Palestine Government, September 11, 1940, Subject: Disturbances at Herzlia, secret, pertaining to alleged robbery by Stern gang members of Hagana weapons, to which the Inspector General added a summary of the gang's background and previous activities such as bank robberies in Jerusalem and in Tel-Aviv to finance its illegal activities. See further most secret memo 59/1809/GS, dated October 10, 1940, probably an internal CID document carrying the header Giles Bey (Arthur F. Giles, the CID's chief, who had used the Egyptian title "Bey" since his days as colonial officer in Egypt).

efforts to reach an understanding with Fascist Italy and about Stern's alleged letter of understanding, which was suggested to the Italian mission in Syria, recommending the arrest of Stern's group. Similar British intelligence sources disseminated at the time about Stern's efforts to create a viable working collaboration with Fascist Italy, in conjunction with Stern's own takeover in Palestine once "liberated" from the British, were found in the Hagana's own counterintelligence files.[54]

Later, after Stern's death at British hands and the arrest of most members of the group, the Sternists were silenced until late 1943, when under Nathan Friedman, Israel Sheib-Eldad, and Yitzhak Yezenitski-Shamir the "Stern Gang" renewed its terror campaign against the British, to be neutralized by cooperation between the Hagana and the British.[55]

Yitzhak Berman, at the time an IZL operative involved in the anti-Stern activities and a future Minister in Menachem Begin's cabinet,[56] soon became involved in bids for cooperation between Raziel, the IZL commander, and British Intelligence, with RAF veterans in Palestine and in Cairo as go-betweens. This cooperation led to Raziel's death in a mission on behalf of the British in Iraq, the Arab country that came for a while under pro-German control.

In December 1941, Berman went to Cairo to offer his support to SOE via the same RAF go-betweens (one of whom was an old admirer of Captain Orde Charles Wingate, the ardent "Zionist" among the British Intelligence officers who had subdued the Palestinian–Arab rebellion of 1936–1939 with Jewish help). Yet, on top of that, RAF interest in cooperation with the Jews was practical. Jews in German-allied nations could indeed be useful, and some, as Berman puts it and the American documentation substantiates, such as the American Jewish G-2 agent de Leon in Bulgaria,[57] were in this regard useful to the Allies.

Neither SIS nor SOE, however, was yet ready to operate in the Balkans, and until late 1942 nothing happened; worse, the IZL idea of making its own network of illegal immigration to Palestine the cornerstone of British espionage and subversion activities in the unoccupied German-allied nations in the Balkans was torpedoed due to the tragedy of the Struma, according to Berman.

The S.S. Struma carried illegal immigrants to Palestine in December 1941, but due to British intervention (the Colonial Office's and the Palestine

54 Hagana Archive, Repository 112, Shai (Counter-Intelligence) Porshim (Stern-IZL files) file 1079, Shai folder 1941, pertaining to Stern–Italian connection.

55 This topic will be addressed in some detail later.

56 Berman resigned this post due to 1982 war in Lebanon; see his memoirs, *Stormy Days* (Tel-Aviv: Ministry of Defense Publishing House, 1993), especially pp. 125–133. The memoir, in Hebrew, however, does not tell his whole story, as Berman referred to Rotstein as M R only.

57 Berman, *Stormy Days*, p. 119.

Government's) it was perceived by Harold Downie as a "Gestapo spy ship," according to Kushner,[58] and was turned away by the Turkish authorities upon British insistence. Later, it was sunk in the Black Sea, probably by a Soviet submarine. It was one of the best-known cases of British White Paper policy and resulted directly in the death of refugees from Hitler's Europe. The public uproar that followed embarrassed the government in London. According to Kushner, the Foreign Office officials finally came to doubt the refugee–spy argument, but the Colonial Office persisted in it. Hence, according to Berman, the British authorities in charge decided to prevent similar cases in the future by refusing to cooperate with the organizers of similar endeavors, such as his IZL colleagues in the Balkans, even for their own military benefit.

Late in 1942, SIS recruited Yitzhak Berman as a major under Colonel Harold Gibson, the station chief in Istanbul in charge of the Balkan operation. Following the Struma affair, which torpedoed Berman's idea of using IZL networks operated in Rumania and Hungary but mainly in Bulgaria for rescue, he and his fellow Zionists created three military, political, and economic intelligence networks, not by directly using Jewish illegal immigration operatives but by exploiting their local connections, which at that time were being used primarily for intelligence gathering. But every now and again illegal immigrants benefited from these activities in small numbers, according to Berman, who immigrated to Palestine via Turkey that way. Berman's activity was an episode (in comparison to the more visible acts and failures of the Yishuv's mainstream emissaries in Turkey) whose rescue efforts and intelligence activities were also related to each other and aimed at getting support from the British and the Americans, primarily OSS, as well.

The American Special Operations (SO) branch of OSS was copied after the British SOE, except that OSS was a centralized agency under the command of William J. Donovan and subject to the Joint Chiefs, after some quarrels with the U.S. Army, which, of course, maintained its own military intelligence and counterintelligence.[59] The Jewish Agency's representatives, especially the head of its Intelligence Branch, Reuven Zaslani, tried hard to mobilize OSS-SO for commando operations behind enemy lines, but no mission was authorized, according to former OSS Major Arthur Goldberg[60] due to OSS Headquarters' refusal to authorize operational deals with the Jewish Agency.

The American Secret Intelligence branch of OSS (OSS-SI) resembled the British SIS except that it was created rather hastily by recruiting a variety of people, some amateurs who learned on the job and some whose expertise

---

[58] Ibid., 153.

[59] For a still valid published work on the early history of OSS, at first as an embryonic office of a "Coordinator of Information" (COI), the final decision to create OSS, and its status, see Bradley F. Smith, *The Shadow Warriors*, pp. 55–139.

[60] Interview with the present writer, Washington, D.C., July 24, 1987.

was needed but who required evaluation by the growing OSS R&A (under historian William L. Langer). Prominent among the R&A's German experts was the noted neo-Marxist economist Franz Neumann, who repeatedly argued that in the hands of the Nazis anti-Semitism was a rather successful tool to unify an otherwise rather divided German society on top of Western mistakes in dealing with Hitler in the 1930s. Thus, fighting Hitler by invoking his own tools in an adverse way (e.g., referring to his most successful tool, Jews) would achieve nothing but trouble from an Allied point of view. Once Hitler had involved the German people in the Final Solution, which allegedly was just the "spearhead" of his much larger aims toward ethnic cleansing and colonization, he was thus the creator of German "collective guilt."[61] Thus, the Final Solution may have indeed helped cement the bond between the regime and the Führer, not only in his own eyes but also in Franz Neumann's eyes.[62]

X-2, or the OSS counterintelligence unit under attorney James Murphy,[63] was a secretive branch copied after or very much influenced by the British SIS Section V, which became a rather formidable but not necessarily effective machine under Felix Cowgill beginning in March 1939.[64] Cowgill was a secretive, opinionated person and is regarded in hindsight as inept.[65] Section V did not comprehend the meaning of SD, the Secret Service of the SS, for quite some time.[66] But its decrypts finally found their way to the close realm of OSS X-2 so that if we had them, or copies thereof, we could at least read

---

[61] See in this regard Barry M. Katz's "American Intelligence and the Holocaust: An Ambiguous Record," in Shlomo Aronson (ed.), *New Records – New Perspectives* (Sede Boker: Ben-Gurion Research Center, 2002), pp. 54–64. For Katz's previous publications on the so-called R&A branch of OSS under historian William L. Langer and especially on the Central European Section thereof, in which "Frankfurt School" members such as Otto Kirchheimer, Herbert Marcuse, and their close associate, Franz Neumann, played a major role, see the text.

[62] See NA, RG 59, R&A Reports, 10/5–11/43, and see report 1113.29, authored by the Central European Section's expert, Krieger, according to which Germany's increased campaign against Danish Jews "spearheaded the inauguration of intensified Nazi control over Denmark," while in fact most Danish Jews were evacuated by the Danes to Sweden in October 1943, and thus rescued. See further report 1113.31, authored by "Frankfurt School" scholar Otto Kirchheimer, period 10/19–25/43, quoting the Reich's Press Chief Dietrich's open justification of extermination of Jews because the Third Reich was at war with World Jewry. Kirchheimer's comment: "This becomes a *pretext* (italics added) for German interference in internal affairs of any country." See further report 1113.34, 11/13/43, authored by Sharp, in which a German POW was quoted, confirming the mass slaughter of Jews in Poland. The details were correct, including the description of atrocities, but the American author found the figures and details exaggerated simply because they were "hard to believe even regarding the Nazis."

[63] See CIA official description of OSS entitled "The Office of Strategic Services, America's First Intelligence Agency" (Washington, DC: U.S. Government Printing Office, 2000).

[64] On Cowgirl and Section V, see West, *MI6*, pp. 128–136. My correspondence with Ralph Erskine made this secretive and rather inept operative more of a real-life phenomenon rather than a shadowy, possibly antisemiticly inclined bureaucrat.

[65] Ralph Erskine's correspondence with the present writer, 2001–2002.

[66] Erskine's evaluation.

German intentions and actions pertaining to Jews and the Holocaust, or traces thereof, in OSS X-2 inquiries.

Both OSS main branches and R&A were under the same OSS overall command, given to William J. Donovan by FDR; the former was personally under British influence from the beginning of the war in various respects, and Donovan's report on his visit early in 1941 in the Middle East, specifically in the Persian Gulf area, stressed the role of the inhabitants of the region as "accomplished cloak and dagger types"[67] "If they trust us, they can be of great help. If they dislike us they are expert saboteurs and wreckers with a history of 5,000 years of practice." Indeed, Donovan was trying at that time to help sustain the British position in that area by stressing American support of the British and dismissed the Arab–Jewish question in Palestine in a conversation with the Iraqi Mufti as a "side issue."[68] But he never forgot the separate American interests to be pursued in due course with, and later possibly without, the British. The pessimistic view of Arabs and Iranians as potentially serious troublemakers was not shared by Churchill, who in May 1941 subdued the pro-Nazi Iraqis and later occupied Iran with minimal forces. The latter country was divided among the British and the Soviets.

The view of Arabs as primitive but weak and wicked, generalized in such simplistic terms, was also represented among Allied experts in the field and was assumed by young Israelis such as Moshe Dayan, who had fought the Palestinians under Orde Wingate in the 1930s (and the Vichy French in Syria as a British scout when the British decided to expel the Vichy French from that country in July 1941 and prevent it from becoming a German asset in the neighborhood of Iraq). But most American experts, such as the World War I Marine Lieutenant Colonel William A. Eddy, who became the first high-ranking OSS representative in North Africa,[69] World War I Lieutenant Colonel Harold Hoskins,[70] who toured and worked in the region on behalf

---

[67] See Bradley Smith, *The Shadow Warriors*, for the sources of Donovan's messages to Secretary Frank Knox on his Middle East and Balkan messages, and NARA, Diplomatic Branch, 740.0011 EW 1939.

[68] Quoted in Smith, *The Shadow Warriors*, p. 48. His source is the American legation in Baghdad to Near East Division, Department of State, February 21, 1941, 740.00118 EW 1939/230, Diplomatic Branch. However, in an internal report on his tour, Donovan offered his, or a British, opinion that the Jews wanted to expel the Arabs back to the desert from which they came; in North Africa, Arab anti-Semitism was grounded in specific reasons "since Moslem occupation thereof" and the alleged Jewish role in Spanish and French colonial rule in the area, NA, RG 165, Entry 77, box 3027.

[69] About Eddy's activities in North Africa, see for example NA, RG 226, Entry 108, Cairo reports, box 83. Among other reports, Eddy forwarded to Washington a report by one Captain Fiot, CIC, Atlantic base station, U.S. Army (who also appears in the files, box 83, as OSS agent 432) that blamed the Jews for France's misfortune, promised that they would not occupy a key position in the future, and stated that the main danger for the Western Allies by now was the Bolshevik threat.

[70] See Hoskins' own and other British-originated reports on the Middle East "explosive" situation following Zionist activities, and pro-Zionist statements made by Wendell Willkie, as made by PICME and local OSS and American diplomats throughout the region and

of OSS, and the State Department's Middle East experts, were very much of different opinions. They appreciated the Arab culture as a living civilization compared to what seemed to them to be Zionist efforts to revive a dead one. They appreciated the weight of Arab masses, were conscious of their potential violent habits should they "dislike us" because of the Zionists, and several of them were involved, directly or indirectly, in the oil business.

As far as the State Department was concerned, the official policy with regard to Jewish refugees who might find a haven in North Africa when liberated by the Allies and on the Palestine question was formulated by Near East Section Chief Wallace Murray, Harold Hoskins, and others. They recommended to Secretary Cordell Hull, after a visit by General Pat Hurley as FDR's personal representative to King Saud, to freeze the issue of the refugees and to avoid any possible step that may damage Arab interests in Palestine or elsewhere.[71]

The second generation of OSS Middle East experts was comprised of people such as Stephen B. L. Penrose, the future SI Chief in OSS headquarters in Cairo (Chief Intelligence officer).[72] Penrose was already there in the early stage of OSS establishment in Washington, actively fighting the Zionist aspirations for a Jewish army and for a Jewish state in Arab Palestine.[73] Penrose used Theodor Herzl's (the founding father of Zionism) interim solution for the Jewish Question (i.e., a haven in an African territory), by itself an idea that brought about an open rebellion among Herzl's followers (Weizmann on top), and suggested Cameroon as a Jewish home to his superiors.[74] Penrose and his colleague Lewis Leary had been active in the Arab world since the late 1920s and educated either in the American college in Beirut or in Cairo.[75] Donovan's newly arrived representatives in the Middle

compiled into: "Chronology of Events Pertaining to Palestine and Related Issues Threatening the War Effort and American Interests," as presented by Major General George V. Strong, Assistant Chief of Staff, G-2, to Judge Samuel I. Rosenman (FDR's counsel) at the White House, August 17, 1943, FDR Library, Rosenman Collection, box 13. See further Hoskins' role in regard to an alleged agreement between the Zionists and King Ibn Saud of Saudi Arabia, exposed by Hoskins as almost a Zionist fraud, and the related correspondence with Dr. Weizmann, FDR Library, Rosenman Papers, box 4, folder Dr. Ch. Weizmann.

71 See Michel Abitbul, "North Africa and the Rescue of Jewish Refugees in the Second World War: The Failure of the Fadala Plan," in *Contemporary Jewry: Studies in Honor of Moshe Davis*, edited by Geoffrey Wigoder (Jerusalem: Institute of Contemporary Jewry, Hebrew University, 1984), pp. 115–124.

72 See History of the Near East Section, OSS, Cairo, from May 15, 1943 to September 15, 1944, RG 226, Entry 210, box 275, and oral testimony of Prof. J. C. Hurewitz to me, July 14, 1987.

73 See RG 226, Entry 210, box 389, Penrose correspondence with various American public figures, protesting against their support of Zionist activities.

74 Ibid.

75 See for OSS personnel Cairo in the main period of my research (June 1944), RG 226, Entry 171, box 09. The Station Chief and Strategic Services Officer, Colonel John Toulmin, was also in charge of various outposts such as Istanbul. OSS Cairo had been divided

East were thus pro-Arab on their own and open to British influence until well into 1943, when they at least developed their own means of reporting. The desk officer in charge at OSS-SI, the Secret Intelligence Division, was Gordon Laud, also an old Middle East hand, whose namesake had dug the remnants of Armageddon (Megiddo) in the valley of Jesrael in the late 1920s. The Middle East desk chief at R&A was Professor Efraim Avigdor Speiser, a noted expert on ancient Assyria and Babylon at the University of Pennsylvania, who would recruit an old acquaintance, Professor Nelson Glueck, a renowned Middle East archaeologist, head of the Hebrew Union College in Cincinnati and one of the leaders of the American Jewish Reform movement, to serve as OSS agent in Palestine (codenamed "Hicks") next to Harold Glidden (codenamed "Laing"), an American resident in Palestine whose pro-Arab attitudes were pretty explicit in his reports and private correspondence.

Late in 1943, R&A engaged a young Jewish scholar, Dr. Charles Irving Dwork, as a sort of "Jewish Desk Officer'" in charge of collecting data on things Jewish, the Holocaust included, for the purpose of the debated issue of war crimes trials. His most important source, the whole Gestapo archive of Eichmann's representative in Rumania, which he received toward the end of the war via OSS channels, was never used at Nuremberg, however.

Another OSS outfit – the Foreign Nationals Bureau (FNB) – under DeWitt C. Poole, to be discussed in chapter 13, monitored the Jewish organizations in America, at least with regard to their contacts with the Palestine Zionists or with communists as ONI conducted similar monitoring of Jewish organizations in the United States.[76]

X-2 was a separate unit under the overall command of the OSS Director, as described earlier, but also worked very closely with British MI6 and with ISLD. They had to reckon with the U.S. Army's CIC and with G-2's JICAME, which also was under British influence and yet represented traditional Army prejudices and also had their doubts about OSS, the new outfit. The relations

---

beforehand into a Middle East headquarters under Toulmin and a North African, later also Italian, HQ located at Algiers and later at Caserta, Italy, under Colonel Edward Glavin, who succeeded Eddy. Once Glavin stopped fighting General de Gaulle and moved to Italy, the Zionists tried to create working contacts with him toward the use of Zionist commandos in Nazi-occupied Europe. For the rather complex birth of OSS operations in North Africa, possibly in the whole Mediterranean area, and regarding British supremacy in intelligence matters in Allied HQ, see Bradley F. Smith, *The Shadow Warriors*, pp. 227–228.

[76] See "List of Names Submitted to Censorship by the Foreign Intelligence Branch (O.S.S.) of Individuals whose Correspondence that Branch Would like to Receive," List A, RG 226, Entry 210, box 97, folder 390, no date. The names included those of Dr. Chaim Weizmann, Rabbi Stephen Wise, and the Bergson group activist Pierre van Passen. Regarding ONI and FBI's surveillance of Jews and Jewish organizations within the United States, see Joseph Bendersky, "National Security Rationalizations in the U.S. Army's Response to the Holocaust: New Evidence and Cautionary Lessons," paper submitted to German Studies Association Annual Conference, Washington, D.C., October 2001.

with the British, however, especially in regard to espionage and to subversive and otherwise politically colored operations in the Balkans, were not smooth and could even generate enmity and actual friction between the Allies. This rivalry would play a role in OSS activities in Hungary before and during the German occupation of that country, which is a central issue of this book.[77]

"Torch" – the planned landing in North Africa – made both Allies more interested in the Middle East and in keeping the Arabs neutral. This alone explains the large amount of information gathered about Jews, including their secret activities to rescue Jews from Europe, and German activities in which Jews were involved. These sources must be studied on top of the Yishuv leadership's own deliberations, so carefully analyzed by Dina Porat, in order to come to balanced conclusions regarding the behavior of the Yishuv's leadership since the outbreak of the war.

As mentioned earlier, today there exists an impression in Israel and abroad that the Zionist leadership was negligent, unable to rise to the needs of the hour, and absorbed in its own affairs during the Holocaust. Ben-Gurion is one of those who supposedly failed that supreme test. Among other things, he is accused (also by historian Dina Porat) of not having assumed the chairmanship of the Yishuv's "Rescue Committee," which was established after long and difficult deliberations in January 1943.[78] The Rescue Committee was a coalition of the Zionist parties, including Jabotinsky's Revisionists, chaired by Yitzhak Gruenbaum, a former leader of the Polish General Zionists. Gruenbaum's person and methods were not appreciated very much by Ben-Gurion, and thus the whole work of his committee was not seriously supported by the actual leaders of the Yishuv and the World Zionist movement.[79]

Yet Porat's study and the more recent one conducted by historian Tuvia Friling were based on a method of research that treated the rescue as a separate issue from the general trap situation in which the Nazis dictated the basic trap and the Allied role made it look as if they could have mitigated the disaster, whereas the Allies added their own contributions to the trap situation and vice versa. Porat did mention the Nazis' central role and did briefly allude to the war and Allied politics related to it, but the impression remains that the Allies could, and should, have done much more than they did. However, rescue became entangled, as we shall see in the Hungarian case, not just with previous prejudices, images, and reputations of Jews and Zionists and with other political and strategic calculations but with actual intelligence and espionage complexes, the adequate study of which requires the use of foreign archives and not just the Zionist ones. Porat's impressive

77 See Bradley Smith, *The Shadow Warriors*, pp. 238–239.
78 See Dina Porat, *An Entangled Leadership: The Yishuv and the Holocaust 1942–1945* (Tel-Aviv: Am Oved, 1986), pp. 101–116 (in Hebrew).
79 Porat, *An Entangled Leadership*, pp. 111–116.

research is largely based on the Zionist central archives and the open discussions, public speeches, and behind-the-scenes deliberations contained in
them, which were made under conditions of hostile British rule, British Intelligence efforts (mostly successful) to obtain information on those meetings,
or were collected from Zionist witnesses or persons involved later. However,
rescue was no separate matter but was an integral part, historically, of a
much larger picture.

12

The Jewish "Refugee Traffic"

The Road to Biltmore and Its Ramifications

To some leading Labor Zionists, such as Bernard Joseph, the Jewish Agency's counsel,[1] the Holocaust seemed primarily to be damaging the Zionist cause since the Nazis decimated the millions of Jews "that we are claiming home for them . . . after the war." Yet the Zionists cultivated hopes that many would–be victims might escape the Holocaust even in Poland, because the process of the Final Solution there was gradual and some ghettos such as Lodz were maintained almost until the end of the war, and that the Jews in the German-allied nations, primarily Rumania and Hungary, might survive.

On the other hand, if the Zionist leadership (once it internalized the Final Solution to its depth, while the "world" remained on one hand too sensitive to everything Jewish but at the same time silent to Jewish pleas for help) conveyed the depth of the trap to the Yishuv, many would blame them for succumbing to it and accuse them of weakness, neglect, and passivity. Their own Zionist credo pushed them to all kinds of rescue efforts that later may have seemed to be mere lip service to the cause or even as searches for an alibi if they were combined with the political aspirations to be discussed in this section. On the other hand, the Allies perceived them as war-damaging or as irrelevant, disturbing, side issues on their own and as being related to the Zionists' political goals.

At the same time, a responsible political leadership operating under British rule, although hated by many, had to recognize that the British did the fighting that actually saved the Jews of Palestine and others, if they survived, in Europe and many in the agitated Arab countries under British control. Such a leadership, which ignored this while admitting helplessness in the face of the Catch-22 situation, would not only have twisted the actual truth around (that is, that the Germans and not the British were the cause of the multiple trap) but may have driven its own masses to political activity

---

[1] Quoted by Gelber, November 11, 1942, *The History of Voluntary Mobilization of the Yishuv*, p. 147n.

that, having no other outlet but in Palestine proper, must have found its outlet in action against the nearest target: the British rulers. A Jewish rebellion in the middle of World War II against the British, fighting the Nazis, would have associated the Zionists with the Nazis themselves, and apart from Arab reaction to it and the expected British countermeasures against the 450,000 strong Jewish community in Palestine, it would have rescued no Jews from the Nazis. Hence, Ben-Gurion had to draw an extremely fine line, supporting the British while verbally condemning them, which he did rather seldom when the Holocaust's actual depth became clear to him. At the same time, he was trying to force them to do more for rescue, against their own interests, without losing control over his own, sometimes desperate Jewish community facing the Holocaust when it became fully known.

On the other hand, the Yishuv's leadership tried to maintain contact through neutral countries with the Zionist youth movements and work together with Zionist individuals in German-allied nations to enhance illegal immigration into a country closed by the British to large-scale, free immigration due to reasons related to the conduct of the war as they saw it. The Yishuv had to fight suspicions and arguments, which survived even after World War II in narratives written by serious British historians,[2] such as Christopher Sykes, a former intelligence officer stationed in Cairo during World War II, that the Zionists and the Nazis had more in common than the Zionists and the Allies. Sykes maintained that the "Jewish mass movements" from Germany, German-dominated countries, and German-allied countries continued until the end of the Nazi regime,[3] while the hate and the hysteria cultivated by the Nazis had no other object but malevolence, according to his post-Holocaust judgment. If there was any real goal, Sykes added, it was to empty the center of the ruling Teutonic race from Jews. There was one mitigating factor, and that was some kind of goading of the Jews to leave the European hell. On this opportunity jumped the Zionists, the Nazi believers (i.e., the "real" Nazis), and like them the profiteers. There is no way to know (and probably never will be) exactly what was the role of each of these factors in this immigration, and *whether the Nazis encouraged it because of real faith in the Nazi credo or because of corruption.*

Sykes, whose narrative was published in the 1960s, when there was "a way" (more than one) to do serious research on Hitler's forced emigration policy and on the future "deals" regarding human trade that supposedly were

---

[2] See Christopher Sykes, *Cross Roads to Israel: Palestine from Balfour to Bevin*, Hebrew translation (Tel-Aviv: Ma'arachot Publishing House, 1966), p. 208, and see discussion in text.

[3] There were no "mass movements" – as the Nazis forbade them. The British tried their best to prevent them until late in 1943, while most of the last-mentioned Jewish communities did not initially want to leave for Palestine in contrast to those in Poland and the Soviet territories.

offered in the wake of the peak years of the Holocaust, reflected here wartime intelligence mentality. Intelligence and censorship reports[4] – including from the peak years of the mass murder – about Adolf Eichmann's previous emigration tactics, which were at first the official strategy of the Third Reich, were still in circulation when the Nazis dropped forced emigration in favor of the Final Solution. The tactics of forcing Jews out by arresting them first, confiscating their property, and sending them abroad by using intermediaries, Jews among them, who supplied tickets or traded old boats for much money, were known to the British. The Zionists had used such contacts in spite of their dubious and sometimes corrupt character.[5] Sykes might have also seen, in his wartime capacity, intelligence reports on individual Jews who allegedly bribed their way out of Nazi concentration camps in collaboration with Hermann Göring, Robert Ley (the head of the Nazi "Labor Front"), and "Gestapo-Müller" himself, baseless as they were, or received copies of reports on the "Dreyfus Affair" in Switzerland, which in fact was torpedoed by the British.[6] It might have been one Rudi Scholz, a German Intelligence operative in the Balkans who seemed to the Zionists to offer a very promising, direct contact to the ghettos in Poland or a variety of rescue options that seemed to be serious, whose actual role will be discussed later. At any rate, the main source of the talk on refugee traffic was Zionist rescue workers, who were believed sometime in mid-1943 to have been on the verge of such a movement entailing a "large number of refugees." In fact, these were daydreams because the Final Solution meant that the Jews were forbidden to leave Nazi-dominated Europe and later were to be killed. Yet there were some deviations from this universal rule, which may have resulted in much misunderstanding later.

Late in 1942, Hermann Göring, in his capacity as economic czar of the Third Reich, along with the head henchman of the Final Solution, Heinrich Himmler, approached Hitler about it and received his permission to allow a few wealthy Jews to leave abroad in exchange for "large sums of foreign

---

4 See, for example, the report entitled "HIAS-HICEM (Refugee) Traffic in Near East," OSS Censorship Division, 17 February 1944, RG 226, Entry 210, box 208, folder 2.

5 See Dalia Ofer, *Illegal Immigration during the Holocaust*, pp. 160–204. see also Berman, *Stormy Days*, p. 39.

6 See, for example, OSS files RG 226, Entry 110, box 53, report on a Rumanian disguised as an American, who allegedly had bribed Göring, Ley, and Müller to free rich Jews from German concentration camps in the 1930s. Several names mentioned therein, such as Margot Klausner (a rich heir of a shoe business in Berlin, who became a well-known filmmaker in Israel), seem genuine. OSS seemingly authenticated the story in 1943 when the Rumanian person involved reached the United States. See RG 226, Entry 210, box 101, folder 420, an exchange between FBI Director J. Edgar Hoover and Captain James Roosevelt, Office of Coordinator of Information (future OSS), October 1941, regarding one Isidor Lazarus, alias Lee Lane, a Rumanian-born Jew who pretended to be a naturalized American. Roosevelt was interested in the case as a possible anti-Nazi propaganda tool.

currency."[7] The related suspicions among Allied security officers were anchored in previous conspiracy theories. One learns from Sykes that Nazi triumphs, and especially the fall of France, ascribed to French inner weakness and to Fascist influence, which was largely anti-Semitic as well, deepened the suspicion in Britain that mass Jewish emigration may represent "fifth column" activities against them while they were preparing to resist Hitler, who made the Jews responsible for British resistance against him. The Yishuv leadership then concentrated upon the rescue of children since the British authorities perceived adolescent Jewish refugees as possible enemy agents. Such efforts, which included mass immigration schemes from German-allied nations such as Rumania, yielded no results, mainly due to Nazi efforts to prevent the Jews from leaving and also to British maneuvers, including interventions in the transit countries such as Turkey, to restrict their arrival and make it as difficult as possible.[8]

The Yishuv had tried, as its own duty and obligation, bearing in mind its future interests, to join the Allied cause by invoking two kinds of secret activities in collaboration with the SIS and SOE. One was a sustained effort to obtain every piece of information on Axis Europe from Jewish refugees who did manage to arrive in Palestine and later, in neutral countries such as Turkey, on their way to Palestine as mentioned earlier, where they were concentrated in Haifa and in the Atlit Camp nearby.[9]

The Hagana-SIS-SOE secret cooperation continued on several levels, mainly with regard to intelligence gathering in the pro-Axis Middle Eastern countries such as Syria but also in Turkey and Iran, where Yishuv emissaries were asked by the British to build intelligence cells among local Jews should these countries come under Axis influence or be lost altogether.[10] The second

[7] See Richard Breitman and Shlomo Aronson, "The End of the 'Final Solution'? Nazi Plans to Ransom Jews in 1944," *Central European History* 25, No. 2 (1993), 177–203. See source NA, RG 242, T-175/R94/2615065, Himmler's agenda notes prepared in advance of the meeting: "Loslösung gegen Devisen [,] bin nicht dafür [,] bedeutende[r] als Geiseln." Translated into English, Himmler wrote that he was "against freedom in exchange for foreign currency, more significant [would be to hold the rich Jews] as hostages."

[8] For details, see Friling, "David Ben-Gurion and the Catastrophe of European Jewry," pp. 49–77.

[9] See for the early history of the Haifa Investigation Bureau under Ing. E. Wilenski, Yehuda Bauer, *Diplomacy and Underground in Zionism*, pp. 101–102, according to which this office operated from July 1940 until November 1944, and see Yoav Gelber, *The Standard Bearers: The Mission of the Volunteers for the Jewish People, Volume 3, History of Voluntary Mobilization* (Jerusalem: Yad Izhak Ben-Zvi, 1983), pp. 134–144 (in Hebrew), which includes a short description of the early cooperation between the Yishuv and various British foreign intelligence operations. Professor Gelber also kindly helped me in discerning the role of MI9 regarding the future mission of Zionist volunteers in the Balkans.

[10] One of them was Eliahu Epstein-Elath, a member of the Jewish Agency's Political Department and later the first Israeli ambassador to the United States. Elath indeed cooperated with the DSO Palestine, John Teague (later stationed in Cairo), who mobilized him for a variety of intelligence operations in Iran, Iraq, and Turkey, according to detailed testimony given to

activity was supposed to allow Zionist commandos to help their brethren in occupied Europe to rise against the Nazis. During the high tide of German victories in the Western Desert, there was a degree of limited cooperation between the British military authorities, but ironically enough, British victories in the Western Desert put an end to it, and the campaign against the illegal Hagana, especially the searches for illegal arms, was pursued every now and again, as its very existence, and inflated numbers about its strength, were now used by British officials to prevent the Americans from adopting pro-Zionist policies in the wake of the radicalization of the Yishuv as seemed to be the case in the face of the Holocaust.

At the same time, the British mandatory authorities and their counterparts in Cairo kept wondering if the refugees who had managed to enter Palestine, or those in whose name the Zionists claimed interest in immigration therein, did not prefer to go elsewhere and continue their previous Diaspora existence as usual.[11] They claimed that their own Jews, groomed on the "emancipation contract," were mobilized maybe to the Zionist cause due to the Holocaust, but in fact "most of the leading British Jews are either non- or anti-Zionist. They are keeping silent at the present time but would probably express open opposition to the creation of a Jewish state."

The most devastating argument raised by British bureaucrats in deliberations with their American counterparts as late as April 1944 in this connection was the following one:[12]

There has been a noticeable increase in anti-Semitism in England during the war stimulated partly by the behavior of many of the thousands of Jewish refugees in the United Kingdom, and particularly by the predominance of Jews in connection with prosecutions for black market operations. Sir Morris (Peterson, British Undersecretary of State for Foreign Affairs, in charge of the Eastern Department) expressed the view, however, that no organized or violent Semitism [sic] would develop in Britain unless the British should be called upon one day to establish a Jewish State with British military force [italics added]. ("Report on Jewry," NA, RG 59)

From this we learn that the refugees allowed to enter Britain since Hitler's rise to power, about 70,000 according to Kushner, many of whom were women

---

me, and when active in Istanbul, Turkey, he created a local favorable base of cooperation between the Jewish Agency's operatives, Teddy Kollek and others, with MI6 Station Chief Gibson and MI9 Station Chief Wolfson. See also Eldad Haruvi, "British Intelligence and Secret Cooperation with the Yishuv during WWII," Master's Thesis, Haifa University, 1999, pp. 40–72.

[11] See Imperial Censorship intercepts relayed to the U.S. Department of State, dateline London, July 5, 1944, "Report on Jewry," NA, RG 59, State's decimal file 811.111 Refugees, Visa Division 7-21-44 1940–1945: "Many refugees who had announced their intention of settling in Palestine are now more anxious to go to Canada or the United States, and the relief organizations have been given a good deal of trouble in consequence; in general, however, it is clear that the latter have very little to do compared with their frenzied activity in the earlier years of the war" (as most European Jews were dead by now, one may add).

[12] "Report on Jewry."

and children and some of whom were interned by the British government in 1940, still had a reputation problem. Anti-Semitism in England itself was a political weapon against its victims and the Zionists, who had to operate within these realities, especially when some American ears followed this line of British argumentation against the idea of a Jewish state or had their own reasons to reject and actively fight it as an issue separate from the European Holocaust, which the Zionists tried hard to combine.

The Palestine Government and the British Palestine experts in Cairo did not concentrate upon Stern's group alone. In fact, as we are told by Ron Zweig and his sources,[13] the British High Commissioner for Palestine, with the support of members of the Minister of State's Office in Cairo and of various intelligence and censorship agencies, had launched rather early in the war a campaign to abolish the Jewish Agency itself. Describing the leadership's political behavior as if they were working toward the creation of a "national socialist (i.e., Nazi) state," they invoked terms such as "Zionist Juggernaut" and "Todt Organization" (the Nazi slave service). In fact, Sir Harold MacMichael, the British High Commissioner, rightly understood that the Jewish Agency perceived the Jewish "refugee problem" in Europe as the main target of the Zionists "after the war." He combined it with what he perceived to be the growing radicalization of the Yishuv, with "the almost Nazi control" allegedly exercised by the Jewish Agency, the Histradrut (the General Federation of Labor), and Mapai (the Labor Party) over the Yishuv. MacMichael warned that since this leadership was no longer aiming at creating a "Jewish National Home" only, as stated in the Balfour Declaration of November 1917, but rather at the creation of a national socialist state, "the Zionist Juggernaut which has been created with such an intensity of zeal for a national state will be the cause of very serious trouble in the Near East."[14] Hence, he wanted the mandatory regime, which allowed the Jewish Agency to function as a semiautonomous body overshadowing the British government of Palestine itself, as he saw it, to be replaced by transforming Palestine into a regular Crown Colony. This went too far, as far as Churchill's cabinet was concerned.

The growing tension in the Yishuv following the news about the Holocaust, which was made publicly known late in 1942, when combined with the official endorsement by the Zionists of the new political agenda known as "the Biltmore Program" in May 1942, about a year after it was anticipated by MacMichael, revived the argument about the illegal armed strength of the Yishuv on its way to creating a "national socialist state" if the Jewish Agency was not suppressed in order to avoid unrest among the Arabs and leave British options open until after the war. At least the Foreign

---

[13] Ibid., 152–167.

[14] See MacMichael's "Note on Jewish Illegal Organizations, Their Activities and Finances," FO 371/31375 E2026, and MacMichael's introductory letter to it, October 16, 1941, sent to Colonial Secretary Lord Moyne.

Office decided to vigorously pursue the political action to curb Zionist efforts in America, while the full meaning of the Final Solution was slowly imposing itself on the Yishuv and on American Jews. For the British, and for many American officials, these remained two separate issues.

For his part, David Ben-Gurion had concentrated on the Americans since late in 1941. He harbored three main objectives: a Jewish army fighting in Allied ranks, the immediate transfer of millions of Jews to Palestine, and the demand for Jewish political independence, which, however, had not yet been endorsed by the Zionist executive when he left nor by Mapai, his own political party, when he arrived in the United States early in 1942.[15] He hoped, rather naively, to meet FDR personally, thanks to Justice Frankfurter's intervention or maybe to the support of Judge Sam Rosenman, a close aide of the President, but to no avail.[16] He then concentrated on preparing a general Zionist Conference, held in May 1942 in the Biltmore Hotel in New York. It adopted his grand schemes in cooperation with Chaim Weizmann, President of the World Zionist Organization. Yet Weizmann tended to perceive in the Palestinian Arabs a silent majority led astray by "politicians" such as the Grand Mufti and believed further that some kind of accommodation, which included transferring them to neighboring countries, could be negotiated with them.[17] Ben-Gurion, on the other hand, postulated urgent Jewish needs against Arab givens – the former were in dire trouble, whereas the latter lived in homogenous concentrations in enormous territories, partly empty and partly hardly inhabited, as he argued. Jewish settlement in Palestine did not harm Arab interests but on the contrary generated quite a growth in Arab population where Jews had settled, and thus mass Jewish immigration will not harm the interests of Arabs, whose rights must be observed. At any rate, the Arabs would have to accept the new reality when it was imposed on them by the Anglo-Saxon powers due to the moral significance of Jewish claims, so there would be no need to negotiate with Arabs, who would flatly refuse to acknowledge any Jewish rights in Palestine, or would even attempt to force the Jews out.[18]

Thus, Ben-Gurion decided to make a major step forward in America, which might in turn influence the British to accept a Jewish state, during the

---

[15] See Tuvia Friling, *Arrow in the Dark*, Volume I, pp. 71–92, about Ben-Gurion's visits to London and the United States in 1941–1942, and see Yoav Gelber, "Zionist Policy and the Fate of European Jewry, 1943–1944," Studies in Zionism, A Journal of Israel Studies, No. 7 (Spring 1983), pp. 133–167 and Zweig, *Britain and Palestine during the Second World War*, pp. 152–153.

[16] See Ben-Gurion's letter of February 10, 1942, to Judge Rosenman, sent from the Ambassador Hotel, Washington, D.C., FDR Library, Rosenman Papers, folder Palestine, box 13, in which he tried, among other things, to portray the Arabs as pro-Axis. In fact, this was indeed a major reason, in Allied eyes, not to help the Zionists.

[17] See David H. Shapiro, *From Philanthropy to Activism*, p. 163.

[18] Ibid.

war, and also immediate, free Jewish immigration of millions. This was his main goal within the framework of his social democratic credo. Ben-Gurion thus concentrated on America and its Jews, its Zionists, and its popular leaders in order to unite them behind a simple, large enough idea: Jewish independence, to be pursued now.

Ben-Gurion's future critics would ask what he was doing in America and in other Western countries for many months in 1940, late in 1941, and in 1942, when the bulk of the European Jewry was being slaughtered. The answer was that at that time he still perceived the European Jewry and the Zionist networks operating among them as a living body and even a possible asset for the Allies.[19] Ex post facto one can answer this question with a typical Jewish counterquestion by asking what Ben-Gurion could have achieved in this respect in Palestine when the official British policy remained what it was. Several intelligence services (the Americans had just entered the picture) were collecting every bit of information about the Yishuv and its leadership,[20] the regular cable traffic and letters mailed abroad were censored by the "Imperial Censorship," no independent channels of communication existed between the Yishuv and the European continent, and decisions were made in London, Washington, Moscow, Rome, and Berlin.

This issue must be examined within the timetable of the Final Solution first, as Ben-Gurion left Palestine for his extended stays abroad before the Final Solution was decided upon and later developed into a full-scale operation. The first reports on the mass slaughter and its magnitude reached Ben-Gurion while he was in the United States but penetrated the heads of the Yishuv's leadership only after Ben-Gurion's return to Palestine from the United States later in 1942. Perhaps the best evidence for that is produced by Tuvia Friling when he tells us about Ben-Gurion's semilegal efforts, while in the United State, to transfer funds from America to Zionist centers in Nazi-occupied Europe, perceiving them as parts of a living Jewish body that may survive.[21] In fact, the timetable of the Final Solution dictated the liquidation of Polish ghettos in which Jews were mobilized to work for the German war machine late in 1943. The need for slave labor slowed down the Final Solution in 1942 in several cases, so 1942, following Pearl Harbor, harbored some conflicting messages. The entry of the United States into the war, which

---

[19] See Friling, *Arrow in the Dark*, for details.

[20] Ben-Gurion's written program, which culminated a year later in the "Biltmore Conference" in New York, about which he – and Weizmann – spoke candidly with the British Colonial Secretary, Lord Moyne, in August 1941, was taken from Ben-Gurion's luggage by British agents when he left Britain for America in November 1941 and copied. See Zweig, *Britain and Palestine during the Second World War*, p. 152n.

[21] See Friling, "David Ben-Gurion and the Catastrophe of European Jewry," pp. 96–97, and about the period between October and November 1942, pp. 87–90, including the priority given at that time by Ben-Gurion to the adoption of the Biltmore Plan by the Zionist Executive and Mapai's organs.

would help destroy Nazi Germany, could indeed be seen in Zionist eyes as a great step forward toward enhancing Jewish interests, as Nazi Germany would now certainly be destroyed. But that the Jews would be slaughtered en masse before this happened, and in connection with it, was a nightmare that even Ben-Gurion was hardly able to foresee or, once he understood it, to influence. He did entertain some hopes that some Jews in Rumania, Hungary, Bulgaria, and Slovakia, Germany's autonomous allies, might escape the Holocaust and that perhaps some may have even survived elsewhere. The Yishuv itself could have been inclined to make the British government of Palestine the target for their helpless pain and sense of horrible frustration in the face of the situation in Europe, especially since late 1942. The leadership encouraged this at first by mounting a campaign against the limits imposed by the British on immigration. But this might have pushed the Yishuv to a disastrous campaign against a Western power that after all did not initiate, nor could have seriously influenced, Hitler's politics and emotions unless it negotiated with him on his terms.

As before, Ben-Gurion was thinking in terms of transforming the disaster (as he had done since Hitler's rise to power) to a crusade for mass immigration into Palestine, the only haven close enough and practical enough not only due to history, religion, and legal arguments but due to Zionist settlement efforts and social achievements already made in the country. This remained his public answer to the Holocaust, as he was able to follow it after he had accomplished what he wanted in America – an American Jewish commitment and later a general Jewish campaign toward the adoption of the "Biltmore Program."

First, a positive political goal that was clear and big enough for American tastes and as simple as possible had to be formulated once the circumstances had changed, and that was the immediate creation of an independent Jewish "Commonwealth" in an unpartitioned Western Palestine. Second, mass and immediate transferring of "millions" of Jews from wherever possible had to be pursued. Such a change in favor of the Jews – transforming the Arabs into a minority – would allow the Arabs to accept the facts and stay in the country as lawful citizens. A consensus among world Jewry had to be secured to support both; parallel to this, the Zionist leadership would be reorganized and a power base shaped within the Yishuv itself to lead and convince the public to accept the necessary political programs as dictated by the ever-changing reality.

Soon afterward, Ben-Gurion found himself in a desperate race with the reality of the Final Solution, which he could not see how he could influence except by publicly fighting for a Zionist goal, a positive and clear-cut vision of Jewish sovereignty, that could give some hope to those trapped behind the brown curtain and unite the Yishuv itself and free world Jewry behind it. Alas, in retrospect, this could be seen as a distasteful, petty political game while millions were dying, just as other activities of the Yishuv in conjunction with the Allies could be degraded as "collaboration" with those who closed the gates of the country to the victims and while other cooperative activities did not save many Jews.

In fact, the adoption of the program exposed serious cleavages within the Yishuv and the world Zionist movement itself. Hashomer Hazair, the Marxist kibbutz-oriented movement, rejected it due to its pro-Soviet stances and its previous hopes that some kind of a binational Jewish–Arab entity could be forged in Palestine. Ichud, or Brit-Shalom as they were known previously, an even more radical pacifist group, was ready to give up unrestricted Jewish immigration if the Arabs were ready for some accommodation – say to a Jewish canton in an Arab federation – with the Jews of Palestine.

Even Mapai's own left wing and possibly also some members of the leadership were not ready to fully support an officially endorsed political plank. This typical behavior drove David Ben-Gurion and Berl Katzenelson, Mapai's spiritual leader, to reiterate (which Ben-Gurion did many times by threatening to resign from his offices and by actually resigning for a while) what they called "Zionist discipline," which was perceived by the Left as "acts of dictatorship."[22]

When the Holocaust penetrated the minds of Zionists, both moderates and radicals alike, the outcome was a certain radicalization of Labor Zionism, in various directions. Ben-Gurion's direction was to create a viable domestic political base for immediate and longer-range decisions, which would require separation from the Left and general elections later on.

The Holocaust also influenced the revival of Stern's radical Zionism, which led to terrorist campaigns against the British. Later, Menachem Begin's IZL declared its "rebellion" against the British, which played into the hands of the anti-Zionists and anti-Semites alike in the West and was suppressed by the Labor-dominated leadership.[23]

Arab governments and the Palestinian Arab leadership reacted to Biltmore and to any sign of American positive response to Zionist claims (such as positive remarks made by the Republican leader Thomas Dewey in his Republican Party's Convention in 1944 and by the president in response to them and to Zionist pressure) with a storm of protests and threats that engulfed Roosevelt and seem to have made a serious impression on him.[24] Churchill, however, remained loyal to his Zionist past and seemed in late 1943 and early 1944 to be able to neutralize his own "Arabists" in Cairo due to Allied victories in North Africa and the declining political power of the Arabs

---

[22] See the rather accurate GSI Main HQ Ninth Army Weekly Military Newsletter No. 36, 11-17-42, RG 165, Entry 77, box 2726, Confidential, Palestine Report 3700.

[23] See PICME Report "Jewish Illegal Organizations in Palestine, PIC Paper No. 2, P/I/C 261/31, August 30, 1943, most secret, PRO XC 189967, ref. WO/169/8311.

[24] See letters of Arab leaders addressed to the president in this regard in the FDR Library, Collection OF 76c, and see the text.

themselves as a result of it. In addition to Churchill's "Zionist" obligations, shared by a few colleagues at cabinet level such as L.S. Amery, he seemed to have hoped to be able to shape the Middle East as a British-influenced, even controlled, sphere of influence, while the Holocaust contributed to creating an atmosphere of sympathy toward the Jews now that victory in the war seemed assured.[25] By the end of 1943, this led to a British decision, first made in secret and then made public by Colonial Secretary Oliver Stanley, to allow Jews who could come on their own to enter Palestine – within the White Paper's quota – and stay in the country. Yet the Cabinet Committee carefully created by Churchill for the purpose of transforming Palestine and the whole Middle East operated under the screen of utmost secrecy and coupled a change in Britain's Palestine policy with the establishment of various new entities in the region, all of which were connected with each other in a variety of agreements and were supposed to be connected with Great Britain by individual separate agreements.

This confidential plan was devised by Lord Moyne, a former Colonial Secretary, a close friend of Churchill's, and now Deputy Minister of State in Cairo, and explicitly called for the creation of a Jewish state in a partitioned Palestine. The idea was indeed to combine some Jewish claims and realities created by them on the ground with at least some pan-Arab aspirations that would lead to the birth of Greater Syria, a Christian Lebanon, and a separate entity in and around Jerusalem.[26] Yet the Foreign Office reacted quite effectively, under Anthony Eden's leadership, as Moyne's plan was conceived without consulting the French, who formally held the future of Syria and Lebanon in their hands as mandatory power. Syrian nationalists would not agree to a "Greater Syria" under the British-friendly Emir Abdullah of Trans-Jordan, as Moyne had first thought. Embroiled in all of these problems, the Palestine partition plan seemed at first to be the only idea that could be carried out during the war. But by now the "Cairo Club" of Middle East Arabists, led by Miles Lampson and Kinahan Cornwallis, was up in arms against partition, and Churchill could not prevent their views from being presented to the cabinet. Other ideas circled in the tense air of a cabinet getting ready for the invasion of Europe in the early summer and coping with the anticipated German missile attacks. Finally, everything was shelved until after the war even though the cabinet adopted the idea of partition on January 25, 1944.[27]

Churchill himself seemed to have lost patience with the Zionists following the assassination by the Stern group in Cairo late in 1944 of Lord Moyne, who had become in the meantime British Minister of State in the Middle

[25] See Porath, *The Test of Political Reality*, pp. 138–162.
[26] For details, see Ilan, *America, Britain and Palestine, 1939–1945*, pp. 140–141.
[27] See Zweig, *Britain and Palestine during the Second World War*, p. 175.

East. This assassination is of great importance to us since it was linked to a large rescue scheme allegedly torpedoed by Moyne and allegedly was not pursued by the Labor Zionist leadership but neglected and missed by them altogether. This issue is of further interest for us because the rescue scheme was aimed at saving the Jews of Hungary through Zionist action, a major subject of this book, and became a topic in the Kasztner trial in Israel, which made Labor publicly guilty of collaboration with the "Nazo-British" and with the Gestapo itself.

Moreover, the Zionist effort involved in Biltmore and its follow-up activities allegedly consumed much time and energy of the Zionist leaders while millions were dying. This was true, although from early 1943 the leadership was very much involved in all kinds of (largely futile) rescue issues. At the same time, they were accused by the local British authorities and by American intelligence operatives of almost Nazi "militancy" by streamlining the Yishuv's body politic toward independence while trying to rescue Jews, possibly behind Allied backs. This militancy was described to the Americans as if it might have even brought about a general Jewish mutiny in the country. The Labor Zionists under Ben-Gurion assumed a threatening posture against the hostile Palestine Government but did not pursue a rebellion against it in real terms. They would not stab the British in the back in their war with Hitler, as the Sternists and Menachem Begin's IZL seemed to do in various ways, and instead worked for actual rescue of the European Jews into Palestine as best they could at the time. However, they were accused then and later by their own right-wing rivals of "collaboration" with the "Nazo-British."

Seemingly nothing that was done then could have been done right; even when the Roosevelt administration was moved to do something directly toward a formal rescue in January 1944, not much came out of it. Indeed, the U.S.-based relief organizations were operated by American citizens, and thus their efforts had to be recognized as legitimate within the democratic rules of the United States. The year 1944 was an election year, and the Republican candidate, Thomas Dewey, seemed to be even more sympathetic to the Jewish cause than Franklin Roosevelt. This presidential election, feared by FDR and his aides as uncertain and preceded by the invasion of Europe, by itself a rather uncertain venture, constrained efforts toward rescue in the sense that it never assumed top priority among Western leaders, nor were extraordinary efforts to be expected from the top leadership. The invasion could be a major defeat, and it required at the least a very broad national consensus on the war goals, coined in the simplest terms of a struggle for liberty. Any real American involvement in rescue efforts thus waited until later in 1944, and even then it proved to be rather problematic in terms of its possible foreign strategic and domestic political ramifications and in terms of German demands on the rescue issue. Yet the very birth of a special agency – the War Refugee Board (WRB) – in January 1944 to deal with rescue could have raised Nazi expectations or have been viewed by them as a challenge to the Final Solution itself. On the other hand, the birth of the WRB raised (mostly unfounded) Jewish expectations. In fact, the WRB was born into circumstances and attitudes that were not essentially changed from those of several years before.

13

American Wartime Realities, 1942–1943

While in the United States early in 1942, David Ben-Gurion (and most of world Jewry) did not yet seem to realize the full extent of the Final Solution, partially due to its staged development into a full-fledged genocide. Ben-Gurion and the head of the embryonic Foreign Intelligence Service of the Hagana, Reuven Zaslani-Shiloah, used their visit in New York for the Biltmore Conference to meet with Arthur Goldberg, a labor lawyer in peacetime and the OSS Liaison Officer to foreign labor movements and social democratic parties. They suggested cooperation with the OSS in occupied Europe thanks to the Zionist network on the Continent that was mentioned earlier. Allen Dulles, the head of the OSS New York office, was interested in intelligence gathering, but nothing came out of that. Both Dulles and Goldberg were transferred abroad shortly after the meeting.[1] Goldberg's main concern at the time was "to fight Fascism," and later, following the American–British breakthrough from the Normandy beachhead, he perceived the war as being as good as won and returned to practicing law at home about a year before the war ended and with it the Final Solution.

Allen Dulles became the chief OSS agent in Europe and the recipient of rather early heartbreaking reports on death camps in Poland, which he does not seem to have forwarded to Washington. His view of the war was typical and significant: It was a struggle for the interests and the values of America but was an unnecessary war because the United States had withdrawn from European affairs after World War I, although having imposed on

---

[1] Interview by the present writer in Washington, D.C., and July 24, 1987, about Dulles in Bern, see *From Hitler's Doorstep: The Wartime Intelligence Reports of Allen Dulles*, edited and annotated by Neal H. Petersen (University Park: The Pennsylvania State University Press, 1996), p. 601n, in which the editor referred to Dulles in another connection saying "this issue provides additional support to the argument that Dulles was inadequately sensitive to the reality of the Holocaust."

the Continent an international regime that could not survive without American involvement.[2] Such a typical liberal Republican view was correct, but it had no room in it for the plight of the Jews, which Dulles was observing with sympathy from his New York office.

In his capacity as director of OSS operations in Bern, Dulles later in the war was decidedly against overburdening his Swiss base with a rescue effort aimed at saving Jews, even if he was largely free of anti-Semitic prejudice.[3]

In the Unites States, 1942 marked growing activity by the OSS at home, besides the regular FBI surveillance, aimed at gathering information on foreigners or American organizations working for or linked with foreign causes. Here we find Dewitt Poole, a Princeton scholar of "WASP" (White Anglo-Saxon Protestant) origin and aristocratic manners, and a former American diplomat in the early days of the Soviet regime, who joined the State Department upon returning home.[4]

Poole descended from seventeenth century New England English stock of which he was very proud, especially of his father, who "as the only white man in five hundred miles," "governed thousands of Sioux 'just by moral force.'"[5] This frontier "army background," which included Poole's officer brother, "exemplified to him a 'special aspect of a social discipline that is very pervasive in the United States, but lacking among the immigration from 1890 to 1920' of 'Bohunks' who remained 'city dwellers [and] did not go out into the country the way the Germans and Scandinavians did.'" On top of that, these newer immigrants reelected Roosevelt – "a calamity."[6] Roosevelt demonstrated that he shared Poole's view, though not entirely, when he launched the secret "Project M." In November 1942, the president established an "Anthropological Committee" to deal with the problem of foreign refugees without committing the United States to absorbing them. Roosevelt's sensitivity to the restrictionists (his conservative rivals' possible criticism) was manifested in the complete secrecy in which the project was conducted. The committee's work, which remained secret until after the war, was named "Project M" – for migration. Its chairman was the president of Johns Hopkins University, Isaiah Bauman, a non-Jew. The director was the archaeologist and anthropologist Dr. Henry Field.[7]

---

[2] See NA, RG 226, Entry 190, Bern-OSS-OP-21, "Rappard," box 24.

[3] See Bern files, memo dictated on August 14, 1943.

[4] See Bendersky, "*The Jewish Threat*," pp. 70–71.

[5] Ibid., 70.

[6] Ibid., 71. See details regarding Poole's activities in Soviet Russia and ensuing State Department responsibilities, where he became Director of the Russian Desk soon after the Bolshevik Revolution. Under Poole, the Russian Division "came as close to verifying a worldwide Jewish conspiracy theory as would be possible without actually crossing the line into categorical affirmation of the plot's existence."

[7] See FDR Library – PSF (President's Secretary's Files), John Franklin Carter Reports folder, August–December 1942.

In his letter of appointment, FDR referred to Jews as a formerly "pastoral" nation that was relatively recently confined to ghettos and big cities; hence Jews might be welcomed in empty South American or African plains and thereby fears of their becoming a dominant factor in the cities could be avoided. Secretary of State Cordell Hull finally objected to Project M since the South American governments did not want the refugees and in fact were pushing them "on us." The African option may have been Penrose's idea of using Cameroon as a "Zionist solution." Historian Henry Feingold sees Roosevelt's interest as an effort to attract Zionist support and financing for a "Jewish supplemental national home" without interfering with British Palestine policy.[8] Yet nothing came out of the many studies conducted within the framework of Project M while American Jews rallied behind the Zionists at exactly that time.

Dewitt Poole's FNB, formerly a State Department outfit, continued to shadow the Zionists in America rather closely and received regular reports on meetings of foreign Zionists such as Weizmann and Ben-Gurion with American Jewish (non-Zionist) organizations such as the American Jewish Committee and B'nai-Brith.[9]

One of the FNB draftees in charge of the liaison with such organizations was Dr. Abraham Duker, a Polish-born scholar of significance, who was in charge of Polish affairs.[10] Duker, who worked for the American Jewish Committee before he was drafted into the U.S. Army and trained at Fort Meade, was at first sent to the front and made a sort of education officer following the initial setbacks of the American forces in North Africa when the "kids – who had no idea what the war was all about" were slaughtered first by the Germans at the Kasserine Passes and then were properly indoctrinated – certainly not to fight a "Jew's war."[11]

Duker further recalled the resentment, almost the hatred, of German refugees of at least partial Jewish origin such as Franz Neumann, an associate of the Frankfurt School group at the OSS-R&A branch, who developed at that time his "spearhead" theory regarding the role of anti-Semitism in Nazi politics, which made the Jews only a forerunner of a much larger campaign against other nations by the Nazis. In Duker's words, the issue was even worse, as those assimilated neo-Marxist Jews active in OSS-R&A would privately make the "Ostjuden" (i.e., Jews of East-European origin, some of whom migrated to Germany after World War I) responsible for the most virulent anti-Semitism that befell Germany. Officially, Neumann could not see how the German people, already involved in the Holocaust, could be moved

---

[8] See Henry Feingold, *The Politics of Rescue: The Roosevelt Administration and the Holocaust, 1938–1945*, (New Brunswick, NJ: Rutgers University Press, 1970), pp. 85–87.
[9] See FNB files stored at the NARA, RG 226, Entry 100.
[10] See entry for Abraham Gordon Duker in *Encyclopedia Judaica*, Volume 6, p. 266.
[11] "Abe" Duker's testimony to the present writer, New York, 1986.

any further by Allied threats, as demanded by Yitzhak Gruenbaum of the Zionist "Rescue Committee" from Palestine and from Jewish organizations in America to stop the killings, and whether the corruption of the German upper classes, industry, and the army gave them any outlet from the grip of the SS.[12]

Neumann disliked Duker's East European Jewish appearance almost physically, and being acquainted with the latter's interest in the Holocaust and possibly with his sympathy for the Zionists and his actual contacts with them, used to ask Duker about "his Jews," rolling the "s" sharply on his tongue, whenever he met him or his colleague Charles Irving Dwork, a University of Southern California Ph.D. in Jewish studies recruited in 1943 to monitor the crimes against the Jews at OSS-R&A in order to build the case against the perpetrators after the war.[13] But Dwork, too, had to live with Franz Neumann, his immediate boss, whose views of Germany and Jews were heard at least by General Donovan, if not by the president himself.

Any study on FDR's own Jewish policy must distinguish between his rather active role in criticizing Nazi atrocities such as Kristallnacht before the outbreak of World War II, the creation of the Intergovernmental Committee on Refugees (IGCR) and the efforts to settle European Jews elsewhere, and the period after September 1, 1939.

Roosevelt's biographer Robert Dallek argued, in his published work[14] and in a conversation with the present writer, that in 1939 the president seriously contemplated a permanent solution to the Jewish Question by developing a space for the absorption of refugees in large numbers. He presumed that this general idea would gain public support, having given it a universal rather than a specific Jewish character. He returned to the same idea in 1943, having created Project M ahead of it in late 1942. Roosevelt approached the IGCR in the belief that worldwide support for the resettling of some 20 million refugees in some empty place somewhere could be mobilized, but it was to no avail. The British and the French argued that victory in Europe would solve the problem, and among the Jews the response was negative. Roosevelt at that time believed, according to Dallek, that British opposition to the Zionist claims made Palestine a nonstarter and developed the idea (probably in conjunction with the Project M planners) of an alternative absorption place, or of "another Jewish homeland" next to Palestine, against Zionist wishes. But even when the planners agreed to this alternative, no place was

---

[12] See OSS R&A 1113.9, Psychological Warfare, written by Neumann.

[13] Dwork served in OSS R&A until mid-1945 as a member of the OSS team preparing the Jewish parts of the IMT (International Military Tribunal) indictment to be presented at the Nuremberg Trial. Since important parts of his knowledge were based upon information received from Dr. Kasztner via OSS and OSS-affiliated WRB operatives such as Herbert Katzki, we shall deal with him in due course.

[14] See Robert Dallek, *Franklin D. Roosevelt and American Foreign Policy, 1932–1945* (New York: Oxford University Press, 1979), pp. 444–445.

found in South America or elsewhere. Roosevelt did not want to push the idea when he needed a Congress that would allow the high degree of American involvement in international affairs now deemed necessary. Here, in addition to FDR's efforts in neutralizing Congress by invoking military arguments and working with military institutions, he made a trade-off with Congress in practical terms by leaving the Jewish issue aside in exchange for more freedom of action for himself on other international issues. The restrictive immigration policy had been maintained by Congress for decades and was tightened to avoid the entry into the United States of unwanted aliens during wartime. Large-scale Jewish emigration to North Africa or to Palestine would jeopardize relations with the Arabs.

Roosevelt saw no practical means of rescue in a way that caught his focused and sustained attention. He certainly was not ready to compromise the unconditional surrender demand from Nazi Germany, possibly being the main lesson learned from Woodrow Wilson's armistice accord of November 1918, or to endanger the coalition with the Soviets. Hence he would have rejected any direct negotiations on rescue (entailing danger to both). He was not ready to risk domestic and foreign political controversies that might in his view have prolonged the war, but early in 1944 – at the outset of an election year – he was ready to demonstrate more action, under pressure from Secretary Morgenthau (and his key non-Jewish aides, who were appalled by the British view of the Holocaust). Roosevelt then created the War Refugee Board, limited as it was in its actual working, which we will discuss separately.

Anti-Semitic repercussions at home were not uncommon anyway,[15] but the issue was not limited to domestic anti-Semitism. It was a practically important political issue pertaining to the Nazis themselves in the first place. If the president openly addressed the rescue issue, what would Hitler's response to it be? The Jews were the alleged cause of the war, and hence FDR was their alleged tool. If FDR and the Jews wanted the Holocaust to stop, they should stop their war against the Third Reich and its "natural rights," meaning also its hegemonic "rights" in Europe and the Soviet territories. Later, it would mean the quest for world domination and an unavoidable struggle with the United States. Responding to the Final Solution in a way that would play into Hitler's hands either by justifying his "Jew's war" allegation or risking what could be viewed as making concessions to Hitler because of Jews would have been not only unthinkable in principle but a contradiction in terms in the sense that the dying Jews would be used to enhance Hitler's goals in his struggle with those who were supposed to work for their rescue.

Roosevelt could capitalize on the notion of self-defense when Japan and Nazi Germany started a war against the United States and threatened vital

---

[15] The FDR Library contains many examples of such wartime mail, addressed to the president and sometimes prompting angry denials on his part.

interests of most Americans. Indeed, real action became possible once the
Japanese and Hitler opened fire against their Fort Sumter. Like Lincoln,
FDR could mobilize his William T. Shermans to fight the enemy "rebels"
rather than fight at the outset for the Emancipation Act, for which Lincoln
had waited two more years. True, the president proclaimed his "Atlantic
Charter" rather early, and then his "Four Freedoms," which might not have
pleased the conservatives, but he took no action in particular to help Jews,
who were put to death in Soviet territories at first and in secret, or let their
cause intervene too directly in the hostilities. Later, when America was at war
and the Holocaust became known, did FDR indeed "abandon" the Jews? In
fact, he may have even thought that by not mentioning their catastrophe in
public as a specific case, and not intervening in an impractical and dangerous fashion in their favor, he was serving their cause. He might have believed
that if he had spoken about their plight in public, it would have caused Nazi
wrath and thereby not have helped the Jews while also giving Hitler some
hope that his home front would become even more aware of the war as being
fought by the Allies "for the Jews." Certainly the Nazis, if FDR read Franz
Neumann's recommendations, tainted the war as "Jewish" also to cement
their own home front. The president may have calculated that any activity
that he undertook that might support that argument would cement it further,
create problems on the Western home front, and possibly add new ones regarding the maintenance of the Grand Alliance. The opinions at home were
indeed various and conflicting; some expressed deep apprehension, although
many did not, including those who maintained anti-Semitic traditions and
cultivated anti-Semitic conspiracy theories aimed against FDR himself. The
president seemed to have been unimpressed by these opinions, but when it
came to actual rescue and its related complications, or to the Zionists, he
simply reacted to various pressures from various sides according to his political agenda and the changing fortunes of the war, bearing in mind his main
priorities: maintaining a consensus about the war at home, maintaining his
own power to win it both in Congress and in the various elections untill after
the start of his fourth term, maintaining the Grand Alliance, and working for
a better world order. When the Zionists succeeded in uniting many segments
of the Jewish communities in America behind them and started to use their
political muscle toward the implementation of Biltmore, Americans such as
Mrs. Doris McQueen wrote in a private letter mailed from Jerusalem to a
friend back in Denver, Colorado, which was opened by the combined British–
American censorship offices and circulated by the U.S. Military Intelligence
Division (MID) to several government agencies:[16]

The Jewish problem is a difficult one. I can see no hope for it; but that the Arabs
& Jews must unite [and create a binational confederation, not acceptable to Arabs
and most Zionists – S.A.], but with the extremist Jews demanding the whole country

---

[16] NA, RG 165, folder 3800, Palestine, box 3029, dated September 1, 1943.

that's impossible – however bitter the experience, the Jews never learn. They are fearfully angry about the Allied powers not saving the Jews from Europe. – I've told a lot of my friends that if they'd only suggest once that <u>all</u> [underline in original] the persecuted in Europe be saved, it would go over better, but they only want the Jews saved to bring them to Palestine, and the Arabs are going anti-American, because the Jews put so much in their papers about what America, including Wendell Willkie, are saying about the Jews & Palestine. This is a tragic almost a cursed country. (NA, RG 165, folder 3800, Palestine, box 3029, September 1, 1943)

A typical view of the Jewish question among American officials at the time was that Zionism in particular and Jewish involvement in general did not concur with and could even endanger the shaping of the post–World War II world according to the Atlantic Charter. This opinion is expressed in a U.S. Army intelligence report from December 1942, as follows:[17]

All of our Allies make no [illegible] about demanding American-born leaders whose ancestors came to America at least two generations ago. They do not trust naturalized nationals who have migrated to America as leaders to be trusted.... They are also very much afraid that our representatives to these countries for post war reconstruction will be appointed from the mass of Jewish refugees who came out of these European countries and will be looking for a job in the post war world. They insist that if the American government does not insist on non-refugee personnel of two or three generations in America . . . the great percentage of our advisers for post war reconstruction will be the unwanted Jews. They realize that the *American of several generations will be more certain to have the American idea of justice and fair play but that on the other hand he will naturally desire to stay in his homeland and let Aaron or Isaac to go over to Europe . . . or influence things in the Middle-East according to Aaron's or Isaac's is distorted sense of justice* (italics added). (NA, RG 226, Entry 106, box 4, folder 34)[18]

---

[17] NA, RG 226, Entry 106, box 4, folder 34.
[18] See a verse written by Dwight Chaplin, a member of the Foreign Office's Enemy Branch, in response to a letter by a Mr. S. Sass, a German Jew now living in Colombia, offering his services as a former steel executive in the Rhineland to reorganize the German steel industry after the war:

> "From Africa's shore, from Colomb's sunscorched strand,
> Urgent there streams an eager Hebrew band,
> Imbued with our desire to serve the aims
> of Allied justice, see them stake their claims
> to jobs in Germany. They know the ropes . . .
> 'Till Hitler came and rudely thrust us forth
> 'We helped the men who laid the powder train' . . .

and so forth. Chaplin was probably referring to German Jews such as Walther Rathenau and to German-Jewish patriotism during World War I and before, which was manifested among other activities in intelligence gathering by Jewish-owned companies such as Mannesmann abroad, including in North Africa. The above quoted verse was taken from Tom Bower, *Blind Eye to Murder: Britain, America and the Purging of Nazi Germany – A Pledge Betrayed* (London: Paladin, Granada Publishers, 1983), pp. 169–170.

Here the tragedy of the "chosen people" "who never learn" is apparent, combined with the perception of the war as being fought – at the height of the Holocaust – for the sake of "all the persecuted in Europe" but neglected by the Jews, who as usual were screaming about their own people and alone were interested in saving them in order to bring them to Palestine, which they wanted all for themselves, and by manipulating their standing in America for that purpose while damaging American interests, and the fear that postwar Europe would be governed by Jewish refugees in their own, un-American way.

Turning our attention to the American Jews, an interesting example of their behavior at the time could be cited when we realize that many among them were drafted into the U.S. Army, and even those among them who seemed to have been close to occupied Europe not only could not help but as intelligence officers their war efforts only worked against Jewish interests.

The Honorable Arthur Goldberg occupied an important position in the OSS London office as head of its "Labor Desk." I have interviewed him, especially regarding his role in sending an OSS mission, codenamed "Sparrow," to Hungary on the eve of the German occupation of that country in March 1944.[19] The story of the "Sparrow mission" itself requires more than a verbal testimony and hence belongs to the Hungarian chapters of this book, but it should be noted here that Goldberg was involved in a mission, justified perhaps in military and political terms, that not only failed miserably but could be used by the Germans as a pretext to occupy Hungary, which they did and in the process destroyed the last great Jewish community remaining alive.

As a well-known labor lawyer, Goldberg had his connection with the Jewish Labor Committee and with key American–Jewish labor leaders, who had their own ties with exiled German Social Democrats such as the future SPD (the West German Social Democratic Party) Chairman Erich Ollenhauer. Thus Goldberg, who had at first no idea about intelligence work and learned some basic rules from the Canadian William Stephenson together with Allen Dulles in New York, became head of the OSS' Labor Desk in London in August 1942. At that time, as quoted earlier, his only interest was focused on "fighting Fascism." Goldberg's main effort centered around the training and possible use of young Germans to influence Germany's postwar future. During the breakthrough from Normandy in summer 1944, Goldberg tried to have his German "kids" sent into the seemingly open frontiers of a defeated Germany. In his view, the war was over, and after a short while he asked his superiors to deactivate him. He did his best, he said, for three years, and now his family needed him in Chicago. He had no money – one could not raise a family on an Army Major's salary, he said – and he indeed returned home to practice law before the war was over.

[19] The interview took place in Washington, D.C., on July 24, 1987.

Goldberg's story is one among many telling us what American Jews did at the time. The reasons for his resignation from OSS may have been different from what he chose to tell me.[20] Yet many Jews were simply away from home, their war effort aimed at defeating Fascism first and above all, and most of them had no access to the knowledge that Major Arthur Goldberg might have acquired about the Holocaust in time or comprehended the possible Jewish ramifications of the Sparrow mission.

Back home, however, FDR was approached, reminded of, or asked to take action in several ways to save Jews almost daily; his attention to the Holocaust was supposed to have been drawn by a ceaseless stream of pleas, of ideas, and indeed of blessings by common Jewish individuals, whole communities, and numerous groups. Whether his real attention was indeed drawn to the Holocaust by this mail, which was usually diverted to the State Department, is hard to say; yet some of it did reach him, and he had to deal with Jewish and Zionist pleas to a growing degree from 1943.[21] The Zionist solution, in spite of doubts and many frictions among American Jewish leaders, seemed now to have been endorsed by most of them and by many among the rank and file because Palestine was the only recognized Jewish "national home," because America itself was closed as a matter of course for immigrants and far away from Europe while Palestine was so close, and because of the rigorous Zionist efforts to unite American Jewry behind their cause.

Indeed, the Palestine problem loomed as an issue by itself in addition to the rescue problem. Both were highly political, even if the linkage between the two proved to be a double-edged sword from a Jewish point of view. Both issues – rescue and Palestine – were positively interrelated for the Zionists and now for many American Jews. For many others among the Allies, they were negatively interrelated, or in the case of FDR, seemed impractical.

Ben-Gurion's "Biltmore" strategy, aimed at giving the Jews and the Zionists among them an agreed goal that combined immediate and unrestricted Jewish immigration to Palestine on its way to becoming an independent Jewish "commonwealth," a goal around which they could unite and act to mobilize support in America, was quite problematic in America itself, although it had some chance of political success among Jews, including American Jews, in the face of the developing catastrophe in Europe. (Ben-Gurion left the idea of partition aside, although he would later return to it as the only realistic solution.) Open American rescue efforts, in terms of negotiating with Hitler or threatening him or the German people, proved to be pipe dreams and could even have been counterproductive. Ben-Gurion, on the other hand, concentrated on the creation of an independent Jewish state during the war, as a

---

[20] See RG 226, Entry 190, Bern box 31, G. O. Pratt, Chief, Labor Desk, London, on Goldberg's "troubles above," December 1944.

[21] See, for example, FDR Library files, collection OF 76c, "Jewish" folders.

precondition for rescue efforts independent of British and American Arab-related calculations, while working for emigration from the Arab countries and whatever could be done in Europe. He became involved in trying them all, almost to no avail except for some success in bringing in Jews from the Arab countries, even if he was later blamed for seeking a state for its own sake, and for not having even tried to work for rescue. Yet the Zionists did accept several arguments about Jewish habits and behavior in the European Diaspora, and hence they had anticipated a sort of catastrophe for the Jews of the Continent since the birth of Zionism. Thus David Ben-Gurion and Berl Katzenelson – the spiritual leader of the Labor Zionists – were talking not only of external political efforts toward the creation of a sovereign Jewish state but of an internal change, the creation of the "new Jew," which they had aspired to be socialists from the beginning. Having the psychological and emotional tools to face the disaster without sinking into anarchy and despair, and acting as a mobilized community toward independence at the height of the anticipated disaster, which became a catastrophe, was typical of Ben-Gurion and his generation, and yet the "new Jew" was twisted by British officials and American Army officers to sound like Hitler's "reborn German."

14

Bermuda, Breckinridge Long, G-2, Biddle, Taylor and Rayburn, and Palestine Again

Franklin D. Roosevelt seems to have been exposed to conflicting views, from Hitler's former intimate friend Ernst "Putzi" Hanfstaengel's description of top Nazi behavior in terms of "Jewish self-hatred"[1] to images of threatening, corrupt, and almost criminal elements among the European Jews who might be allowed entry into the United States. Hanfstaengel's view of Nazi Germany was that of a "dynamic chaos" caused by power-obsessed, cynical exponents of lower middle-class degeneration, some of them allegedly Jewish in origin, such as Hans Frank (Governor General of occupied Poland), whose great-grandfather was supposedly Jewish. Nazi Foreign Minister Joachim von Ribbentrop was accordingly "close" to rich Jewish circles before he discovered the "Nordic soul" and moved away from them. Nazi "chief ideologue" Alfred Rosenberg was allegedly 95% Jewish. "One could ascertain indeed certain Jewish characteristics among aggressive anti-Semites."

But usually the president deferred everything related to the rescue of Jews to the State Department, which he in fact did not trust very much but used now to take the heat of criticism at home, loudly made in some key media and in the rally at Madison Square Garden against the administration's inaction on rescue matters.[2]

---

[1] See FDR Library, PSF, box 163, according to which FDR, who had known "Putzi" personally since both studied at Harvard, refused to meet him after he had broken with Hitler and found refuge in England but read his memos when he was transferred to the United States. According to Bradley F. Smith, after initially being enthusiastic, FDR turned cautious on the Hanfstaengel project in early 1944, and later in the year, funds for "Mr. Sedgwick" were cut off and he was handed back to the British. See Smith, *The Shadow Warriors*, p. 270. Others perceived in him a valuable source for State, OWI, G-2, ONI (Office of Naval Intelligence), and OSS, and the latter used Hanfstaengel for its psychological research on Hitler; see boxes 126–139.

[2] See Feingold, *The Politics of Rescue*, pp. 178 ff., also concerning the State Department's role regarding information on the Final Solution and its relations with the Treasury Department and the British toward the Bermuda Conference of 1943.

Matters related to the rescue of Jews and refugee problems usually fell into the hands of Assistant Secretary of State Breckinridge Long, who worked behind the scenes to curb Jewish immigration to the country by arguing that there were dubious elements among the would-be immigrants. Long went so far as to try and block the reports from Switzerland on the Final Solution and falsify information about these efforts.[3] Long lost his control over the Visa Division and his fight against the creation of a special agency to deal with rescue following a complex and strange battle in Congress and in public, described by Henry Feingold and others, in which he saw himself victimized by a Jewish "conspiracy" aimed against him personally. In this battle, Long invoked a typical tactic, maintaining that the State Department had done its utmost to save Jews and had granted about half a million visas since 1933 to Jewish refugees. This number was immediately found to be misleading – deliberately or not – as it was the total number of visas granted during that period. This incorrect figure frightened restrictionist senators such as Carl Mundt (R-North Dakota), but Long assured him that, except for some gestures probably done to allow some prominent and useful people such as Albert Einstein to settle in the United States, the "immigration laws remained intact" (i.e., America remained safely closed).[4]

Breckinridge Long's attitude contained an element that went back to his service as American ambassador in Rome in the mid-1930s and that he had shared with Joseph P. Kennedy in London, namely that the Nazis were almighty and could not be defeated nor stopped in their schemes in Eastern Europe.[5] Hence, the Final Solution could not be stopped anyway, and Jews who may have escaped from it, such as possibly those in Rumania, should not become a burden on the United States. Rescuing Jews belonged to the variety of anti-Jewish feelings in America and England that included a most venomous current, namely that the Jews had brought their misfortune upon themselves, or at least their tragedy made them look "egotistic" and "particularistic" while others were fighting to save the world – and them – from the Axis. Yet there was no such thing as a "Jewish people" who could be dealt with in normal political terms, as they had no country of their own, no government of their own, and were divided among themselves to a degree justifying historian Feingold's methodology of describing American Jews' rescue activities along with a parallel description of the disunities among them during the Holocaust as if unity might have enhanced rescue. It might have robbed several opponents, and possibly Roosevelt himself, of an argument

---

[3] See Feingold, *The Politics of Rescue*, pp. 180–181. As a result of these machinations, Long was removed from exclusive control of the Administration's rescue-related activity, which more and more concentrated in the Treasury Department, but in my view to not much avail either.

[4] On this topic and the ensuing intervention of the Treasury Department against the State Department, which led to the creation of the WRB, see Feingold, *The Politics of Rescue*, pp. 233–239.

[5] For Long's background and previous career, see Feingold, *The Politics of Rescue*, pp. 131 ff.

regarding the Zionist claims that they represented American Jewry and hence free entry into Palestine was the only practical and just avenue of rescue. Yet in reality the unity or disunity among American Jews had no influence on Hitler except that the creation of the WRB by FDR in January 1944 may have added to his resolve to kill the remnants of the European Jewry, especially in Hungary.

Efforts undertaken by the "militants" or "nationalists" among Jews to gain a state of their own during the war were not shared by all Jews and seemed by others to be incompatible with the very "anti-nationalistic" character of World War II itself. Nor were these efforts free of the most complicated ramifications in terms of American interests. Thus, a huge rally of American Jews and their supporters, sponsored by the Church Peace Union, the AFL and CIO labor unions, and many other groups mobilized as a result of Jabotinsky's mission to the United States mentioned earlier, was held on March 1, 1943, in Madison Square Garden. Its first demand from the administration was, as quoted by Feingold, "negotiate with Germany and her satellites through neutral agencies and nations regarding the rescue of Jews." "Negotiate with Germany" would have been forbidden by the "unconditional surrender" declaration of the Casablanca Conference later the same month, but the Bermuda Conference held later that year indeed responded to this demand in the most negative fashion conceivable. Henry Feingold, by describing the State Department's maneuvers against the Madison Square Garden demand to negotiate with the Germans, simply offers his opinion that State Department officials "could not fathom an order of priorities, which placed the rescue of Jews above the winning of the war." Indeed they could not, and in fact they might have perceived in "negotiations" a two-way street making Jews a Nazi trump card to extract concessions from them if they wanted Jews to survive. Entering into such negotiations with Hitler, even indirectly, in the middle of what seemed to be and was described to have been a "crusade" to save liberty and democracy, might have contributed to the myth of a war waged by Allies on behalf of the Jews and if successful would have made the United States responsible for their future.

Caught in this web, the Jews were a fact, and a rather major focus of attention, that required much caution in identifying with them in practical terms unless the Arabs agreed to the Zionist claims. Dealing with an issue as complex as a Western responsibility for rescue of the Jews, at least before victory in the war was convincingly assured, seemed to be unwise and politically dangerous due to the domestic repercussions. Whether Hitler's anticipated use of any public move in this direction that might have been interpreted as an overture to him to stop the massacre and pay a price for it was also a major consideration of Breckinridge Long or President Roosevelt we do not know, but the Bermuda Conference ruled out any negotiations with Germany. However some public steps could be undertaken at least to demonstrate good will and silence liberal and Jewish outcries without any effective action following them. Even when Breckinridge Long suddenly interpreted the Bermuda Conference decisions as if they did allow negotiations with Germany and declared under pressure in a congressional hearing that Bermuda had indeed recommended the reactivation of the defunct IGCR and given it a mandate to negotiate with the Germans, this interpretation was immediately denied by Sir Herbert Emerson, the IGCR's Chairman, and his American deputy.[6] The president himself was ready to issue pro–Zionist declarations on the eve of elections until the creation of the WRB in January 1944 under heavy Treasury Department and public pressure. Had this finally broken the logic of the multiple trap? Was at least the Allied part of the trap removed? We shall discuss these questions in due course.

In addition to the pioneering work offered by Feingold, Wyman, and other scholars, a document explaining Bermuda's practical inaction should be added here.[7] Entitled "Memorandum on Bermuda Conference on the Refugee Problem held April 19 to April 29, 1943," the duplicate found in the WRB files is not the whole original memo but just its first page. We thus cannot tell who wrote it, except that it suggests a responsible State Department officer such as Breckinridge Long, who could hardly hide his motives. The writer started by saying that:

Until late in 1942 the Department of State followed the policy of withholding atrocity stories received by it from Europe on the theory that confirmation of such stories was lacking. But on September 28, 1942, Rabbi (Stephen) Wise [at the time the most prominent Jewish leader in the United States – S.A.] made public a communication received from one Riegner in Europe transmitted through the State Department and which Wise, either mistakenly or deliberately, stated had official State Department sanction. (Memorandum on Bermuda Conference on the Refugee Problem)

This resulted in a flood of mail to the president and the State Department aimed at procuring: (1) a joint declaration by the United States and the United Kingdom censoring barbarism and promising retribution; (2) opening Palestine to the Jews; (3) removing all barriers to the immigration of Jewish children; and (4) exchanging Jews in occupied Europe for interned Axis nationals. The last point was emphatically disapproved by the State Department: "In the first place, there are not enough Axis internees to make such a project possible. But most important, the exile governments could be expected to *object to this favoring of Jews over non-Jewish nationals*. This latter point *could also be used by the Germans for propaganda claims that the war is being fought for the Jews*" (italics added – a report made in this regard is mentioned in parentheses as having been submitted on December 15, 1942).

[6] See Feingold, *The Politics of Rescue*, pp. 234–235.
[7] FDR Library, WRB files, Container 26, duplicate – the original was prepared on February 22, 1944, courtesy of Richard Breitman.

The memo then criticized a study of rescue submitted on January 9, 1943, by "United States Jewish organizations for the files," as if this study "shows primarily the diversity of aims of such organizations": "The American Jewish Congress *looks toward action by the Jews as a race including the sending of delegates to any peace conference following the war*" (italics added). They also "seek to establish Palestine as an independent nation and to maintain a separate Jewish Army during the present conflict." Hence, the issue of "action by the Jews as a race," taken for granted by Hitler in principle even if it was far from operational reality, was a source of apprehension among the Allies. But this was not the only argument explaining Bermuda's basic inaction, which by itself is missing in this duplicate: "The communists [sic] organizations appear to be making use of the Jewish sentiment to further general communistic [sic] rather than Jewish ends." Indeed Stalin had used Jews such as writer Ilya Ehrenburg to enhance Soviet images and ends, but always in the framework of an "anti-Fascist" rather than Jewish committee, and always blurring the Jewish Holocaust with the general catastrophe inflicted on the Soviet peoples as a whole by the Nazis.

The military and strategic dimension, given top priority in FDR's mind anyway, could rationalize a political decision that the previous Jewish-friendly and superficially pro-Zionist Roosevelt had made since he realized that the American people would have to fight and when he endorsed a strategy of direct, enormous pitched battles with the Wehrmacht in North Africa as an overture and on the European mainland as the decisive battle. The moment of truth in this respect was yet to come – in June 1944.

At the same time, our OSS and G-2 reports disclosed the emergence of the United States as a great power, including in the Middle East, the Balkans, and elsewhere, striving to create a modified Wilsonian world order. This emergence of the "American Century," including some kind of understanding with the Soviet Union, preoccupied the idealist president and also dictated his other priorities in addition to the domestic mobilization of a peaceful, unready nation to fight.[8]

Roosevelt went out of his way to declare World War II as almost a domestic affair, due to the attack on Pearl Harbor, and to deny that it was a

---

[8] See FDR Library, PSF, regarding the initial confusion, missing coordination among various federal agencies, complaints about labor policies, and war profiteering early in 1942, and see folder Bernard Baruch, letter by Baruch to the president's secretary, General "Pa" Watson (no date): "I can see the great unorganized mass getting organized and moving slowly forward.... We have to keep control of the sea and the air and the others cannot win even if the U.S. is left alone. Germany and Japan can never bring peace to their people until America is beaten and that can never happen.... All we have to do is get wisely prepared for a long fight and hold on, and on, and on, and we will lick 'em." All of this required national consensus and wisdom dictating caution in Jewish affairs, while Baruch himself was a symbol of Jewish power in Nazi eyes.

"foreign war" at all.[9] At the same time, the World War I precedent as well as its peace arrangements were to be avoided at all costs. The combination of nationalism, mass politics, and wrong economics with horrendous front-line casualties not only destabilized the world order but also had given birth to both Bolshevism and Fascism. The German variation of Fascism was making use of anti-Semitism quite successfully, and therefore one could think that focusing on Jews could serve the enemy rather than help Jews. The Soviet Union could now be brought into some kind of an understanding to work together in the face of the common Fascist threat. This could allow a new world order to emerge within the charter of a new, revised, League of Nations, the future United Nations, which would endorse and implement "postnationalistic" values and norms. These were big schemes, and the issue of the Jews could have been seen here to be rather a side issue. The trouble was, and remained, that some Jews perceived their civilization, their history, and now their disaster to be a legitimate issue, not a "particular" one, that should be radically taken care of before the "new world order" was implemented. The Zionists among them, having mobilized growing support among American Jews, simply would not endorse the secret Project M, nor any other benevolent ideas pursued by FDR, but stuck to Palestine.

G-2, on the other hand, had its own views of the Jews and the Middle East situation. Acting very much under British anti-Zionist influence, General Russell A. Osmun, the head of the American Joint Intelligence Collection Agency, Middle East (JICAME), a branch of G-2 charged with coordinating regional intelligence activities,[10] met David Ben-Gurion and Moshe Shertok, who naively enough had tried to enlist his support for rescue and for the Zionist cause. In turn, General Osmun said about both of them: "They are tough boys. . . . If they'd been born in Chicago, they'd have been part of Al Capone's mob."[11] Osmun's G-2 man in Jerusalem was the already mentioned Lieutenant Nicholas Andronovich, the Orthodox Russian who, according to Joseph Bendersky, still spoke English with an accent. Disguised as an American censor working together with the Imperial Censorship, Andronovich boasted of having "established excellent relationships . . . with many prominent and well placed British" and "befriended the Arab elite."[12]

According to Bendersky, G-2's "authority" on Palestine was Major Edwin M. Wright, a Middle East scholar closely connected with the American University in Cairo and with Arab leaders. He delivered orientation lectures at the American University and in several military outfits. In one he is quoted as having referred to Theodore Herzl as a "crackpot" eventually "repudiated by his own people" and having made a "huge joke" out of explaining

[9] FDR Library, PSF, FDR's file.
[10] See Bendersky, *The "Jewish Threat,"* p. 320.
[11] Ibid., 104.
[12] Ibid., 320.

how Germans and Poles were dumping Jews back and forth across their borders in 1938. The repeated argument made by people such as Wright and OSS resident in Palestine Harold Glidden was that the Palestine problem was caused by Jewish repression in Europe and not a natural desire to return to Palestine. The conspiratorial and antidemocratic dimension added to it was that politicians such as Roosevelt only backed the Zionist cause to win Jewish votes under "immense pressure" from well-financed, "influential" Jews with "powerful press" in a way that caused serious trouble in the Middle East, where "well-organized, well-armed Jews with vast resources" were moving against disorganized, ill-armed Arabs with "no one to speak for them."[13]

In their written reports from Palestine, Osmun and Wright examined "Jewish Psychology" and reached the conclusion that during the peak years of the Holocaust "Zionism in Palestine... amounts to an obsession." "Through distorted perspectives emanating from 'fears, real and imagined,' the Jews 'are beginning to persuade themselves... that they are being persecuted again as they were in Biblical times. This gives a tinge of the mystic martyrdom to their activities and explains the spiritual culture in which fanaticism and violence grow."[14] This generalization was further developed in that Jews "displayed deep emotional and 'intense atavistic impulses' that create 'national paranoia.'" Following the Palestinian riots of 1937–1939, the ensuing actions taken by the British in the framework of the White Paper and the Mufti's activities in Berlin, on top of the Holocaust itself, not mentioned in the reports, "a new persecution complex revivifying... the endless martyrdom of the Jewish people by the injustices of others" was diagnosed by the G-2 experts. "The 'modern Jew' cannot be understood 'independent of his past.'" Hence, Jews were after all a sort of people connected to the Holy Land in some peculiar way: "The lawyer or the trader considers himself as part of a universal cosmic process woven about the Jews and is distinctly conscious that he is one of 'a peculiar people.' Anyone standing in the way 'is looked upon with the same animus ancient Jews looked upon a Nebuchadnezzar or a Caesar.'"[15] Indeed, such a "psychology" was typical of the renaissance spirit of Zionism, but G-2 ascribed it to all Zionists in a rather different fashion. The connotation is clear – like Fascists of all colors who returned to their own, pre-Christian legacies, Jews were trying to revive their ancient past and the related cults. Yet Nebuchadnezzar, who had destroyed the First Temple, and the Romans who destroyed Judea had been a living memory among Jews ever since.

As far as the "Zionists proper" were concerned, G-2 experts were sure that they only paid "lip service to democracy and representative institutions."

[13] Ibid., 321.
[14] Ibid., note 108.
[15] Ibid., note 109.

"Aside from moderate democratic types like Dr. Weizmann [in fact rather authoritarian and operating alone behind the scenes – S.A.], the 'totalitarian tendency of all this is unmistakable."[16]

Hence, the Jewish Problem seemed to have threatened established American democratic "rules of the game" in various ways. Breaking these rules in the relations between the executive branch and Congress to allow Jewish immigration in large numbers, if Hitler allowed it, would have been yet another problem, not only because of the British-like "spy scare" and "fifth column scare" but because of existing immigration laws enacted by Congress. Attorney General Francis Biddle warned the president as late as December 29, 1944, against giving Jewish refugees in Oswego, New York, immigrant status since Congress had been explicitly assured by him that immigration laws would not be undermined in this way.[17] The maintenance of the rules in this regard was also based, however, on opinion polls[18] that told the president that the main motive of the American people in this war was material and self-centered, whereas Jews, blamed for self-centrism and materialism, were regarded as not "virtuous" enough by many to break any rules of the game for them, as we also learn from many anti-Semitic letters addressed to the president at the time.[19] In addition, important officials such as Myron Taylor and Sam Rayburn, the American Ambassador to the Vatican and the Speaker of the House of Representatives, respectively, both regarded as friendly to the Jewish cause, made themselves at least the tools of others in FDR's court.[20] Two "case studies" should be mentioned here in this regard, divided from each other by two years of the ongoing European Holocaust.

Ambassador Taylor, who had been involved in various efforts pertaining to the Jewish refugee question in the past, sent the president on July 1, 1942, a copy of a letter by Sir John Hope-Simpson in which the British elder statesman not only argued that the "Jewish question" could not be solved by immigration to Palestine but that the Palestine question itself was too complicated due to its connection to the Middle East and to the East in general. Yet Hope-Simpson added further that "*antisemitism is not confined to Central-Europe and Arab countries as there is a great danger of it in Great Britain and probably in the U.S.*" (italics added). Sir John was a British administrator in India, who later worked with refugee and relief services in China and Greece and also was involved in Palestine immigration matters in the early 1930s.

---

[16] Ibid.

[17] FDR Library, PSF, folder Biddle.

[18] FDR Library, Rosenman Papers, Rosenman to FDR, December 31, 1943: "The public is doubly interested in domestic affairs, in comparison to its interest in foreign affairs. Second, about 2/3 were against foreign aid after the war, should it harm American interests. About 1/2 think foreign aid would harm American interests."

[19] FDR Library, PSF boxes, and see Wyman, *The Abandonment of the Jews*, pp. 12, 327.

[20] FDR Library, collection OF 76c, box 9.

In the late 1930s, he published several books on refugee issues. His view on domestic anti-Semitism therefore did not belong to his actual expertise but reflected establishment opinion. His obvious anti-Zionist views could have been mobilized by the Foreign or Colonial Offices to block the Zionist drive in America following Biltmore.

Speaker Rayburn, on the other hand, informed the president in a hand-written letter on March 7, 1944, attached to protest letters by the president of the Iraqi Senate and the president of the Iraqi Chamber of Deputies, against the opening of Palestine to Jewish refugees and that such an opening would really lead to danger if care were not taken, but he thought that the situation in the House was "under control." The president's answer to Myron Taylor, if any, is not in the files, but his answer to Sam Rayburn is contained therein: "It is merely one of a volume of protests which have come in from practically all Arab and Moorish countries. It merely illustrates what happens if delicate international situations get into party politics."[21]

The president might well have had in mind the Republican Convention's pro-Zionist declarations and the warnings of his Jewish counsel and speech writer, Judge Samuel Rosenman, that the Republicans were offering "the skies" to the Zionists on the eve of the 1944 election campaign, but finally he issued his own pro-Zionist statement at the end of 1943, as discussed earlier.

In this sense, America had to be won over by the Zionists by an un-usual effort in which ethical and practical arguments and the united sup-port of the previously divided Jewish communities had to be tuned to-gether almost perfectly with down-to-earth electioneering considerations of American politicians in both parties rather than the usual support given by Jews to the Democrats. This became the life work of Rabbi Abba Hillel Silver at that juncture as an American Jewish effort in response to the Holocaust.

As far as Ben-Gurion was concerned, he was pursuing the goals formu-lated in 1942 thanks to the "Biltmore Conference," which he perceived to be big and simple enough to be accepted in American (Jewish) terms, but it was the result (in OSS eyes in a report probably authored by Harold Glidden, the principal local resident) of the Holocaust "in Poland" that made it possible for Ben-Gurion to come out openly with such a far-reaching program to justify a Jewish commonwealth in Palestine as a haven for the "remnants of the Polish Ghettos" and also to reunite the Yishuv, at that time torn apart "over comparatively minor issues."[22]

In a survey entitled *Jewish Parties and Their Relationships*,[23] probably deliv-ered to the OSS by the British (due to the spelling of words such as "Labour"

[21] Ibid.
[22] See R&A report 185.
[23] RG 108, Wash-Reg-Int-16 Gr-25, unsigned and without date.

rather than "Labor") late in 1943 or early in 1944, the writer argued that "right" and "left" hardly have the same connotations as abroad among the Jews of Palestine. "For example, the old-fashioned conservatives were considered nationalists, and in certain countries imperialists; while the 'left' were much less nationalistic and even as the Marxist 'internationalist.' "

In Palestine, however:[24]

All Jews are in a sense Zionist and nationalist, though the 'right' wing is more aggressively so, and with the extreme 'right' or Revisionist [e.g., IZL and the New Zionist Organization founded by Jabotinsky – S.A.], is inclined to make the largest claims for nationalistic expansion, and adopt the most direct methods – even military ones.... In part this is deceptive, for even the communists are eager to see Jewish settlement in Palestine expand. *National Socialism in Germany has given us an example of a socialism which is violently and narrowly nationalist; in short, a combination of the mid-left economically with the extreme right politically. It is curious that it is into this class that a large section of the Jews would fall: socialist or collectivist in their economic programme, but strongly Jewish-nationalist in their ultimate aim"* (italics added). (Jewish Parties and Their Relationships)

The writer might have been partially right if he had concentrated on several segments in Mapai and the Histadrut, who emigrated from Soviet Russia in the 1920s, and developed a party "machine" geared toward fighting the Revisionists once a decision had been made to do so and to secure for Labor's leadership the economic and political tools necessary to create a state. In this, several of the Mapai and Histadrut were unscrupulous, and in the 1940s they tried to act more rigorously than ever as the Yishuv was likely to become an independent state sooner rather than later. Yet during World War II the Jewish community remained a voluntary, hybrid structure enjoying unparalleled economic prosperity thanks to wartime investments made by the British and American military in building camps, health centers for soldiers, airfields, and the like. Thus, the Histadrut and Mapai's bosses in it tried to apply pressure on people to volunteer for the British Army. This was not necessarily followed by all,[25] nor did they succeed in organizing the Yishuv for other common endeavors such as harvesting and similar wartime efforts. The admixture of actual economic prosperity with growing pain and despair resulting from the news about the Holocaust is reflected very well in the British–American censorship intercepts, which reveal a picture of a Yishuv torn apart, partially in control of Labor's organization and factions, partially radicalized toward some kind of action in the face of the

[24] The writer probably was aiming at the far-left Zionist Hashomer Hazair, deliberately ignoring the actual Communist Party of Palestine, the PKP, which was vehemently anti-Zionist and anti-British and hence outlawed by the mandatory authorities.
[25] See, for example, Haim Ascher, *Two Rivers and the Great Sea* (Tel Aviv: Publisher, 1996), pp. 140–145 (in Hebrew).

Holocaust, and partially atomized, leaderless, passive, and even sunken into despair.[26]

In discussing Mapai, the writer was closer to some historical differences and cleavages in the Yishuv's most important political party, while tainting it as "National Socialist" (i.e., something like the Nazis) to impress upon American readers that: "They are socialists with a strong Zionist outlook, *and may best be described as National Socialist* [italics added]; that is, in internal economic affairs they adopt the socialist viewpoint and aims, but in external policy they are strong Jewish nationalists." Here, Labor Zionist efforts at creating a true reputation as socialists by insisting on cooperative endeavors, on social services entailing political organization, on workers' control over industrial investments and their actual management, and certainly upon the kibbutz and other agrarian corporations aimed at "making the desert bloom," real reputations that they inflated and transformed to an official series of images, were utilized to create the image of a "National Socialist," a Nazi-like endeavor.

The picture of the Yishuv in 1942–1944, as it emerges from primary sources such as private letters intercepted by the "Imperial Censorship" and read by the Joint (British-American) Censorship Collection Agency stationed on Bermuda, reflected a mixture of helplessness, self-doubt and guilt over several issues, such as the good life enjoyed by some thanks to wartime prosperity, of sheer despair – especially among prominent German Zionists, whose dream of an ideal society seemed to them to have vanished with the dead pioneers in Europe – the reservoir of idealists who were in training or should have been trained to create a beautiful Jewish society in Palestine. Crying for authority and a central, effective government in the voluntary Yishuv that would impose drafting into the British army and identify with the cause of the democracies, at the same time German Jews of those convictions disliked the rough "Ostjuden" running the show. They rejected the Weimar-like party key which weakened the central bodies of the Yishuv, the constant competition between various religious and secular parties on the absorption of a few refugee children in their various and different educational systems.

Yet German–Jewish criticism of Labor–Zionist behavior is a complex matter that might have originated in their cultural-political background, which even drove them to challenge the Yishuv's leadership in an organized political fashion in mid-1942 by creating their own political party, "Alya Hadasha," or New Immigration. Indeed, many of them had difficulties in adapting to the Hebrew-speaking, Eastern European–dominated Yishuv. In addition, their liberal neo-Kantian, German social-democratic, or idealist

---

[26] See, for example, Joint Censorship Collection Agency, G-2 Palestine files, box 3027, envelope 3000–3020 Pal., submitted by R. Cutler, Assistant Reporting Officer, letter dated March 18, 1943, from Dr. Georg Landauer, Central Bureau for the Settlement of German Jews, Jewish Agency, to Kurt Blumenfeld (major German Zionist leader) in New York.

Communist minority status in Weimar Germany made them perceive the situation in Palestine in similar, German terms. Even the early Zionists among them, such as Georg Landauer, himself a member of the Jewish Agency's executive, the philosopher Martin Buber, and in addition to him a gallery of publicists, academics, writers, and artists, such as Robert Weltch, Ernst Simon, Max Brod, and Arnold Zweig, had their doubts and different aspirations.[27] The latter were described in a mid–1942 British CID report[28] as if they "were striving to greater cooperation with H. M. Government and the democracies in internal and external affairs…the abandonment of those Zionist aims which have degenerated into chauvinism [the Biltmore program – S.A.] and the establishment of greater-cooperation between Jews, Christians and Moslems." Accordingly, they advocated the elimination of the various socialist and religious educational systems typical of the Yishuv's hybrid structure and an adequate share in the Yishuv's institutions based on an estimate of about 35% of Germans, Austrians, and Czechs among the Jewish population. In fact, as we learn from the municipal election results in Haifa late in June 1942, the new party won almost half of the seats compared to those won by the Histadrut parties, establishing itself as the second largest party in Haifa thanks to the large concentration of German Jews in that "Red town." This cultivated high hopes for the future, which explained Mapai's tightened regime in Haifa later on, among other reasons due to the illusory Arab policy of the new party and its explicit wish to continue the British mandatory regime.[29] Indeed, Mapai was able to co-opt the new party later on, but coupled with the enormous egos of Martin Buber or of less famous people as quoted by censorship intercepts, their cultural syndrome would be "politicized" in various negative directions in the new Palestine environment in which they found themselves as refugees beginning in the late 1930s. Several among them came to support "Brit-Shalom," a group of intellectuals of various origins who worked toward an understanding with the Arabs first, accepting several limitations on Jewish free immigration and sovereignty. As such, their political group,

[27] See Censorship intercept dated November 11, 1943, from Dr. Lefmann, 35 Hillel St., Haifa, to N. N. Glazer, Roxbury, Massachusetts. Similar examples could be found in OSS reports by OSS agent Gideon Hadari and CIC agent Mordechai Allen. The former also interviewed opinion makers such as "Ha'aretz" owner and editor Gustav Gershom Schocken and prominent lawyer Asher Levitzki. The names hint at Jews who were born in Palestine and later immigrated to the United States.

[28] Inspector General, Palestine Police, CID, to Chief Secretary, Subject: Intelligence Summary No. 9/42, Jewish Affairs. Organized Opposition to Yishuv Leadership, May 19, 1942, secret, Hagana Archive, Repository 47, role 9, frames 328–331.

[29] For the elections to the Jewish Community Council in Haifa on June 23, 1942, see note 28, Inspector General to Chief Secretary, July 1, 1942, CID, Intelligence Summary No. 12/42, frames 342–343, secret. For a preliminary discussion of German-Jewish immigration into Palestine, see Kurt Worman, "German Jews in Israel: The Cultural Situation," *Leo Baeck Institute Yearbook* 15 (1970), 73–103.

Ichud (Unity), attracted much attention among the British and American officials reporting from the Middle East, even when the Holocaust and the activities of the Mufti of Jerusalem in cooperation with Nazi Germany made their plank seem totally out of place. Finally, following the Holocaust (and especially after its Hungarian peak in 1944) and Ben-Gurion's domestic and foreign political steps made then and later toward independence in the face of open Arab and British hostility, most Ichud members were mobilized to support the Yishuv's efforts toward independence, which entailed the war of 1948–1949.[30] Indeed, they wished that the story had developed otherwise, without bloodshed, and without such pain suffered by Arab refugees; they noted, however, that millions of German refugees paid for Hitler's war and were exiled forever from their old homelands.[31] They somehow accepted the norms created by World War II itself within which Ben-Gurion now operated, possibly because of the European experience, Arab behavior, and the Holocaust.[32]

Ben-Gurion seemed at the time not to pay attention to the syndrome of demoralizing pessimism and sometimes despair, reflected in our censorship intercepts, which would return in waves throughout Israel's history, especially among intellectuals, also in conjunction with the appraisal of Zionist behavior during the Holocaust. But in fact Ben-Gurion was very conscious of the dire need for leadership, which must neutralize both right and various leftist groups and operate within the givens of the voluntary Yishuv. He had two plans. One was the public Biltmore Program, which was general enough to please most of the quarreling Labor leaders, who had disagreed on the partition issue since 1937, and aimed without any cosmetics at Jewish independence. There was also the secret "Million Plan," which aimed at the immediate absorption of a million Jewish immigrants from Europe and the Arab countries and would later bring him to his planned visits to the Balkans in 1944. In both cases, Ben-Gurion seemed to have assumed, now that the time was ripe, a plank that was similar to Jabotinsky's program – immediate independence – except that he renounced Jabotinsky's claim over both sides of the Jordan River, and he had worked for independence and mass immigration from 1934 but in his cautious, pragmatic fashion of the 1930s, which had required a social cultural political groundwork

---

[30] The related scholarly research goes beyond the scope of this book, especially with regard to German-Jewish contributions to the Palestine economy, Jewish industrialization, a variety of kibbutzim and other cooperative enterprises, and their massive influence over the arts, the music, and other cultural aspects of Zionist lives.

[31] For the background and the intellectual substance of the idealist Zionists among them, such as Martin Buber, see Hedva Ben-Israel, "National Identity of the Scholar and the Study of Nationalism," *Academia* 11(2002)13–17 (in Hebrew).

[32] The writer Arnold Zweig, who was humiliated in the early 1940 when he spoke in German in a public meeting, left Palestine immediately after the war and returned to Germany. He became an East German public figure for a while.

to be laid in Palestine first. Now the time was ripe to fight for independence in public, at least verbally and by invoking political means abroad.[33] By doing so, Ben-Gurion robbed Jabotinsky's followers of their old demand for immediate independence at a moment in which it seemed justified to make that claim and anchored it in ethical and moral arguments directly related to the disaster that befell the Jews of Europe. Ben-Gurion pursued this rather than political and legal claims accompanied by anti-British acts of violence, as the Sternists and Menachem Begin had done once Begin arrived in Palestine in 1943, and after a while Begin assumed command over IZL.

Ben-Gurion was working to implement his "plans" on several levels, subject to changes, when he tried to remove Chaim Weizmann, who seemed to him to have endorsed a weak, hesitant stance regarding Zionist claims at this crucial moment, from his position as chief spokesman of the World Zionist Movement,[34] while at the same time contemplating a military crusade against the Sternists and Begin's IZL and preparing an electoral showdown with the leftist wing of Mapai under Yitzhak Tabenkin's influence. These leftists resented Mapai's pragmatic socialism, which allowed and encouraged various forms of cooperative efforts outside of the holy kibbutz form of collectivism and idealistic equality among pioneers working on the land as cherished by Tabenkin and his followers. Ben-Gurion refused to allow such ideologically entrenched planks to interfere with actual statesmanship on the one hand and on the other resented the left wing of his party's growing collaboration with pro-Soviet elements still further to the left of Mapai, who were toying with the idea of a binational, Jewish–Arab state in Palestine, possibly under a Soviet–American trusteeship at first, a concept that would avoid partition but was yet another typical illusion in his eyes. These rifts, and the partisan affiliations carried and produced by them, were also reflected in the work of the Zionist bodies entrusted with the rescue of Jews from occupied Europe. For Ben-Gurion, these rifts were typical of the Jewish malady, that Zionism was supposed to cure – the endemic lack of cooperation, the habitual infighting, and the moralizing arguments of the parties, some of whom tried to impose their minority opinions on the majority by invoking their "private virtues." The issue of majority–minority relations also governed Ben-Gurion's view of Arab and Jewish coexistence in the same country, which he hoped to secure

---

[33] See OSS report of October 2, 1943 on a meeting of the Zionist Executive "late in 1943," in which Moshe Shertok-Sharett reported on his talks in Cairo shortly before with Lord Moyne and the Iraqi pro-British premier, Nuri Said, and later about his visit to Turkey, RG 165, Entry 77, G-2 Regional File, box 3029. The "source" quoted in this report implies that OSS or rather British Intelligence, had an informer within the ranks of the close circle of the Jewish Agency's executive, see CID Intelligence Summary No. 15/43, Hagana Archive, Repository 47, Role 9, frames 429–441, Subject: Jewish Affairs, Moshe Shertok, September 14, 1943, secret.

[34] All of these moves were reported with acerbic interest in British and OSS intelligence reports almost on a daily basis.

by transferring at least a million Jews into Palestine during the war instead of transferring the Arabs outside of it.[35]

However, later in 1944, when Ben-Gurion created the power base necessary to accomplish his own, changing goals by means of elections to the Histadrut Council and to the Yishuv's representative body, he and other Jewish leaders abroad would be perceived to have been too conventional, calculating, and absorbed in parochial Zionist politics to rise to the height of the emergency situation created by the Holocaust. In fact, Ben-Gurion could not and did not drop rescue in favor of domestic politics, but in regard to rescue the Zionists failed as everybody else did.

---

[35] See OSS reports regarding "Transfer of Arabs from Palestine," RG 226, Entry 108, Wash-Reg-Int-16 G-3500. Shertok was quoted therein as if the idea had originated in the executive of the British Labour Party and that the Zionist movement "was in no way responsible to it." This formulation is much more restrained than others and may reflect the balanced influence on OSS R&A reports of J. C. Hurewitz. See Harold Glidden's reports, Psychological Warfare Roundups, same source.

15

Roosevelt, Stimson, and the Palestine Question

British Inputs

Roosevelt's decisions with regard to Palestine seem easy to follow because he appears to have adopted a shallow, traditional, Wilsonian, pro-Zionist approach at first. During the last two years of World War II, he adopted a rather reserved, if not negative, view of the Zionist endeavor, but on the face of it he promised everyone almost everything in this regard. This strategy was very much influenced by the delicate military and political situation in the Middle East, in Europe, and in other parts of the world that were Muslim to a considerable extent. Roosevelt was also influenced by opinions such as the expertise of a Lieutenant Colonel Harold B. Hoskins, the OSS-affiliated State Department adviser,[1] and by reports (some already mentioned) made by Colonel William J. Donovan, the future director of OSS, who toured the Middle East early in 1941 and gained the impression that the Palestine "Jews wanted to push the Arabs back to the desert from which they had come," an idea that FDR himself seemed to have endorsed for a while in favor of the Jews.[2] The idea itself originated in a 1937 report on Palestine by the British Royal Commission, headed by Lord Peel, which had recommended the removal of Arabs – by force if necessary – from the territory of the Jewish state in a partitioned Palestine.[3] However, FDR also listened to the State Department's opinions, expressed by military experts and State's Near East Division's "Arabists," many of them products of the American colleges in Beirut or in Cairo, and/or by officials close enough to the oil business, as well as to the anti-Zionist views of Secretary of War Henry L. Stimson, which might have been Stimson's own or influenced by U.S. Army officials and Army Intelligence.

---

[1] See Ilan, *America, Britain and Palestine*, pp. 114–115. See Ilan's note on Hoskins' alleged role as Chief, OSS FNB. In fact, the Chief was DeWitt Pool.
[2] See further Ilan, *America, Britain and Palestine*, p. 135.
[3] See Shabtai Teveth, *Ben-Gurion and the Arabs of Palestine: From Peace to War* (Tel Aviv and Jerusalem: Schocken, 1985), pp. 296–298.

Stimson was a major figure in FDR's cabinet, a moderate Republican "elder statesman" who recruited or helped install several key figures in the American war and foreign policy machines such as John J. McCloy, his Assistant Secretary of War.[4]

In order to understand Stimson's mind, its possible shaping, and the way it worked in practice with regard to a specific issue, we should cite here Stimson's response to a Zionist initiative in Congress early in 1944 calling for congressional hearings and a resolution based on the Biltmore Program of 1942.[5] Having discussed "S-1," or the enormous financial needs of the "Manhattan Project," with FDR's scientific adviser, Vannevar Bush, and Generals Styer and "Gross" (General Leslie A. Groves, director of the atomic bomb project), Stimson then "found that the Jews were raising trouble in Palestine again." The Zionists had brought on a resolution (the Wagner–Taft Resolution) of a most drastic character calling for immediate and unrestricted immigration of Jews into Palestine in order to eventually set up a completely Jewish commonwealth in Palestine. This went much further than the resolution that had been adopted twenty-two years before, in 1922, and it violated – according to Stimson – all the experience that the British have had involving the necessity of restricting immigration. The resolutions have been brought before the Senate Committee on Foreign Relations and the House Committee on Foreign Affairs. The Senate Committee under the chairman, Senator Connally of Texas, was responsive and considerate to Stimson's warnings: Connally said that, if the Secretary of War would write a letter in general terms saying that *"the conduct of hearings and the passage of the resolution would be a military danger"* (italics added) at the present time, his committee would take no action. Stimson had conferred with the Army's Chief of Staff, General George C. Marshall, and found that he was very apprehensive of the result of any such action. Stimson continued by saying that in fact the danger was manifest: The situation between the Arabs and the Jews in Palestine had long been acute and explosive, and the present resolution would set it off like a powder mine for there are at least a million Arabs in that country as opposed to a minority of probably less than five hundred thousand Jews. The Jews want to drive out the Arabs and take possession. It would produce immediate hostilities and war and would require retaining in Palestine to keep the peace a large number of Allied troops, which were at present much needed in other parts of the world to fight the Germans, particularly in the invasion of France. Thus, one may conclude that the invasion of France, a supreme war aim cherished by the Jews as the means to destroy Hitler, their worst enemy, handicapped Zionist interests, even when

---

[4] On Stimson and the "young guard" that he mobilized during World War II, see Walter Isaacson and Evan Thomas, *The Wise Men: Six Friends and the World They Made* (New York: Simon and Schuster, 1986).

[5] See Stimson Diaries, microfilmed in the U.S. Library of Congress, Volumes 46, 52–55, role 8.

Jews were the only nation dying at Hitler's hands – among other reasons because they had no country of their own. In fact, the Jews remained a regional, non-Arab minority, who claimed sovereignty in the Arab Middle East and thus threatened the Arab sense of security and supremacy in the region. Furthermore, among the various "solutions" to the Palestinian Arab problems, their transfer to other Arab countries, to be revived in several forms afterward, was taken for granted by Stimson. In fact, the Zionist executive in Palestine had discussed the idea among themselves and raised it with other Zionist leaders abroad, Weizmann included[6] (since it was mentioned by the British in Peel's Commission report in 1937), but Ben-Gurion finally shelved it publicly once he adopted in May 1942 the idea of an immediate transfer of two million – later one million – Jews to Palestine and its transformation into a Jewish "commonwealth," which would solve the issue of an Arab majority therein as a matter of course.[7] However, coming back to our "case studies," Moshe (Sharett) Shertok, the Jewish Agency's Political Department head, did mention the option of transferring the Palestinians elsewhere in a conversation with a high-ranking American official, probably the OSS-SI chief in Cairo, Stephen Penrose, or his deputy, Lewis Leary, on February 6, 1944, which might have reached General Marshall and fed Stimson's fire. Stimson's diary entries quoted earlier were made on February 14.[8] Various other constants in the ensuing Arab–Israeli conflict were mentioned in that conversation as well, coming from the British PICME Chief, Brigadier C. D. Quilliam, who also attended.

The meeting, which took place in Cairo, opened when Shertok was asked straightforwardly by the two intelligence officers about Zionist propaganda efforts in the United States, aimed at Congress, which they described as counterproductive from a Zionist viewpoint, and he responded that the Jewish Agency was helpless in a country that put such stock in the freedom of the press that all attempts to curb free expression of opinion were useless.

"Frankly," wrote the American party in his report to Washington, "I think he is telling a deliberate lie. I cannot believe that the Jewish Agency would be unable to stop the activities of its American Associates. . . . Shertok is a very charming and a very plausible talker but quite frankly he impressed me as a rogue and a liar."

Shertok then spoke "with surprising frankness" of Zionist aspirations. He was quoted as having said that "the Zionists laid claim to all lands

---

[6] See Bauer, *Diplomacy and Underground in Zionism*, pp. 66–67, on Weizmann's early efforts in America (1940).

[7] Bauer, *Diplomacy and Underground in Zionism*, p. 200, and see Shabtai Teveth, *The Vanished Years and the Black Hole* (Tel-Aviv: Dvir Publishing House, 1999), pp. 245–287.

[8] See RG 165, G-2 Regional File, Entry 77, box 3029, folder 3800, orig. Pal 5940-P, A 23310-P C 1975.

occupied at any time by the twelve tribes of Israel." Accordingly, "such claims embraced Lebanese territory including the area around Tyre and Sidon."

Shertok was then quoted as if he said that Iraq "could easily support all the Arab population in Palestine if that population were to be uprooted and transplanted thither." The formulation here could be interpreted by a nonexpert reader such as Marshall or Stimson as if Shertok clearly aimed at "uprooting" the Arabs and "transplanting" them by force, even if he then spoke "enthusiastically" of raising Jewish money "in order to act as a magnet to attract the Arabs from Palestine into Iraq."[9] Thus Shertok gave his interlocutors, willingly or not, sharp ammunition against the Zionists.

A rather interesting controversy then developed between Shertok and Brigadier Quilliam regarding the coexistence of Arabs and Jews in a sovereign Jewish state – a critical issue to this very day. Quilliam reflected doubts already expressed years before, since the very inception of Zionism, whether the Jews, thanks to their typical "narrowness," would be capable of respectfully treating others as sovereign rulers of an independent state when Shertok said that "the Jews would be only too willing and glad to have a certain percentage of the Arab population remain in Palestine." The PICME Brigadier responded that this was "out of the question and entirely impracticable."

Quilliam then charged Shertok with two motives underlying his desire to maintain an Arab minority within a Jewish state. The first of these motives, Quilliam said, was the necessity of proving to the world how well the Jews could treat a minority within their own lands. Shertok "admitted" that, reflecting the defensive posture so typical of the Catch-22 situation of Jews in those days, which made the Jews look like sinister oppressors even while they were being slaughtered by the arch enemy of civilized humanity as a hated minority. Quilliam, however, was quick to make his point, aimed at his American colleague: "He doubted whether this good treatment would last for more than five or six years at the maximum." "Shertok denied this vehemently, but neither Quilliam nor I [Penrose or Leary – S.A.] were convinced. Quilliam accused him quite openly (I believe absolutely correctly) [parentheses in original] of hoping to maintain an Arab minority in Palestine to be used as slave labour in the development of Jewish industry and agriculture." This Western anti-Semitic perception of Jews as slave drivers and exploiters might have been derived from common European images and stood in contradiction to the Labor Zionist credo of "Jewish Labor," a postulate aimed at creating a real reputation for Jews as physical workers, "new Jews," who renounced the old images and reputations that Jews have radiated in the Diaspora. Yet this very effort would be interpreted as a means to push the Arabs out of jobs altogether.

---

[9] See in this regard the various plans discussed at the time to solve the Palestine question within a larger regional framework in Bauer, *Diplomacy and Underground in Zionism*, pp. 204–223.

By itself, that credo combined Labor Zionism's drive to make the Jews themselves farmers and workers, when they accepted various critical arguments about Jewish life in the Diaspora, with its aim to refrain from exploiting the cheap local work force while avoiding dependence on it. The ensuing campaign to remove Arabs from working for, and being exploited by, private Jewish entrepreneurs would be described as a Jewish drive to "take possession" of the country and uproot the Arabs in a specific colonialist–imperialist fashion. "Shertok naturally denied this, but neither Quilliam, nor I, were impressed" (the "I" once again being Penrose or Leary).

A second conversation between the American party to the preceding conversation and Shertok took place at Grosvenor House in London later, this time without Quilliam's direct involvement but typed in British English on the same typewriter (probably by the British Intelligence hosts), on February 19, 1944, exactly one month before the Nazi occupation of Hungary.

The idea was to make Shertok appear even worse and probably achieved a reasonable degree of success. His interlocutor reported to Washington[10] that Shertok "denied ever having suggested to me in Cairo that the Zionists had any interest in [Lebanese – S.A.] territory. This was truly a startling revelation. . . . I believe he told the truth by mistake in Cairo and was lying to me this evening." The rest of the conversation revolved around the issue of the industrial development of Palestine that would "lead to bitter commercial rivalry between a Zionist state and England for Middle East markets." We have no room to quote the document in its entirety, but one passage related to the agricultural development of Palestine and the limited water reserve even when the Jordan River was dammed and Lake Tiberias was exploited for that purpose. Shertok did mention the Litany River in Lebanon and Syrian sources as a possible solution, which prompted the eager question of whether the Zionists wanted to settle there, too, as a proof of their lust to expand beyond Palestine itself. Shertok denied this, emphasizing agreement resulting from "pressure" on the Arabs to cooperate with the Jews. The American asked whether this was military pressure, and Shertok replied no, that it was "moral and practical."

The exchange continued: "He proclaimed a passionate faith in the ability of the Jew to live alongside of the Arab in peace and friendship;" indeed this was one of Shertok-Sharett's aims then and later – to show to "the world" that the Zionists, and he personally, were doing their best to prove it. "I observed a missionary tone in [Shertok's] voice which suggested that he would like me to think that the Jews would do so much for the Arabs living in the areas adjoining the Palestinian frontiers, that in the end current hatred would be transformed into permanent affection and lasting cooperation. His arguments . . . were slick and plausible. He spoke with great fire, grace and conviction. Nevertheless, I cannot help but fear that his hopes and this

[10] G-2 box mentioned in note 8, orig. Pal 5940-P.

burning faith of his were ill-founded and I got a definite impression that he himself knew that this was so." Armed with this, and possibly with similar information dating back to 1943 and supplied by Army Intelligence, to be soon quoted, Secretary Stimson and General Marshall were ready to torpedo the Zionist initiative in Congress later in 1944 when Marshall declared before the Senate Foreign Relations Committee on February 23 that further action on the Palestine resolutions at that time would be prejudicial to the war effort.

The Zionists continued their drive, however, and late in 1944 the new Secretary of State, Edward R. Stettinius, Jr., was in the forefront to oppose them. The story is discussed in the scholarly literature elsewhere,[11] but its final outcome can be quoted here from an interesting primary source:[12]

The Wagner–Taft Palestine resolution [the renewed Zionist effort in the Congress – S.A.] was blocked before the Senate Foreign Relations Committee by Stettinius who appeared in person to explain why it was impolitic to pass it at present, and was deferred until the next session. . . . The State Department has issued a statement saying that in view of the 'delicate international situation' involved, it would not be wise to pass this resolution now. I learn that this appears to follow on a letter received (and kept confidential) [parentheses in original] by Senator Wagner (D-N.Y.) from the President whom he had consulted on the matter, in which Mr. Roosevelt said that he had been told that rash action now might precipitate a massacre of Jews in Palestine. (*Washington Dispatches*, p. 479)

Roosevelt had been exposed to previous arguments such as that of a possible Arab military threat to Allied interests made by Colonel Hoskins or made independently by G-2 yet also coined in terms of a possible disaster awaiting the Jews of Palestine (and hence transmitted to Judge Rosenman by the head of Army Intelligence, General George V. Strong).

Strong's own arguments went back to summer 1943.[13] On August 5, 1943, he wrote to his chief, General Marshall, that the "horrendous facts" gathered in an attached "chronology" of events by British PICME, by G-2, and by other intelligence and diplomatic channels in the region refute the growing "militant Zionist propaganda" in the United States, which already involved it in partisan interests related to a region that could thus sooner rather than later face a civil war. Strong argued further that, after all, there were sixteen

---

[11] See Ilan, *America, Britain and Palestine*, pp. 157–165.

[12] *Washington Dispatches 1941–1945: Weekly Political Reports from the British Embassy*, edited by H. G. Nicholas; introduction by Isaiah Berlin (Chicago: University of Chicago Press, 1981), p. 479, cabled on December 18, 1944. Berlin wrote most of the reports and was personally close to Dr. Weizmann and to the Zionist cause as well, but at the time he also loyally served his country in Washington, echoing British and American perceptions of the "militant Zionists" striving for full independence.

[13] NA, RG 165, Entry 77, G-2 Regional File, box 3029, folder 3800, Palestine IV, "Memorandum for the Chief of Staff," Subject: "Jewish–Arab Controversy," including the "chronology" mentioned in the text, sent separately by General Strong to Judge Rosenman.

million Jews in the whole world [he did not mention the Holocaust, which decimated them daily at that very time – S.A.], whereas 320 million Muslims [this included Turkey, Iran, the Dutch East Indies, and the "3% Moslems" in the Philippines – S.A.] inhabited an enormous global belt reaching from Casablanca to Manila in which hundreds of millions of natives cultivated the highest degree of self-consciousness (the Muslims were the "largest, the most self-conscious bloc of native people in the world"). Should American policies enrage them, the results could be catastrophic in three respects: threatening major supply routes to Russia, causing trouble in the Allied rear while the Allies were preparing for battle in Europe and in central Asia, and endangering the global oil reserve in addition to the possible damage to a trans-Arab pipeline planned at the time. One could try and subdue them with much direct military effort, which would engage the troops needed elsewhere and whose success would be questionable. The other option would be an American intervention toward solving the Arab–Jewish dispute, but the British had tried it unsuccessfully for twenty years. From a military point of view, Arabs and Jews were of American interest as an issue of military security alone. Priority issues should be given their due priority, and victory in the war should be the first goal. From a military point of view, the only reasonable course should be an official American declaration to the effect that the United States would not commit itself to any party; it should refuse to be involved in partisan issues and demand that the partisan sides (i.e., the Zionists) cease their propaganda activity.

For us, the central point here is not only the fear of Arabs, which might seem legitimate in wartime, but the comparison made between Muslim culture and political behavior – deliberately simplistic as it probably was formulated – and Jewish civilization, denying the latter, complex and hybrid as it was, any "national" rights in general and in particular in Palestine, as reflected in OSS reports.

16

The Views of Harold Glidden and/or British Intelligence, Consul General Pinkerton, and Rabbi Nelson Glueck

OSS-R&A Report 185 on "Zionism – Aims and Prospects" was an American, not just a British copied, report. It might have been very much influenced by the British, but the report assumed a distinctly American character.[1]

First, the anonymous writer dismissed the Balfour Declaration of 1917 as a British affair, a concession they made "at the heat" of World War I, without mentioning its endorsement by the United States Congress and by the League of Nations, even if the State Department indeed had viewed it – and the Zionists – with open hostility since the early 1920s.

The writer then moved over to British calculations in regard to the Zionists, which had to consider not only Arab reactions to concessions made to them but Muslim–Indian reactions and even American reactions to commitments made to third parties that might involve the United States as well. Then the author described Zionism within the larger context of Jewish problems in general:

Jews living in Axis-dominated Europe are frantically seeking havens of refuge. Their first choice of refuge is usually the US. Their second a British possession far distant from Europe, their third choice South America and their fourth Palestine. Only because Palestine seems to be somewhat... [closer – S.A.] than other lands have many Jews turned in that direction. Their numbers may run into millions, far greater numbers than Palestine can support, even if Transjordan were annexed and the Arab population expelled. ("Zionism – Aims and Prospects")

The "catch" in the Zionist claim, that they represented millions of Jews, is apparent because what the Zionists perceived since Hitler's rise as their most convincing argument could be the most frightening one for the British establishment, for Americans, and of course for Arabs, even while in fact the millions were dying. However, the report continued, a Zionist "dream state" could not possibly solve three problems facing the Jews of the world.

---

[1] See NA, RG 226, Entry 190, box 76, folder 70.

The first was that Palestine is too small and barren to settle even the Jews of Eastern Europe, who indeed might be willing to come. Second, if Judaism aligns with nationalism, it can expect the same fate as other forces at odds with the centralized modern state, "which tolerates only with reluctance and suspicion even the mildest forms of divided loyalty." Third, the Jewish community is a religious, not a cultural, entity; there is no common language or a way of life, and any semblance of cultural unity in Christian or Muslim lands is the result of persecution and segregation. This view was exemplified by such statements as "Even the Jews expelled from Germany by Hitler remain essentially German in thought and feeling, as well as in language" and "The Arab world, on the contrary, is a cultural unity, if not a uniformed unity, thanks to the Arabic language, to Islam and to the literary tradition." These arguments, which eventually conceded that the Eastern European Jews (who were being killed at that time) may have something in common and may be willing to create their own state in their ancient homeland, concluded like most other reports that Palestine was perceived by the Arabs as theirs from time immemorial and warned that Arab sympathy with Nazi Germany and Fascist Italy could hurt the Allied cause and that Arab revenge aimed against America would follow if the United States stupidly got involved in "British promises" and Churchill's "Zionism."

This attitude of British and American Arabists toward Zionism and Zionists has been dealt with in the scholarly literature for decades. My contribution to this literature, and the quotes from intelligence reports in this regard, are aimed at one major point: that Judaism as such, and Jews in general, were denied the right to be a legitimate civilization, a legitimate nation, an equal entity in comparison with the Arabs. The Zionist experiment in challenging this historical reality was transformed into "Nazi-like" nationalism during the time when the Nazis were killing all members and descendants of this civilization they could reach in cooperation with the former Mufti of Jerusalem, the most important Palestinian leader of the time. His involvement on the Nazi side made Arab threats against the West in many eyes more, not less, convincing politically and morally. On the other hand, the carnage made Jews endorse Zionism more than ever before, and those living at the time in Palestine developed quite a sense of revenge toward Palestinians and other Arab leaders who officially fought Zionist rescue plans, while in fact the former could do very little to rescue the dying and the few who were still alive.

An "expert opinion," expressed by OSS agent 203 in Palestine, Harold Glidden, codenamed "Robert Laing,"[2] a future CIA and State Department

---

[2] See NA, RG 226, Entry 108, Cairo boxes, box 83, Index of OSS code names and numbers. I also corresponded for a short while with Mr. Glidden in 1986–1987 and tried to interview him by phone, without much success, as he seemed to be interested in Israel's problems at the time in Arab Jerusalem.

specialist and one of the "Arabists" of both agencies, echoed the arguments put forward by the British High Commissioner for Palestine, Sir Harold MacMichael, equating Labor Zionists in principle with the Nazis due to their socialist regime and "extreme nationalism" as manifested toward others,[3] while in fact the "nationalistic" nature of the "modern nation state," prohibiting divided loyalty such as Jewish support of a Jewish state as just mentioned, was taken for granted as justified.

The American diplomatic representative in British Palestine at the time, Consul General Lowell C. Pinkerton, alluded to this trap in a conversation with visiting officers from the War Department by creating a clear-cut contradiction between Allied war aims and the Zionist dream:[4]

"Pinkerton agrees... that *the influence of Zionism in America* [underlined in the original] is at present being highly exaggerated out here by British, Jews and Arabs alike, but at the same time he feels that the amount of pressure which the Roosevelt administration is prepared to bring upon Britain in favor of Zionism is unpredictable. As he tartly remarked, Felix Frankfurter may well catch the President off his guard at any moment – or some miserable rainy morning, for example, or when suffering from a passing spell of dyspepsia – and convince him. He agrees with me [his interlocutor, a Major Snyder from the War Department – S.A.] that *a Zionist state as that advocated by the Jewish Agency would be a festering sore on the face of world peace after the present war is ended and would merely establish that very ape of nationalism which we are at present striving to destroy*" (italics added). (NA, RG 165, Entry 77, G-2 Regional File 1933–1944, Palestine, box 3027, January 1, 1944)

Pinkerton further said that the Jewish Revisionists and other radicals might declare a rebellion against the British if the White Paper of 1939 were not replaced with free immigration. The Palestinian Arabs, on the other hand, who had been subject to machinations by the wrong "engineers" in the last twenty years, were totally demoralized, leaderless, and not organized, lacking a "sense of corporate responsibility." Yet should the Jews risk a mutiny, when faced with British machine guns they would soon put their tails between their legs and run for home, while the Arabs would go to the hills and generate serious and durable trouble. Pinkerton's final advice was to issue a joint British–American declaration on Palestine (to overcome British misgivings about American pro-Zionist statements made behind their back), but leave its implementation to the British alone, in order to avoid the

---

[3] Agent "Laing" wrote a large report on the Arab–Jewish problem in August 1943, and made it available to ISLD, which may have been OSS Report 185 cited previously. Brigadier Iltyd N. Clayton, who at that time was in command of PICME, was very much interested in publishing Laing's "tractatus" and in giving it the widest publication possible in America. See OSS-SI Chief Whitney Shepardson's warning to Gordon Laud, the SI Desk Chief in Washington, against the publication of the "excellent" August 1943 report on Arabs and Jews in Palestine, as the issue was too sensitive and "thousands" of interested people might harm the interests of OSS as a result of it. NA, RG 226, Entry 190, box 76, folder 70.

[4] NA, RG 165, Entry 77, G-2 Regional File 1933–1944, Palestine, box 3027, January 1, 1944.

unthinkable "burdens" that the United States might assume if it became directly involved in the Palestine question. As Amitzur Ilan puts it, Pinkerton's view that the issue should remain in principle a "British matter" was in fact endorsed and maintained by Franklin D. Roosevelt until his death.[5]

In addition to Consul General Pinkerton and OSS agent Glidden, another figure, Rabbi Nelson Glueck, OSS agent 201, an eminent archaeologist and one of the leaders of the Jewish Reform movement in America, was active in Palestine at the time, first as a surveyor. Following the Biltmore Resolution, Glueck realized that the Zionists, very probably because of the Holocaust and due to the emergence of Rabbi Abba Hillel Silver as a driving force in the "American Zionist Emergency Council"[6] in spite of constant infighting with his antagonist, Rabbi Stephen Wise, were close to uniting American Jewry as a whole behind Biltmore. The instrument for that was an "American Jewish Conference," which held its first meetings in August–September 1943.[7]

For Rabbi Glueck, the very idea of a "Jewish commonwealth" in Palestine as spelled out in the Biltmore Program and endorsed for the first time by mainstream Zionists and non-Zionists abroad was intolerable. After all, the Balfour Declaration promised only a "national home" to the Jews, and the idea of an independent Jewish state was perceived as a narrow, nationalistic, separatist solution, and not only by Glueck himself, but it reflected a whole scale of Reform Judaism's search for a "universal" rather than a "particularistic" Jewish, American way of life in the New World.[8] But now it seemed that in their rage over the Holocaust, American Jews would endorse that state and involve Glueck's people back in the United States with problems of divided loyalty on top of everything else. He even asked his OSS superiors in Cairo to be granted permission to go home and fight it, having submitted a formal bid for resignation from his post in Palestine, and they supported his action fully until his return to the region early in 1945.[9]

---

[5] Ilan, *America, Britain and Palestine*, p. 136.

[6] See David H. Shapiro, *From Philanthropy to Activism*, pp. 265–294.

[7] See RG 208 L.Vs/o.9, Entry 368, box 350, U.S. Memoranda no. 235, December 25, 1944, Press Opinion – plus commentary – on Jewish Affairs November 1943 – December 1944, issued by Research Department, Foreign Office, London, declassified in the United States in 1982.

[8] For a detailed discussion, see Ofer Schiff, *Assimilation in Pride: Antisemitism, Holocaust, and Zionism as Challenges to Universalistic American Jewish Reform Ideology* (Tel Aviv: Am-Oved, 2001) (in Hebrew).

[9] See NA, RG 226, Entry 190, box 76, folder 70, OSS-SI Cairo to Gordon Laud, SI Washington: "Hicks [i.e., Glueck] is an executive of the Association of Reformed Rabbis," in whose absence from the United States a substitute was at work who drove those Rabbis toward the Zionists. Hicks's friends who were opposed to the Zionists put pressure to bear on him to return and alleviate the situation, and as a result he submitted his resignation (from OSS). OSS Cairo was very much in favor of accepting Glueck's bid to return and fight the Zionists for those reasons. Glueck returned to Palestine about a year later, and his detailed reports to Lewis Leary in Cairo were released by NA, RG 226, Entry 210, box 175, folder 126. Since the

Glueck's arguments, as he communicated them to the Reform movement in the United States from Jerusalem in a private letter opened by the Imperial Censorship, which had no idea that the writer was an OSS agent, were against a Jewish state as a "Fascist solution" and against the British White Paper, which he condemned as well, but in favor of Jewish immigration that would equalize the number of Arabs and Jews in the country and allow a Jewish province, or a canton, to emerge in a Middle East federation. By itself, this idea was not new and had been raised before by a variety of British Middle East experts to avoid full sovereignty for the Jews and also prevent trouble with the Arabs. This Rabbi Glueck recommended in September 1943 when the Holocaust made the Zionists indeed the spokesmen of many American Jews if not all of them.[10]

Glueck's arguments in his letter, that in fact the main aim of Reform Judaism should be "the strengthening of the movement in America," otherwise a normal priority and a traditional aim of a Jewish group of that kind very much concerned with accusations of divided loyalty, must have sounded somewhat hollow, even in the eyes of the Reform movement's own rank and file, in the face of the Holocaust. Thus, at least among Jews, including American Jews of liberal and far left affiliations, the doubt and possibly even the aversion against Zionism and its open quest for an independent Jewish state were melting down.

Whether the Zionists could have achieved more in regard to rescuing the dying candidates to inhabit that state, the European Jewry, by pushing or even fighting FDR on the matter depended on forces beyond them, the American president, and even the British. Nor could Felix Frankfurter, so respected by Consul General Pinkerton, save the European Jews even at that late stage, as the Hungarian chapter will tell us.

Felix Frankfurter was the symbolic figure of a Jewish liberal gray eminence behind the scenes of FDR's long rule and as such was an object of doubt and suspicion among the American State Department and army officers. In fact, he was instrumental in one affair related to the Zionists (i.e., in shelving a joint British–American statement initiated by Colonel Hoskins and endorsed by FDR in August 1943 to the effect that any (Zionist) propaganda before the end of the war does damage to the war effort, that nothing should be done to change the status quo in Palestine before then, and even then that all parties concerned would be fully consulted).[11]

The Jewish personalities involved were not only Frankfurter but Bernard Baruch, Herbert Lehman, and Henry Morgenthau, Jr., and they were

---

British and the Zionists used Glueck in 1945 as a channel to the Americans, he met most of the key figures in Palestine around at the time. His illuminating correspondence with OSS Cairo awaits a separate article.

[10] See Ilan, *America, Britain and Palestine*, pp. 86–104.

[11] Ilan, *America, Britain and Palestine*, p. 119.

horrified by the condemnation of Zionist propaganda as damaging the war
effort and perceived in it a sheer anti-Semitic argument, a typical State Department product, rather than positively endorsing Zionism. Frankfurter
was a declared "Zionist," Lehman was more sympathetic toward the Zionist
idea, Baruch much less so, and Morgenthau had been sympathetic.

The above-mentioned achievement of gaining American Jewish support
for the Zionist idea late in 1943 was not enough, and it could even have been
counterproductive in the sense that the president himself leaked Stimson's
letter to Connally to the press and thus indeed made the Zionists appear
in public as if their cause were damaging to the war effort. The result
was a straightforward Zionist threat, made by Rabbi Silver, not to vote for
the Democrats in election year 1944. Roosevelt responded by bluntly asking
the Zionists if they wanted a Jihad in which many would die.[12] Nevertheless, the president issued a pro-Zionist statement in which he referred to the
British decision to allow Jews who were able to arrive in Palestine to enter
and stay in the country. A storm of Arab protests engulfed him as a result
of this, and hence FDR's view of the future of Palestine remained largely unchanged. The Holocaust could not make America use force to create a state
for the Jews, as Army Intelligence and OSS agents warned the president that
the United States would have to assume the military consequences of endorsing Zionism.[13] At the same time, the Zionists and other Jewish groups failed
in their bid to mobilize at least one Allied military arm that seemed to be
able to rescue Jews – the Allied bombing machine.

[12] See for the whole subject Ilan, *America, Britain and Palestine*, pp. 158–159.
[13] See General Strong's "chronology" and its sources: 4 June 1943 – Bulletin No. 2 from
British Political Intelligence Center, Cairo, Egypt, states that "Ben-Gurion remains fanatically
nationalistic.... Further confirmation has been received of the intention of Hagana to play a
large part in Palestine politics. 12 August 1943 – JICAME fears armed outbreak in Palestine if
Britain and U.S. declare in favor of Jewish Political State. Danger of attacks on Jewish property developing into Anti-Christian and Anti-foreign riots. Military transients will require
convoy under guard. Serious political and economic effects inevitable. 14 August 1943 –
Teheran states in event of armed conflict between Arabs and Jews in Palestine, Moslems
would stage Anti-Jewish riots and disturbances. Iraq government would assist Arabs." See
R&A Psychological Warfare Roundup, Europe-Africa Division, Near East-African Section
1090.3, April 17, 1943, authored by Glidden, p. 20: "Psychologically our position among
Arabs very poor... We have to convince the Arabs that they'll get a fair deal vis-à-vis Jews
at peace table." See further no. 1090.11, June 1–7, 1943 also authored by Glidden: "Jews
are not fighting for U.S. or Britain but for themselves." See also report 1090.16, July 6–13,
1943 (undisclosed author): "Shertok impressed with advice of British friends not to confuse
question of rescue of European Jews with Zionist demands, as was attempted at time of
Bermuda Conf."

17

Various Methods of Rescue

Albert Speer, Hitler's architect and Minister of Armaments, had the task, among other things, of repairing bombing damage during the war, which he accomplished with a considerable degree of success.[1] Once he was released from Spandau Prison, I asked him what would have been Hitler's reaction to an air raid against a German city as a reprisal for "say, the transport of Jews which left the other day to one of the killing centers in the East." Speer answered: "He would have exploded. He would have hit the roof. He always blamed the Jews for the bombing raids against German cities. Now he would have had his proof [in printed leaflets supplied by the Allies – S.A.]. He then would have reacted. He would have taken his revenge, and even accelerated the 'Final Solution.'"

To my astonished question of how the Holocaust could have been "accelerated" when the Nazis already invested in it an enormous effort and diverted manpower, vital transportation facilities, and other irreplaceable resources at the expense of their war machine to accomplish the murder (an image that was created following Hannah Arendt's arguments against the Judenräte, who allegedly had done nothing to at least make the smooth working of the machinery of destruction more difficult since the initial mass killings in Russia), Speer answered with facts and calculations that he had prepared in advance of our interview: "It is not true that the 'Final Solution' required an extraordinary effort of any special significance – and hence it could have been accelerated. I have calculated the amount of railcars, which was necessary to ship two and a half million people during two and a half years to Auschwitz. [This was the length of time in which this factory of death was mostly active – S.A.] The number is about sixty to one hundred railcars a day" (out of about 190,000 cars at Speer's ministry's daily disposal

---

[1] Film interview at Speer's home in Heidelberg, July 11–14, 1972, and ensuing correspondence. Parts of the film interview were broadcast by Israeli TV. I published most of the transcript of the film interview in the Ha'aretz newspaper shortly after the airing of the TV interview.

supplied by the Deutsche Reichsbahn alone and not including foreign railway systems under German control or under German influence).

Speer continued:

And so was the rest – the victims were totally at the mercy, as unarmed civilians, of a mobilized great power at war, whose troops were ready and deployed everywhere anyway, who occupied the living space of those victims and who did not need to be mobilized especially to take care of them. A mobilized, armed great power could kill millions of civilians without any extra effort, just as a by-product of its own state of preparedness.

In response to my question about the possible interruption of the railroad system leading to Auschwitz by aerial bombing and the eventual destruction of the railway bridges serving them, Speer said that the railroads "would have been repaired in a matter of hours or less, if at all they could hit them – and bridges in such distances could hardly be attacked effectively due to their strong structure, air defenses and the weather."

Adding to that the "great surprise" of the Warsaw ghetto uprising in spring 1943, Speer said that no one in Hitler's inner circle expected the Jews to rise against the Nazis, but the result was a victory for the most radical element in the SS, which wanted to annihilate them all, and a defeat to the more moderate element, which wanted to use some for labor and rejected the idea that the outright annihilation of all Jews be given top priority. Whether this "moderate" element really existed in the SS (according to Speer, it was centered around Oswald Pohl, the head of the Concentration and Death Camps System, who was also entrusted with Heinrich Himmler's economic ambitions and did spare some Jewish lives for this purpose) is a question beyond the scope of this book. However, according to Speer's testimony, Jews in Poland who were spared at the time of the Warsaw ghetto uprising as laborers in specific ghettos or camps were murdered afterward. Himmler ordered this operation in summer, fall, and winter 1943–1944, but the connection created by Speer between these killings and the Warsaw ghetto uprising may be misleading. In fact, the labor camps were under Speer's indirect control, but he was present at the meeting in which Himmler told his henchmen that it had been decided to liquidate these Jews as a part of Operation "Erntefest" of fall 1943, which probably followed the liquidation of the Treblinka death camp but not the Warsaw ghetto uprising almost half a year before. Himmler described this decision in terms acceptable to "comrade Speer."[2]

For the Yishuv in Palestine, the Warsaw ghetto uprising was a source of Jewish–Zionist pride since many among the ghetto fighters were Zionists.

[2] Source – Himmler's speech cited from his NA files, T-175, roll 85, frames 0152–0200, published in Bradley F. Smith and Agnes Peterson, *Heinrich Himmler: Geheimreden 1933 bis 1945* (Berlin: Propyläen Verlag 1974), p. 170. In this interview, Speer did acknowledge knowledge of the "Final Solution" as a sort of a "matter of course" in Hitler's court.

Yet the Yishuv leadership was also aware of some labor camps in Poland and of some ghettos that remained alive until "Erntefest" and afterward. Hence, the issue was not just to get ready to send them money, letters, and moral support from Palestine but to do it by using secret channels, which seemed available to the Zionists in Istanbul, Turkey. This proved to be the case when "Erntefest" silenced most of the centers of Jewish life remaining in Poland.

In fact, the "Rescue Committee" in Palestine and rescue workers sent by the Yishuv to Istanbul in 1943 did not pursue a simplistic, "heroic," Samson-like approach like the Warsaw ghetto uprising but undertook a variety of actions, including protests and pleas aimed at the Allies and fund raising to negotiate possible deals with the Germans when possible or to finance whatever activities the Zionists in occupied Europe might decide to pursue. The whole complex of activities undertaken by the Yishuv's leadership from 1943, and especially its meager effort to help the dying Jews of Europe to rise against the Nazis by training commandos and actually sending a few of them to occupied Europe, in cooperation with British Intelligence and the OSS, created a myth of armed resistance against the Nazis organized or at least very much enhanced by the Yishuv. This in fact was hardly the case since the efforts were local, resulting in no meaningful success but creating the myth, which proved to be badly necessary to transform the Yishuv into a fighting community after the war in order to meet the Arab challenge.

The Holocaust-related efforts were not linked together in reality. There was a "collaboration" with the Allies regarding intelligence, subversion, and resistance, which yielded some results that allowed token immigration. This was imperative because no activity related to occupied Europe was possible without British (and American) consent, knowledge, and support, a fact that by itself prohibited an open "rebellion" against the British by the official Yishuv.

Instead, the Yishuv's mainstream leadership fought IZL and the Sternists. But even the Yishuv's leadership efforts to steer resistance in Hungary, by sending a few commandos to Budapest thanks to cooperation with British MO9, assumed the image of a heroic effort that had been allegedly torpedoed by their own man on the spot, Rezsö Kasztner, and later covered up.

But what was the actual historical reality of the time? Who remained in early 1944 when a huge percentage of Jews were already dead? Mainly Jews in Rumania and Bulgaria, about 50,000 in Theresienstadt, those living in Western Europe who had not yet been deported or found some hiding place, and the large Hungarian Jewish community. The Hungarian Jews managed to stay alive in a pro-Nazi but politically independent country, which was invaded and occupied by the Germans in March 1944. In about six weeks, the preparations undertaken by the Germans and by the Hungarian authorities were completed, even if not necessarily initiated in many cases by the Germans but by the Hungarians, who compensated themselves for the German takeover on Jewish account:[3] Jews in the provinces outside of Budapest were compelled to carry the yellow star to identify them as Jews, isolated from the outside world, from the other ghettos, and from the capital, and then deported to Auschwitz.

[3] See in this regard Christian Gerlach, "The Ghettoization in Hungary, 1944, and the Jewish Response," paper delivered at the 25th German Studies Association Conference, Washington, DC, October 25, 2001, and see Christian Gerlach and Götz Aly, *Das Letzte Kapitel Der Mord an den ungarischen Juden* (Stuttgart and München: Deutsche Verlags-Anstalt, 2002).

PART III

THE SELF-DEFEATING MECHANISM
OF THE RESCUE EFFORTS

18

Istanbul, Geneva, and Jerusalem

Let us now discuss the rescue mission established by the Yishuv's leadership in Istanbul, Turkey, in spring 1943, in addition to and in cooperation with the regular representatives of the Jewish Agency under the most difficult conditions of Turkish neutrality and dependence upon the British, whose standing in Turkey was relatively higher than that of the Germans. Another rescue mission established itself in Geneva, and both were connected with each other, with rescue workers in the Balkan countries, and with the Zionist leadership in Palestine, as well as with non-Zionists abroad.

Dina Porat[1] gave us the names and the political affiliations of the twenty people who were involved in this effort between 1942 and 1945. Tuvia Friling expanded the scope of this research by looking in much detail at the differences between the Zionist representatives in Turkey and their composition and ties with the Jewish Agency's own inner and hybrid structure at home.[2] Friling's conclusion is that, under these circumstances, a small, secret system of decision-making was created within the Yishuv's leadership, comprised of David Ben-Gurion, Eliezer Kaplan (the Jewish Agency's "Minister of Finance"), and Moshe Shertok (the head of the Political Department). This small, compact group made decisions outside of the public Zionist bodies due to their diverse nature and British (plus American) surveillance of their activities. Thus, not much is available in terms of records that this inner group may have left behind. We shall find the traces of its activities – including a major rescue effort opened by Shertok in August 1943 when he visited Istanbul to start the campaign – in Nazi records. The tools of operation were the rescue emissaries working in Turkey and rescue operatives working in Budapest, Bucharest, and Switzerland. To learn about them, we have access to some of the mail they sent back home at the time or sent to the Jewish communities and Jewish leaders in occupied Europe. This mail

[1] Porat, *An Entangled Leadership*, pp. 219–221.
[2] See Friling, *Arrow in the Dark*, Volume I, especially pp. 369–377.

fell into either German or Allied hands. There are also some of the Zionists' own records.[3]

Turning to the Allied records, we realize that the arrival of Teddy Kollek, the future mayor of Jerusalem, whose task was to combine rescue work with intelligence work for the Allies, in Istanbul in summer 1943 generated suspicion.

A certain "Mr. Kowlik," representing the "Jewish Relief Agency" in Istanbul (i.e., Kollek) was mentioned on October 27, 1943, as having met "Cereus" – Archibald J. Coleman (an operative of the Secret Intelligence section of OSS Istanbul). OSS Istanbul was supposed to be cautious due to a "wire from London no. 00321 dated September 23, in which they caution us regarding the Jewish groups because of the fact that their intelligence can be colored by political motives." In spite of the expectations that "there is something to be gained by cooperation, I think we have to be quite careful of dealings with them because of (our) close relations with the British."[4] The cooperation between Kollek and the OSS and British SIS developed in the meantime to information gathered by Allied intelligence from Jewish refugees who reached Allied territories and were allowed to continue to Palestine and from contacts still existent between the Zionists and their colleagues in the Balkan countries.[5] Yet out of this emerged perhaps one of the most tragic trap cases. One key to this tragedy was Alfred Schwarz, a Jewish businessman of Czech origin turned American agent, who had created a chain known as the "Dogwood" network, believing that he had a mandate to topple Hitler, shorten the war, save Europe from the advancing Soviets, and stop the Final Solution. This "grand design" may have had its perfect logic in Kollek's eyes, and in the eyes of his superiors in Jerusalem, but Allied logic proved to be different, so we must leave its story aside until it reached its tragic climax later in 1944.

---

[3] See, for example, RG 226, Entry 120, box 31–7, file TC 319.1, Origin: Cairo, Subject: Jewish fighting Force for Europe, Date: September 16, 1944, Sender: Captain Habeeb, Theater Censor, secret, contains list of cables from and to Shertok regarding "Jewish Partisan Groups for the Balkans," difficulties with the (British) authorities. See also files of SS Hauptsturmführer Gustav Richter and discussion of their transfer to OSS in August 1944 and other examples cited.

[4] RG 226, Entry 148, box 33 – Holland SI, Istanbul O.S.S-AD-1, O.S.S-INT-1, O.S.S-OP-1.

[5] Among other things, Kollek was able to contact Bucharest by phone and obtain daily weather reports as guidance for Allied plans or obtain information on bombing results and names of captured Allied fliers, see Barry Rubin, *Istanbul Intrigues: A True Life Casablanca* (New York: McGraw-Hill, 1989), pp. 212–213, regarding Zionist efforts to convince the Allies that Jewish refugees could be of intelligence value. Regarding a later period, see, for example, RG 226, L 42777, July 28, 1944, most secret (indicating British source) on conditions in Hungary, rescue efforts undertaken by various Jewish–Hungarian groups into Rumania, including Jewish hideouts in the Carpathians, in Yugoslavia, on Jews and Marshal Tito, on communist sabotage acts, and on the circumstances of the Jews' escape.

The Kollek group was a secretive cell within the Yishuv's mission in Istanbul. The mission was a colorful group of individuals, working for various organizations, who cultivated rather independent opinions about their duties, so close to the dying Jews of Europe.[6] They also discussed their problems with a variety of leaders in Palestine, which was typical of the Yishuv's political structure, in which the same people, such as David Ben-Gurion, nominally governed the Mapai Party, the kibbutz movement, the Histradrut, and the Jewish Agency. Ben-Gurion, however, had no complete control over his own party in the voluntary Jewish community and much less control over the kibbutzim, and he cooperated with growing friction especially with those on his Left, who emphasized their kibbutz affiliation or the Histradrut rather than the Jewish Agency, the supreme world Zionist body.

In Geneva, an isolated outpost in the midst of occupied Europe, conditions similar to but more unfriendly than those in Istanbul, and rather tense internally,[7] governed the relations between representatives of the World Jewish Congress, the Jewish Agency, private Jewish rescue bodies, and one of the Zionist–Socialist organs, which happened to be represented alone in this crucial outpost by Nathan Schwalb.[8]

The picture that emerges from Schwalb's early letters[9] in 1941 through the peak of the Holocaust in Poland in 1943 is that of a continued effort in terms of the previous Zionist work: training of young Jewish pioneers even under Nazi domination in order to keep the pioneers alive and continue their training by means of sending money, political news, and cultural material by couriers and then by means of helping them to find refuge in less endangered countries such as Slovakia, Hungary, and Rumania, by obtaining British immigration certificates to Palestine, which was the primary Zionist goal, or by obtaining foreign passports.[10] All of this and more, such as armed resistance in Poland as planned and in fact carried out in the ghettos of Warsaw

---

[6] See in this regard letters by Venia Pomerniz (i.e., Pomeranz, beginning in February 1943) and letters signed "Menachem" (Bader), Venia (Pomeranz), and Ze'ev (Shind) in the Hagana Archive, including a list of letters from "Moladti," the code name of the Labor Group in Istanbul, in the same file plus explanation in the following Hagana Archive holdings: "Moladti" files – repositories 14/61, 14/798, 14/153א, 80/187f/32. These files contain correspondence between rescue workers abroad and the corresponding bodies and leaders at home. "Moladti" means "my homeland" in Hebrew.

[7] See Yehuda Bauer, *American Jewry and the Holocaust: A History of the American Jewish Joint Distribution Committee, 1939–1945* (Detroit: Wayne State University Press, 1981), pp. 390–393, and see Richter's Gestapo sources.

[8] Schwalb kept his wartime records to himself for many years or prevented access to them otherwise at the Lavon Institute of the Histadrut in Tel-Aviv. Interviewed by Shabtai Teveth for the latter's *Ben-Gurion and the Holocaust* in 1995, he somewhat modified the statements he had given to me but still argued that more money could have saved about 200,000 more victims.

[9] AZ S/6/2801.

[10] Ibid., letter of July 2, 1943.

and elsewhere in 1943, required much more money than Schwalb was receiving from the start, as he believed and argued at that time and later. Operating almost alone in wartime Geneva as the representative of the Zionist youth movements, he ran into bureaucratic difficulties at home, and the money he received at last was a subject of permanent strife between the Zionist groups fighting to get their meager share of the cash appropriated by a variety of reluctant non-Zionist organizations at first, such as the AJDC, operating within the limits of Allied economic warfare.

Orthodox peculiarities, such as taking care of the learned and the rabbis first and the separation of men and women, continued even in those temporary havens such as independent Hungary in which they and nonbelievers found refuge with or without Schwalb's help or with the help of non-Zionist organizations in Switzerland.[11]

Schwalb was sure, however, that his Swiss-based operation and contacts with the Jewish organizations in the German-allied nations such as Slovakia, Hungary, and Rumania that served as liaison channels to the occupied territories were completely safe, as he used to write back home. He was wrong, to a degree, which exposed much, if not most, of his, the Zionists', and the general Jewish secret rescue operation conducted from Geneva and Istanbul to the Gestapo and SD as early as 1941. The source of our information in this regard is the German Legation archive in Bucharest.

The story of the German Legation archive captured intact in Bucharest is by itself a historiographic tale that should be told. When Rumania switched sides and joined the Allies in August 1944, the new Rumanian regime took over the German Legation building. Shortly afterward, an OSS mission was sent to Rumania, which had tried to develop ties with the West when facing the victorious Red Army but finally succumbed to Soviet control. In the interim phase, the OSS mission was able at least to receive copies or the original documents taken from the German Legation archive. Its head was Frank G. Wisner, a New York lawyer and reserve U.S. Navy Lieutenant Commander, who several months before had run the OSS station in Istanbul and had previously served in the OSS Middle East center in Cairo.

Wisner was given access to the German Legation records by the Rumanians, who might have kept the originals of the same records of the Nazi attaché in charge of Jewish affairs, SS Captain Gustav Richter.[12] Wisner was rather uneasy about the Richter documentation. He believed that some of Richter's material, including Richter's own reports and those of Gestapo

---

[11] Ibid.

[12] If they did, this may explain how Jewish organizations abroad and Dr. Chaim Posner, a Zionist representative in Switzerland, obtained several of Richter's files, which were then used by the Israeli historian of the Rumanian Holocaust Dr. Jean Ancel (Ancel's testimony to the writer), and thus they or some of them reached "Yad-Vashem," the Israeli Holocaust Memorial Authority, independently.

agents to him, forwarded by Richter to Adolf Eichmann personally at his Jewish Referat in Berlin, were "sensitive" in the sense that they seemed to reveal internal Jewish problems and illegal money transfers by Jewish organizations abroad to Nazi-controlled territory.[13]

The Gestapo files contained the names of almost all of the Zionist and non-Zionist personalities involved, such as those of Richard Lichtheim, the Zionist office director in Switzerland, Dr. A. Silberschein, the representative of the World Jewish Congress in Switzerland (in addition to Gerhart Riegner), Saly Mayer, the Swiss resident representative of the non-Zionist American Joint Distribution Committee (AJDC), of whom we shall hear more, and that of Nathan Schwalb, of course. The names of these people are properly spelled because of authentic letters bearing their signature and intercepted by the Gestapo, i.e., by Gustav Richter, in his capacity as the Judenberater, or "adviser on Jewish Affairs" in Rumania. This was the official title of Gestapo officers in charge of the Final Solution in those German-allied nations that retained a degree of autonomy from the Nazis and whose governments had to be handled with some care. SS Captain Richter, the Judenberater in Bucharest, reported directly to Adolf Eichmann's Jewish section of the SS Reich's Security Main Office.

Other names were sometimes misspelled, such as the names of Chaim Barlas, the Jewish Agency immigration officer in Istanbul, who was promoted to "Dr. Charles Barlas," and that of Venia Pomeranz, the rescue operative on behalf of Hakibbutz Hameuchad, the leftist branch of the kibbutz movement, whose name was misspelled "Pomerianz." The reason for the errors could be oral reports given to the Gestapo by double agents. The names of most Zionist Hungarian rescue workers at the time were correct and known to the Gestapo, such as those of Samu Springmann and "Jenoe" Brand, as well as the names of the Rumanian non-Zionist and Zionist activists. The role that was played in saving the Rumanian Jewry itself by the former president of the Rumanian Jewish communities, Dr. Wilhelm Fildermann, an established major figure even after his replacement by a submissive "Judenrat-like" body, becomes clear thanks to this documentation. His role was of course of utmost interest to the Gestapo representative Richter, as Fildermann was blocking his Final Solution mission by finding support within the Rumanian Court and government system itself. Zionist activists who tried to get the Jews out of Rumania were also of great interest to SS Captain Richter, and he knew a great deal about them. They included A. L. Zisu, Misu Benvenisti, Shmuel Enzer, and David Tannenbaum, a young Zionist activist

---

[13] See RG 226, Entry 88, box 495, Wash-Commo-R+C-381–382, London–Bern–Ankara–Istanbul; the box also contains documents from OSS substations Izmir, Sofia, Bucharest, and Jerusalem. For the current location of the Richter records, see *Holocaust-Era Assets*, compiled by Greg Bradsher (College Park, MD: United States National Archives and Records Administration 1999), pp. 217–218.

and now Professor Emeritus David Tene of Hebrew University. The Gestapo records also contain items concerning "Judenschmuggel": photostatted lists and intercepted letters to Dr. Silberschein in Geneva, Schwalb's colleague in this respect, concerning the smuggling of Jews from Poland (mainly from Lvov (Lemberg)) into Rumania.[14]

Schwalb's name was in fact contained in a batch of twenty-one files dating back to 1941 and covering 1942–1944 in which other rescue workers such as Samu Springmann in Budapest were prominent. "Information Reports on the Jewish Question," issued by the RSHA itself in Berlin and pertaining to international Jewish organizations and mainly to the Zionists, which were captured in Richter's Bucharest archives, might have been at least partially drawn by the Nazi authorities from the dedicated informative activity of Schwalb and other rescue workers in Istanbul, including a detailed report on the "Baltimore [sic] Program of the 'Emergency Committee for Zionist Affairs' in New York, headed by Weizmann, Wise, Ben-Gurion, and others."[15]

Further, individual letters sent by Schwalb to rescue workers in Rumania in December 1943, and notations of a correspondence between Schwalb and "Menachem" at that time, were at the Gestapo's disposal. Menachem Mendel Bader was a key rescue person in Istanbul, and later we shall briefly discuss his future role in the Hungarian Holocaust.

Schwalb was not the only one under Gestapo surveillance, however. Saly Mayer, the AJDC Swiss representative, closely associated with Schwalb and with the rescue and relief work financed by the AJDC, had been known to the Gestapo as "Franz Keller."[16]

Istanbul, too, supplied the Gestapo with information such as "Correspondence concerning the activities of the 'Jewish Agency' in Palestine, headed by Mosche Schertok [sic], includes a 7-page summons given in Istanbul, late August 1943, on the rescue of the European Jews, 1942–1943." This was the exact date of Shertok's visit to Turkey and his drive to pursue rescue also by means of dealing with the Germans, intelligence gathering, and resistance by using the channels that seemed to have been opened to occupied Europe.[17]

An issue by itself is the breaking of Allied codes by the Germans, especially the American diplomatic cable traffic to and from Switzerland and other countries, which was partially used for reports on the Holocaust and pertained to rescue efforts as well. This matter requires separate research that goes beyond the scope of this chapter. Some of this was done by the Oberkommando der Wehrmacht's (OKW) Chifrierabteilung and some by the code breakers in the German Foreign Office. More could have been done by the so-called "Göring Bureau" in charge of listening to and wiretapping

---

[14] RG 242/1010, NA Microcopy T-175, DGesBukarest XL 13172, roll 660, frames 85–302.

[15] Ibid., roll 657, frames 55–193.

[16] Ibid., roll 657, frames 622–780.

[17] Ibid., roll 660, frames 762–1183.

the phone networks under German control when we consider that although we have no clear picture of the distribution system, the decrypts, and the information gathered by Ribbentrop's and Göring's services, we can assume that copies may have been made available by them to the various SS outfits, including the Gestapo and SD.[18]

Not only did the Germans know about Schwalb but the Allies also, especially the British, thanks to wartime censorship that they later shared with the Americans in a "Joint Censorship Collection Agency" stationed in Bermuda. The Allies controlled and sometimes intercepted by other means Schwalb's and other Yishuv emissaries' letters and cables back home and interpreted them their way in reports such as the following:[19]

A good deal of evidence concerning the activities of the Jewish Underground [meaning the Zionist youth movements and their mother parties in Palestine – S.A.] has come from Poland and Central Europe. Many volunteers are sent by the various Zionist groups in Palestine, who it is said perform the most amazing feats of aspiring away deportees, obtaining faked documents... and even penetrating into the concentration and death camps to aid inmates to escape. ("Report on Jewry," July 5, 1944)

On top of these myths, which circulated at that time in the Yishuv and inflated their rescue effort, this report did reflect some of Schwalb's real efforts by quoting reports on the activities of the Zionist youth movements that he represented in Switzerland: "The Hechalutz Halohem (The Fighting Pioneer) operated in Western Galicia (Poland) and was at one time affiliated to the Polish Workers Party (P.P.R.). This was not however a success. . . . The Hechalutz published a newspaper which gave details of [Jewish – S.A.] traitors, and of successful acts of sabotage of their organization."[20]

Acts of resistance by Zionist groups were indeed widely publicized in the Yishuv thanks to Schwalb. He also spoke for Ichud, the umbrella organization of Labor Zionists abroad, and according to the British censorship intercepts, based very probably on his own reports that they intercepted and summarized in their "Report on Jewry":[21]

They use 'grapevine' system of communicating with their branches in these countries. This movement... maintains departments of relief for those of their members who are interned or doing forced labour. Their main object, however, as opposed to the active participation in partisan activities... is to keep the Zionist idea alive and to prepare themselves as thoroughly as may be to eventual emigration to Palestine.

---

[18] We have at our disposal only several testimonies given in this regard by Walter Schellenberg, the head of the SD's Foreign Intelligence office after the war. See Schellenberg's interrogation reports by U.S. Intelligence: RG 226, Entry 125, box 2, folder 21, copy to OSS Stockholm from SAINT, London, original to SAINT, Washington.

[19] See, for example, "Report on Jewry" of July 5, 1944, originated in London.

[20] Censorship intercepts.

[21] Ibid; see Chapter 12, note 11.

In essence, although both resistance against the Nazis and preparation for emigration to Palestine could combine with each other, the report fits well with Schwalb's activities, and indeed the report originated in Palestine itself and could have also been drawn at least partially from official Zionist publications. At the same time, the real personal and partisan relationships between Schwalb and Dr. Silberschein, between the latter and Richard Lichtheim, a veteran Zionist leader based in Geneva, and between Schwalb in Geneva and Pomeranz in Istanbul were, as Dina Porat tells us, extremely bad. They were not able to cooperate with each other within one streamlined rescue operation in spite of the Jewish Agency's repeated plea for them to get organized properly.[22] What Rezsö Kasztner was trying to do in Budapest – create at least one working rescue operation under the control of Mapai and himself – never materialized in Geneva.

As far as rescue worker Venia Pomeranz, stationed in Istanbul from 1943, is concerned, we have the record of his and his colleagues' talks in Istanbul with several couriers who were supposed to deliver Zionist mail to Jewish addressees in occupied Europe because these "couriers," several of whom were Gestapo agents, reported to the Gestapo representative in Bucharest in charge of Jewish affairs, the above-mentioned SS Hauptsturmführer (captain) Gustav Richter, who in turn reported them to his boss, Adolf Eichmann, in Berlin. Such Gestapo agents, most of them Swiss subjects, betrayed in a similar way Zionist and non-Zionist rescue workers and representatives of Jewish charity organizations in Switzerland, who were in touch with the Jewish Agency's executives in Palestine and with Jewish operatives in the United States, and then betrayed their Jewish interlocutors in Bucharest and Sofia and reported about their colleagues in Budapest.

One can safely argue that the Gestapo knew enough about the rescue organizations and activities undertaken from Istanbul, Geneva, Bucharest, Budapest, Jerusalem, and New York as early as 1943 (i.e., upon the inception of the rescue efforts). But the Nazis failed to stop them not because the SS was really interested in them or willing to extend to them some kind of a deal, as some interested survivors believe and historians may argue today. The Gestapo simply had no direct control in Hungary until March 1944 and in Bulgaria and Rumania – both unoccupied allies – to the end of the war. This is to be understood in the context first of the changing policies of the Rumanian and Bulgarian governments plus the wisdom and influence of Rumanian Jewish leaders such as Dr. Wilhelm Fildermann, whose activities were reported to the Gestapo representative in exact detail by local agents, and the above-mentioned "couriers" who helped save the lives of the bulk of Rumanian Jewry. Their own governments in fact protected the Jews of Rumania and Bulgaria, provided that Hitler did not occupy their countries, as he would do in the case of Hungary.

---

[22] Porat, *An Entangled Leadership*, pp. 216–217.

In any case, the Gestapo informer net was open wide and deep, and in this sense Istanbul and Geneva supplied them with the information necessary to prevent large-scale rescue rather than enhance it.

In April 1943, rescue operative Venia Pomeranz, just arrived, met in Istanbul with a Swiss subject, Karl Gyr, officially described as the representative of the Swiss Press Agency in Bucharest, who acted as a liaison between Jewish leaders in Bulgaria and Rumania and the Zionist rescue workers in the neutral countries.[23] Pomeranz treated this man, who in fact reported the contents of his various meetings with the Zionist rescue workers immediately to Gestapo representative Richter in Bucharest, with complete confidence, whether because he was pretty inexperienced in the underworld of intrigue in which he found himself in Istanbul or in accordance with his belief, as conveyed to the present writer, that the "Germans and the Hungarians and the Rumanians should have been oiled with all the money in the world, and everything should have been done in their full knowledge." That is to say, "we, the rescue workers, meant to tell the Germans that we aimed at dealing with them." The trouble was that Pomeranz himself was not sure about German intentions and was rather skeptical at that time, though not later, about the Slovak "Europa Plan," which seemed to offer major rescue options[24] and will be discussed in chapter 19. On the other hand, Pomeranz could not know what the Allies would think about his ties with the enemy or rather believed that his holy mission should have been appreciated – or at least tolerated – by them.

Gestapo agent Gyr also met Chaim Barlas, the Jewish Agency's immigration officer in Turkey.[25] Barlas was pretty cautious but not free of his own illusions. He wanted to know whether the Rumanians were serious about protecting their Jews and wanted to use Rumanian dictator Antonescu's groping toward the Western Allies, as he put it, to save Jews. Barlas wanted to visit Rumania and showed Gyr documents to the effect that he had British certificates of immigration for 4,500 children and 500 adults from that country (which fell within the unused White Paper quotas). Even the Germans knew that Barlas was a British subject and an immigration specialist, and therefore they "had nothing against him." Barlas argued that the Germans, too, wanted to have the Jews leave their sphere of interest. He further maintained that more certificates could be obtained for immigrants from Rumania and other Balkan nations. By this he meant the rescue of children from Nazi-dominated Europe – a plan endorsed by the Jewish Agency. Barlas hoped to get British permission for child immigration beyond the White Paper's

---

[23] OSS RG 226, entry 154, box 26, folder 374.

[24] See Dina Porat, *The Blue and the Yellow Star of David* (Cambridge, MA: Harvard University Press, 1990), p. 181 (English version).

[25] See Haim Barlas, *Rescue during the Holocaust* (Kibbutz Lohamei-Hagetaot: Lohamei-Hagetaot Publishing House, 1975) (in Hebrew). Nothing is said therein about Gyr.

quota, children being acceptable to the British because adults could be enemy agents and spies. Barlas further stressed yet another scheme adopted before by the Jewish Agency, the rescue of Jews who had already been deported to Transnistria, the German–Rumanian occupied territory in the Soviet Union. He distinguished between the Rumanians and the Germans, presupposing that the Germans would not let the Jews go but "maybe, he said, they would be practical after all and maybe benefit from it after the war." In other words, Barlas did not exclude the possibility that Gyr was an enemy agent and that his overtures about the Germans "being practical" in saving Jews would reach Nazi authorities, which they did. He was trying to argue that even Nazi Germany should be interested in helping these "innocent people" to survive in order to "make clear that they could be humane after all and use it after the war."[26]

How could Barlas believe that the Nazis would spare the Jews of Transnistria, or any other community within their reach, while the Jews of Poland and the rest of Europe were at the same time in the process of being wiped out? As noted earlier, at this stage some ghettos and labor camps in Poland survived, waiting for their turn to be eradicated late in 1943 and during 1944. Barlas thus hoped for a German interest in sparing Jewish lives at this stage of the war (e.g., after El Alamein and Stalingrad). Yet this may have meant a trade-off of Jews at Allied expense or just Jewish "flood" into Allied spheres of interest.[27]

In fact, the amateur rescue workers sent from Palestine to Istanbul in 1943 were soon embroiled in the underworld of espionage, intelligence trade, contraband, and rumor mongering typical of a wartime neutral center such as Istanbul.[28] They knew that they were under surveillance by the Turkish Secret Service Emniet[29] in their homes. They figured that some of their mail to the Jewish ghettos in Poland and centers in Hungary, Rumania, and probably Bulgaria, too, the three unoccupied Nazi allies, must have been read by the Abwehr and Gestapo, according to the testimony of Venia Pomeranz, the Kibbutz Hameuchad rescue worker in Istanbul, to the present writer, adding that this did not bother him. "We were trying to save Jews, and we were transferring money to aid and save them. We were ready to deal with the Germans, and our letters indicated such readiness."

---

[26] Richter documents, RG 226, Entry 154, box 26, folder 374.

[27] See British Foreign Office to the State Department, Memorandum of January 20, 1943, Source: CZA, S25/7570. The internal British deliberations are described by Bernard Wasserstein, and by Martin Gilbert in his book *Auschwitz and the Allies: A Devastating Account of how the Allies Responded to the News of Hitler's Mass Murder* (New York: Holt, Rinehart, and Winston, 1981), and hence I have refrained from repeating them here in any detail.

[28] See Rubin, *Istanbul Intrigues*, pp. 49–62.

[29] Venia Hadari-Pomeranz's testimony to the author.

According to the same testimony, which in this regard is also documented,[30] Pomeranz – later Professor Hadari, a nuclear physicist – returned to Palestine from Istanbul several times in 1943–1944 to discuss rescue plans; he wrote regularly to the Histadrut bodies and met personally with Ben-Gurion, Katzenelson, and others to make them do more for rescue. His main demand was much more money, and Ben-Gurion's answer in one crucial case was – according to Pomeranz – "it's placing money on a deer's horn."

In fact, the Jewish Agency appropriated more and more funds for rescue from 1943 onward, as Porat has shown,[31] and Friling explains how and why.[32] As documented in Pomeranz's own letters quoted earlier the amount was more than the other much wealthier Jewish communities in the free world provided but not enough in Hadari–Pomeranz's view and in the view of his Geneva colleague Schwalb.[33]

More money might have made quite a difference, both continued to argue years later (Professor Hadari–Pomeranz passed away late in 2001). Pomeranz seemed not to be that sure, when interviewed, whether the missing funds would have rescued many more Jews, in contradiction to his stated firm belief in print about that, arguing that the chief SS henchman himself, Heinrich Himmler, already acknowledged Germany's defeat in 1943 and was ready to deal after that.[34] But Pomeranz kept insisting that at least a major drive should have been launched in the United States once the means at the disposal of the Yishuv were exhausted, and more efforts should have been invested, even in vain. He had already adopted this moral–political line in his letters at that time, with due skepticism, and changed almost 50 years later when he adopted the view that the SS was in fact ready to deal and that bribes indeed saved Slovak Jews, at least for a while.

---

[30] Several of Pomeranz's letters, and letters mailed by other members of the Istanbul rescue mission or by the Geneva rescue operatives, were diverted at first to the Gestapo by Swiss couriers, copied, and their content reported to the Gestapo headquarters in Berlin. Only then were the originals delivered to their Jewish recipients in Bucharest or Budapest. See Richter documentation.

[31] Porat, *The Blue and the Yellow Star of David*, pp. 117–189.

[32] Friling, "David Ben Gurion and the Catastrophe of European Jewry," pp. 131–182.

[33] Interview with the author, 1985.

[34] See Zeev Venia Hadari, *Against All Odds: Istanbul 1942–1945* (Tel-Aviv: Ministry of Defense, 1992), especially pp. 134–135 (This work is Hadari's memoir.)

19

How the Holocaust in Slovakia Was Suspended

The "Europa Plan"

We have here several issues: Was the Slovak "deal" a deal at all? Who initi-ated it? The Germans? Jews? Were bribes offered by the Jews effective then and later? This was the political and practical side of the matter, whose answer is to be sought in German documentation, when possible, because whether the Jewish side had initiated the bribes or not, the success of such deals depended on the German side and on their autonomous allies. The moral and political issue, however, seems to be detached from the practical one. One should have paid the Germans; even for nothing, if this would have finally proved to be the result, as long as one was not entirely sure about it, and even for the sake of rescuing one's image or reputation in the eyes of future generations. Yet "not finally sure" may be an indefinite, self-defeating procedure in which the other side may always be given the opportunity to maintain that your side could have done more, a strategy adopted by Eichmann himself regarding his alleged Hungarian ransom of-fer, to be discussed as the "Gestapo Deal," in his trial in Jerusalem. Thus, he sought to transform the victim and third parties, who were supposed to deliver the goods, into collaborators in the victim's own doom. But for what actual purpose? Eichmann certainly did not prepare for his trial in Jerusalem in the early 1940s during the Hungarian Holocaust, and hence other rea-sons for his apparent willingness to negotiate the Gestapo Deal must be explored such as propaganda gains and political goals aimed at splitting the Allies.

Ransoming was a matter of priorities, too. It was a very practical issue for the small Zionist community in Palestine and not a moral issue alone; nor could one forget the Yishuv leadership's current responsibilities and fu-ture demands for the sake of much more remote reputation debates (which might or might not take place when a Jewish state might be born and absorb those who might survive the current disaster) if the money were wasted. In fact, Ben-Gurion was at first more taken by the practical considerations, which accompanied his view that the Nazis crossed the Rubicon; money was not the issue for them. Yet at the same time he had his hopes, recognized the moral and political aspect of the disaster, and endorsed the raising and appropriation of more funds in Palestine itself as well as abroad (but never enough from the point of view of the rescue operatives in Istanbul and Geneva),[1] swallowing his initial doubts about their actual effectiveness. The Allies' response to such deals that might have given the Germans foreign exchange needed to buy war material abroad must be examined in due course.

Pomeranz's colleague in Geneva, Nathan Schwalb, sounds today even more definite: "If we had had more money, we could have rescued more Jews, in direct proportion. The Nazi system was not that uniform. There were different people out there, and some of them could have been bribed. Some needed an alibi, and some were simply corrupt. Money was the problem."[2] Even during the war, Schwalb had argued that even Polish Jews, whose fate was in the hands of a separate, local SS killing machine not directly under the control of Eichmann and his deputies, such as Dieter Wisliceny's alleged control in Slovakia, could have been saved if more money had been available. This was possibly due to Wisliceny's own assurances that Eichmann had taken charge over the fate of the remaining Jews in Poland as well and due to Eichmann's own apparent willingness to exchange 1,000 Jewish children from Byalistok, who indeed were transferred to a special ghetto in Theresienstadt.[3] But soon enough these children were deported to Auschwitz and killed there. The story behind this episode is told by historian Sara Bender based on the relevant German records.[4] Accordingly, the British Government had approached its German counterpart through Swiss mediation and asked for the release of 5,000 Jewish children from occupied Poland and their emigration into Palestine in July 1943, as well as the release of Jewish children from German-occupied territories in Western Europe. The German response, as discussed between SS Chief Himmler and Foreign Minister Ribbentrop, seemed to be positive, provided that the children would be exchanged with German POWs. They would not be admitted into Arab Palestine but into Great Britain, provided that such an exchange were authorized by the British House of Commons. The German side had informed the former Mufti of Jerusalem of the expected deal, about which they had very few hopes, but for the time being they did exempt about 1,000 Bialistok children from the "Final Solution." Adolf Eichmann, in charge of their transportation either to Auschwitz or elsewhere, had them sent to the ghetto of Theresienstadt until a further decision on their fate could be made. The decision soon was

---

[1] See Friling, "David Ben Gurion and the Catastrophe of European Jewry."
[2] Interview with author.
[3] See Bauer, *Jews for Sale?*, pp. 88–89.
[4] See Sara Bender, *Facing Death: The Jews in Byalistok, 1939–1943* (Tel Aviv: Am-Oved, 1997), pp. 285–289. In Hebrew.

made to kill them all upon the Mufti's insistence. This sad story incorporates in it various aspects of the multiple trap: German hopes to use a few Jews in order to make the British side officially endorse their release into Britain by a public act, and thus taint itself as a Jewish tool, apparent British refusal to go ahead with this game, German benefits in terms of the release of POWs, and finally intervention of the Mufti, who did not trust either side and feared that the children would finally arrive in Palestine.

As far as Slovakia, over which the Germans had no direct control, was concerned, the situation was different and seemed to have allowed Jewish rescue activities with Eichmann's man in Bratislava as their target. According to the available German, Jewish, and Zionist documentation and testimonies, Wisliceny was approached in fall 1942 by a Jewish person representing Rabbi Michael Weissmandel, the Slovak rescue operative, who pretended to speak for the AJDC's Swiss representative. Wisliceny promised to no-longer pursue personally the deportations from Slovakia. The first bribe, of about $20,000 (U.S.), might have been paid at that time. Shortly afterward, in October 1942, the same middleman paid Wisliceny $20,000 (U.S.), about which the latter informed Eichmann and wrote a report for SS Chief Himmler. Since around that date the deportations indeed stopped, the Slovak Rescue Committee linked both separate actions together. Himmler ordered Wisliceny via Eichmann to stay in touch with the Slovak rescue workers, who then approached him directly, asking him to convey the principles of the "Europa Plan" to his superiors: cessation of the Final Solution altogether in exchange for several million dollars to be raised by world Jewry.

Wisliceny might have known about the rescue efforts circulating around him from Jewish and specific Zionist letters and cables intercepted by German intelligence. Eichmann knew even more thanks to the intercepts of the Gestapo/SD, while the Jewish side did not know that the Nazis knew its plans in such detail. According to Wisliceny's own postwar testimony, he never received any answers from Himmler in response to the ideas contained in the Europa Plan. He was allowed to gather information about the Jews but promise nothing in exchange until September 1943, when he was explicitly ordered to stop the "negotiations."[5]

Hitler himself had authorized ransoming of "rich Jews" in exchange for "large sums of foreign currency" at the end of 1942. Hence, the offer made by the Bratislava Rescue Committee to Wisliceny, following their irrelevant bid to stop the deportations from Slovakia, to ransom other Jews could have fallen into that category at best.

It could be speculated that Himmler saw in such exchange deals an opening toward negotiations with the West on a separate peace, capitalizing on

---

[5] For details, see Bauer, *Jews for Sale?*, pp. 62–101, and see Wisliceny's Nuremberg testimony in Volume 12 of John Mendelsohn's *The "Final Solution" in the Extermination Camps and the Aftermath* (New York and London: Garland Publishers Inc., 1982) (no page numbering).

Hitler's limited permission to exchange a few Jews for much money. The requested sum was thus an opening for much more in terms of the very connection thereby created between Himmler and the West using Jews for his genuine political purpose, separate peace, following El Alamein and mainly due to the German defeat at Stalingrad, as argued by several parties involved such as Pomeranz in his postwar memoir and by some scholars ex post facto. One may further argue that Himmler recoiled when Hitler proved to be as adamant as ever in regard to the Final Solution whenever possible. Yet the connection to Stalingrad is refuted by German hopes for major victories in the East in summer 1943. One could add to this Nazi fears later on that the home front might yield to Allied pressure from all sides, and hence the Final Solution, which was carried out with fury (except in Slovakia) all over during the Europa Plan negotiations, became an open secret inside Germany, possibly in order to galvanize German resistance to the Allied threat and meet German expectations for some revenge. In accordance with the extreme anti-Semitic propaganda beamed at the West in 1943, admitting the Final Solution openly as justified in response to the alleged "Jew's war" waged against Germany, Himmler might have toyed with the Europa Plan negotiations as a tool to make Allied peoples believe that Jews enjoyed preferential treatment at Allied hands while non-Jewish combatants were fighting the alleged "Jew's war." In fact, no real exchange deals of significance took place. Another reason not to accept the Europa Plan concept seriously, in spite of the talks between Wisliceny and the Rescue Committee, was Wisliceny's relatively low rank and complete subordination to Eichmann, having no direct contact with Himmler. On the face of it, Wisliceny seems to have become personally interested in some deal early in 1943 and might have pocketed some of the money paid. In fact, Wisliceny's involvement in the plan and his bid to save Jews in the final stages of the war, when Eichmann's apparatus practically fell apart, were honored by some rescue workers with due reservations, in comparison to Rabbi Weissmandel's complete faith in him and in the scheme as a whole, which made him accuse the mainstream Jewish and Zionist leadership abroad of criminal negligence in this regard.[6]

Pomeranz in Istanbul, Schwalb in Geneva, and several members of a Zionist "Rescue Committee" in Budapest, among them Joel Brand and Rezso Kasztner, came to share a similar concept, or at least adopted for various reasons a similar hope, that a deal (or several separate deals) with the Germans was possible. Such deals depended on outside funding or on the delivery of Allied goods. Once Wisliceny appeared in occupied Budapest with a letter of

[6] In fact, Weissmandel made such accusations in letters to Schwalb during his 1943 negotiations. A manuscript repeating them entitled *Under Duress* (New York: Emuna Publishers, 1960) was not published by Weissmandel but others published it posthumously, and it has since been used by ultra-orthodox circles to incriminate the Zionists for actual rescue failures.

recommendation from Rabbi Weissmandel in Bratislava and was approached by the Hungarian Rescue Committee to renew negotiations he had broken off in August 1943, telling his Slovak counterparts that he might renew them in the future,[7] these rescue advocates sincerely believed or at least argued that such deals should be pursued. Thus, the ensuing Gestapo Deal concerning the ransoming of the Hungarian Jewry might have been born first in their minds, then returned to them by the Germans as a "real" possibility, and then suggested as such to the suspicious Allies, who, in turn, would look into the matter and finally turn down the suggested "deal."

On the face of it, there was evidence to the effect that bribing the SS did work, at least in the cessation of the deportations from Slovakia in 1942, a fact believed to have been the result of a bribe "deal" with Wisliceny. Out of this grew the so-called Europa Plan, which was supposed to exclude the rest of the Jews of "Europe" from the gas chambers in exchange for money offered to Wisliceny by Slovak Jewish leaders.

The so-called "rescue debate" seemed to have found here a solid ground. This was especially true when Rabbi Weissmandel's view of its chances, Wisliceny's alleged serious intentions, and Wisliceny's superiors' alleged willingness to negotiate (if the Slovak Rescue Committee at least had something serious to show in terms of money) were shared by other rescue workers, even if with less bitterness and crusade-like emotions. Some kept repeating that a chance was missed and that rescue in general could have been enhanced if more money had been appropriated by the "conventional" Jewish leadership. In fact, the Zionist leadership and AJDC representatives in Europe invested much thought and energy in regard to the Plan, and in spite of their grave doubts about its origins and purposes, they invested in it the requested advances (although not at the speed believed necessary by the Bratislava Rescue Committee).[8] The Plan and its collapse became a combined religious and emotional case personally for Weissmandel, whose accusations were posthumously published by ultraorthodox leaders in order to explain the Holocaust their way – as a result of the secularization process among Jews, which led on the one hand to the catastrophe of the European Jews as divine punishment and on the other to the alleged betrayal of Jews at the hands of secular Jews.

All of the rescue workers in Istanbul and Geneva were aware of the cessation of the deportations from Slovakia, which indeed took place late in 1942, but they had no idea why they were stopped. In fact, they were stopped, according to the German sources at our disposal, due to Slovak decisions made by the Slovak government against explicit German wishes. Hence, bribes paid to Wisliceny played no role in this decision, but bribes paid to

---

[7] See for details, Bauer, *Jews for Sale?*

[8] See Bauer, *Jews for Sale?*; Porat, *The Blue and the Yellow Star of David*, pp. 328–346; Friling, "David Ben Gurion and the Catastrophe of European Jewry," pp. 113–130.

the Slovaks possibly did.[9] About 60,000 of the 95,000 Slovak Jews were deported to death camps in Poland until August 1942, when the SD branch (Abschnitt) in Bratislava advised its head office (Leitabschnitt) in Vienna that about 59,000 had been deported, about 8,000 had fled to Hungary, and the lives of the remaining 22,000 had been spared by the Slovak authorities. In fact, the deportations continued for several months afterward and then were finally stopped. Indeed, said the report, the number of Jews had shrunk by 67,000, but it should be noted that most of the deported Jews were "small Jews," who had few connections, whereas the rich and influential Jews to a large extent remained in the country. This argument entirely refutes Weissmandel's assumption, and his posthumous allegation, that the Germans were successfully bribed to stop the killings. The SD report offered other explanations for the cessation of the deportations. Many Jews had converted to Christianity (in order to enjoy the church's protection, as the Slovak regime was in fact a Catholic–Fascist combination). Almost all had a Slovak work permit, a certificate of indispensability for the Slovak economy, or a letter of amnesty issued by the Slovak President Tiso. Since all of these Jews were freed from the compulsory duty to carry the yellow star the impression was created, said the report, that the Jewish problem had been fully solved, while the Jews themselves behaved "in a provocative and outrageous fashion." They rode in the streetcars again in large groups, crowded the sleeping cars, and pushed themselves all around. "The corruption, whose origin was to be sought among the Jews, involved large circles and was the reason for repeated anger and criticism among the people." SD Bratislava then reported on efforts made by the Slovak Minister of Interior, Mach, to renew the deportations following a police action that uncovered a Jewish "center for issuing false papers" and a letter of protest issued by the bishops of the Protestant church in Slovakia against the deportations, which allegedly angered the Catholic president very much.[10] Yet on August 11, 1942, said the SD report, a meeting of the council of ministers was "suddenly" ordered by Prime Minister Tuka in which both the minister of economics and the secretary general of the industrial union declared that they maintained the continuation of the deportations of Jews as "impossible to sustain" (untragbar) for the economy. The Council of Ministers decided to stop the deportations and to continue the action after the end of the war. This, and not the bribing of the Gestapo/SD henchman in Slovakia, saved

---

[9] See NA, Microcopy T-175, *Records of the Reich Leader of the S.S. and Chief of the German Police*, RG 242, Role 584, SD-Leitabschnitt Wien, no frames, letter by SS-Untersturmführer Urbantzke to SD-LA Wien, Abteilung III B, z.Hd. SS-Hauptsturmführer Herrmann, den 22.8.1942, Betr. Judenaussiedlung (i.e., resettlement of Jews), and see Bauer's discussion of the Slovak bribes and especially of Wisliceny's role in *Jews for Sale?*, pp. 62–101.

[10] The story of the Church's (Catholic and Protestant alike) intervention in the Slovak Holocaust to save at least converted Jews is more complicated than that and was told by Bauer, *Jews for Sale?*

the remaining Slovak Jews, for the time being, even if the bribing of Slovak officials by Slovak and Hungarian Jews might have played a decisive role in their deliberations in addition to the intervention of the churches and Slovak humanitarians.

In fact, Prime Minister Tuka, so we are told in the same report, had informed the SS officials in the German mission in Bratislava, SS Major Grüninger and SS Captain Wisliceny, about the positions taken by the Minister of Economics and by the secretary general of the industrial union before the meeting of the Council of Ministers but said nothing about postponing the deportations until after the war. Tuka did say that as a result of a newly made check (Überprufung) the deportation of Jews would continue in three stages until the end of the year, except for about 380 Jews needed by the industrialists and 2,000 with their families needed by the economics minister who could stay behind. Hence, he took two contradictory positions – one in the Council of Ministers in favor of the cessation of the deportations, and the other in favor of deporting most of the remaining Jews, as demanded by Grüninger and Wisliceny. At least, we realize that Wisliceny was not alone in this bloody business, and a higher SS officer was directly involved in the talks with the Slovaks on the continuation of the deportations, so that bribing him alone was pointless. Yet Wisliceny seems to have adopted a realistic view of the Slovak decision to stop the deportations, which he, as a Judenberater in a formally independent, allied nation, had to live with. Wisliceny was said in that report to have agreed that the number of the remaining Jews, if calculated with their families, about six persons per family, should be about 14,000–15,000. The SD reporter added his view that the figures both for those Jews vital to the Slovak economy and their family members were too high, quoting the president of the Slovak grain producers, who estimated the number of "vital" Jews to be about 500–600 and added that even four members of a Jewish family was much too high an estimate, as those relevant "Intelligenzjuden" had few children. Thus, the acceptance of the six person family also calculated the parents, cousins, and the like (who should have been killed as a matter of course). The SD reporter then calculated the relevant numbers:

Total number of Jews in Slovakia before the deportations	95,000
Converted before 1941, married to non-Jews, etc.	6,000
Remained	89,000
Out of which already deported (ausgesiedelt)	59,000
Fled to Hungary	8,000
Remained in Slovakia	22,000
Out of which vital for the economy+families	14,000–15,000
Remained for following deportations	6,000–7,000

The SD reporter criticized the German diplomatic mission in Bratislava under Hans Ludin in general because they "strangely enough" adopted an apathetic position toward the deportations of the (remaining) Jews and refused at first to bring pressure upon the Slovaks, arguing that such pressure was rejected by Berlin. The mission, however, remained involved and also discussed other things related to the deportations, so we are told in the same report, including missing railcars, but Wisliceny has declared that the railroad authority in Breslau (in charge of Auschwitz) had given him enough railcars. Finally, the SD report expressed higher hopes with regard to Slovak President Tiso compared to the German mission itself. Tiso spoke publicly in favor of the continuation of the deportations on August 16, 1942, a position that he hoped would fully isolate Tuka and force him to limit the number of "vital" Jews to 4,000–5,000 against his previous 14,000–15,000. SS Captain Wisliceny summarized his view in favor of the continued deportations, adding that "the mission should adopt the German demands made in Wisliceny's summary and submit them to the Prime Minister, so that continued deportations in this year could be expected." In this matter, the August 1942 SD report proved to be wrong. Most of those who survived in 1942 remained in Slovakia, but not thanks to bribes paid to an SS captain. They survived, as Bauer tells us, until September 1944 thanks to a combined set of inner Slovak calculations and bribes paid to key Slovak persons in charge of the deportations, Vatican pressure, and their relatively insignificant number compared to the other priorities of the SS at the time.[11] Their fate was finally sealed – most were sent to Auschwitz and gassed by the end of September 1944 – in connection with the Nazi policy toward the Jews in the last phase of World War II, related to the destruction of the Hungarian Jewry that began in May following an anti-German uprising in Slovakia in summer 1944. To this we shall return in due course.[12]

I believe that the key document just cited may help to explain the actual historical situation and prove Rabbi Weissmandel's allegation about the cessation of the Holocaust in Slovakia as being due to bribes paid to SS Captain Wisliceny, and about a possible deal with the SS to save the remaining European Jews, as completely detached from the historical reality.

However, Nathan Schwalb not only tried his best to give some future meaning to the deaths of those who could no longer be saved in his correspondence with Weissmandel by making them martyrs but himself seems to have believed that some deals with the Germans could have saved Jews if he and other rescue workers had been given more money – a view that in fact corresponds with the one adopted by Weissmandel. In his conversation with the present writer, Schwalb added to the Slovak "deal" a Jewish pioneering

---

[11] See Bauer, *Jews for Sale?*, pp. 91–101.

[12] About the final "action" against the remaining Slovak Jews, see NA, T-175, roll 584, SD Pressburg, note dated September 29, 1944: "Half of Pressburg [Bratislava] was on its feet this morning to watch the show of the Judenevakuierung... so was the kick, administered by a S.S.-man upon a tardy Jew received by the large crowd... with hand claps and cries of support and encouragement..."

outfit in Silesia, financed by means that he had managed to smuggle there and that existed until late in 1944. Rescue operative Venia Pomeranz even talked shortly before his death about a broader definition of "Europe," pertaining to the negotiations with Wisliceny, to broaden the alleged Slovak deal to include other European Jews, which for him probably meant the Balkans and maybe Western Europe, too – but not Poland. "It might have been a mistake to mention Poland to them," Pomeranz said, tears in his eyes: "We might have been mistaken, when we demanded from Eichmann to include the Polish Jews in the rescue efforts aimed at saving the Rumanians and the Hungarians. He was not ready to let Polish Jews go, because, he said, 'that it might become known.'"

"Known" to whom? Probably to Hitler, who was supposed to be kept in the dark by Himmler, who might have been ready to deal on his own following Stalingrad. This vision of Himmler's alleged pragmatism is not supported by any serious study of the man and his relations with Hitler so far, based on his own records[13] or on my interviews with Albert Speer and Dr. Werner Best, the former deputy director of the Gestapo, to be cited in due course.

The idea of allowing a few rich Jews to leave abroad for "much foreign currency" had been authorized by Hitler himself late in 1942, while Himmler was against money deals, preferring the taking of some rich Jews as hostages. Bauer, Porat, and lately Friling, on the other hand, created the impression that Himmler might have been more serious than was indicated by the incomplete documentation available. Hitler had indeed authorized the ransoming of some Jews, following Göring's and Himmler's inquiries; but this was the exception, not the rule, and some related cases became known to Allied intelligence.[14] This would complicate rescue deals in the future, especially when the Allies perceived in them Jewish-initiated acts authorized by the Germans to enhance German – and Jewish – interests but not those of the Allies.

One of the first American documents dealing with rescue in 1943 was a U.S. Military Attaché Report that originated in British Intelligence sources in Cairo and was circulated by G-2, United States Armed Forces in the Middle East (USAFIME) on April 19, 1943, in which the "Jewish refugee traffic" was discussed, "largely between Europe and the Americas," as supported by three "chief agencies": the American Joint Distribution Committee (AJDC), the Hebrew Immigrant Aid Society (HIAS), and Jewish Refugee Society (HICEM). Therein "a note of warning was sounded," based on counterintelligence reports stemming from "British Intelligence sources"[15]

---

[13] Breitman and Aronson, "The End of the 'Final Solution'?," p. 181n.

[14] The best-known case, to be discussed separately, was that of the Hungarian Weiss family; others will also be mentioned in due course.

[15] G-2 Palestine box 2724, evaluated "A-2," usually the highest grade.

concerning "the possibility of their use by the enemy for the planting of personnel for espionage and other subversive purposes."

The conclusion that was to be drawn from "available evidence" was that "while these three organizations are in no way officially connected with German plans, their operations must be closely scrutinized, (1) because of the unsavory character of certain individuals connected with them; and (2) because of the undoubted opportunity afforded the enemy for making use of them in introducing agents into America" (underlined by reader in original). Thus, even when Jews were to be saved by Germans who disguised the rescue operations as useful for espionage and sabotage in the United States or elsewhere but in fact were given an excuse to be allowed to leave, they must have been perceived by Allied intelligence as a source of trouble. Such rescue operations were ascribed by recent scholars to Abwehr officials such as General Hans Oster, Dr. Hans von Dohnanyi, and even to Admiral Wilhelm Canaris himself, who is supposed to have obtained Hitler's permission to use refugee Jews for intelligence purposes in America.[16] Such rescue efforts undertaken by Abwehr officials contributed to their own downfall and replacement by a combined Gestapo/SD operation.

However, several remarks made by rescue worker Pomeranz, when he spoke of having "mentioned to them" rescue deals and his comment quoted earlier that his mail to occupied Europe was meant to be read by the Gestapo,[17] led the present writer to the conclusion that Pomeranz was aiming at what the Allies were afraid of by adopting a strategy of negotiations with the Gestapo and believed that money would have saved Jews as it might have done in Slovakia. In a letter to the Histadrut's Executive mailed from Istanbul on March 10, 1943, he quoted information received from Rabbi Weissmandel and Gizi Fleischmann, a Zionist activist in Bratislava much trusted and appreciated by everyone, to the effect that if Wisliceny were not bribed, he would deport the remaining Slovak Jews immediately and implement the Final Solution in Greece and in Bulgaria as well. "The letters are crying to heaven," Pomeranz continued, quoting Fleischmann further that if bribed Wisliceny would stop the deportations also from the Czech "Protektorat" and Poland itself. Pomeranz was not sure about the larger scheme, known to us as the Europa Plan, but he seemed to have been sure at that time that the deportations from Slovakia itself had been stopped "due to such means." Moreover, in terms of immigration certificates issued by the British within the terms of the White Paper itself, Pomeranz wrote that "many certificates" were available then, but the Jewish Agency's immigration

---

[16] The issue of Abwehr's officers, such as Hans von Dohnanyi, and Jews, including Dohnanyi's efforts to save several individuals by getting them into neutral countries rather than exploit them as spies, is discussed by Winfried Mayer, *Unternehmen Sieben* (Frankfurt: Filo Verlag, 1993).

[17] Testimony to me.

apparatus abroad, under Chaim Barlas in Istanbul, for example, the Zionist youth movements, and the rescue teams were hardly able to coordinate their efforts and tried to run their own operations separately.[18]

On the face of it, the strategy of rescue by ransom was reasonable and concurred with Ben-Gurion's own scheme before and after Biltmore to support a variety of rescue schemes, such as the "Children Plan," an anxious bid to the British made late in 1942 and repeated in 1943[19] to avoid the security risks involving alleged Jewish spies by allowing children to emigrate from Nazi-occupied Europe when possible. Ben-Gurion combined the rescue of Jews from specific territories such as Transnistria, due to its special status as a Rumanian–German occupied territory, from Rumania proper, and more generally the goal of bringing a million survivors to Palestine as soon as possible and absorbing the refugees coming from Europe with his bid for independence.[20] Yet this required not just Allied consent but primarily Nazi interest in ransom deals.

---

[18] Hagana Archive, Moladti Collection, Repository 14/61; see also file 857/33, which includes Rabbi Weissmandel's cries for ransom from Bratislava relayed through Nathan Schwalb.

[19] For details, see Friling, "David Ben Gurion and the Catastrophe of European Jewry," pp. 220–246.

[20] See Devora Z. Hacohen, *The Million Plan* (Tel-Aviv: Ministry of Defense, 1995). According to Mrs. Hacohen, the "plan" was kept secret to avoid British intervention and became a blueprint for Ben-Gurion's efforts toward mass Jewish immigration to Palestine after the war, but in fact it was designed to be carried out during World War II itself if possible.

20

The Significance of the British Decrypts

Apart from Himmler's activities in fall 1943, which culminated in the liquidation of most Polish Jewry late in 1943 and early in 1944, and his infamous speech before the SS generals in Posen discussing the Holocaust as an act of bravery on October 4, 1943, which contradicted any serious attempt on his part to negotiate the end of the Holocaust with the West, we have at our disposal British decrypts concerning murderous activities by the SS at that time outside of Poland. These decrypts were made available to the Americans out of many thousands more that are stored at the British Public Record Office. According to these documents, when Wisliceny was supposed to have negotiated the Europa Plan in September 1943, the Germans were busy introducing "measures" against the Jews of Rome in spite of their fears that these measures would combine with the other, seemingly serious problems that they faced by suddenly taking over a former ally and its capital.[1] By October 10, 1943, the Nazi official in charge – SS Captain Herbert Kappler – pretty much aware of the local conditions and possible trouble if the deportation of Rome's Jews was to be carried out at that early stage, reported to Berlin that at least "50 gks [kilograms] of Jewish gold are being dispatched to CdS" (Chef der Sicherheitpolizei – Gestapo and Criminal Police), expressing his hope that "as far as the Reichsbank is concerned this will facilitate the supply of Devisen [foreign currency – S.A.] for our purposes."[2]

Reporting about local complications, Kappler radioed Berlin that the Vatican has "sold Spanish, Argentine, Portuguese and Mexican visas to Jews who wish to smuggle themselves out" on a train in which the Spanish

---

[1] See Rome to Berlin, RSS 42/29/9/43 no. 6921. The RSS was the Radio Security Service/Section in charge of intercepting enemy radio messages beginning in 1941 and was controlled by MI6. The actual decrypting was done by Bletchley Park's code breakers. The number given to the decrypt next to the RSS one is Section V's or Bletchley's. The American copies are stored in RG 226, Entry 122, box 2, Italian Decodes.

[2] Rome (Kappler) to Berlin, RSS 157/7/10/43 decrypted as no. 7256.

diplomats traveled home after the fall of Mussolini. Reporting on this late in September, SS Captain Kappler promised, amid the chaos and fears of Italian resistance, disarming the Italian police, and his other duties, to attempt to ascertain "who these Jews are."[3]

What we learn from this is that this tough and able product of the SS system was conscious of the local conditions, and thus he started with looting Jewish gold – as historian Richard Breitman quoted from his defense in a postwar trial, plus the relevant scholarly research on the Holocaust in Italy, in a *Holocaust and Genocide Journal* article – instead of arranging for the immediate deportation of the Italian Jews. The looting of gold could be seen perhaps in connection with the need of foreign currency for the SS's own purposes, which might have been the development of SD Ausland to replace Admiral Canaris's Abwehr[4] and had to wait until later in 1944.

Thus, the decrypts tell us about the dispatch of Eichmann's aide Theo Dannecker to round up the Italian Jews and ship them to Auschwitz on the same date – October 10.[5]

The significance of these decrypts is not to be sought on the British or American sides, whose inaction in regard to them is the only fact we can ascertain. What these decrypts do reveal is the situation in Rome, where Kappler, the so-called police attaché in the German embassy and in fact the local representative of the SS Main Office RSHA (Security Police – Gestapo, Criminal Police, and SD), served as the main communication officer for all of the other SS outfits after the fall of Mussolini and the immediate German intervention in Italy.

Berlin (RSHA or Himmler's Secretariat – we do not have the details) told Rome that according to a report from Budapest "binding agreements" existed between Hungary and Italy in regard to dropping out of the war.[6] In this connection, Himmler ordered an investigation regarding an alleged long telephone discussion between Pope Pius XII and President Roosevelt.

For his part, Kappler reported the seizure of the records of the Italian Foreign Ministry and about "a corresponding rumor on an alleged agreement between [Marshal Pietro] BADOGLIO [capital letters in the original] and Hungary.[7] The significance of this for us was that the fall of Mussolini focused German attention to a growing degree onto Hungary. After having been taken by surprise by the Badoglio negotiations and final agreement on

---

[3] Rome to Berlin, RSS 27/25/9/43 no. 6728 dated September 24, 1943.
[4] Kappler was able to collect anti-Canaris information from SIM, the Italian Secret Service, and transmit it to his superiors; see Rome to Berlin, RSS 13-14/5/9/43, no. 5446 (also another number is attached to this one underneath – KFL 3614).
[5] See Rome to Berlin, RSS 32/7/10/43, original date October 6, 1943.
[6] Berlin to Rome, RSS 263/15/9/43 no. 6047, dated September 15, 1943.
[7] Rome to Berlin, RSS 152/16/9/43 no. 6089.

a separate peace with the Allies, the Germans would not risk such a surprise in Hungary.

Another decrypt tells us that the Croatian soldiers who found themselves in Italy, as a result of the collapse of the Italian–German rule over parts of the former Yugoslav Federation, including the so-called Croat independent state, were ordered by Himmler to be returned home. But "an offer is to be made to the Mohammedan Croatians only, of the opportunity to join the Waffen SS in conformity with the order of the Grand Mufti."[8] Decrypts concerning the Mufti's whereabouts in Italy and his possible help in raising an "Arab Legion" are numerous here. Also preparations ordered by Himmler to liberate Mussolini were mentioned, as well as Rumanian soundings toward the possible mediation of Pope Pius XII toward a separate peace but described as having been rejected by the Holy See. Yet an important part of these decrypts deals with the destruction of the Italian Jewry. Kappler reported on a "disguised" (as Aryan) Jewish concern smuggling Jews across the border into Switzerland. The German ambassador in Rome, Rudolf Rahn, however, and Kappler himself, according to a message delivered by Fritz Kolbe, an American agent in Ribbentrop's Foreign Ministry to OSS Bern, were informed about orders given in the meantime to deport all of the Jews of Rome, but both suggested using the Jews "as in Tunis" for fortification work and the like.[9]

In response to this, SS General Ernst Kaltenbrunner, the head of RSHA, radioed Kappler [cable quoted here verbatim as decoded – S.A.] that it was:

... precisely the immediate and thorough eradication of the Jews in ITALY which is the special interest of the present internal political situation and the general security in ITALY. To postpone the expulsion of the Jews until the CARABINIERI and the Italian army officers have been removed can no more be considered than the idea mentioned of calling up the Jews in ITALY for what would probably be very improductive labour under responsible direction of Italian authorities. The longer the delay, the more the Jews who are doubtless reckoning on evacuation measures have an opportunity by moving to the houses of pro-Jewish Italians of disappearing completely ... (line corrupt) ITALY (has been) instructed in executing the R.F.S.S. [Himmler's – S.A.) orders to proceed with the evacuation of the Jews without further delay. (Cable Berlin to Rome to Kappler, signed Kaltenbrunner, Org. (SS Obergruppenführer, RSS 256/ 11/10/43 7458)

The other decrypts tell us the story of the "action" taken against the Jews of Rome, "after the release of those of mixed blood, of foreigners including Vatican citizens, of the families in mixed marriages including the Jewish partner, and of the Aryan servants and lodgers," the exact dates and

---

[8] Berlin to Rome, RSS 353/17/9/43 no. 6209, signed by Ernst Kaltenbrunner, the head of RSHA.
[9] Doc. 2–105, Telegram 1496–97, Dulles to OSS Washington, December 30, 1943, reprinted in Petersen, *From Hitler's Doorstep*, pp. 189–190.

route to Auschwitz were detailed.[10] Thus, in spite of being careful not to arouse trouble with the Italians by deporting those mentioned, Himmler's and Kaltenbrunner's insistence on the Final Solution in Italy hardly supports the thesis that Himmler authorized any bargaining regarding the Europa Plan and that he was trying to use Jews at the same time as a tool for negotiating a separate peace with the West.

[10] See Rome to Berlin, RSS 113/10/10/43 no. 7412 KFL 4052 signed Kappler, Berlin to Rome to Kappler, signed Kaltenbrunner, Ogr. (SS Obergruppenführer) RSS 256/11/10/43 no. 7458, Rome to Berlin decrypts no. 7668, no. 7682, no. 7724, no. 7754, signed by Dannecker, and no. 7834 and no. 7846, signed by Kappler, regarding the rail route of the Jews to Auschwitz via Brenner-Innsbruck.

21

The "Small Season"

Begin's Rebellion

While in and around occupied Europe there were rescue efforts requiring passive or active support by the Allies should some hole or holes be punched one
way or another in the German wall, in Palestine in early 1944 a "rebellion"
was declared by Menachem Begin against the British as those who were
preventing rescue. Here the revival of Jewish terrorism by a dissident group
seemed to endanger the majority's politics and even its rescue schemes.

In a long memorandum submitted early in 1945 to OSS, its author, on behalf of the Jewish Agency (the thirteen-page document remained unsigned),
started the history of Jewish terrorism in Palestine.[1] As such, the document
explains milestones in the history of relations between Left and Right in
Israel until this very day and the birth of a still-existing argument that Labor
Zionists, led by Ben-Gurion, were in fact "collaborators" with the British
while allegedly doing nothing for rescue.

Having described the history of the National Military Organization, or
Irgun (abbreviated IZL for the Hebrew "Irgun Zvai Leumi") until the outbreak of World War II and the emergence of Avraham Stern's terrorist group
afterward, the writer or writers continued: "Stern propagated the continuation of activities against the British . . . and the establishment of contact with
Germany and Italy," which he indeed did,[2] while IZL commander David
Raziel was able to win support among most Revisionists (e.g., Jabotinsky's
followers organized in the "New Zionist Organization"), "who accused the
Stern group of being supported by Germany." The group continued its activities alone and mainly carried out robberies for the accumulation of funds

---

[1] See memo entitled "Jewish Terrorist Gangs in Palestine," submitted on January 15, 1945, by
the Jewish Agency to OSS Cairo, the related correspondence between the Labor Desk officer
in charge, Leonard Appel, and Teddy Kollek, the responsible Jewish Agency official, now
back in Jerusalem, and between OSS Cairo officials among themselves in this connection in
RG 226, Entry 190, box 73, CAIRO-SI-OP-4-7.

[2] See, among others, CID Chief Arthur F. Giles to J. B. Griffin, the Solicitor General, June 3,
1941, CID doc. 59/1809/2/GS, CID collection, Hagana Archive.

but also attacked British police. In one of these incidents, two Jewish and one British police officer were murdered in February 1942, and thus the "Small Season," an organized Yishuv action to eliminate the Stern gang, had begun, in cooperation with the CID – the British Police Intelligence. The Hagana members involved, described in this memo as "volunteers," were provided with police uniforms without being placed under the command of the British Palestine Police. Lists of nearly all of the active members of the Stern group, containing names, descriptions, and their hideouts, were compiled and submitted to the authorities, thus enabling them to effect extensive arrests. In April 1942, the remnants of the Stern group prepared a series of attempts on the lives of high-ranking police officers. Warnings were given to the authorities by the Yishuv leadership, and the people engaged were arrested. The police shot the leader, "Yair" Stern, at the time of his arrest in Tel Aviv. It is hard to conclude from this document whether Stern, who became a sort of martyr to the whole Revisionist movement and is acknowledged as such in the post–Ben-Gurion Israel, was in fact denounced by the so-called Jewish "volunteers" just mentioned and in fact by the Hagana, even if they did not expect his death at the hands of the British Police.

The British, according to our source, differentiated between the Stern gang and the IZL and tried their luck with several of the Stern group's leaders, still in detention, who refused freedom in exchange for a promise not to engage again in terrorism. The memo named Nathan Friedman, "a friend of the late Stern," a Polish-born engineer and editor, as the leader; in fact, there emerged a troika of leaders consisting of the leftist Friedman, the Nietzscheian mystic Dr. Israel Sheib, and the operator Yitzhak Yezernizki-Shamir, a future Prime Minister of Israel. All of them were born in Poland, and the latter two were influenced by both Jabotinsky (before breaking with him due to his British orientation) and by the romantic-ultranationalist poet Uri-Zvi Greenberg. Shamir made good his escape, together with various IZL leaders, by the end of 1942 from British jail, and the group reorganized and commenced at first verbal terror activities against the British. About a year later, a larger group of Stern gang members was able to flee from British prison. Later, the leading troika ordered the assassination of Lord Moyne, the British Minister Resident in the Middle East, invoking his alleged roles in preventing rescue and closing the gates of Palestine to Holocaust survivors as the reason for the crime.

When the IZL saw the success of the Stern group, continued our Jewish Agency source, it decided to renew its activities as well. It hoped to make capital out of the embitterment of the Jewish public that had piled up because of the closing of Palestine's borders to the remnants of persecuted European Jewry, the overzealous application of the White Paper restrictions, and the staging of the arms trials. The British indeed searched for illegal arms in various Hagana hideouts once the German threat was over, fearing Arab unrest, and accused the Jewish Agency and Ben-Gurion of personally running a military underground and of being "active in movement to smuggle immigrants into Palestine," plus Ben-Gurion's vigorous campaign for full independence after Biltmore.[3] The political dynamics of the Yishuv becomes clearer here when we realize that the small Stern gang was able to push the larger IZL at its direction by demonstrating a degree of public success in their anti-British actions when they managed to kill some constables and Jewish and non-Jewish police officers, while remaining at large, and having a martyr – Stern – to give their small outfit an image larger than life. The IZL under Ya'akov Viniarsky-Meridor remained rather inactive until Menachem Begin took over late in 1943. The competition from the Stern group remained a factor in IZL calculations and obviously in those of the Jewish Agency.

The Yishuv's leadership calculated its response to Jewish anti-British terror when the Sternists and the IZL resumed their activities with the Holocaust as their main "raison d'être." In the words of our Jewish Agency source, "The Jewish public again summoned its strength," a biblical expression that was typical of Moshe Shertok, "to stamp out terrorism, in cooperation with the (British) Palestine Authorities." By then the Holocaust had become IZL's major political asset, crowned by the Hungarian Holocaust. This carnage, which seemed to have harbored rescue options, allegedly doomed to fail because of British machinations and Labor Zionist failures bordering on treachery in Palestine and in Hungary itself in the far-right Zionist vocabulary, requires our in-depth study.

[3] See, for example CIC, USAFIME, transmitted by G-2, RG 165, Entry 77, box 2726, "Hagana" Activities, Cross Reference Sheet Synopsis, May 10, 1943.

22

The Origins of the Budapest "Rescue Committee"

The Zionist "Rescue Committee" in Budapest, known by its Hebrew name "Va'ada," came into being in 1943 following the initiative of local Zionists. This effort was coordinated, with typical difficulty, by the Istanbul Rescue Mission, which reported about it to the Jewish Agency and its subsidiaries dealing with rescue in Jerusalem. The Va'ada also entertained direct ties to the Rescue Committee in Bratislava and maintained contact, by various means with the Zionist emissaries and the AJDC's representative in Switzerland.

The Budapest situation was no different from the others in that the Committee had to coordinate the efforts of independent and autonomous Zionist bodies, which hardly accepted central authority. Rather, partisan interests dictated the distribution of available emigration certificates issued by the Palestine government.

Rezsö Kasztner, the local Mapai representative, finally intervened in this and other matters pertaining to rescue in order to impose such an authority – and himself – upon the Budapest Palestine Office, the official Zionist immigration outfit, as best he could when he actively joined the Rescue Committee later in 1943, thereby creating long-lasting enmities.[1]

Rezsö-Rudolf Israel Kasztner was a rather well-known Labor Zionist operative in Rumania, where he enjoyed public recognition and respect, but much less so later in Hungary, when Germany transferred his native Transylvania to its rival neighbor.[2] In Hungary, Kasztner belonged to the small Zionist minority and made a living as a salaried functionary of a

---

[1] See "Moladti" collection, Hagana Archive, Repository 14/153', letter pertaining to problems with "Jaari" "Mizrach," probably sent by Samu Springmann, dated April 12, 1943, and see the situation of the Zionist Youth Movements in Poland therein: "The [Polish] Zionist movements could not agree among themselves until this very day. The others, except us [Mapai] and . . . [the small youth movement associated with a liberal party] are interested only in their share in the [Palestine immigration] certificates, and this poisons everything since years."

[2] Interview with Kasztner's niece, Professor Rivka Bar-Yosef of Hebrew University, 1985.

Zionist fund, a position that hardly earned him any respect in the eyes of the high-minded Hungarian Jewish leadership.[3]

At first, he was active among the Zionist youth movements in Hungary, absorbing refugees from Poland and Slovakia – following a period of compulsory service for the Hungarian Army – when the Istanbul Rescue Mission instructed the Va'ada to distribute the finances of rescue "according to the needs" rather than being given to competing partisan interests. Rescue from Poland should not be dictated by "absolute affiliations" with the Zionist youth movements alone.

The Committee members operated in a semilegal manner to rescue Jews, sheltering them first in Hungary itself and later moving them to Palestine.

Kasztner was more than a rescue operative; he had grand political interests and tried to put the Committee's work within a larger perspective. His analysis of the war situation in April 1943 was typical, as were his complaints about the lack of cooperation and solidarity among the various Zionist groups and their difficult relations with the Hungarian Jewish establishment.[4] He took it for granted that "aunt Moledet" (aunt homeland – a code word for the rescue mission in Istanbul) was doing "everything possible" for rescue from occupied Europe and promised similar efforts on his side. Kasztner warned that the war could reach Hungary itself, and thus he expected a "special pressure" to be exercised upon the Jewish community therein, but added: "hopefully we shall be saved from the fate of the others," as "on the other hand one could... feel that the fortunes of the war took different directions than the [Nazis] hoped for."

In his April 1943 letter, Kasztner wrote that the Zionists were trying to exert more influence on the Hungarian Jewish leaders. The established Jewish communities, which were largely non-Zionist, were busy helping Jewish conscripts to the "Labor Companies" of the Hungarian Army in the Eastern Front, an activity in which they were rather successful, even if many hundreds died in this service to the Axis, and in helping victims of isolated pogroms (especially in Hungarian-annexed territories of Yugoslavia). Immigration to Palestine seemed, according to Kasztner's own analysis, as a rather irrelevant, even dangerous, sideshow to the assimilated Jews and the orthodox notables who could maintain Jewish life in this German-allied

---

[3] Kasztner himself referred to it in a German written report about its activities as Vaadat Ezra Vo-Hazala Bo-Budapest (i.e., The Rescue and Relief Committee in Budapest). The confidential report carried no date but was probably ready in 1946 in connection with an accusation made against him immediately after the war that Kasztner in fact "collaborated" with the Nazis. Henceforth it will be quoted as Kasztner's 1946 Report entitled *Der Bericht des jüdischen Rettungskomitees aus Budapest 1942–1945* (hereafter "Bericht"). The accusations led to an internal Zionist inquiry leading to no open charges or further investigations. See for this and the ensuing legal battles in Israel, Yehiam Weitz, *The Man Who Was Murdered Twice: The Life, the Trial, and the Death of Dr. Israel Kasztner* (Jerusalem: Ketter Publications, 1995).

[4] Same archival source as in note 1, letter of April 12, 1943.

nation largely without serious interruption thanks to the Hungarian bid for independence from complete German dominance in cooperation with the upper, non-Jewish classes. The official center of Zionist activity was the local "Palestine Office" (i.e., the Jewish Agency's official in charge of Zionist immigration), which functioned prior to the Rescue Committee and collaborated with a coalition of the leftist Hashomer Hazair and the national religious party "Mizrachi" – with Mapai pushed aside. One of the reasons for this was that the religious party, a small minority in Palestine, held the majority among Hungarian Zionists. The immigration officer was Miklós Moshe Krausz, of whom we shall hear more, "whose ambition and egoism ('Geltungsgier') knew no limit, as a former Yeshiva scholar." "He is very shrewd, but has no (general) Zionist sense of responsibility, is unscrupulous and thus very dangerous."[5] Indeed Krausz, the orthodox functionary, would fight Kasztner's bids to establish Mapai – and himself – as a pivot among the Zionists as best he could, claiming that Mapai was the majority party in Palestine itself. Later he would oppose also Kasztner's rescue strategy and after the war fight him to the bitter end, thus preempting Kasztner's criticism of his own behavior at the time. In 1943, Krausz – according to Kasztner's letter mentioned earlier – divided the Palestine immigration certificates between his party and the far Left people by keeping the Palestine Office's partisan structure unchanged in spite of the changed European map and the changed tasks. The tactic was partially grounded in Krausz's direct responsibility to the Immigration Department of the Jewish Agency, which developed typical cautious bureaucratic habits, and its Hungarian official had enjoyed a degree of autonomy for years before as a knowledgeable man with important local connections, including non-Zionists.[6] "The elegant letters" of the Istanbul immigration officer Chaim Barlas did not move Krausz, whose interests were clearly aimed at specific religious groups and who had his own ties with the Hungarian government, threatening from time to time to use them to maintain his power.

The mainstream Laborites engaged in rescue in Budapest were Shmuel Samu Springmann, a Polish Zionist who immigrated to Hungary in the 1920s. A clever diamond dealer, he carried the main burden of helping Zionist youth movement refugees from Slovakia and Poland by providing them with financial help from Palestine and Switzerland and by helping them (absorbed in their own affairs and always demanding more, as he recalled years later)[7] to acquire official Hungarian papers and avoid expulsion while

---

[5] See note 1, same archival source.
[6] Ibid.
[7] The present writer held a series of interviews with the German-speaking Springmann in his Ramat-Gan home in 1985 and recorded them in writing. Springmann corrected my original notes, submitted to him in typed form. The typed manuscripts are in my possession and will be quoted as "Springmann 1985."

they were preparing to leave for Palestine. Springmann further maintained contact with various couriers who carried Zionist mail and money to and from Budapest, including to Zionist labor camps, which still survived in Poland at the peak of the Holocaust in that country, and with helpful foreign diplomats as well.

According to Friling and his Zionist sources,[8] Springmann was the one who created the initial contacts with four couriers of significance to our trap thesis: a German called Rudi Scholz, who was supposed to be a "Gestapo" official (in fact, he is described as the head of Abwehr Station Budapest, but no trace of him in such a position is found in the available records), Joseph Winninger, believed to be a half Jew, an Abwehr operative, Erik Popescu, or Erich Wehner, also believed to be a half Jew associated with the Abwehr;[9] and Bandi or Bondi Grosz, alias Andor Giorgy, a converted Jew of Hungarian origin, who had served the Abwehr, the Hungarian Intelligence Service, the Zionist Rescue Mission in Istanbul, and the Americans as well, whose role in the Hungarian trap situation would be central, next only to that of another "courier," Fritz Laufer, who was also believed to be Jewish or half Jewish.

Another rescue worker in Budapest was Joel Brand, a businessman-adventurer type, as described by Yehuda Bauer,[10] who was born in Hungary, raised in Germany, became a communist functionary, was expelled, and then went back to Hungary, where he eventually joined the tiny Zionist minority and found himself involved in rescue matters due to family connections and his adventurous nature. Rezsö Kasztner was also involved in this rescue work. Soon enough, Kasztner intervened as Mapai's representative in the Krausz controversy and joined Brand (the latter without an eligible vote at first) in the Va'ada to become the executive director thereof under a respected Hungarian–Jewish figure, Otto Komoly, who served as president, together with several other Zionists. At any rate, the "party key" of the Zionist parties was changed in Mapai's favor.

Kasztner's analysis of the war situation and of the chances of the Hungarian Jewry in mid–summer 1943[11] is easy to criticize due to our obvious hindsight. But it does reflect a typical optimistic view of his world, which colored it according to the wishes of the writer, possibly a personal but also a Jewish–Zionist trait in the sense that Jews and the Zionists among them did hope and acted according to an optimistic perception that they tended to rationalize. Hope was one of their sources of survival but also a source of their doom, in many cases, which may explain Jewish passivity but not Kasztner's own activism. The personal trait demonstrated by Kasztner here was his self-confidence, or rather his unrestrained belief in his own judgment and to

---

[8] Friling, *Arrow in the Dark*, Volume I, p. 447n.
[9] Bauer, *Jews for Sale?*, p. 130.
[10] Bauer, *Jews for Sale?*, p. 152.
[11] Moladti letters, repository 14/153', dated July 18, 1943.

a degree in his and his new Hungarian community's good fortune, which he mixed with an impressive analysis of the Hungarian conditions that de facto seemed to have been wrong from the beginning almost to the end of the war. In Istanbul, and in Jerusalem, Kasztner's optimism was greeted with skepticism, however, when he wrote in July 1943: "This Community could be grosso modo already now regarded as saved" – that is to say "there is no danger of a domestic political development [that would] allow an extreme radical direction to take over" and implement similar "wild" anti-Semitic measures in Hungary as was the case in the neighboring German-allied nations, such as Slovakia, Croatia, and Rumania. The situations in these countries varied widely, but Kasztner meant local pogroms, the extradition of most Slovak Jews to the Germans, the deportations to Transnistria of many thousands of Rumanian Jews, and possibly local mass killings by Croat Fascists. Kasztner then quoted the Nazi press to the effect that the Danube was the border of "Fortress Europe," and thus he foresaw the transformation of Hungary into a battlefield but added that "politically" the Germans could not "influence our fate decisively." The whole analysis offered by him was based on the domestic Hungarian situation, not upon Hitler's possible moves, which he still regarded as those of the dangerous "wounded lion." He thus offered a political and economic analysis of the situation of the Jews in Hungary, estimating their assets as about one quarter of the national wealth. He further explained to his readers in Istanbul and in Palestine the historical reasons – as he saw them – why the Hungarian Jewry was a sort of "special case." After World War I, Hungary developed as an industrial nation, increasingly aspiring to Carpathian predominance, free of complete German domination, thanks to the cooperation between its aristocracy, high finance, and rich Jews. The pro-German elements were rather weak and alien to the national interest, in spite of Hungary's inevitable involvement in World War II. Anti-Semitism was always there, "but it worked also in the past with gloves."

In September 1943, Kasztner was more realistic when he identified the main political and strategic problem in terms of a German "intervention" in Hungary[12] while informing the rescue team in Istanbul about the inner Zionist and inter-Jewish conflicts that were typical of the Hungarian community about six months before its fate was sealed by the Holocaust.

Kasztner, together with two or three other signatories, thus wrote something representing a common effort, "an Moladti" ("to: Homeland"). This group, according to Hagana historian Gershon Rivlin, was the combined Labor rescue team in Istanbul: Ze'ev "Danny" Shind, Menachem-Mendl Bader, and Venia Pomeranz. Sometimes Teddy Kollek and Ehud Überall-Avriel were also part of it, but their main assignment was to maintain contact with British and American Intelligence in Turkey. They called themselves "Homeland" when addressing the general interest of the Jewish people,

---

[12] Moladti letter dated September 9, 1943.

as they understood them as Zionists, whereas when they dealt with the Histadrut (i.e., with pure Labor matters), they signed "Ovdim" (Laborers). Having thus smoothed their own relations among themselves as best they could by invoking a triple signature by representatives of the three main wings of the Labor camp, they tried to make their Hungarian counterparts repeat the same strategy and procedure. However, they kept separate contacts with their partisan movements in Hungary, Rumania, and wherever they could, but then they signed their letters personally.[13] The whole correspondence seemed to have been intensified and became rather regular thanks to the courier service established by Springmann, including services rendered by the perviously mentioned Bandi Grosz, a Hungarian-Jewish smuggler and intelligence agent for a half dozen different agencies operating in the Balkans, and by other couriers such as Winninger, Popescu, and Laufer, who were able to cross borders even during the war thanks to their contraband and intelligence-related activities, about which the Zionists seemed not to be bothered. In fact, such ties seemed to the Zionists to be rather valuable and thus would get them into serious trouble later.

Kasztner first told "Homeland" about negotiations between the Zionists and the Hungarian government under Miklós Kallay to allow the former a larger freedom of action and complained again about the assimilated Jews who had managed "in the period 1897–1918" to equate Zionism with antipatriotism and also intervened in practical terms against the Zionists, while preparing themselves for the "peace negotiations." Second, Kasztner complained about the division ("chaluka") of Zionist money from abroad among the youth movements according to their relative partisan strength, which created serious trouble among them. The intermediate outcome was a kind of parity between the youth movements in spite of the differences in strength among them. The creation of a supreme Zionist body – a Central Committee (Va'ada Merkazit) on top of the Youth Movement Committee – instead of the old committee in which Krausz was running the show was, however, difficult to achieve due to the Movement's opposition so that both bodies existed next to each other.

Another subcommittee was now in charge of the so-called "trip" (Tijul) (i.e., rescue from Poland), which was financed through several couriers. Joel Brand's letter in this regard of early September 1943 to "Homeland"[14] reveals a number of Jewish camps and ghettos still in existence in Poland and hopes of getting more inmates into Hungary. Later, the Zionists would distinguish themselves from the Hungarian Jewry as the only ones who did something for rescue in this respect and acknowledge the Yishuv's initiative and pressure in this regard. In regard to Poland, Brand mentioned in his letter five Jewish camps and ghettos into which aid was coming from Palestine

---

[13] My interview with Rivlin, 1990.
[14] Moladti letter dated September 9, 1943.

through Budapest and rescue to Hungary was attempted: Stryj (this was true until June 1943); Bochnja (as well); Chenstochowa, "where a bigger Kibbutz of Jaari's" (Hashomer Hazair) still existed, to which the Geneva rescue operative Schwalb was probably referring in his interview with the present writer as an example of survival and rescue possibilities from Poland itself; Crakow, "where many are still alive"; and Lemberg/Lvov. One can, however, assume that most of those survivors were put to death either in summer 1943, later during that year (Operation "Erntefest") or finally during 1944. Those who escaped to Hungary, if they were able to leave before March 1944 for Palestine or find refuge in Budapest city thanks to the efforts of the Rescue Committee, may have survived. This depended upon their legal status in Budapest, the local Zionists' ability to legalize them (indeed a money matter but not just that due to Hungarian and Jewish politics), and the availability of British entry certificates, which at that stage were rather available to the small numbers involved, and transit visas through Rumania and Turkey.

The Hungarian rescue effort and the Zionist mail in general were carried to Istanbul late in 1943 (according to an unsigned letter to the Istanbul rescue team very probably also written by Kasztner) by Bandi Grosz, the Hungarian Jewish smuggler, among others Grosz was employed at the same time by several intelligence agencies: his country's, the German Abwehr, the American OSS, and also sometimes the British, of whom we shall hear a lot more.[15] Grosz demanded exclusivity in his courier activity, probably because he had some doubt about other couriers used by the Zionists, who indeed fully or partially betrayed them, but his advice was ignored, whereas he himself was rather dubious in the eyes of the Zionist Left in Budapest. The grand picture of the war, especially Allied victories in North Africa in May 1943, might have contributed to the streamlining of the Zionist activities in Hungary. A letter from Kasztner and two other activists in November 1943, refers to the "liberation from the nightmare, when we learned that (Palestine) was finally far away from the bad guy,"[16] an important notion when we want to understand why non-Zionists in a relatively safe place such as Hungary were reluctant to leave for an unsafe place in their eyes such as British Palestine.

On December 18, 1943, Springmann, Brand, and Kasztner gave vent to their anger against Krausz without mentioning names.[17] Krausz still controlled the British entry certificates into Palestine and divided them among (as

---

[15] Moldati letter dated September 9, 1943, in which the writer thanks "Gros" for his connections with the Hungarian GHQ, which allowed him to be transferred to the capital during his active service in a labor company. Since this letter is a part of Kasztner's correspondence, he could have written it himself.

[16] Moladti letter dated November 11, 1943.

[17] Moladti letter dated November 11, 1943.

they said) the ultraorthodox and even the anti-Zionist. The Jewish Agency was obviously too careful to remove a local immigration officer with ties to the Hungarian government and influential Jewish circle altogether. On top of this problem, the three reported about successful negotiations with the representative of the Red Cross (abbreviated ICRC), Dr. Jean de Bavier, who was recommended to them by the AJDC's Saly Mayer and by Nathan Schwalb in Switzerland, on the creation of public halls (Warmesäle) for the growing number of refugees from Nazi-dominated Europe and about the Hungarian "serious" response to their pleas to send food to survivors in Poland itself under strong pressure from Istanbul to do more and more for rescue. Whether their efforts remained unknown to the Gestapo, and in fact made the Germans more – rather than less – determined to stop these efforts and also destroy the only Jewish island left intact within Hitler's hegemonic territory, is a question to be dealt with separately. However, the very enhanced rescue effort may give a new dimension to the multiple trap in the sense that the Yishuv and the Jewish leadership abroad had to act and do more and more for rescue, which, on the other hand, could have driven the Nazis to become even more aware of these efforts and use them for their purposes.

In Kasztner's words late in January 1944, things seemed to have worked nicely so far:[18]

Exactly one year is over, since you [the Yishuv's leadership through its Istanbul emissaries – S.A.] appealed to us, to mobilize all our powers in the service of rescue and aid. We have tried to follow this holy impulse. Since then more than 2,000 refugees from [Poland – Kasztner used a simple code word instead] came here, and when we look back we can securely ("ruhig") state that the rescue of these brothers and their... well being were impossible... [without] the biting heart and helpful hand of the Yishuv... behind us.... The few among us, who were ready to cooperate in the rescue work, would have been sentenced to inactivity due to the cold lack of cooperation of the majority among the Hungarian Jews, if the spiritual and material power of the Yishuv did not prove itself. The rescue workers, the rescued, and the supporters – and those who remained here have learned... the meaning of the Yishuv for the Jewish people. (Moladti letter, January 30, 1944)

Kasztner's criticism of the Hungarian Jewry was genuine and stemmed not only from his status as a "foreigner" (Transylvanian) Zionist in the eyes of the Hungarian Jewish elite, who despised him as such and had their traditional doubts about double allegiance and immigration to an alien country claimed by foreign Jews as a political entity. He in turn maintained his own – Zionist – contempt for them, and yet he was pretty conscious of the meaning of the Hungarian Jewry if almost a million such Jews survived to enhance Zionist claims in Palestine.[19] At the same time, Kasztner had to combine his

[18] Moladti letter dated January 30, 1944.
[19] Moladti letter of January 7, 1944.

compliments to the Yishuv with bad news about the actual meager rescue possibilities from Poland while telling his readers that the very fate of the Hungarian Jews themselves was soon to be decided. He reported further about partisan difficulties among the members of the Rescue Committee in regard to money matters. By now, however, he had established himself as Executive Director of the Rescue Committee,[20] whose president was Otto Komoly. The other committee members were a representative of the Zionist–Orthodox party Mizrachi, two representatives of Mapai – Joel Brand and Kasztner himself – and a representative of the leftist Hashomer Hazair. However, very soon the able and experienced Springmann left for Palestine (and was interned by the British in Cairo for interrogation for a while, released, and thereafter lived in Palestine and later in Israel without any public notice of him). Kasztner's power in the Committee grew accordingly, but he was never its only spokesman nor its all-powerful single policy maker. In fact, Brand was the more practical rescue worker among those who remained behind, whereas Kasztner perceived himself more as the "statesman" among the two – a characterization that Springmann found years later to be rather problematic due to Kasztner's combination of arrogance and a certain degree of educated naiveté.[21] At the same time, the rescue workers in Hungary and elsewhere could have derived much hope from the creation of the American War Refugee Board, in charge of saving Jews, in January 1944.

[20] Moladti letter of January 20, 1944.

[21] According to the Springmann interview in 1985, he brought Kasztner with him to a business meeting (pertaining to semilegal transit visas for Jewish refugees bound for Palestine) with a Turkish official in Hungary. Kasztner got bored after a while and suddenly asked the Turk when his country would abandon neutrality and join the Allies. The dumbfounded attaché took Springmann aside and demanded an explanation "why you brought this guy here to ask me stupid questions on high politics."

23

The War Refugee Board and the Extension of the Trap
The "Dogwood Chain"

Much has been written about the origins of the War Refugee Board (WRB) and its official creation in January 1944.[1] The present writer has first one important document to add to the published literature, found in the papers of Undersecretary of State Edward R. Stettinius, Jr., dated January 7, 1944, and already partially quoted earlier, which carried the heading "Summary of Recommendations for Specific Action":[2]

I. <u>Release of Persons from Axis Europe</u> (underlined in original)

1. The President or the Department [of State] should enter into negotiations with Hitler or the German Government, through the Pope or through the heads of the Governments of Switzerland or Sweden, to reach an understanding which would permit the release of Jews at a certain rate per month consistent with the capacity of available neutral shipping and of Spanish and Turkish railroads. If initial negotiations on humanitarian grounds fail, consideration should be given to further appeals offering a quid pro quo to the Germans such as hope of less severe peace terms or the possibility of reduced bombing of certain cities or areas.

Next to this first paragraph and underneath, a single handwritten word was added: "No." We do not know whether the document was a summary of Jewish demands made possibly by Peter Bergson, alias Hillel Kook, of the IZL Mission in the United States and communicated to Stettinius by Assistant

---

[1] Feingold, *The Politics of Rescue*; Wyman, *The Abandonment of the Jews*; Breitman, *Official Secrets*; and see Ronald W. Zweig, "Feeding the Camps: Allied Blockade Policy and the Relief of Concentration Camps in Germany, 1944-1945," *Historical Journal* 41, 3 (1998), 825-851. Whereas most authors value the work of the WRB as "too late if not too little," they perceive in the creation of the WRB at least a major move toward an "activist" rescue policy, which however was very much constrained by the Allied refusal to give Jews preferential treatment (anchored among other reasons in German refusal to do so) and due to their own policy of unconditional surrender and of economic blockade against Germany.

[2] Edward R. Stettinius, Jr., Papers, University of Virginia, courtesy of Richard Breitman.

Secretary Long, to be rejected by both or by a higher authority, or by another State Department official, as it seemed to have given Hitler what he might have wanted to achieve among other things during the Final Solution: a sense of emergency among the Western Allies, as influenced by the Jews as they supposedly were to do it, to make concessions to him if they wanted Jews to be saved from his mills of death, or to supply him with official evidence that the war was about Jews. At least that is how Allied officials would perceive such ideas on top of the possible military ramifications of an Allied promise to declare a part of Germany "bomb safe."

The memo further recommended a major change in Allied treatment of those who managed to escape by constructing "healthful and attractive receiving centers," the transportation of the "appropriate persons" once "carefully classified as to skills and experience" to countries "where labor shortages exist." Finally, the authors of the memo foresaw "negotiations . . . with neutrals to obtain shipping to transport refugees to Palestine or to other havens of refuge." This last sentence prompted yet another handwritten rejection "in view [of] the Zionists in the Arab World."

When one reads this document in conjunction with the arguments of the (non-Jewish) officials in the Treasury Department who worked toward the establishment of the WRB and threatened Roosevelt that he might be exposed (in an election year) as an accomplice of the British in their monstrous refusal to allow Jews to survive,[3] one cannot help but expect these recommendations never to be accepted, at least those related to the negotiations on a "quid pro quo" with Hitler. Indeed they were never endorsed by the State Department or by higher authorities.

We have at our disposal only indirect evidence in this regard when a day later Stettinius wrote a memo to Assistant Secretary Long in which he mentioned Long's own memo of December 27 "relative to the discussion with and communication from Mr. Peter Bergson." Having studied the file, Stettinius decided "not to send a letter to him (Bergson) at this time," but he was "still considering the possible telegrams to neutrals and the possible warnings to the satellite governments – regarding rescue – and will be in touch with you on these matters later." Stettinius was of a tentative opinion, however, that "it might be advisable not to send one at this time [due to the possible change in its orientation – e.g., a possible separate peace with Budapest – S.A.] to Hungary."[4] This memo at least indicates no interest in the far-reaching recommendations for a "quid for quo" in negotiations with Hitler regarding rescue.

Soon enough the whole issue was turned over from the State Department to the WRB itself, which was created separately, seemingly as an independent agency, in January 1944 but "too late" and doing "too little," as David

---

[3] See Wyman, *The Abandonment of the Jews*, pp. 178–182.
[4] Memo dated January 8, 1944, Stettinius Papers, box 215, folder Asst. Sec. Long October 1943, courtesy of Richard Breitman.

Wyman put it. In fact, the WRB had to work with the State Department and coordinate its efforts with the U.S. Army, the OSS, and others.

Yet my interpretation of the impact of the creation of the WRB on the Germans is that the very birth of a special agency to deal with the rescue of Jews, even if Jews were never referred to in its title, might have given Hitler – and Himmler – a sense of having some trump card against the Allies: some among the remaining Jews of Europe. The creation of the WRB might have been seen in Hitler's eyes as a typical challenge: If FDR wanted to save Jews, he should have tried to do it in a way that would expose the American president as if he was fighting a "Jew's war," and if possible a wedge could be driven between the Allies by using Jews for that purpose without allowing any meaningful number of Jews to survive.

Hitler did not give up on victory until very late, and once he did only very few Jews would be left alive because he was determined to destroy as many as possible until the very end. At least until the end of 1944, when he was getting ready for his big surprise attack in the Ardennes, he had a source of information on the WRB's rescue efforts and similar endeavors hereto unknown to us, meaning the intercepts made by his OKW/Chifrierabteilung (OKW/Chi).

The significance of the OKW/Chi decrypts of American diplomatic messages (one code entitled "black" was broken late in 1941, others sometime late in 1943, and they ended about a year later) is to be understood in terms of my "kaleidoscopic" methodology (e.g., the reflection of reality as perceived by the enemy and by the so-called "third parties," thanks to the information made available to them by decrypts and other sources).[5] In addition to these records, American and sometimes British, Jewish, and Zionist records will be quoted that deal with the same or related issues.

The OKW/Chi VN (verlässliche Nachrichten – reliable news) decrypts available at the U.S. National Archives – captured after the war – reveal only a partial picture of what the Germans might have known from this and also from other sources, some quoted earlier and some, like those read by the decrypting division of the Nazi Foreign Office, that are not yet available to us. Hitler read OKW/Chi decrypts, as we are told in an American–British postwar study of its operations.[6] We cannot, however, prove which decrypts he read, nor which actions he took as a result. Further, we do not have the distribution list of the decoded messages, but we can assume that Himmler, his foreign intelligence chief, Walter Schellenberg, and others had to be extremely careful with whatever plans they might have toyed with behind Hitler's back if and when they did so.

---

[5] For the early history of OKW/Chi, see David Kahn, *Hitler's Spies: German Military Intelligence in World War II*, paperback edition (New York: DA-APO Press, 2000), pp. 191–203.
[6] See Note on the Sources for a detailed discussion of the dissemination of the OKW/Chi decrypts within the Nazi hierarchy.

At the same time, the OKW/Chi decrypts tell us in their way what the Allies were doing in various ways, including the hectic activities of WRB's operatives upon its inception. Thus, the following cable from Washington, dated February 9, 1944, from the State Department and signed by Secretary of State Cordell Hull but in fact sent by the WRB to the American Legation in Bern, dealt with funds made available to the International Red Cross (ICRC) in Geneva to help Jews in Rumania, Croatia, Hungary, Slovakia, and Theresienstadt by the Joint Distribution Committee (AJDC), as authorized by the Treasury Department.[7]

On March 11, 1944, a cable that was sent to the American Ambassador (William Averell Harriman) in Moscow from the WRB[8] was intercepted and decoded within two weeks afterward. Accordingly, the WRB was explicitly given the task by the President of the United States of "immediate action" and help to be rendered to the "Jews of Europe" and other victims of the enemy's persecution. Hence, the WRB was trying to mobilize Soviet help as well, but Harriman was instructed not to put pressure on Moscow "to do more than they are doing now" and yet to ask for their cooperation in various programs now under consideration. Thus, Ira Hirschmann, the WRB's representative in Turkey, has discussed two matters upon the suggestion of Ambassador Laurence Steinhardt with Vinogradov, the Soviet Ambassador in Ankara. One was to join the WRB in its efforts to put pressure to bear on Bulgaria and the other Nazi "satellite states" to treat Jews humanely and also approach the Turkish government to allow the use of a vessel in order to evacuate refugees therefrom. Vinogradov was ready to "informally" discuss the matter with his Bulgarian colleague, but in both relevant cases he referred Hirschmann to Moscow, and thus this message was cabled to Harriman plus a high-powered declaration of intent to warn all the "satellites" against cooperation with this "organized murder" against the Jews and others, especially Rumania, Bulgaria, and Hungary. Speaking in terms of a "crusade," the WRB also referred – with the necessary caution – to the fact that many refugees living under satellite control (such as in Transnistria) should be evacuated to Turkey, "if the governments thereof will allow it," and repeated the term "crusade" as if not only the governments of the related countries but also their peoples should be warned against collaborating with the Nazis in this regard. This cable was distributed by OKW/Chi about a week after the occupation of Hungary by the Germans.

The situation in Bulgaria was unique. The small community of Jews in Bulgaria proper (not those who used to live in the annexed parts of

---

[7] OKW/Chi V.N. No. 1746/2.1994 F., received February 11, decrypted on February 28, 1944, top secret. Source: RG 457, Entry 1032, HCC, box 211.

[8] OKW/Chi V.N. No. 2167/3.1944 F. Sent on March 11, 1944, received by OKW/Chi on March 14, decrypted on March 28, 1944, Geheime Kommandosache (i.e., top secret): Source NA, RG 457, Entry 1032, box 205.

Macedonia, all of whom had been deported) remained alive due to internal conditions to which the Germans might have been alerted but had no power to change. Otherwise, the OKW/Chi decrypts read like a mirror reflection of those of WRB, the U.S. Embassy in Ankara, and Zionist officials, as well as Kasztner's own cables as follows (organized by dates). The first that should be mentioned is a cable sent by Shaul Meirov-Avigur, the head of the Zionist Mossad (organization) for Immigration via the State Department from Istanbul to a Zionist colleague in New York, dated February 2, 1944,[9] in which he detailed the rescue actions "in this critical moment" (following the establishment of the WRB) that needed to be presented according to "our gained experience" to the United Nations. First, the Slovak Jews could flee to Hungary in order to immigrate further therefrom . . . (rest illegible). Second, emigration from Bulgaria was still possible. Third, neutral (e.g., Swedish and Portuguese) vessels should collect refugees from Slovakia, Rumania, and Hungary in Rumanian and Bulgarian ports, next to Red Cross . . . (decrypt incomplete). Fourth, the population of the occupied territories should be warned daily through radio programs neither to allow the persecution of the Jews nor to support the Germans in this regard. This should be an Allied policy in the sense that the relevant nations will demonstrate in this way their intention to depart from Nazi Germany. Fifth, the radio stations of the United Nations should call upon opposition groups and the churches in these countries to shelter Jews, while the Red Cross was expected to enlarge its operations with regard to refugee children and food parcels and appoint a special commissioner in charge of the rescue of refugees. That most of this was a sort of daydream becomes clear from an OKW/Chi decrypt of Swiss efforts on behalf of the WRB to save Jews under German occupation control who pretended to be foreign passport holders when the Germans told them that most had forged visas and thus would be treated "by police methods" like any other local Jews, let alone help saving hundred of thousands of Hungarian and Slovak Jews later in 1944 (most of the Slovak Jews who had survived since mid-1943 were deported late in 1944) by appointing a commissioner or by radio broadcasts, or by most of the other means already mentioned.[10] The Rumanian Jews were a special case: at this stage, even many deportees to Transnistria were allowed to return to Rumania proper, while the Zionists were trying to get as many as possible to Palestine, with a limited degree of success. The German Foreign Office tried its best to stop the immigration to Palestine until the final break between Rumania and Germany in August. Indeed, German power did not suffice at this stage to impose itself on Rumania.[11]

[9] Same source as in note 8, folder 17.
[10] RG 457, Entry 1032, box 206, Volume 5.
[11] See Randolph L. Braham, *The Politics of Genocide: The Holocaust in Hungary*, Volume II (New York: Columbia University Press, 1981), pp. 908–910.

Another cable, dated March 22, 1944, from the American Consulate General in Zurich, promised entry visas for refugee children from France – when and if such children could reach the American consulates in Switzerland at that early date, one might add. But it was a step forward, at least in the sense that the Swiss authorities would allow them entry. However, the Germans knew about these efforts and more, thanks to rescue efforts that started before the creation of the WRB and that the Board had tried to enhance upon its birth. Its very birth and early rescue efforts may have encouraged the Germans to finish off those Jews who were supposed to be rescued, while pretending to deal with them through the Zionists and the American intelligence network established by Alfred Schwarz, codenamed "Dogwood."

When we turn our kaleidoscope toward the rescuers, we shall see that a basic common denominator seems to have been shared by Alfred Schwarz, Teddy Kollek, and Rezsö Kasztner. All three were men of action. His ties with Schwarz, "shahor" in Hebrew, were certainly known to Kollek's Jewish Agency superiors,[12] possibly offering a breakthrough: a Jew placed high in the American intelligence network operating in occupied Europe.

Out of the three, only Kollek escaped calamity then and afterward. The two others were perceived – even tainted – from two different angles, that of the Allies and that of contemporary Jews, to have been or to have become enemy tools. The story of both was a subject for extensive research, much more so Kasztner's role during and immediately after the Hungarian Holocaust, because each became politicized before, during, and following his trial in Israel and his ensuing violent death.

Schwarz's case was studied first by Barry Rubin, then by Jürgen Heideking and Christoph Mauch, and by Yehuda Bauer, who interviewed him and gained a personal view of this interesting person. Tuvia Friling has also recently contributed his share to this research. My contribution to this previous scholarship is based not only on their work but on primary sources used by them but interpreted in my own way, due to new sources that I have added on Kasztner, Kollek, and "Dogwood."

Alfred Schwarz, a Czech-born Jewish intellectual turned businessman,[13] settled in Turkey in 1928. As described by Bauer, he had decided since the outbreak of World War II to dedicate his energies to fighting the Third Reich. According to his self-portrait, supplied to OSS X-2 following the decline of his power and initial success as an American intelligence operative,[14]

---

[12] See Friling, *Arrow in the Dark*, p. 447.

[13] See his short bio as published by him in Alfred Schwarz, *Der Mensch im Widerstreit mit sich selbst* (Vienna: Verlag für Wissenschaft und Kunst, 1981). The title translates as "Man in Conflict with His Own Self." This was his second published book – the first one, entitled *Irrungen des Geistes – Der Verrat am Leben*, was published in 1979. Both books show the influence of Karl Popper and Bertrand Russell – in a rather amateurish fashion.

[14] RG 226, Entry 210, box 53, folder 217. This document was withdrawn from previous OSS records but declassified in 2001 and released in the fall of that year.

Schwarz was born in 1904 and from 1924 had been engaged as advertising manager of a Czech concern "on the strength of lectures on Mass Psychology and the Psychology of Advertising." He won a public competition for advertising circulars and from 1926 to 1927 was adviser on advertising to the Czechoslovak machine industry. Schwarz was not exactly an intellectual, or a better-educated man of the European World, as he at least perceived himself to be. But he harbored such self-perceptions and ambitions as would be seen as rather typically Jewish, and in his way they were. In 1928, Schwarz was sent to Turkey as the representative of Czech and Austrian industrial concerns, was active until 1938 in Turkish business as the representative of the two largest Czechoslovak concerns, a large Austrian engineering company, and as a contractor to the Turkish government. Having had his ties with German, Czech, and Austrian exiles in Turkey, and being pretty ambitious intellectually and politically (not unlike Rezsö Kasztner), Schwarz was at least exposed to their dreams, knowledge, and hopes.

According to his OSS dossier, he was representative plenipotentiary of a large English engineering firm in Turkey between 1938 and 1942, but from 1942 to 1943 he was acting as "adviser and collaborator of the British Military Intelligence Department for Central European questions" (e.g., for Colonel Harold Gibson's MI6 Istanbul station). It is possible that prior to this stage he established relations and trust with one Frantisek-Fritz Laufer, who will become a central figure in this story as possibly the key to the emergence and failure of the rescue efforts in Hungary and beyond and possibly other tragedies. Laufer was Jewish or half Jewish, or believed to be by the Western Allies, and at least since May or June 1944 the British and the American counterintelligence services had regarded him as a full-fledged enemy agent.[15] Laufer is described by Bauer to have been "reportedly" a former waiter in a Prague Café[16] who was recruited by the Abwehr in exchange for "Aryan" papers, having betrayed Czech resistance operatives to the Germans. If true (the records available to me could not corroborate this as yet), Laufer may have had early ties with the Gestapo and SD-Inland,

---

[15] See SAINT London to SAINT Istanbul (SAINT means "Intelligence" in general; however, the contents of the message reveal OSS X-2 as its originator in London and recipient in Istanbul), Subject: London Fortnightly Report, dated June 13, 1944, RG 226, Entry 214 (AI-174), declassified May 9, 2001. This document contains a list of names and issues, many based on British information, including that of Friederich [sic] Laufer, who has here a previously unknown alias (Ludwig Hermann). According to this source, "Laufer is popularly regarded as a 'Gestapo' agent in Budapest, as he appears to be persona grata with the Germans in spite of being a Jew, and has suddenly shown signs of great wealth." The same document contains a sharp criticism of the missing cooperation between X-2 and the other field branches of OSS, using the Schwarz case as an example of the ensuing damage. Laufer, who served OSS as a "Dogwood" agent, is exposed here as an enemy tool not without connection to the preceding criticism.

[16] Bauer, *Jews for Sale?*, p. 129.

whose job was to fight resistance in the Czech Protectorate, and with the Abwehr. As such, his Abwehr and Gestapo/SD superiors would have been Captain Erich Klausnitzer and Captain Gerhard Clages,[17] both of whom operated in Prague, and we shall meet them again in Budapest with Laufer in due course.

Schwarz's description of Laufer was different.[18] According to Schwarz, Laufer was born in Prague in 1900, graduated from a Gymnasium, and studied in a "School for Agricultural technique." He then worked in his father's food import firm and as administrator the family estate. Later, he became "Director of the Import and Export Department of a Prague department store, which dealt with textiles." Indeed, in his dealings with the Zionists later on behalf of his German masters, Laufer used the alias "Direktor Schroeder" among others.

According to Schwarz, Laufer in 1938 was sent by his department store to Belgrade, where he directed its export business until "the city was bombed." Then he moved to Budapest, "where he conducts purchases in Balkan countries on behalf of Swiss import firms, and has of late conducted compensation deals with Swiss and Balkan firms." As a man of means, Laufer also developed business ties in Bulgaria and Turkey, had contacts with the heads of the German diplomatic mission in Rumania and its mission chief in Greece, but since 1940 "he has been in touch with the Allies, and closely associated with them since 1942, working under the instructions of one who is now a close collaborator of ours." No further information was given on this "collaborator," who could, however, be Teddy Kollek.[19] "He is an objective, realistically-minded, serious man, extremely enterprising and not without a certain adventurous vein," Schwarz continues. As such, Laufer might have been used by the Germans to handle contraband deals across borders and purchase for them strategic goods, which enriched him on top of his

---

[17] Klausnitzer's identity remains a mystery. Whereas Clages's personal file clearly identifies him as an SD/Gestapo officer, to be quoted later, there is no "Erich" Klausnitzer file existing in the BDC (SS) personal files at NARA. A file was found only on an Alfred Klausnitzer, who indeed was active as an SD agent within the Czechoslovak Army before the annexation of the Czech "Protectorate" by Nazi Germany and was commissioned by RSHA Chief Heydrich to SS Lieutenant in 1942 after having served as an SD agent in occupied Czech territory. It could be a case in which an SD agent was serving in the regular German Army as an Abwehr officer, but the SS personal file ends with Alfred Klausnitzer being promoted by Heydrich in 1942.

[18] RG 226, Entry 210, box 104, withdrawn until August 2001, original box 439, folder 2, Schwarz's description of his agents, with Laufer as flower name "Iris." There were several instances in which the rather secretive "Dogwood" was finally forced by X-2 and other bodies, including Harry Harper, rapport officer in OSS Istanbul, to reveal the true names of his "flower agents" plus short descriptions of them, which we find in various (not just one) OSS entries.

[19] See "Dogwood" Schwarz list of his agents under code name "Iris," RG 226, Entry 210, box 104, folder 2.

previous fortune, and he was also used by the Zionists as a courier to and from Budapest.

In the meantime, Schwarz sold his firm and became "Dogwood," a full-fledged American intelligence operative, among whose agents Laufer was regarded by "Dogwood" Schwarz as one of the best, if not the jewel in the crown.

Yet his description of Laufer's business ties could have been a cover supplied by the Abwehr, or by the Gestapo/SD, for Laufer's real objectives among his contraband duties – to spy on Allied intelligence and betray his contacts, including those serving Admiral Canaris's Abwehr (and the Zionists as well). Indeed, Laufer's location in Budapest would have brought him in touch with both. However, he did become "Dogwood" Schwarz's most trusted agent and courier, under the code name "Iris." According to Samu Springmann in an interview with the present writer, it was Laufer who sometime in 1943 advanced the idea of ransoming Jews in occupied Europe in exchange for Allied goods such as trucks. Springmann's affidavit is supported by Dogwood's own testimony in an interrogation after the collapse of his chain in summer 1944, at which time he told OSS Rapport officer Harry Harper, Jr., that Laufer "has proposed using a Jewish refugee deal, in which refugees in Central Europe would be exchanged for either material or money."[20] In Harper's opinion, "this scheme has apparently never been more than a wild dream." On top of the interesting fact that Laufer may have referred to Jews in "Central Europe" alone, not those doomed already in Eastern Europe (e.g., Rumanians, Hungarians, and Bulgarians, who at that stage were not under direct German control), at least a few of them might not have been removed from Laufer's world of contraband activities. The Germans of course tried hard to have the Jews of Rumania, Hungary, and Bulgaria destroyed like all the others. Especially in the case of the Kallay government in Hungary, which allowed the Jews a reasonable degree of normal life, the German reaction to this was one of outspoken anger. Yet trading with a small number of Jews was another matter. It is hard to guess whether ideas such as Laufer's truck proposal could be connected to Hitler's own order, issued late in 1942, that a "few rich Jews" could be exchanged for "large sums of foreign currency," as described earlier. Still, a small number of Jews was always possible barter for a deal if the German side could hope for much larger material or political gains, or both, in exchange.

Nothing came out of this except the myth of the Slovak "Europa Plan," but the idea remained in the mind of Springmann, and possibly other rescue workers, until it was renewed (or so it seemed) by the Germans upon the occupation of Hungary in March 1944. It seems, however, that Laufer's ties

---

[20] RG 226, Entry 210, box 53, folder 217. Harper's devastating report on "Dogwood" was released to the NA before the above-cited new release at Entry 210 and is quoted by Bauer in *Jews for Sale?* from Entry 148, box 34; see his Chapter 8, note 18.

with the Nazis, when they became known to his Zionist interlocutors, did not disturb them, nor "Dogwood" Schwarz, but for different reasons – Schwarz was sure that Laufer was *his* loyal agent and not a German-operated traitor.

For the Zionists, Laufer might have been a loyal "Dogwood" agent or primarily an enemy agent, but the idea that one must negotiate with the enemy to save lives had taken root among the Zionists, and others were talking about it at least since the mass rally at Madison Square Garden late in 1942, which even called for negotiations with the Germans to stop the carnage. Ransoming of Jews was by itself an idea not foreign to Jews since time immemorial, and the assumption was that enough corruption and loopholes existed on the Nazi side to try it not just in Slovakia.

Whereas Schwarz blindly trusted Laufer, the Zionist rescue workers wanted to get to the heart of the enemy, combining this with intelligence work for the Allies. The rescue operatives in Istanbul, such as Z'eev Shind and Teddy Kollek, who joined them in May 1943,[21] thought that they could sell such contacts to Allied intelligence or be allowed to pursue them in exchange for other services. Thanks to Samu Springmann's contacts in Budapest, they engaged as a courier one Rudi Scholz, who went as far as the Polish ghettos to deliver Zionist mail and money, in addition to others who joined the Zionist "courier service" such as Bandy Grosz, Joseph Winninger, and Charles Popescu. Scholz, Winninger, and Popescu were associated with the Abwehr. Grosz – a converted Jew – was known to have served the Hungarian intelligence service as well. The Zionists believed similarly to "Dogwood" himself, who made Kollek one of his own American network agents, codenamed "Gerbera,"[22] that such Zionist–Nazi ties could help the Allied cause for intelligence and even be used for political purposes. In fact, Joseph Winninger became Schwarz's agent "Begonia," while Grosz became his agent "Trillium."

According to X-2's post-"Dogwood" inquiries, based on British-supplied information and Grosz's own interrogation by the British and the American CIC and OSS[23] after his arrest by the British in May 1944, Winninger was a German courier and agent of the Abwehr Ast III.F (Ast is the abbreviation of Abwehrstelle – Abwehr station) in Vienna, who "worked for the Jewish Agency in Istanbul, and for the British and the Americans in Turkey." Known to the Zionists as "Joszi," Winninger was believed to be half Jewish.[24] He had been based in Vienna according to the X-2 report in Budapest since at least early 1943, when "Trillium" (i.e., Grosz) first met him. "Trillium"

---

[21] See Friling, *Arrow in the Dark*, Volume I, pp. 447 ff.

[22] See Schwarz's description of his agents, RG 226, Entry 210, box 53, folder 217.

[23] See in this regard the X-2 summary on Winninger, contained in Appendix A: "Dogwood Chain's Personalities," p. 72, withdrawn from the original X-2 report, pp. 53–54, made by Major Pfaff (see note 9 in Chapter 24) but available now thanks to the Nazi War Crimes Disclosure Act.

[24] See Friling, *Arrow in the Dark*, Volume I, pp. 326–328, 445–471.

encountered Winninger when he was looking for someone to transport Zionist mail and money to Poland and Slovakia. Winninger arranged for this service (possibly paying off Wisliceny among other things), first notifying his chief, Dr. Schmidt (Chief V–Mann of IIIF, Vienna in Hungary, the Abwehr operative in charge of undercover agents in Hungary). Under Winninger's plan, Ast Vienna retained 40% of the Zionist money; most of the reminder was divided among Winninger, Abwehr courier Popescu, and "Trillium." Winninger also cheated the Zionists on the exchanges from gold or dollars into Reichsmarken. "Trillium" stated that he warned the Zionists against Winninger, telling them that the Abwehr was controlling all their mail and funds, but the Zionists apparently disregarded his warnings.

The Zionists were trying desperately to reach Poland and Slovakia at all costs. Moreover, Kollek had succeeded in convincing "Dogwood" that he was operating in Istanbul, as the Jewish Agency's own Intelligence Service was doing "in Syria and in Iran" in collaboration with the British.[25] "Later it was decided to extend and develop the organization and transplant it to Europe, where the existence of some remaining positions of influence in Jewish hands (Hungary, Rumania, Slovakia – parentheses in original), and the movement of emigration from Europe to Palestine via Turkey offers favorable openings for intelligence work."

Referring to a rather limited local cooperation between the Jewish Agency's representatives and MI6's Colonel Harold Gibson, his deputy Arthur Whittal, and MI9's Commander Wolfson, the impression was created that the British supported the Zionists at least regarding intelligence gathering, and hence there was no problem in "finally" securing an agreement on close cooperation "with our Department" (i.e., the "Dogwood" chain), reached following Shertok's visit to Istanbul in August 1943.

"Dogwood," and his superior "Cereus" Coleman, went so far as to endorse Kollek's political overtures toward the American government against Zionist fears of the British mandatory government of Palestine. It should be repeated here that in mid-1943, upon Kollek's arrival in Istanbul, the relations between the Yishuv and the British authorities in Palestine itself deteriorated following local and regional developments. It is thus not surprising that Kollek tried his luck with the Americans, which resulted in "Dogwood's" memo just quoted. In essence, Kollek argued that the Jewish Agency's intelligence effort, compared to the "passive or hostile attitude of the Arabs" to the Allied cause, should be recognized in addition to the "confidence" expressed in the United States for an "honest and sympathetic attitude" toward the Zionist claims and goals in Palestine and the "Jewish Question in general," beyond the "exclusive dealings with this [Dogwood's]

---

[25] See Report on the Desirability of our Co-operation with the Jewish Agency, dated October 27, 1943; source Cereus; subsource Dogwood; date of information, the same. Source RG 226, Entry 92, box 591, file 5.

Department." Fearing British postwar refusal to honor the Zionist contribution to the Allied cause, Kollek suggested (or "Dogwood" did on his behalf) that "during the journey of an American emissary in special mission to Palestine Shertok should be notified in consultation with our Department that the contributions of his organization are appreciated and conscientiously recorded by the competent American Government Departments," so that they "will not be forgotten when the future of the Jewish nation in Palestine . . . and elsewhere will come under discussion by the Allies." "Dogwood's" memo went so far as to suggest "further consolidation and deepening of the connection with us" that "might be recommended" to the Jewish Agency "on this basis," and that "official contact should be made in USA" with Dr. Nahum Goldmann, the American representative of the Political Department of the Jewish Agency:

> . . . to let him know that the help given by the J. A. through Teddy Kollek in Turkey to the representatives of our Department, Dogwood, is known and appreciated, and that it represents a very positive argument for the Jewish protagonists in the USA. Shertok should then be notified in a suitable manner that such an assurance has been given to Goldmann in the USA [underlines in original]. (RG 226, Entry 92, box 591, files)

These political activities were to be carried out in "great urgency" "in the interest of the valuable results held out for US intelligence in the immediate future."

Thus, "Dogwood" Schwarz made himself, in hostile British eyes, a Zionist agent, and therefore one may speculate that they and their X-2 colleagues would act to destroy his credibility if he gave them a chance to do so, with Kollek's involuntary help.

At the same time, the Jewish Agency's embryonic Intelligence Service was desperately forging plans to fight the Germans by landing commandos behind enemy lines within Allied ranks, and at the same time Kollek and his associates were helping Allied intelligence by supplying strategic information (weather conditions and the like plus details on Allied flyers shot down in Rumania thanks to their cable and telephone connections with Zionist operatives in that country) and in interrogating Jewish refugees for their own military benefit. All of these activities were sort of contradictory, or supplementary, if we want to discern the spirit of those terrible times.

At any rate, the first contact with the dying Jews in Poland made through Rudi Scholz created much hope and emotion among the rescue workers. Rudi Scholz was supposed to have been head of Abwehr station Budapest,[26] and the Zionists sensed that he might have had no altruistic motives in serving them. In fact, they even thought that he was a Gestapo officer, but the emergency justified emergency measures and could create various

---

[26] Friling, *Arrow in the Dark*, p. 447.

justifications for dealing directly with the enemy in the hope that in this case the man was after Springmann's young secretary and/or was an anti-Nazi in disguise. At the same time, they were aware of the alleged Europa Plan negotiations, and these were held with Dieter Wisliceny, a Gestapo officer, who seemed to be ready and able to do business. Yet both Springmann and Bandi Grosz, when interrogated by the British later in 1944, belittled Scholz's person and real service for the Zionists since in reality he was a subaltern Abwehr operative, a contraband dealer who was involved in efforts to smuggle Jews out of Switzerland to Spain and enriched himself without delivering.[27]

In the meantime, Schwarz and his existing contacts in Turkey and in occupied Europe became "Dogwood" in summer 1943 as a full-fledged American network operative under the supervision of Archibald "Cereus" Coleman, who had worked for OSS in Spain and in Mexico without much success but seemed this time to be able to pursue a big game.[28]

According to Coleman's post-"Dogwood" report made to X-2, OSS-HQ initiated the penetration of Axis countries from Istanbul since previous efforts of that kind undertaken from Switzerland, Sweden, and England had proved unsuccessful.

Early in September 1943, Teddy Kollek initiated a meeting with the American Consul General in Istanbul, offering intelligence work with the Americans, according to Coleman. Finally Kollek found his way officially to "Dogwood," although the two had already been in touch beforehand and had used Grosz as a courier to Budapest as well.

Thus, Kollek suggested to Coleman to use Grosz either as a courier or as a source of military intelligence, in cooperation with British Intelligence at first. Nothing much came out of this, but for his part Grosz was eager to talk to the Americans on another matter – as an envoy of Hungarian officials interested in a separate peace.

At the same time, "Dogwood" seemed to have been able to penetrate Nazi Germany itself, working toward a major coup that might have ended the war soon enough. Combining his views of the war goals in general, of the future of Germany, and of his desire to save as many Jews as possible as soon as possible, Schwarz had his ties with German opposition circles in Istanbul and acted as an intermediary between them and his American superiors, starting with "Cereus" Coleman, then working directly with OSS

---

[27] See SIME Report No. 2, Andor Gross, SIME/P.7755, PRO reference KV/120; no date on this record, but interrogation dates are given as June 6–22, 1944. See also extracts from SIME Interrogation Report No. 2 of May 25, 1944 (Received June 3, 1944) – "Personalities known to Springmann in Budapest and Istanbul," PRO reference KV/130, according to which Scholz was an unreliable smuggler and possibly an Abwehr V-Mann (Subaltern agent). Reference courtesy of BBC4.

[28] See Coleman's report to Major Lee M. Sharrar, Executive Officer, X-2, dated December 5, 1944, entitled "Dogwood Project, Istanbul Mission," declassified May 9, 2001.

Station Chief Lanning Macfarland (codenamed "Juniper"), and all the way to General William Donovan and his top aides.

According to the related OSS records, published by Jürgen Heideking and Christoph Mauch,[29] "Dogwood" had endorsed late in 1943 a far-reaching, dramatic, "one blow" strategy to end the war in the West, avoid the "Bolshevization" of Germany by the advancing Red Army and allow it to adopt a democratic, Western-oriented postwar regime, save hundreds of thousands of Allied lives, and – obviously – stop the Holocaust, although this was never mentioned as his goal. The German opposition leader, who was supposed to represent a group of various anti-Nazis "in high positions," ready and allegedly able to collaborate with the Western Allies in implementing this "one blow" strategy, supposedly in conjunction with current Allied invasion plans, was Helmuth James, Count von Moltke, a scion of the Prussian military aristocracy. "Dogwood" thus endorsed, or even devised himself, in negotiations with von Moltke's German refugee contacts in Istanbul a seemingly sophisticated strategy of a separate peace between Germany and the Western Allies, which may have become known to Fritz Laufer, his trusted agent, and to other "Dogwood" agents as well, and thus it might have been returned to the Allies later on in a fashion to be discussed in chapter 29.

The "grand design," as formulated by "Dogwood" in a letter to General R. G. Tindal, the American military attaché in Ankara, on December 29, 1943, anticipated that Allied invasion plans were nearing completion. Hence, President Roosevelt, Army Chief of Staff Marshall, and OSS Director Donovan were supposed to be informed and prepared for a decisive meeting with the German group "no later than January 1944" toward a new strategy in the sense that a protracted invasion of the Continent, similar to the endless one fought in Italy, had to be avoided but replaced with a combination of external pressure and internal German support. Possibly the Balkans should have been the target, but this was never spelled out in concrete terms.[30] In a supplemented exposé on the "readiness of a powerful German group to prepare and assist Allied Military Operations against Nazi Germany" attached to this letter, "Dogwood" outlined the new strategy in terms of a massive Allied invasion into Europe that would prove to the German people that Hitler was militarily defeated in order to avoid another stab in the back myth, accept "unconditional surrender" in order to meet Allied official policy principles, allow Germany as a whole to be occupied up to the

---

[29] Jürgen Heideking and Christoph Mauch, "Das Herman-Dossier, Helmuth James Graf von Moltke, die Deutsche Emigration in Istanbul und der Amerikanische Geheimdienst Office of Strategic Services (O.S.S.)," *Vierteljahreshefte für Zeitgeschichte* 4 (1992), 567–623.

[30] The reader is referred here to the relevant records cited verbatim by Heideking and Mauch, while I shall add to this narrative only the ones found and printed here either for the first time or mentioned by Bauer in *Jews for Sale?*, in which the way of interpreting them is different.

Tilsit–Lemberg line, thus stopping the Russians short of invading Germany proper and parts of Poland, and transform Germany into it to a Western-oriented democracy thanks to the active involvement of the German group in Allied service. In practical terms, the idea was to combine the giant Allied invasion of the Continent proper, in addition to the endless campaign in Italy, with a military act supporting the invasion and a domestic German uprising of sorts. The elimination of Hitler would also stop the Holocaust, about which "Dogwood" was careful to say nothing in the name of his German interlocutors, possibly to avoid the impression that he was aiming at his own, Jewish-specific cause. For Yehuda Bauer, this was a sign of the Moltke conservative group's own lack of interest in Jews, but the trap theorem explains the situation better than that – "Dogwood" could not appear in General Tindal's eyes, or those of his superiors, as someone whose main interest was related to Jews when high strategic and political matters of that kind were on the agenda. But soon enough "Dogwood" would be exposed as such, be dismissed, and even be denounced as a Nazi spy. Here, the Laufer and the Kollek connections proved to be fateful. In fact, according to one of Grosz's interrogations by the British Security Intelligence SIME,[31] Kollek was in touch with "Dogwood" already in May 1943, and at that time he supplied Grosz with Zionist mail, "including a letter from SCHWARZ... for a certain Fritz LAUFER, BUDAPEST." A few days afterward, Grosz received an urgent call from Anton Merkly, the Deputy Director of Hungarian Army Intelligence, one of his employers, who inquired about Laufer and asked him about Schwarz's letter, which he in fact gave to rescue operative Samu Springmann with the rest of the Zionist mail. Having recovered the letter from Springmann, an angry Merkly told Grosz that henceforth all the Zionist mail should pass through his hands since Laufer, "Chief V–Mann of AST.III, PRAGUE" had recently called with Captain Klausnitzer, head of Ast III, Prague, to complain against Grosz's "working with American Intelligence." Thus, the praxis disclosed here was a typical double-agent work – Laufer reported to Klausnitzer, and both complained to Hungarian Intelligence, whose operative Ferenc Bagyonyi told Grosz later that "LAUFER was a CZECH emigrant [as was "Dogwood," and hence a connection was hinted here by SIME – S.A.], alias Ludwig Mayer, and a first-class GERMAN agent."

Turning our kaleidoscope back to Washington, precisely at that period of time, the U.S. Congress endorsed the president's scheme to establish the WRB. The WRB went into action with a high degree of enthusiasm, hoping at least to save the entire Balkan communities, such as those of Hungary and Rumania. Soon enough, the Germans were reading the WRB's cable traffic from Turkey, the major base of WRB's operations, while the British were reading at least the SD/Gestapo cable traffic from and to Rome after the fall

[31] See extracts from SIME Report No. 3, OSS record in RG 226, Entry 210, box 105, folder 447.

of Mussolini, in which a clear-cut linkage was feared by the Germans between Italy and Hungary. In other words, once the fall of Mussolini triggered
the separate Italian–Allied peace, countered by the German occupation of
northern and central Italy, Hungary seemed to the Nazis to be the weakest
spot in their armor. The Allies seemed to have been eager and ready to exploit this weakness, but one should have calculated the German response to
such a danger, even with those Rome decrypts.

Ira Hirschmann, a New York department store executive, was likewise
not alarmed ahead of the German invasion, when he got prepared to assume
his WRB job in Ankara, and neither were other fresh WRB field operatives.
On the other hand, by the end of 1943, Allied victory seemed to be remotely
but not finally secured. Nor was General Donovan convinced that the situation was all too rosy. Nobody anticipated a successful German invasion
into Hungary. What Donovan – and Moltke – may have realized after the
fall of Mussolini was that the Germans were able to transform an initial disaster into a victory by easily occupying Italy and confining the Allied armies
within the mountainous peninsula. If the invasion anticipated for 1944 were
to be carried out in a similar fashion – protracted to endless battles afterward toward the fortified German border – the Nazis might at least create
a standstill of very serious ramifications. Hence there was an initial interest
on Donovan's side in the Moltke scheme. With regard to Hungary, OSS
Washington, London, and Bern were planning their own mission to Hungary,
codenamed Sparrow, whose official goal was gathering intelligence.[32] At the
same time, "Dogwood" had his own Hungarian operation, aimed at detach-
ing Hungary from the Germans, and there were ties with underground cells
in Austria, three seemingly different and promising operations.

In fact, Moltke himself and his "Kreis" had no real influence in Germany,
but if the coup itself succeeded, future historians could have believed[33] that
Moltke's involvement in what became the July 20, 1944, "Putsch" against
Hitler was known to Heinrich Himmler – the head of the SS and mass
murderer of the Jews – in advance, maybe thanks to Laufer. Accordingly,
Himmler allegedly waited to see whether the coup might succeed and did
nothing to prevent it. On the contrary, he might have perceived himself as
the one who could succeed Hitler and use Jews as trump cards for a separate
peace. Thus, the link on the one hand to von Moltke, who was arrested in
January 1944 by the Gestapo without any harm done to him as yet, and to
German agents making peace offers or suggesting all kinds of "deals" to save

---

[32] On the Sparrow mission, see General Donovan's cable to EXDET, Algiers, dated March 24,
1944, RG 226, Entry 210, box 462, in which the OSS Director defended the mission and
described its nature in the face of British, and possibly State Department, criticism. Obviously,
he described Sparrow to be an intelligence team, having no authority to act in political
matters.

[33] Rubin included; see his *Istanbul Intrigues*, pp. 172–175.

Jews in exchange for goods or even as hangers for separate peace talks, even when made by Jews who would prove later to be enemy agents such as Laufer and even if unrelated to each other, could be described by "Dogwood" as lost chances for shortening the war and of saving many Jewish lives. This view would be endorsed at least as a possibility by Yehuda Bauer.[34]

[34] See Bauer, *Jews for Sale?*, pp. 102, 104–112, 117–119, 126, 164–166.

24

The Double Hungarian Debacle

General Donovan was informed about the Moltke connection, and a series of consultations were conducted by General Tindal, by the OSS Director himself and his closest aides, and outside consultants even after Count von Moltke was arrested by the Gestapo in January 1944. It appears that he may have been betrayed by Fritz Laufer, "Dogwood's" own and much trusted agent.[1] For his part, the OSS Director was advised not to deal with some opposition groups in and outside Germany whose aims, strength, composition, and influence were questionable.

Behind this advice one could discern the fear that such a Western German coup could have blurred the principle of proving Nazism as a complete military and political disaster inflicted on Germany by Hitler's military in-competence combined with his ideology, thus avoiding another November 1918 situation that not only left Germany with its army intact but indeed created the political climate that allowed it to claim a military defeat as a lost victory or misuse American commitments made by President Wilson as if they had been broken all the way to Versailles, creating a rift with the Soviet Union.[2]

Hitler was certainly doing his best to prevent a second November 1918, which was the crucial experience in his life that transformed him into a "Politiker," and he would use any means possible to avoid the collapse of the home front and split the Allies by using propaganda means as well,

---

[1] This part of the narrative is based on Heideking and Mauch, "Das Herman-Dossier," as well, but not the speculation about Laufer's possible role in the arrest.

[2] This, in broad terms, was the view expressed by Alexander C. Kirk, the American Minister in Egypt, who had served in the American Embassy in Berlin before – see RG 226, Entry 88, box 420, also quoted by Bauer. Von Moltke, who knew Kirk, tried to meet with him beginning with his mission to the West but was rebuffed. Other separate peace soundings that go beyond the scope of this chapter were undertaken by various German parties, all of which were rejected by the Allies and hence became food for revisionist historians to argue against "unconditional surrender" from various angles.

including the "Jew's war" slogan, which was primarily aimed toward the West. The Western Allies might have learned from the same period and the ensuing infighting among themselves, plus the previous fall of Czarist Russia and the Stalin–Hitler Pact, to do everything in their power at least to bring this war to a definite conclusion while maintaining their alliance.

"Dogwood" had a good reason to believe that his initial mandate when his chain became an official American intelligence operation included toppling Axis governments, and this might have meant Germany itself to begin with, which explains his negotiations with Count von Moltke.[3] But he was also allowed to try and set underground cells in Austria and break the enemy's own coalition by dislodging Germany's allies, such as Hungary, from the Axis camp. In this case also, which should have saved the Jews of Hungary as well, the results were tragically either counterproductive or irrelevant. Yet in mid-1943, with the Battle of the Atlantic hardly won, and the Tunisian campaign not yet over, with "Dogwood" having created a network of agents, spies, informants, and anti-Nazi activists in Turkey and in the Balkans, in Austria, and in the Czech Protectorate that seemed to be a huge success, his views and standing seemed to be rather high among his American superiors.

The related OSS records will be cited in due course, but the main figures in "Dogwood's" Hungarian enterprise (i.e., dislodging this Nazi ally from the Axis camp) were his network agents, several among them Jews or half-Jews who served the Zionists as well, plus Teddy Kollek and some Hungarian officials probing the possibility of a separate peace with the West following the fall of Mussolini in the West while the Red Army was approaching from the East.

For the Zionist rescue workers, this network seemed to be rather promising now that through "Dogwood's" agents and other agents they could reach occupied Europe in order to achieve their contradictory goals of dealing with various Nazis on the ground, gathering intelligence for the Allies, working with local anti-Nazis, and helping to organize resistance among local Jews.

---

[3] This mandate is acknowledged as such even in the postwar evaluation of the "Dogwood" chain by X-2, SSU, dated May 1946, in which Schwarz was declared to be "a member of the Gestapo" by two German Intelligence agents allegedly active in Hungary during the war who were interrogated later by OSS after V-E Day. "Dogwood's" chain was blamed both for the failure of the "Sparrow mission" and the arrest of Franz Messner, the brain of an Austrian anti-Nazi cell, which in fact was "Dogwood's" own creation to a large extent. See "Penetration of O.S.S. by Foreign Intelligence Services," RG 226, Entry 210, box 241, folder 6. The German Intelligence agents quoted above, a "Kriminalrat Nohl" and one Grete Totter, have not been identified by me as such in the BDC personal files at NARA so far. Indeed, "Dogwood" might have been sloppy and unwise in handling his agents. Making him a "Gestapo member" would be at least a fantastic allegation, or rather the transformation of Laufer's role into that ascribed to "Dogwood" himself, which may have been the result of Nohl's and Totter's investigation.

According to Tuvia Friling, Moshe Shertok himself gave these various actions enthusiastic support on his visit to Istanbul in August 1943, about which Gestapo representative Richter was informed in due course, while David Ben-Gurion may have been motivated by the news about "Dogwood's" network and its connections to raising money for rescue by invoking emergency measures.[4]

Yet the fall of Mussolini and the ensuing strategic changes in Italy turned German attention onto Hungary no less.[5] An invasion of "Fortress Europe," to be undertaken in northern France, was perceived even by the then rather pessimistic Field Marshal Erwin Rommel, who soon became GOC of Army Group B, as having fair chances of being defeated on the beaches (with whose fortification he was entrusted).[6] Hence, the Balkans may have been perceived as the soft belly of German defenses, and this required action on their side once the Hungarians tried to walk away in addition to their preparations along Fortress Europe.

In this situation, "Dogwood" and his Istanbul station chief Macfarland, OSS Washington, plus OSS Bern and OSS London, were simultaneously working without informing each other on two separate Hungarian schemes, which in return helped trigger the German counter action and sealed the fate of most of the Jews of Hungary.[7]

The OSS's Hungarian schemes developed into a mess in which the Hungarian General Staff was involved, plus the Hungarian Intelligence Service, the German Abwehr under Admiral Wilhelm Canaris and its various operatives, plus Richard Klatt, a sports journalist whose real name was Fritz Kauders,[8] and who was believed to be of Jewish extraction, working for the German Air Force Intelligence and the Abwehr in Sofia, the "Dogwood" chain with its Jewish and half-Jewish agents on the American side, plus Teddy Kollek on the Zionist side, and the OSS-SI in Washington and London, Major Arthur J. Goldberg included, inspired by OSS Bern under Allen Dulles, which was working separately on the "Sparrow" mission.

---

[4] Friling, *Arrow in the Dark*, Volume I, p. 458n, and his Zionist source.

[5] See "German Estimate of Allied Intentions," Boston Series No. 1041, no date, RG 226, Entry 210, box 442, folder 7, and "German Speculation on Probable Allied Action in the Balkans and Eastern Mediterranean," Boston Series no. 1100, no date, RG 226, Entry 210, box 442, folder 8, but both dealt with the time span between late 1943 and early 1944. The "Boston Series" were original German diplomatic messages copied by Fritz Kolbe, alias George Wood, an anti-Nazi official working in the German Foreign Ministry, and delivered to OSS Bern; see Bradsher, "A Time to Act"

[6] See Erwin Rommel, *The Rommel Papers*, B. H. Liddel Hart (ed.) (Norwalk, CT: Easton Press, 1988), p. 463, containing Rommel's letter to his wife, Lu, dated March 31, 1944; see also p. 464, containing the entry in his diary dated May 15, 1944, "I telephoned...the Fuehrer for the first time a couple of days ago. He was in the best of humours and did not spare his praise of the work we've done in the West."

[7] See Petersen, *From Hitler's Doorstep*, pp. 96–97, 138–139, 198–199, 599–607.

[8] See Bauer, *Jews for Sale?*, p. 125.

In the ensuing OSS–X-2 investigation, submitted to OSS Director Donovan on July 28, 1944[9] the roots of Dogwood's Hungarian adventure were described in the following terms:

For the purpose of obtaining Axis military intelligence out of Istanbul, the so-called "DOGWOOD–CHAIN" [capital letters in original] was created by 550 [code number for Station Chief Lanning Macfarland – S.A.] in July 1943. This chain was to penetrate Germany and the Balkan Axis powers (Austria, Hungary, Rumania, and Bulgaria). In addition to obtaining military intelligence, it was hoped that this chain would be able to collaborate with resistance groups and eventually effect the overthrow of the Axis governments and their satellites. (Signed by Roger E. Pfaff, Acting Chief, X-2, box 352 Branch, RG 226, Entry 211, Folder Wn 19902)

The X-2 author, Major Pfaff, thus referred to Dogwood's German and Austrian contacts and moved over to "Dogwood's Hungarian Operations," finally combining them all – including the ensuing "Gestapo deal" or the so-called Brand Mission to exchange the Hungarian Jews for Allied strategic goods such as trucks – into one big serious intelligence blunder caused by "Dogwood," declared to be an enemy agent, and handled miserably by OSS Station Chief Macfarland:

DOGWOOD, presumably early in July 1943, established contact with a *Hungarian–Jew* [italics added], who was given the flower name, IRIS (Friedrich Laufer – parentheses in original). Through IRIS, the Hungarian General Staff was contacted some time before October 4, 1943, which agreed that a conference would be held in which American and trusted emissaries of SZOMBATHELY [General Ferenc Szombatelyi – S.A.], Chief of the Hungarian General Staff, would participate. (Pfaff, RG 226, Entry 211, folder Wn 19902)

X-2's Major Pfaff, the author, went on to say that Lieutenant Colonel Otto Hatz (self-description Otto von Hatz, Hungarian Military attaché in Sofia) was designated negotiator for the Hungarian side once he was appointed military attaché in Turkey. When we compare this document with Hatz's own description of his initial meetings with the Americans that he gave to the Germans, we find there "Dogwood" Schwarz and Theodor Kollek, and possibly also Kollek's aide and successor in Istanbul, Ehud Überall-Avriel. Bandi Grosz, the Hungarian Intelligence agent and Zionist courier (Dogwood's") agent codenamed "Trillium") became the liaison between Hatz and OSS-Istanbul (also when the former moved from Sofia as military attaché in Turkey) and the Hungarian General Staff.[10] For OSS X-2 Washington, Hatz's

---

9 Signed by Roger E. Pfaff, Acting Chief, X-2, box 352 Branch, RG 226, Entry 211, folder Wn 19902. My summary contains also heretofore withdrawn parts of this inquiry in Entry 210, box 35, which was the location after declassification thanks to the Nazi War Crimes Disclosure Act as previous "withdrawals" from available records, now open to research.

10 See Boston Series no. 1164 (original German report made available to the Americans by Fritz Kolbe, no date), entitled "German Conversation with Hungarian Colonel Hatz," RG 226, Entry 210, box 442, folder 9. According to this report, Hatz reported to Colonel Wagner,

reports delivered to the Germans on his negotiations with OSS-Istanbul were proof of his loyalty to the Nazi cause.

The Zionists, however, such as Kollek and Überall, who wanted Hatz to be an ally and met with him when the initial contact with him was created via the good services of Zionist courier Bandi Grosz, seemed to have been involved now in a big game, securing Hungary (and its large Jewish communities) to Allied plans in the Balkans if designed properly. Yet, according to X-2's Major Pfaff, "as early as December, 1943, 550 [station Chief Macfarland] was warned against von Hatz as an agent of the Axis, and as subsequent developments have clearly shown, von Hatz was in collusion with the Abwehr as early as December 14, 1943."

For his part, Macfarland wrote to his superior in Cairo, Colonel John Toulmin,[11] in January 1944 about his own doubts concerning Colonel Hatz and even called for X-2 intervention in this regard by "loosening up on a few of their trained agents" in order to "follow up matters of this kind." "I might add also," wrote Macfarland, "that we are quite aware of his [Colonel Hatz's] association with Andreagyongy [i.e., Andor Gyorgy, alias Bandi Grosz, whose name he was hardly able to spell right, or he did not bother to correct his dictation to a secretary – S.A.], *who acts as a runner for the Jewish agencies in supplying Jews in Europe with funds to flee the country*" (italics added).

Yet at least until early February 1944, Macfarland seemed to be interested in the negotiations with Hatz and was not bothered much by the Grosz connection. In a "final" meeting with Hatz on January 20, 1944, he tried to convey to the Hungarian military the idea, developed by "Dogwood" and "Cereus" Coleman, that they should take over from the politicians and lead the country toward a separate peace with the Allies. This seemed to be a legitimate military matter (i.e., an operation conducted within the official competence of OSS, which was primarily military).[12] Nothing much came out of this except that the Germans became alarmed enough to invade Hungary on March 19, 1944. All of the previous intelligence activities, such as Sparrow,

---

the Abwehr Chief in Sofia, that "through the intermediary of the Hungarian agent, Andreas Gyorgy [Bandi Grosz], the British and Americans had established contact with Hatz . . . early in October 1943. . . . Hatz met two Englishmen, one of whom, he thought, traveled constantly between Istanbul and Cairo [or rather Palestine – S.A.]. His name sounded something like Kellock [Kollek]. Both of these men tried, in a rather clumsy confidential fashion, to induce Hatz to engage in espionage against the Reich. Hatz had refused bluntly." A similar report was made to Admiral Canaris, the head of the Abwehr, around that time.

11 "Superior" in an administrative sense, as Macfarland had his direct line to General Donovan in Washington, reporting to Cairo at the same time; see RG 226, Entry 190, box 74, Cairo-SI-OP-7-10.

12 See the letter by Macfarland to General Donovan dated February 8, 1944, summing up the talks with Colonel Hatz as having led to a final meeting on January 20, the only one in which he personally participated, RG 226, Entry 210, box 344, folder "Hungarian Chiefs of Staff" no. 250/64/28/2-3.

seemed now to have been either exposed by the Germans or by some traitor or traitors or had become very much controlled by the Germans, among them "Dogwood's" agents "Iris" (Laufer) and "Trillium" (Grosz).

Suddenly, in mid-May 1944, the same Bandi Grosz came to Istanbul with Joel Brand, the Zionist rescue operative based in Budapest, on an official German mission offering separate peace talks between the Nazi SD and the Western Allies. Joel Brand suggested the ransoming of the Hungarian Jews for trucks and other commodities.

Who had recruited Grosz among others for this mission? "Iris" Laufer. Laufer was now exposed as a full-fledged Gestapo/SD agent, who was behind the Brand mission itself – named the "Gestapo Deal" by Allied Intelligence services – as proved to be the case from Grosz's and Brand's own interrogation by the British. A very unpleasant Jewish–Zionist–Gestapo/SD ploy could develop here, in Allied eyes, rather than rescue.

When we reconstruct the developments leading to such a conclusion drawn by the American OSS–X-2 and the U.S. Army's Counter Intelligence Corps, we discern here a number of phases. Hatz, who was supposed to represent the Hungarian General Staff in the separate peace negotiations late in 1943, reported about his meeting to the head of the Abwehr station in Sofia, Colonel Wagner (alias Dr. Delius). Since this was a political situation, the matter was referred also to the German Minister in Bulgaria, Adolf Beckerle. Possibly Hatz himself met with the minister. Beckerle gave Hatz's version of the meeting to his superiors in the German Foreign Ministry on December 14, 1943, and the report was made available to the Americans thanks to Fritz Kolbe, a German working in Ribbentrop's own office. A connection, not yet fully confirmed, was created here thanks to the same Kolbe report annotated by Allen Dulles in Bern between Hatz, his personal loyalty to the Germans, his way of life, and his Jewish contacts, as cabled by Dulles to Washington on January 2, 1944: "Hatz is reliable pro-German. However, he is short of funds and has numerous affairs with women. There is also an unconfirmed report to the effect that he is in touch with Jews who are paid by Hungarian Intelligence and that he shares in the profits which he makes from smuggling currency."[13]

The X-2 version of Beckerle's report seems to be shorter than the original but repeats its contents in most cases verbatim because it originated with Fritz Kolbe, an independent American intelligence source.

The significance of Kolbe's reports is that it took quite some time for Colonel McCormack of G-2's "Special Branch" to accept him as a bona fide, anti-Nazi German official who had direct access to his Foreign Ministry's cable traffic, which was copied and brought by him or delivered to Allen Dulles in Bern. But finally Kolbe's materials were accepted as high-level, authentic

---

[13] See Doc-2-109, Telegram 1534-38, January 2, 1944, reprinted in Petersen, *From Hitler's Doorstep*, pp. 190–191.

German records, later to be incorporated into "Ultra" messages. According to Kolbe's reports, there were several meetings – sort of negotiations – held between Hatz, Coleman, Schwarz, and Kollek about which he told the Germans (Minister Beckerle, Admiral Canaris) that he resisted the Americans' attempts to use his services for gathering intelligence and rather stressed "the fact that it was none other than the National Socialist Party and the Fuehrer who had instilled this unprecedented will to fight into the German army and had given it the inspiration for its mighty military performance," adding that "the Americans were extremely impressed by this argument and asked Hatz repeatedly if he really believed that National Socialism and the Fuehrer were at the bottom of this spirit of resistance."[14] For his interlocutors, especially "Dogwood," whether Hatz meant what he said or not, the elimination of Hitler following a successful Allied landing on the Continent, supported by elements within the German army itself as proposed by Count von Moltke, would indeed become a lost opportunity to shorten the war, save millions of lives, and stop the Soviets at the gates of Central Europe.

Parallel to the Hatz negotiations, General Donovan sent the OSS mission, organized by OSS Bern and codenamed "Sparrow," in which Major Arthur Goldberg, his Labor Desk chief in London, was involved as well,[15] to Hungary early in March 1944. Soon after its arrival, with the Germans already occupying Hungary, the mission members were arrested and handed over to the Germans.

OSS did not assess the imminent invasion properly but tried to encourage the Hungarians in January 1944 to "become a non-belligerent and cut off German transportation at the same time that Russian troops reached the Carpathians on the Hungarian frontier. Hungary would (therefore) render invaluable services – cutting the Southern German armies from the northern.... Germany cannot spare from 10–15 divisions which would be necessary to occupy Hungary."[16]

---

[14] See Boston Series No. 1165, "German Abwehr Report on Colonel Hatz's Activities," no date, RG 226, Entry 210, box 442, folder 9. This folder contains more German reports on Hatz that doubt his sincerity and loyalty to their cause later in 1944.

[15] See for details RG 226, Entry 97, box 35, which contains the history of the "Sparrow" mission from November 1943 and according to which the "Sparrow" team, consisting of one lieutenant and one master sergeant, had strict military intelligence objectives to be carried out in cooperation with a Hungarian general. See also RG 226, Entry 190 – Caserta-SI-OP-58-67-box 172, and Rubin, *Istanbul Intrigues*, pp. 194–195. The mission head, however, became a Colonel Florimond Duke. Donovan imposed Duke, who was described as being too old for the job, on the mission's planners in spite of his lacking the needed experience and training for such an endeavor. See the report made by an unidentified Labor Desk operative to Arthur Goldberg in London dated January 25, 1943 (must be 1944, letter received on February 4, 1944), RG 226, Entry AI-174–214, box 5, folder 24.

[16] Entry 97, box 35, incoming cable MC no. 338 from Bern, action Donovan and Macgruder (Deputy Director, OSS).

This indeed was the primary reason for the German preemptive invasion of March 19[17] but not the only reason, as OSS Bern (Dulles) summarized them in a cable to Washington on March 21, 1944: "(1) They knew that the Hungarians were carrying on discussions with Anglo-Saxons; (2) they did not want a 'Badoglio' in Hungary; (3) there were approximately 1,000,000 Jews behind the German armies and this the Germans could not stand."[18] Thus, American actions aimed at neutralizing Hungary and trapping the "southern German armies" fighting in Russia at the time, which certainly did not take into account the results of such actions on the last remaining large Jewish community in Europe and only helped to trap it, while the Germans needed much fewer forces to occupy Hungary than estimated.[19]

In occupied Hungary itself, a pro-Nazi government was established in Budapest. Admiral Miklós Horthy remained chief of state but was largely neutralized. A degree of Hungarian sovereignty was observed by the Germans, at least on the surface. In Budapest city, in cooperation and sometimes in friction with the Nazi–Hungarian Gestapo, which had come into being since the occupation, the SS had replaced the Abwehr after a short while. Agents who reported to the Abwehr or to the Gestapo/SD from a free base, not under direct German control as Budapest used to be in some cases, and to Hungarian intelligence had to confine themselves to various SS outfits such as Eichmann's special death squad, which arrived in Budapest upon the occupation, and deal also with special SS emissaries such as Kurt Andreas Becher, who came to Budapest on an economic mission.

Since the von Moltke project was dead, "Dogwood" was as active and as desperate to get results in Hungary, and possibly in Austria and Slovakia, by using Grosz, Winninger, and Laufer as best he could, and this involved him and others in a seemingly careless if not irresponsible treatment of his agents, who allegedly would betray the "Sparrow" mission and Schwarz's

---

[17] See for preparations for Fall Margarethe I (i.e., the German occupation of Hungary) and Hitler's talks with Regent Horthy in Percy Ernst Schramm (publisher and commentator), *Kriegstagebuch des Oberkommandos der Wehrmacht 1944–1945*, Teilband I (Bonn: Percy Ernst Schramm, no date), pp. 828–865.

[18] See note 15, box 35, cable no. 2548-2549.

[19] See NA Microfilm Guide no. 18, RW4/ 584; OKW 1905–1908, 34 – German occupation of Hungary – "Einsatz der Kräfte und deren Aufgabe," according to which the invading force consisted of three Kampfgruppen, including elements of three Waffen SS divisions, elements of several army divisions, police, and border police battalions. According to OKW Chief Keitel's occupation order of March 18, 1944, received courtesy of Bundesarchiv Koblenz, Budapest city was not to be occupied in order to maintain at least the impression of Hungarian autonomy and thus of acceptance of German occupation. The same archive supplied the present writer with documents related to the German order of the battle in Hungary until September 1944, when such documentation was hardly available due to the situation at the fronts.

own Austrian underground to the enemy. In the X-2 report on "Personalities in Dogwood's Chain," the parts dealing with Joseph Winninger, Bandi Grosz, and Fritz Laufer seem to be rather incriminating. In the case of Winninger, the report continued, after having described him as a full-fledged German tool who cheated the Zionists of their rescue money, that "WINNINGER was also used by DOGWOOD . . . whom TRILLIUM reports to have warned against subject, saying that he told everything to his Nazi masters. DOGWOOD is said to have replied that subject was doing excellent work and that he had 'complete faith in him.' "

However, after the German invasion, Winninger and his Abwehr chief, Dr. Schmidt, conducted Grosz's interrogation when he was arrested after his return from a trip to Turkey and inquired at length into his dealings with the Allies.

WINNINGER and SCHMIDT are reported to have extorted vast sums of money out of the Zionist representatives in Budapest, BRAND and KASZTNER. . . . Finally, they were stopped by IRIS, of the S.D., who wanted to make use of BRAND and KASZTNER and who also wanted to prove the S.D.'s authority over Abwehr personnel. IRIS reportedly had WINNINGER arrested in mid-May. . . . According to information dated 20 September 1944, subject is still under arrest in Budapest. (Pfaff, RG 226, Entry 211, Folder Wn 19902)

From this report, we learn that the SD had taken over the Abwehr, and that Laufer had become – if not beforehand – a full-fledged SD operative. We further learn that Laufer wanted to use Joel Brand and Rezsö Kasztner for bigger purposes than cheating the Zionists of their money (e.g., strategic goods, possibly political aims formulated by his superiors all the way to Walter Schellenberg, the head of SD Ausland).

Indeed, the above-cited X-2 report tells us that "Early in July 1943 subject [Laufer – S.A.] became a member of the 'DOGWOOD ORGANIZATION' and worked as personal 'friend' and 'trusted agent' for DOGWOOD. In July 1943 TRILLIUM is said to have told DOGWOOD in Istanbul that LAUFER was a 'double crosser,' to which DOGWOOD is said to have replied that that was impossible since subject was his 'best agent.' " The report mentioned further Dogwood's efforts to supply Laufer in Budapest with radio codes in March and with a transmission set after the German invasion in April, using Grosz, possibly Colonel Hatz, and Hungarian contacts who all "shared the feeling, according to the X-2 report, that DOGWOOD had badly compromised them by telling his 'trusted friend LAUFER' all about their activities." The report went on to disclose Laufer's ties with Gerhard Clages, described as the "SD Chief in Budapest" after the occupation. According to Grosz, "LAUFER and KLAAGES [this misspelling of the name clearly indicates that the source of the information was one of Grosz's interrogations by SIME, to be discussed later – S.A.] negotiated at length with TRILLIUM and with Joel BRAND, the latter a leading Zionist representative in Hungary, and in late May sent both men on separate missions to the Allies in Istanbul."

Thus, Grosz's reappearance with Brand in mid-May seemed to have completed the circle. Here came Grosz, now an SD tool in the hands of Laufer, with a bid for a separate peace between the Western Allies and Germany. This was a distorted version of "Dogwood's" own grand design as negotiated with Count von Moltke, apparently involving the rescue of many Jews, aimed at driving a wedge between the Allies and the Zionist Brand, too, with an offer to allow a million Jews to leave Hungary in exchange for Allied trucks and other commodities.

Around this time, the British interrogated Samu Springmann, the Zionist rescue operative in Hungary who had secured the services of all of the "couriers" mentioned and had been arrested by SIME on his way to Palestine, and reached the conclusion that a Jewish-inspired conspiracy involving "large movements" of refugees from Hungary was taking place in cooperation with enemy agents.[20]

SIME certainly interrogated Brand and Grosz, having had their own information about the latter's ties with "Richard Klatt," a half-Jew who had run an espionage network in Sofia for the German Air Force and for the Abwehr, whose main effort was directed at the Eastern front but who also gathered intelligence on Turkey and the Middle East. The British had decrypted not a few of Klatt's messages at least since mid-1943, which they had given to the Americans as well, and they had a good picture of other Abwehr officials such as Colonel Wagner, or "Dr. Delius," who was the local station chief.[21] Thus, any "Dogwood"–Klatt connection via any of "Dogwood's" agents, who also served the Zionists as couriers, was bound to raise quite a problem for "Dogwood" later on.

For his part, Klatt seemed to have been, and to have remained, a loyal German operative, later described as having tried his best to be "an Aryan," but Hitler forbade the use of Jewish agents at all costs, so when his Jewish ancestry became known he was moved by his superiors to the service of their Hungarian allies.[22] Whether Klatt's removal had anything to do with the decline of the Abwehr and the campaign launched against it by RSHA chief

---

[20] See extract from SIME Interrogation Summary No. 4 of May 30, 1944, Samuel and Ilona SPRINGMANN, PRO Reference number KV2/130; record contains file number SF.52/Middle East/3 6a.

[21] See British decrypts of Group VII/62, Ankara-Sofia February 23, 1943 to February 12, 1944, mostly signed by Klatt. The contents of the reports are at best a sort of wishful thinking, such as an expected Soviet collapse "reckoned in Allied circles by October 1943 if Germany avoids the same mistakes as last year;" see decrypts 59540 (no further details known when and how it reached OSS), stored in RG 226, Entry 210 Army, box 6, folder XIV. On Klatt and Schellenberg, see the text.

[22] See Schellenberg's interrogation, RG 226, Entry 125, box 2, folder 21.

Kaltenbrunner and SD Ausland chief Schellenberg, accusing the Abwehr of using Jews (without success) or half-Jews, we do not know.[23]

The nature of Klatt's connections with Grosz remains unclear and could have been personal or business-related (e.g., contraband) thanks to their freedom of movement during wartime between German territories, German allies, and neutrals.[24] Klatt's postwar career requires too much space here since he was supposed to become an American agent in Vienna, according to oral information given by historian Timothy Naftali, but was arrested by the Americans and also became a subject for separate Soviet and British inquiries.

We even find Laufer's name as a double agent serving the American Strategic Service Unit (SSU– the OSS's postwar heir) as part of an anti-Soviet operation in Vienna,[25] while Bauer's Czech sources maintained that Captain Klausnitzer shot him in Prague's central jail by the end of the war because he knew too much.[26]

---

[23] For Klatt's background and intelligence work for the Nazis, see David Kahn, *Hitler's Spies: German Military Intelligence in World War II*, paperback edition (New York: DA-APO Press, 2000), pp. 312–317, 369.

[24] See in this regard the X-2 summary on Grosz contained in Appendix A: "Dogwood's Chain Personalities," p. 72, withdrawn from the original X-2 report made by Major Pfaff but now available thanks to the Nazi War Crimes Disclosure Act, RG 226, Entry 210, box 35, according to which Grosz acted as a money courier between Klatt and one of his contacts in Istanbul.

[25] See War Department, Strategic Services Unit, from Vienna to Washington, signed Ulmer, July 27, 1946, top secret control regarding Wash no. 0883 and Wash no. 1903: "1. Laufer believed definitely identical with Laufer of LSX-171 [probably an SSU name file – S.A.]. 2. Laufer former Gestapo agent. Now working in Austrian Staatspolizei Vienna as subagent for N.K.V.D. 3. Has been used approximately 1 month as subagent on probationary basis by this office for contemplated project to penetrate communist network in Staatspolizei. 4. Work as double agent highly satisfactory. To evidence of his playing against us, extreme care being used...." Cable no. 0883 dated June 6, 1946, signed Quinn, indeed asked whether "your Laufer has any connection Friedrich or Fritz Laufer of Dogwood case and unsavory Zionist fund transactions including Schmidt, (and) Gross...."?

[26] Bauer's information was given in a conversation with the present writer.

PART IV

THE BRAND–GROSZ MISSIONS WITHIN THE LARGER PICTURE OF THE WAR AND THEIR RAMIFICATIONS

25

The Zionist Initiatives

The Yishuv representatives in Istanbul such as Venia Pomeranz and Menachem Bader were not necessarily aware of the differences between the Nazi occupation authorities and intelligence bodies. In the past, they had used every contact possible, including couriers who had served OSS as well, such as Bandi Grosz, in order to reach Nazi-occupied or Nazi-controlled Europe. For Pomeranz, it might have made no difference that could help the cause of rescue. On the contrary, one had to talk to the killers themselves and somehow try to deal with them. This was an extremely sensitive matter, and it involved money, if not goods, to be supplied to Nazi Germany in exchange for Jewish lives.

Seemingly anchored in the assumption that the Germans were ready to deal, Joel Brand wrote to rescue emissary Nathan Schwalb in Geneva upon arrival in Istanbul that in fact this is what was left to the Va'ada to pursue under the new circumstances of Nazi occupation.[1] Indeed, Brand – and Bandi Grosz – were in touch with several Gestapo/SD operatives, discussing with them various deal options before Adolf Eichmann himself seemed to have endorsed them. One option, to try and exchange Jewish lives for Allied-supplied goods such as trucks, had been raised already in 1943 by Fritz Laufer.

The truck option surfaced again after the German occupation, but we do not know whether Laufer suggested it first to Brand, who conducted most of the talks with the Germans alone,[2] promising that the Allies would be willing to pay the price.

---

[1] Hagana Archive, Division 14, file 798, Brand to Schwalb, Istanbul, May 31, 1944.

[2] See Kasztner Report 1946, p. 36, in English translation: "The negotiations were carried out from May 8 through May 17 by *Brand* alone [italics in original]. I was neutralized" (arrested by the Hungarians).

Yet Brand wrote to Schwalb that he undertook the "mission" because the Va'ada had no other option left and thus transferred the onus of action to the Zionists abroad, who would have to deal with the Allies.[3]

According to Himmler's economic emissary in Hungary, Kurt Andreas Becher, Brand heard about the deal aimed at transferring a major Jewish-owned armament factory to SS control in return for the owners' lives, a deal with the property of the Jewish Weiss family, and then Brand offered to him as well a large number of trucks, to be supplied by the Allies, in exchange for the lives of Hungary's Jews.[4]

The Va'ada leaders, especially Joel Brand and Rezsö Kasztner, were at that early stage subjected to harassment and blackmail by Abwehr officials, who robbed the Va'ada of its Zionist money.[5] According to Brand's own report to Moshe Shertok of the Jewish Agency when they met in Aleppo, Syria, they tried to reach members of Eichmann's staff, notably Dieter Wisliceny, and SS Lieutenant Colonel Hermann Krumey, who intervened and restored the monies, minus huge commissions, seemingly offering a deal between the Gestapo and the Va'ada, that at first was aimed at allowing those who already were in possession of Palestine entry certificates to leave the country.[6]

Here we are introduced to the topic that finally became known as "Kasztner's Train" – a group of 1,684 Jews, many of them dignitaries or rich people, who were allowed to go to Switzerland and were labeled as the few who were saved by Kasztner, while he neglected most when Brand failed to return from his mission, and thus the fate of most Hungarian Jews was sealed.

Eichmann was accordingly supposed to have given Kasztner a few hundred Jewish lives, including his own and his family's, in exchange for his actual collaboration. No effort was made by Kasztner to tell the bulk of the Hungarian Jewry what was approaching; no effort was made by him to warn them to run for their lives or to rise and fight. Even worse, Kasztner did nothing to prevent the persecution and execution of the Yishuv's own emissaries sent over to help them fight, among them the legendary Hannah Szenes, who parachuted into occupied Yugoslavia and then entered Hungary. Worse still, having sold his soul to the devil, Kasztner even saved one of the Nazi henchmen, SS Colonel Kurt Andreas Becher, after the war and testified

[3] See note 1.
[4] See Interrogation No. 2710-a: Vernehmung des Kurt BECHER vom 2.3 1948, in John Mendelsohn (ed.), *The Holocaust: Volume 15, Relief in Hungary and the Failure of the Joel Brand Mission* (New York, London: Garland Publishers Inc., 1982) (no page numbering).
[5] Grosz's interrogation, Public Record Office (PRO), doc. FO 371 42811, file SIME /P. 7755, dates of interrogation: June 6–22, 1944, and see note from, Budapest Va'ada to Moladti; see Chapter 29, note 19.
[6] See Hagana Archive, Division 14, Repository 153א, Zionist Rescue Mission Istanbul (Moladti) to Jewish Agency, Jerusalem, May 14, 1944, which combined this opportunity with previous efforts to negotiate barter deals with Eichmann's aide Dieter Wisliceny.

at Nuremberg in favor of two others, Eichmann's direct subordinates, including SS Lieutenant Colonel Hermann Krumey.[7] This package of allegations could be easily attached to the acceptance by Israel around that time of German reparations, as if the Labor Zionists had no soul and were ready to trade Jewish blood for German money. It was if Kasztner's own motives, as rumored before his trial, in testifying for Becher in Allied courts at Nuremberg after the war were the recovery of Jewish monies he had given Becher in Budapest as a part of the train deal for Mapai's own purposes.[8] Moreover, attorney Shmuel Tamir combined, with the great help of journalist Uri Avneri on the one hand and that of the American writer Ben Hecht on the other, all the events related to the Holocaust in Hungary into one "system," or "modus operandi," as far as the Yishuv's leadership was concerned. Why had Brand's mission failed? Because he was extradited to the British by the Jewish Agency's operatives such as Ehud Überall-Avriel, who had accompanied Brand from Istanbul to Palestine. Why had he done this? Because shortly beforehand Menachem Begin had proclaimed his "rebellion" against the British; had Brand's offer become known, the people would have massively joined Begin in trying to force the British to save the Hungarian Jews. But the Yishuv's leadership "collaborated" with the British and was also afraid of losing power at Begin's favor.

The "Great Season" – the extradition of Menachem Begin's IZL and Stern group operatives to the British by the Yishuv's leadership – which occurred several months after the failure of Brand's mission, could be brought in as yet another act of collaboration with the British in the context of the Holocaust in Hungary.

Following Brand's arrest in British-controlled Syria, he was brought to the British Middle East HQ in Cairo. Lord Moyne, the British Minister Resident, was murdered by the Sternists because of his previous anti-Zionist activities, given up by now, to which the allegation was added ex post facto that he was involved in killing Brand's mission. At least Brand quoted Moyne as if he, Brand, had personally made the "Gestapo Deal" offer known to Moyne in Cairo and that the British Minister responded to his mission by saying, "And what shall I do with a million Jews"?[9] This sentence became one of the

---

[7] For the most recent accusations in this regard made by Rudolf Vrba, one among two Auschwitz escapees who authored "The Auschwitz Protocol," which was supposed to warn the Hungarian Jewish leadership about the reality of the death camp in April 1944, see "The Preparations for the Holocaust in Hungary: An Eyewitness Account, in Randolph L. Braham with Scott Miller (eds.), *The Nazis' Last Victims: The Holocaust in Hungary* (Detroit: Wayne State University Press, 1998), especially p. 95.

[8] See Weitz, *The Man Who Was Murdered Twice*, pp. 93–98.

[9] See Joel Brand, *In the Mission of the Sentenced to Death* (Tel-Aviv: Ayanot Publishers, 1956), p. 155 (in Hebrew), and see a later English version by Alex Weissberg, *Advocate for the Dead – The Story of Joel Brand* (London: A. Deutsch, 1958), p. 167, in which Brand wrote that the person who exclaimed "And what shall I do with a million Jews" was not Moyne but

best-known figures of speech pertaining to the "world's" attitude toward rescue in the post-Holocaust Israeli Jewish world. I found no evidence to substantiate Brand's claim that he ever met the British Minister of State in Cairo. Indeed, the high-level British attention given to the Brand mission first by Moyne himself but later by the Foreign Office and Embassy in Ankara, as described by Martin Gilbert, was rather skeptical to begin with, but London could not ignore it altogether due to WRB interest in it and the public attention that could have been aroused owing to a missed opportunity to save a large number of Jews, whose possible influx into the Middle East worried them very much indeed.[10] But the British needed evidence that the whole "mission" was a ploy instigated by enemy agent Laufer in collaboration with the Zionist rescue workers themselves, and they received it from Brand and Grosz when they were interrogated by SIME.

An SIME agent – Royal Artillery Lieutenant Strachan according to my PRO records – was the only one who interrogated Brand in Cairo. Later, other British officials did, according to Brand's own version. Yet the role of counterintelligence agencies in "killing" Brand's mission was decisive – if the "mission" itself was serious. They had Brand arrested in Syria. They interrogated him and Grosz separately in Cairo. The inquiry was related to a much bigger intelligence complex, about which attorney Shmuel Tamir knew nothing.

Others, among them Miklós Moshe Krausz, the former Zionist immigration officer in Budapest, who had accused Kasztner of "collaboration" immediately after the war[11] following his infighting with Springmann and Kasztner, who in turn had accused him of idleness and of misusing his position as Director of the Palestine Office in Budapest for narrow partisan purposes, were waiting to take their own revenge on Kasztner and claim credit for themselves. For his part, Kasztner took credit not just for saving the 1,684 Jews of "Kasztner's train." He claimed that he had saved many thousands of Jews who were sent to Austria for work and did survive, that in fact he stopped the Final Solution in Hungary, and finally saved the remnants of the European Jewry by negotiating their fate with Heinrich Himmler through Kurt Andreas Becher and by enlisting Becher to protect the Budapest Ghetto from Hungarian Nazis. No one dismissed Krausz's successful efforts at that time in collaboration with the Swiss Consul General Charles Lutz and the Swede Raoul Wallenberg backed by the WRB, the Red Cross, and others to protect Budapest Jews during the final stage of the Holocaust in Budapest.

---

another British official. In fact, Moshe Shertok, while trying to negotiate with the British in London on the fate of Brand's mission, summed up the British attitude by using this formulation in a Mapai meeting in Haifa upon his return at which Brand was present.

[10] See Gilbert, *Auschwitz and the Allies*, Chapter 24: The Gestapo Offer: "Unmanageable numbers."

[11] See Weitz, *The Man Who Was Murdered Twice*, pp. 55–57.

Yet instead of burying their enmities, Krausz and Kasztner – and other survivors – emerged out of the Holocaust seeking revenge on each other. Seeking credit in such matters as who saved whom and when or whether the Final Solution was ordered to be halted or stopped altogether was a matter of historical realities that in most cases were hidden from the best-informed – and most involved – victims and rescue operatives alike.

In fact, the alleged "Stopp der Endlösung" was not a simple matter.[12] More will be said about it later, but during the Jerusalem trial in which the State of Israel sued Malkiel Gruenwald for spreading and inflating the rumors against Kasztner as a tool in the hands of the Nazis, Shmuel Tamir as Gruenwald's defense attorney transformed Kasztner into a "collaborator" with Eichmann's staff who finally, at the very end, tried to save the meager remnants of the European Jews as an alibi for himself and for Eichmann's own aides, Becher included. District Court justice Binyamin Halevi in fact endorsed Tamir's line: Kasztner was made to be a symbolic figure of Labor Zionist "collaboration" with the Gestapo itself. Aiming at his political party, Mapai, and at its leaders Moshe Shertok-Sharett, at the time Prime Minister of Israel, and David Ben-Gurion, still the acknowledged leader of Mapai and the founding father of Israel in a partitioned Palestine (anathema to Tamir and his Zionist–Revisionist tradition), past and present were brought together.

[12] See discussion in text. The argument that the Final Solution was terminated by Himmler's orders thanks to Kasztner's negotiations with Kurt Andreas Becher was spread by Andreas Biss, a relative of Kasztner's who was personally involved in the negotiations. See his memoir, *Der Stopp der Endlösung* (Stuttgart: Seewald, 1976).

26

Rescue, Allied Intelligence, and the SS

The reality with regard to rescue in Hungary was that the rescue workers in Istanbul, Budapest, and Bratislava remembered that "Baron von Wisliceny," as Pomeranz insisted upon calling him decades later (a totally baseless use of the title, which gave Wisliceny some kind of higher rank compared to his relatively low rank as SS Captain), was ready to enter into a ransom deal with regard to Slovakia.[1]

Since "Willy," or the "Shtadlan" (the well-intentioned go-between), as they used to call Wisliceny, had disappeared from sight since August 1943, those trying to rescue the Jews were somewhat relieved when he reappeared shortly after the Germans invaded Hungary in March 1944. According to Brand's own report to Shertok, they did their utmost to reach Wisliceny when he came to Budapest and revived his alleged ransom talks. Willy was equipped with a letter of recommendation from Rabbi Weissmandel in Bratislava. Afterward, his boss, Adolf Eichmann, made an official bid to "exchange a million Jews for ten thousand trucks," as this "deal" was presented by the Zionist rescue workers in Budapest and by Brand himself to the rescue mission in Istanbul and to the Yishuv's leadership. The Allies eventually called it the "Gestapo Deal."

Chaim Barlas, Venia Pomeranz, and other rescue workers received Joel Brand, who later said that he expected the supreme Zionist and World Jewish leadership to wait for him in Istanbul. Pomeranz went to Palestine to see Ben-Gurion and others in this regard. Pomeranz reported later that Ben-Gurion reacted at first with his typical, rather simplistic initial enthusiasm: "Let us have the million Jews; that's how we shall create our Jewish state. Shertok – get your cylinder and visas, and let's talk to the British."

Ben-Gurion was too cautious and too experienced to turn down rescue ideas outright. In fact, he and Shertok would ask the Allies, in spite of their own grave doubts about the suggested truck "deal," to at least try and

[1] Kasztner's Nuremberg interrogation doc.1 No. 2817.

keep the door open. The Western Allies at first, in spite of their own grave doubts about it, seemed to have considered that option seriously until finally turning it down due to intelligence reasons such as the OSS X-2 report quoted earlier and more to be quoted in this chapter. At least the ex post facto accusations about negligence on the Zionist side regarding Brand's mission were groundless. The mission had no chance from the beginning. In fact, it was born in Brand's own mind when he enthusiastically endorsed the truck deal in talks with Fritz Laufer or even possibly suggested it to the Germans. The Allies would also know much, and suspect even more. Hence, Brand's mission evolved into a trap for its own initiators – in real time and ex post facto.

In the meantime, seemingly because Brand failed to return with a positive Allied response, Eichmann pursued the deportations from Hungary to Auschwitz at the rate of 12,000 a day, finally prompting Roosevelt's intervention and American diplomatic efforts with Regent Horthy and his successors on behalf of the Hungarian Jews. The Zionist leadership deliberated whether to ask the Allies to bomb the railroads leading to Auschwitz and the gas chambers.[2] Following Rabbi Weissmandel's accurate information about Auschwitz that was related abroad and his urgent requests to ask the Allies to intervene, the London Zionist office did approach the British, hoping thereby to deter the Nazis and even stop the killing machine altogether.

Yet the timing of such requests – late June 1944 and later in the summer and autumn 1944 – required among other calculations the possible death brought by Allied bombing upon Jewish inmates caused by a Jewish request for such bombing[3] and knowledge of the war situation in some detail.

In early July, Admiral Horthy stopped the deportations from Hungary, so the issue did not seem to the British to be that pressing. The issue of "Anvil," the landing in southern France, prompted internal fighting within the Allied ranks over priorities and the allocation of resources.[4] The stabilization of the German front – and later the "Battle of the Bulge" – prompted the return to the previous bombing policy by the "air barons," which continued while Auschwitz was captured by the Soviets in January 1945. A concentrated offensive on German oil and later on transportation targets in Germany proper finally took place at this stage with the distances between air bases and targets having become rather short. The resulting chaos in Germany, Austria, Hungary, Czechoslovakia, and parts of Poland, however, did not alleviate the fate of Jewish survivors marched by foot into Germany at

---

[2] See Porat, *An Entangled Leadership*, pp. 392–404.
[3] This seems to have been Ben-Gurion's primary consideration at first; see Porat, *An Entangled Leadership*, p. 394.
[4] See Winston S. Churchill, *The Second World War*, Volume 6, Chapter 6: Italy and the Landing in the Riviera, and see Weinberg, *A World at Arms*, pp. 631, 661–662, 677, 682, 695.

that stage or even transported by rail all around, evacuated from one camp to another, a matter that will receive our attention at the end of the book.

Since the Nazi occupation of Hungary in March 1944, the facts, without which the Yishuv's leadership was making decisions as best it could, were largely a matter of guesswork, wishful thinking, domestic political calculations related to maintaining control while putting pressure on the British, pressure from rescue workers in the field, and Allied moves. Most of the latter were related to the overall conduct of the war, to the impending Normandy invasion and its initial problems, to Allied domestic relations and relations among the Allies, plus some hopes and hints coming from the Germans. Such hints were transmitted always by the rescue workers in the field, and thus the rescue workers could have been perceived, in Allied eyes and even in the eyes of the Yishuv leaders, as if the Germans were using them for their own purposes.

Like the Western Allies, we are interested in one figure, Fritz Laufer, who had the German alias Schroeder. Brand saw in Laufer–Schroeder a sort of "friend" and an important Jewish contact with the SD and kept Laufer's real name from Shertok.[5] Thus, for Brand, Laufer's affiliation with the SD was an advantage. Here the Zionists were allegedly dealing with someone who meant business and seemed to have the authority to deal. For the Allies, this very authority and Laufer's possible betrayal of "Dogwood" was just as good a reason not to deal with him. Another option was that the SD Ausland under Walter Schellenberg was ready to deal, and in addition Laufer was involved in the SD–Abwehr infighting, which at this stage could only help the Zionists recover their money and then deal with the winners.

But Schellenberg told his American interrogators after the war that he "knew nothing about Joel Brandt's [sic] offer to exchange Hungarian Jews for trucks with the Western Allies."[6] He thought, however, that Heinrich Mueller (the executive director of the Gestapo, and Eichmann's direct boss) might know something about this. With regard to Jews, he said that Schellenberg's hands were tied by the fact that Hitler had issued a veto "against employing Jews" in his intelligence service: "When Hitler heard, in connection with Russian intelligence material," that Schellenberg's SD Ausland engaged the Jew Klatt in such work, he threatened that if a similar case occurred again he would have Schellenberg shot.[7]

---

[5] See Shertok's report on Brand's meeting with him in Haleb, Syria, following his arrest by the British in Hagana Archive, Div. 80/187f/31 (private archive, Gershon Rivlin, Joel Brand).

[6] See Schellenberg's Interrogation Report June 27–July 12, 1945, RG 226, Entry 125, box 2, folder 21.

[7] "Richard Klatt," according to Schellenberg's postwar papers, was a Hungarian half-Jew whose "greatest wish was to become an Aryan." "His reports on Russian Army matters were good...on political matters devious. He was 'run' by Vienna (Colonel Wiese). The General Staff's Fremde Heere Ost [Generalmajor Reinhard Gehlen, the Chief of the Foreign

As far as rescuing Jews directly or indirectly was concerned, Schellenberg was innocent of any such efforts before October 1944, and thus the earlier efforts such as "Brand's mission" should have been known to him but would have served one goal – the big hope of splitting the Allies. The British quoted in this regard a German official whom they interrogated (codenamed "Dictionary") in April 1945 to the effect that *"Brand's mission was approved by Schellenberg and its main aim was to split the Allies"* (Italics added).

A certain Thibor von Kolasch[8] originally arranged for forty to fifty Jews to be evacuated to Portugal by air from Hungary after they had given up their factories to the SS, who could not appropriate them on account of the Hungarian government. This maneuver led to further black market transactions and to Brand's proposals.[9] According to historian Richard Breitman and his OSS sources, "Dictionary" was a German officer by the name of Karl Marcus, who had served as assistant to Kurt Jahnke, described as a veteran German intelligence official who was a regular advisor to Schellenberg. Marcus deserted and surrendered in November 1944 to French troops in liberated France, where he established contact with the British, offering them valuable information. In fact, Marcus represented himself as Jahnke's envoy to the West, offering to the British the old idea of cooperation with Germany against the Soviets. Disinterested in this, the British recognized that Marcus could supply them with a great deal of valuable information on German Intelligence, so with the explicit permission of Prime Minister Churchill he was brought to England. There he was given the code name "Dictionary" and was repeatedly interrogated by British Intelligence, but only interrogation no. 25 has been found in the OSS archives, probably because of its connection

---

Armies East, German Military Intelligence – S.A.] thought highly of KLATT," even if he had his enemies, such as Colonel Wagner [Delius] (who thought that Klatt was either a British or a Russian agent) in addition to his being Jewish. He was thus moved from Sofia to Budapest and officially was under the control of Hungarian Intelligence. His Budapest network was then closely watched, leading to Istanbul and Bratislava, and from there, allegedly via former white Russians, to Moscow. Klatt was found reliable and resumed his operations for the Germans until Schellenberg lost touch with him. Klatt's ties with General Gehlen, the future head of the West German Intelligence Service, may hint toward the possibility that he served the Americans, too, after the war, at least for some time. His whereabouts later on require a separate inquiry. Otherwise, so we are told by Yehuda Bauer, the old Abwehr had minor Jewish agents elsewhere, and Himmler – who finally took over the Abwehr – might have used them all, Klatt included, to approach the West through a "Jewish" network consisting of Bandi Grosz, through Alfred "Dogwood" Schwarz, who had his connections with Teddy Kollek, without incriminating himself. See Bauer, *Jews for Sale?*, pp. 125–131. My findings here do not confirm Bauer's thesis.

[8] This name could not be found elsewhere in the records, but he could have been an intermediary between the Weiss family and Kurt Andreas Becher.

[9] See document entitled DICTIONARY, information about the U.K. and Eire, interrogation No. 25, dated April 5, 1945, RG 226, Entry 109, box 707, folder b6, declassified August 22, 2001.

to the Brand affair, related as it was to "Dogwood" and his agents.[10] It seems as though the British, through OSS X-2, went out of their way to supply the Americans with incriminating evidence against "Dogwood" and several of his couriers and agents, such as Laufer and Grosz, by using their own behavior as described by them or interpreted by X-2 thanks also to Kolbe's reports. Thus "Dogwood" was finally declared by X-2 to be a Nazi spy. In consultation with "Broadway" (i.e., MI6), previous "Dogwood" reports were checked and found to be either misleading or useless.[11] This was done in connection with the demise of "Dogwood's" Austrian cell when Franz Messner, "Dogwood's" main hope for an underground operation in Austria, who was in Budapest at the time, was arrested by the Germans. This occurred around March 21, thanks to Fritz Laufer, the only one who could bring about Messner's arrest and ensuing execution. Also, the betrayed landing of the American Sparrow mission in Hungary (in which Colonel Hatz, the alleged traitor and German collaborator, had "showed great interest" before it started and its members were arrested) could be interpreted in this connection in an incriminating fashion, as could the Brand–Grosz missions.[12]

The X-2 report was rather cautious regarding Teddy Kollek, who was blamed for just "poor judgment" with regard to his contacts, yet X-2 reached the conclusion with regard to "Dogwood" Schwarz himself that:

There can be little doubt that DOGWOOD is the key to any solution of the penetration of O.S.S. in Istanbul. It is assumed that it was DOGWOOD who . . . gained complete knowledge of all O.S.S. operations, personnel and plans, in Istanbul and elsewhere. It is further believed that DOGWOOD's true name is not Alfred SCHWARZ, but that name is an alias, and that in all probability he is a cunning and crafty double agent in enemy control.

Having thus confused "Dogwood" with Fritz Laufer, X-2 robbed the Zionists of their alleged pillar of rescue in Istanbul, very much under British influence.

---

[10] The relevant OSS files are stored in RG 226, Entry 190, box 756, folder 20.

[11] See 15th Air Force (U.S.) comment on "Dogwood" reports on military targets in Austria and (actual) bombing results in that country, partially originating from "Iris" Laufer and partially from the Austrian anti-Nazi Messner, code name "Cassia:" RG 226, Entry 190, box 74, AIRO-SI-OP 7-10. In Messner's case, he might have tried to save his own or related property from Allied bombing.

[12] See Summary of X-2 report by Major Pfaff RG 226, Entry 210, box 35. This summary had been withdrawn but was released on September 11, 2000.

27

Hungarian Rescue Deals in the Eyes of the Allies

Fritz Laufer's bids for rescue "deals," which he was indeed spreading among Jewish rescue workers upon his visits as a trusted American agent in Istanbul, and his contacts with the SD and the Gestapo, the latter being very probably one of his employers from the beginning in Prague, could have been easily seen in Jewish eyes as if they reflected some change on the Nazi side. But in Allied eyes a rescue "deal" involving the Jews of Hungary could be initiated by the Nazis to enhance sinister conspiracies such as using the Jews to drive a wedge between the Allies and their own citizens. Bring a disaster on FDR's head in an election year – around the uncertain results of the Normandy invasion – to make it seem as if he were fighting a "Jew's war," and drive a wedge between the Western Allies and Stalin. This is how OSS-SI in Washington reacted to Brand's and Grosz's arrival in Istanbul, connecting them as "German double agents" to the precedent of one actual ransom deal authorized by the Nazis in occupied Hungary, that of the release of the rich Weiss family in exchange for its property[1] (see cable 53647, REGIS in Washington to USTRAVIC, London; Copies sent to Director, Deputy Director, OSS, X-2, OSS, offices in the Middle East, Madrid, and Europe):

1. with the complete assistance of the german government, the weiss group mentioned in your (cable) #57377 (#178 to Madrid) reached Lisbon...[further details in previous cables between O.S.S. stations Bern and Washington – S.A.] and also to saint [O.S.S.–X-2 or counterintelligence – S.A.] about report that the signing of a 20-year lease of the weiss works [by the SS – S.A.] was forced as a bargain by the Germans.[2]

---

[1] Archivist Lawrence McDonald of the U.S. National Archives kindly gave the codes of X-2 and the following ones in this cable to me.

[2] The takeover by the SS of the Weiss Works, negotiated by Kurt Andreas Becher, Himmler's "economic emissary" in Hungary, was not that simple due to the sensitivity to Hungarian national interests. For details, see Breitman and Aronson, "The End of the 'Final Solution'?," pp. 183–188.

2. There are additional indications that this may be a portion of a plant by 2 German double agents who reached istanbul on the 5th of the last month [meant are Brand and Grosz, who had reached Istanbul on May 19th – S.A.] with the outlandish proposition that in exchange for a supply of U.S. trucks and other staples they would deliver a group of hungarian jews. *The political move motivating this plant is the implication that american [sic] placed more worth on saving hungarian jews than on the war effort* (italics added).

3. gravely doubt if the particulars you asked for could be trusted or that contact would be wise, no matter how discreet, in view of fact that the arrival of this group under nazi sponsorship may be one or both of the matter listed above. (RG 226, Entry 134, box 254, folder 1499, WASH-SECT-R&C-75)

The cable was sent by REGIS – Reginald S. Foster, SI Washington, serving under SI Chief Whitney Shepardson in OSS HQ Washington, for action to USTRAVIC, London (the OSS mail room in London), confirmation in Washington: SI; information among others: OSS Director, Deputy Director, X-2. Since we know who stood for Regis, we can infer from the cable's contents that OSS-SI Washington, possibly under X-2 pressure, ordered OSS London to stay away from Brand and Grosz as alleged Nazi tools, having brought both of them together with the Weiss ransom deal. Why London? Because this was the center of rescue activity, including that of the Zionists, following Brand's and Grosz's arrival.

The originator of the next priority cable in this regard, sent to the same Ustravic facility in London for its information and OSS Madrid, seems to be clear: OSS X-2 (counterintelligence) Washington sent cable #54234 on July 7 under the heading SAINT to Cairo for action. Here the mix-up with the Weiss group seems to be complete:

Please question brand and georgy about the 'brand plan' as it is called, losing no time in so doing. the german government has assisted about 30 refugees in flying by lufthansa plane from berlin to lisbon. this group is now in lisbon and consists of half a dozen prominent Hungarian Jews and their families [several among them were left behind in Vienna to guarantee the "good behavior" abroad of those who left, but they remained unmentioned here – S.A.]. the germans desire U.S. trucks and other material in exchange for these refugees [the trucks belonged to the separate "Brand mission" – S.A.]. we believe that brand and georgy are aware of this incredible nazi black maneuver, with which their istanbul mission may be connected. *obviously, the project is meant to cause the Allies embarrassment. roosevelt is the chief target, for the nazis claim that he is impeding the war effort by his attempt to rescue Jews* (italics added). (cable 54324, SAINT, copies to London and Istanbul, RG 226, Entry 134, box 254)

In other words, Brand and Grosz were tools of the Nazis, who were aiming at FDR's reputation due to the Nazis' own claim that the president was manipulating the war effort (and hence shedding American blood) in an attempt to save Jewish lives.

Here the trap situation seems self-evident when we remember that Brand and Grosz may have initiated their missions and that the Germans either stood behind them for their own purposes or grasped the initiatives in order to facilitate a speedy Final Solution in Hungary while keeping the Zionists and the Allies busy, possibly accepting a deal for a few Jews in exchange for war material or fighting each other about an alleged "deal" that could always be made public by the German side or even by the Jewish side.

Thus, the British–American decision regarding the Brand–Grosz mission, which was publicly exposed by the BBC later in July as a Nazi ploy and thus buried, should be understood in this context. Indeed, Brand did not come alone but with Bandi Grosz.

Grosz maintained that his was the real mission – a separate peace with the Western Allies, authorized by the SD chief in Budapest, Otto Klages (this is how the name was spelled until recently in the scholarly literature; the actual name was in fact spelled Clages, and the actual Christian name was Gerhard). Clages was described by Grosz as "the SD Chief of Budapest," as if he belonged to a separate (the foreign intelligence) branch of the German Security Police. Yet in his SS personal file, Clages is identified as a Gestapo officer pure and simple at this stage of his career. It is very possible, however, that in Budapest both the Gestapo and SD were amalgamated to serve a common cause.[3] Thus, the SD was amalgamated with the Gestapo in Hungary as it was elsewhere within the SIPO or Security Police, under the Commander of SIPO and SD in Hungary, SS Standartenführer and Oberst der Polizei (Colonel) Dr. Hans Geschke.

A similar name, spelled as Gaschke, was mentioned by Grosz as if he participated in the meeting held between Grosz, Clages, and Laufer on May 15, 1944, a couple of days before Grosz left on his mission.[4] Nothing is reported about Gaschke except the similar name. The only speculation that could be offered here, should the man indeed have been Geschke, is that the close connection between the Gestapo and SD is thus becoming more evident. The information we find on Geschke in his SS personal file is that he was promoted to Oberführer (General) by SS Chief Himmler following the pro-Nazi coup in Budapest in the fall of 1944 and mention in connection with the kidnapping of Horthy's son, in which Clages lost his life.[5]

---

[3] See his BDC personal file, NARA, BDC microfilms. Clages was born in Hamburg in 1902 and joined the Nazi Party in 1931 after serving as "Ingeniuer Assistant" in the Commercial Marine for eight years and allegedly in a "Freikorps" immediately after World War I. He joined the SS in 1934, the SD in 1936, and became Gestapo "Kriminalkommissar" in Prague before he moved to Budapest as one of the local Gestapo/SD operatives. His rank then was relatively low, SS Captain, and only after his "death in action" in the Hungarian capital in October 1944 was he promoted to Sturmbannführer (Major) and Kriminalrat.

[4] See Extracts from SIME Report No. 3, OSS record RG 226, Entry 210, box 105, folder 447.

[5] Geschke's SS personal file, BDC microfilm at NARA. According to his file, Geschke was appointed by RSHA Chief Ernst Kaltenbrunner to his Hungarian command and also promoted on his personal recommendation on November 9, 1944.

Grosz was no fool, and hence he might have devised at least an idea more plausible than Brand's (actually Laufer's) initial "truck deal" in conversations with Laufer himself, possibly counting on Laufer's previous contacts with "Dogwood," which included separate peace talks related to Count von Moltke's plans.

The question that seems here to be crucial is who initiated the deals offered by Brand and Grosz. I maintain that the Jewish side, including the Budapest Rescue Committee, maybe Fritz Laufer, plus Grosz, was the initiator of both missions. Neither Adolf Eichmann nor Heinrich Himmler initiated the "Gestapo Deal." Both used such ideas for their own purposes, which had nothing to do with large-scale rescue of Jews, but indeed Schellenberg may have endorsed it as a political coup to split the Allies, while Laufer may have believed that war materiel and maybe big money would come out of it in exchange for a few Jews. For his part, the clever Grosz may have revived the separate peace ideas dating back to "Dogwood's" efforts with Moltke in order to make himself useful to the Gestapo/SD, who were interested in luring "Dogwood" into believing that the SD was now cultivating the same ideas. At any rate, Grosz thereby managed to get out of Budapest and save his own neck. Himmler, for his part, was not obliged in any way to give anything in return.[6] Hence, rescue ideas initiated by Jews became Nazi traps in Allied eyes and therefore Nazi ploys requiring rejection.

---

[6] See Himmler to Becher in this regard in Breitman and Aronson, "The End of the 'Final Solution'?," p. 187n, Interrogation of Kurt Becher, November 1, 1947, NA, RG 238, M-1019/R 5/534.

28

How the Missions Were Born

According to one of Grosz's British interrogation reports,[1] the story behind his and Brand's mission evolved when several meetings were held early in April 1944 between Brand, Kasztner, Abwehr agent Winninger, and Eichmann's aides Hermann Krumey and Dieter Wisliceny, "always allowing themselves to be cheated out of their Zionist money in the hope that one day the Germans would really do something for the Jews . . . BRAND was acting out of misguided idealism and fright at the same time."

The next day, Laufer told Grosz that he would arrange for "all funds stolen from the Zionists to be returned . . . by EICHMANN to BRAND." Laufer then "expressed the Gestapo's readiness to assist the Jews as much as possible" and instructed Grosz "to draw up a plan of Jewish demands together with BRAND."

On May 5, 1944, Brand met Eichmann, according to Grosz, in the presence of Clages, and both "treated BRAND very civilly." Eichmann said that he would return to him the money and the letters delivered by the Swedish military attaché "intact." Eichmann then:

proposed that BRAND should go to ISTANBUL, and, through the Zionists, arrange for the purchase and delivery of 10,000 lorries, chocolate and cocoa to the Germans via TURKEY, SPAIN, PORTUGAL or SWEDEN. BRAND said that he could easily arrange that. In return, EICHMANN promised the Germans would close the

---

[1] See PRO/FO 371/ 42811/WR 422/9/G, the only SIME interrogation made public by the PRO years ago. See also more recently declassified SIME Report No. 1 on Grosz's interrogation, carrying X-2 ID received on September 25, 1944, RG 226, Entry 190 a, box 5, folder 12, according to which the Germans demanded two billion dollars (Brand is quoted in the document as if they demanded only two million) and ten thousand railcars rather than trucks, a notion that was never repeated elsewhere. Also, Grosz is quoted here as if he had tried to gain Richard Klatt for collaboration with the Americans but was angrily refused. The other interrogations quoted here and the resulting messages by Ira Hirschmann from Cairo and by Lord Moyne (the British Minister Resident in Cairo at the time) are stored in NARA's "Gestapo Deal" files: RG 84, box 110.

ghettoes, stop the deportation of Jews, and see that a number of Jews were given a safe conduct to PALESTINE or elsewhere in N. AFRICA. (PRO/FO 371/42811/WR 422/9/6)

The Zionists then agreed among themselves on several demands with respect to the Jews, mainly the end of the ghettoization and no deportations, while they were still harassed by the Abwehr people and protected by both the Gestapo and SD, when Brand presented Laufer with the Zionists' demands. Laufer was quoted as having responded quite positively, explaining "that HIMMLER had ordered a radical change in the treatment of the Jews, and that if the latter kept their part of the bargain which BRAND had made with EICHMANN, the Germans would certainly do their best to meet the Zionist demands." Nothing in the captured German records lends credibility to Laufer's alleged remarks about Himmler at this stage of the war, when Hitler still hoped to beat an Allied invasion in the West and then turn back upon the Russians, whose spearheads were approaching the Carpathians. Dieter Wisliceny's presence in several of these talks seemed, however, to lend the Gestapo offer credibility. The talks with "Willy," as Brand told Shertok in Aleppo, circled around payments in cash.[2]

Wisliceny soon left the scene to organize the deportations of the Jews from the Carpathian region to Auschwitz as soon as possible. The Budapest Rescue Committee (i.e., the Va'ada) was not conscious of Wisliceny's real role, which we may ascribe not just to Eichmann's zeal but to the Wehrmacht's insistence upon the evacuation of Jews from the Eastern Hungarian province to begin with and Hungarian input.[3] Thus, on May 1, the Budapest Va'ada mentioned "Willy" in a cable to Istanbul,[4] as if the "gifts" for him – money – had been used. Second, the Committee (the cable was signed by four members, including chairman Komoly, Kasztner, and Brand) told Istanbul that:

The negotiations are aimed at <u>avoiding death</u> [underlined by reader] and deportation [two code words were used here – S.A.]. Chance of success exists only when you intervene quickest and positively <u>due to large requirements</u> [underlined by reader; a Hebrew word was used here, meaning "financial requirements"] stop tell <u>Salli</u> [Saly Mayer – the AJDC resident in Switzerland – underlined by reader] and all his people (AJDC, WRB) that delay [Verschleppung] <u>could work here catastrophically</u> [underlined by reader] . . . large immigration to Palestine [code word] from here difficult therefore agreement [re] emigration [to] America necessary via Lisbon. (Hagana Archive, Moladti Files in Repository 14/798)

---

[2] See "recording of a meeting which took place in ALEPPO on [June 11, 1944] between on one hand Joel BRAND and on the other Moshe SHERTOK of the Jewish Agency and Zvi SCHECHTER. A British Security officer was present." RG 226, Entry 196, box 76, folder 196: from Assistant Defense Security Office, Northern Syria, dated June 12, 1944, to Lieutenant Colonel G. N. Kirk, SIME, GHQ, MEF (Middle East Forces).

[3] See *Kriegstagebuch des Oberkommandos der Wehrmacht*, p. 829. "Ostungarn" became "Operationsgebiet" in March 1944.

[4] See Hagana Archive, Moladti files in Repository 14/798.

The cable might have been intercepted both by the Germans and the Allies, whose attention might have been drawn to the target of the deal: large-scale Jewish immigration to America in the middle of the war in exchange for large funds on the eve of "Overlord," the invasion of Europe, which would be a supreme test for Allied troops and their families at home.

On May 2, 1944, the Va'ada cabled Istanbul again,[5] asking for Turkish visas for "joel" and "jozi" – Brand and possibly Winninger – whose code name was "Josi," maybe in order to accommodate the Abwehr as well. They added, however, that the departure of 750 people by ship had been authorized as soon as a chartered vessel was ready at Constanza. Thus, we may say that the SS were indeed promising some kind of a gesture of good will as early as May 2, before Brand's departure and in connection with it.

A couple of days later, the Committee cabled Dr. Chaim Posner, a Zionist representative in Geneva,[6] that the basis of the negotiations was two million dollars and that rescue from Poland "was mentioned" as well, but the chances "were still unclear." The Va'ada further advised Geneva that Brand had already paid "Willy" $20,000 and wrote to Saly Mayer regarding more funds. The 600 Palestine certificate holders whose departure was promised were mentioned and also the German interest in a wholesale Jewish emigration. On May 9, they cabled Schwalb in Geneva about "Willy's" promises to help save Hungarian Jewry and that they had received a special promise from a go-between, without mentioning names (they used the Hebrew word "Sztadlan" – who was in fact Wisliceny), that no deportations and killings would take place. In reality, "Willy" was leaving Budapest at the time on his way to deport all the Jews of Carpathia to their death.

For his part, Fritz Laufer, who probably had fed "Dogwood" Schwarz with similar ideas before, seemed to have believed that Brand would not come back empty-handed. What the Germans would give him in exchange was a different story, as Kurt Becher quoted Himmler: They could take the goods and disappear.[7] Laufer silenced Grosz when he interceded "with the objection that BRAND would not have the slightest chance of obtaining a pengoe's worth of goods from the Allies" and offered his own services as an intermediary between the Germans and Istanbul together with Brand. Brand, however, "reiterated his certainty of success" and told Laufer how he was cheated by Abwehr operatives Schmidt and Winninger; the latter wanted more money and threatened to arrest Brand and Kasztner, whereupon the Gestapo/SD arrested them all and confiscated the stolen money, releasing the Zionists immediately afterward.[8]

Several days later, Clages and Laufer invited Grosz to a café and dinner in a cabaret, where Grosz arranged for "a beautiful plump girl about 30" for

[5] Same archival source as in note 4.
[6] Same source as note 4, no date. Original cables were retyped later.
[7] See note 6. in Chapter 27.
[8] SIME interrogation PRO/FO quoted earlier, pp. 35–36.

Clages and then both "SD chiefs . . . became more serious." They asked why Grosz thought Brand would not be able to buy war material through the Zionists for the Germans. He replied, as he said later, that the Allies would not dream of selling anything to the Germans and objected to Brand's truck mission, but they then agreed that Brand might raise money in exchange for Nazi concessions regarding the Jews.

Clages, now quite drunk, explained "that they had only <u>asked</u> (underlined in original) BRAND if he would be able to buy war material, and he immediately said he could. They had reported this to BERLIN and received instructions that BRAND must be sent on a mission. KLAAGES [sic] went on to explain that the S.D. had identical interests with the Zionists, in that both parties wanted the Jews to leave EUROPE." Indeed, according to Himmler's own definition of the SD/Gestapo's duty, SS officers were expected to act as "political soldiers" of the Third Reich, initiating things within Himmler's general policy. Cheating the Allies out of war material or gaining political capital from dealing with Jews was a legitimate maneuver, even if it had no actual significance with regard to the Final Solution. Having heard Grosz's version, SIME now had evidence how Nazi tyranny and corruption, vividly described by a Jewish smuggler, allegedly combined with German political schemes and with the Zionist philosophy and actual policy coined in terms of "identical interests" with the Zionists and related to the most sensitive political subject on the agenda of the grand alliance on the eve of "Overlord": a separate peace.

Clages then was quoted to the effect that he explained alleged differences between the SD and Gestapo, arguing that his outfit – although "he did not like Jews," was different – yet another reason for some to speculate after the war that Heinrich Himmler, as supreme boss of both the Gestapo and SD, might have played two different games. One would eventually lead to probing for negotiations with the Western Allies thanks to the enormous influence he believed that the Jews had among them, a way of thinking perhaps influenced by the young director of SD foreign operations, Walter Schellenberg. There is, however, no evidence to substantiate this, including in Schellenberg's own testimony discussed earlier. Himmler's other game was the continued pursuit of the Final Solution in such a vigorous fashion as was necessary in Hungary, which was to remain a part of the German Empire in Europe at all costs, and which included the acquisition of the Weiss family works for the SS as if the Third Reich and its race order were perceived to be eternal even at that stage of the war.

Later in May, Heinrich Himmler gave a speech in front of high German Army officers in which he openly addressed the issue of the Final Solution.[9] He said that he was not a bloodthirsty man, but he had to act decisively upon

---

[9] Himmler's own voice, in a gathering of German army officers, Sonhoffen, May 24, 1944, BBC TIMEWATCH documentary 2001, written and produced by Detlef Siebert.

orders received, including with regard to Jewish women and children. The children would have grown up and taken their revenge by "killing us." Thus, *the "Jewish problem has been solved"* (italics added), he said, and was received with warm applause by the Wehrmacht audience. This statement, however, may have allowed a few survivors to be used for political and economic benefits.

Grosz, for his part, used the chance to raise his old idea that he should accompany Brand, "as he could help him bring money (rather than trucks) back . . . for the SD."

The next day, Grosz was invited to meet both Clages and Laufer. Laufer asked him whether "the British and Americans were really keen to help the Jews in occupied EUROPE, and whether there was a possibility of negotiating 'other sort of business' with the Allies through the Zionists." Clages continued by saying, "There was a possibility of a stalemate between the British and the Americans . . . and the Axis," and thus Germany "must combine with these two countries to fight RUSSIA." We interpret this to mean that the strategic stalemate might come as the result of an Allied invasion, which would be defeated, or at least would prove inconclusive.

A meeting between two and three high-ranking SD officers and two or three high-ranking British and American officers for the purpose of opening negotiations on the subject of a separate peace could be raised by no one else but Grosz, who would plant the idea in the heads of the Allies ahead of the invasion or ahead of further Soviet advances without committing the Third Reich. In a way, this was a distorted version of "Dogwood's" own idea of a separate peace as discussed with Count von Moltke and turned down by the Americans about five months before.

Clages declared the SD ready to free Jews for money – $2,000 (U.S.) per capita. Grosz said that was out of the question as far as the Zionists were concerned. Clages returned to his main concern, asking Grosz who could be the best Allied contact man in Istanbul. Grosz then mentioned "Dogwood" Schwarz, and Clages indeed preferred to stick with the Americans alone.

According to Brand's meeting with Shertok,[10] Eichmann was interested in a connection to the American Joint Distribution Committee (AJDC), not to the Zionists proper. Indeed, in all his further talks with Kasztner, Eichmann referred to him, as disclosed in the latter's postwar reports, as the representative of the AJDC, not of the Zionists. The reason for this could have been a decision made by his superiors not to deal directly with the Zionists due to obligations made to the Grand Mufti, who was raising Muslim recruits for the Waffen SS at the time, while the SD prepared to land some Arab commandos in Palestine proper. In fact, two commandos did land early in 1945 and were soon apprehended by the British. The other reason that Eichmann referred to Kasztner's affiliation with the AJDC could be Schellenberg's hope

[10] Hagana Archive, Div. 14, Shertok's report, Brand file.

that the Americans since the establishment of the WRB had become more obliged to the Jewish cause and thus would be vulnerable to German overtures that might split the Allies or damage the Allied cause in the eyes of their own people.

Indeed, upon arrival, Brand and Grosz tried to reach the U.S. ambassador to Turkey, Laurence Steinhardt, as their highest priority, and they used their Zionist connections in Istanbul for that purpose. Laufer and Grosz, however, suggested that both Allies must be approached even if Zionist influence was supposed to be bigger in America. The "Zionist connection" between Jewish criminal types and SS officers, among Zionist operatives, which Allied intelligence officers feared had "identical interests" with the Third Reich, was thus freely discussed in the context of trouble with Stalin on the eve of the Normandy invasion, and revealed to SIME in real time, pending an Allied decision.

Worse still, Grosz's mission – as discussed with Laufer and Clages – cast doubt on Laufer's American Jewish operative, "Dogwood" Schwarz, while he in turn cast doubt on Brand's mission in his SIME interrogation, describing Brand as a Zionist operative easily promising to the Nazis Allied goods (in exchange for Jewish lives).

Thus, Grosz's new "mission," given to him by Clages and Laufer, which seemed to have been based upon his own and Laufer's contacts with Schwarz and with Zionist operatives in Istanbul such as Teddy Kollek, was bound to cast a shadow on Brand and on the Zionists as well.

Brand and Grosz seemed to have become a German team. They were instructed by Clages to try Istanbul Zionists and the Americans. If they failed, they were supposed to try their luck again with Nathan Schwalb in Geneva, known to the Nazis through his intercepted mail and believed to be in close touch with the AJDC's representative in Geneva. They could also operate via Lisbon through Dr. Joseph Schwartz, the European AJDC representative, about whose status the Germans were also halfway informed through intercepted rescue mail. Hence, the Western Allies could infer from the SIME interrogation that they – not actually the Zionists – were the target of the "sinister German ploy" aiming at supplying the Germans with highly sensitive war material such as trucks in the middle of the war and/or further exposing the Western Allies as fighting a "Jew's war."

Laufer was promoted by Brand to a key position in the Gestapo hierarchy, and Clages, the medium echelon Gestapo/SD operative, was promoted by Grosz to be the "SD Chief in Budapest" as if he ran an outfit separate from the Gestapo. For his part, Brand made the survival of the Hungarian Jews dependent on the Allied response to the Nazi offer and hence transformed the responsibility for their fate from the Nazi killers to the third parties, and to the Zionists who should have pushed the third parties to stop the carnage, without a remote connection to the realities on the ground.

In fact, Eichmann had no authority to ransom a large number of Jews in Hungary or anywhere else. His mission was to have them killed. He also was not the only one involved in the Hungarian carnage, but the Wehrmacht wanted the province to become "judenrein" as soon as possible, while Hungarians – starting with state secretaries Endre and Baky and all the way to eager local authorities supported by the Hungarian gendarmerie – were involved in the immediate ghettoization, starvation, humiliation, and final deportation of the Jews in the Hungarian province except in Budapest city.

Both missions combined with an OSS inquiry into "Dogwood" Schwarz's network as a whole. One reason may have been Colonel Hatz's behavior, exposed by Fritz Kolbe as though Hatz was a traitor or at least played a double game. Another reason was Schwarz's ties with Laufer, who was regarded by "Dogwood" as a trusted agent even after the occupation of Hungary, while the head of "Dogwood's" Austrian cell, Franz Messner, the anti-Nazi underground operative, who happened to be in Budapest at the time, was arrested by the Germans in May and later executed. At the same time, Laufer was exposed by Grosz and Brand when interrogated by the British as an SD/Gestapo operative. The American inquiry finally ended in "Dogwood" Schwarz's dismissal in a far-reaching shakeup in OSS Istanbul that included the retirement of the Jewish and non-Jewish members of the station staff, with its chief, Macfarland, on top. Frank G. Wisner succeeded Macfarland, and his opinion of the "Dogwood" chain was no better than that of X-2.[11]

For his part, "Dogwood" felt for the rest of his life, as described by Yehuda Bauer,[12] that the Americans missed promising options that he created, such as the Moltke scheme, to end the war much sooner than it did, to prevent the Soviets from occupying half of the Continent, and to save many Jews. He might have even believed that Laufer was an asset that could be used if handled properly. Being a double agent did not necessarily mean – for "Dogwood" – that Laufer was not primarily his loyal aide, whose great strength rather than weakness was his close proximity to the Gestapo and the SD. After all, if you deal with the enemy, you must deal with someone inside the enemy's system – exactly as Brand and Kollek and other rescuers were convinced as well.

---

[11] The "Dogwood organization" was officially "closed" by Lanning Macfarland on July 31, 1944, but Macfarland himself and all his operatives involved, including "Cereus" Coleman, were fired or transferred immediately afterward; see Wisner's memos in this regard dated July 5 and August 14, 1944, in Istanbul box 34.

[12] Oral information conveyed to the present writer.

29

The Demise of a Rescue Mission

More sophisticated than Brand's or Schwarz's interrogations was the evaluation of both missions made by Reuben B. Resnik, an AJDC representative in Istanbul who was associated with the WRB's effort in Turkey. Resnik met with Brand upon his arrival in Istanbul and also had his connections with members of the Va'ada in Budapest.[1] In his report, prepared at the request of Ambassador Laurence Steinhardt, Resnik – a wise man – expressed his impression that Brand:

... was not as sincere and straight-forward as other observers thought him to be. He had ready and direct answers for all questions and was apparently very cooperative and reiterated on several occasions the seriousness with which he was carrying out his mission. It is important ... to observe that Brand is not completely without anxiety and fear about his assignment and its possible consequences. (Resnik to Steinhardt, June 4, 1944, RG 226, Entry 210, box 105, folder 447)

This description reflects one who initiated or accepted Laufer's mission, and thereby made the Allies and the Zionists seemingly responsible from then on for the fate of the Hungarian Jews, pending his own personal success in that mission.

Resnik mentioned "interviews and conferences" he held with persons "who have had close contact with Mr. Brand during his visit in Istanbul and while he was a resident in Budapest."

Resnik's "possible interpretations" of both missions (he never met Grosz) are rather penetrating. Among other speculations on the German motives in sending Brand and Grosz, such as the possible benefit for a small group of Germans in control of Hungarian matters, or the beginning of peace proposals, Resnik wrote that these "proposals may be designated to enlist so-called Jewish influence to disrupt the present efforts on the part of

[1] See Resnik's Memo to Ambassador Steinhardt, strictly confidential, dated June 4, 1944, RG 226, Entry 210, box 105, folder 447.

the Allies to have neutrals break commercial relationships with the Axis." Indeed, around this time, Turkey was brought under Allied pressure to cancel the vital export of tungsten ore to Germany. Such a consideration would not have been totally foreign to Laufer's mind. The next interpretation is closer to my trap theorem:

These proposals may be designed to place the Allied governments in a position of being unable to comply with the demands and therefore the Germans would be in a position to say that the Allies too are refusing to assist the Jewish people and therefore the anti-Jewish policy of the Germans has validity in that the Jewish people of Europe are in effect ignored by the Allies. (Resnik to Steinhardt, RG 226, Entry 210, box 105, folder 447)

Thus, the creation of the WRB was just a smokescreen in the sense that the Americans were not serious about rescue, thus pushing the Jews to push the Americans even more and hence prove the "Jew's war" theme. The other possibility was that "underground propaganda" in Germany and other occupied territories

... says that Germany is losing the war, among other reasons, because of its strong anti-Jewish policy. By these proposals it can be said that Germany is adopting a new policy favoring the Jews and it would follow that those who were responsible for carrying out the strong anti-Jewish policy could have it said later in mitigation of their acts that they ultimately established a program favoring the Jewish people. (RG 226, Entry 210, box 105, folder 447)

The last option was obviously "effecting a split between the Allies," but Resnik also added that "*one group in Germany prepared to effect some type of a 'Putsch' in order to swing Allied sympathy to their contemplated plans have made this offer.*" "*In this connection, it is thought that possibly Gyorgy may have carried word about the plans of this 'Putsch'*" (italics added). Indeed, Laufer gave Grosz an empty suitcase that included a letter sewn into the linen inside it. This letter was supplied by Krumey, Eichmann's aide, to Grosz in Vienna before he left with Brand for Istanbul and was to be given to "Dogwood."[2]

One can argue that both Krumey and Laufer, Laufer's Gestapo/SD operator Clages, and possibly their superior Geschke were trying to reach "Dogwood" in order to make him believe that his cherished dream of a separate peace was inherited by SD Ausland, and hence some hope of splitting the Allies could be revived as well, while the Gestapo got hold of his Austrian anti-Nazi contact, who indeed was arrested around that time while visiting Budapest.[3] Here the source of Resnik's information on a forthcoming

---

[2] See Grosz interrogation, Public Record Office, document FO 371 42811, file SIME/P. 7755, dates of interrogation: June 6–22, 1944.

[3] See in this regard "Penetration of OSS by Foreign Intelligence Services," X-2 Branch, SSU, Washington, D.C., May 1946.

putsch in Germany may have been "Dogwood," as both were residents of Istanbul at the time.

One may interpret this as if Himmler and his Gestapo/SD operatives knew about the putsch ahead of time and wanted to get in touch with the Western Allies through "Dogwood" in order to capitalize on it for their own overtures toward the West: perhaps a hint about Count von Stauffenberg's attempt on Hitler's life on July 20, 1944, given by Laufer to "Dogwood" in advance. On the contrary, one can only guess that this was "Dogwood" Schwarz's own contribution to the otherwise hopeless mess in which he would find himself when according to Grosz he was very excited when he got Laufer's message and immediately left for Ankara. Accordingly, he may have been motivated to do so thanks to Laufer's letter, possibly aimed at his separate peace dream and allegedly related to his Moltke design. In other words, "Dogwood" might have been told that plans for a German uprising, previously discussed with Moltke, were alive and might be carried out by other elements in the Nazi system or tolerated by the SD. A separate peace with the West, which was in principle Schwarz's own design forged with Moltke, was the subject of Grosz's mission as compiled by Laufer and Clages. Still convinced that Laufer was his trusted agent, "Dogwood" might have swallowed this, trying to revive American interest in an alleged German putsch initiative having possibly been told about it by Laufer in the hidden letter. Since the Allies had rejected the old Moltke scheme, they would hardly accept the alleged SD-initiated one. On the contrary, while a separate peace was anathema to them, Allied attention became focused on Brand's and Grosz's missions, in which the same Laufer and his Gestapo/SD operators played key roles and thus helped destroy both missions and "Dogwood" altogether. For his part, "Dogwood" perceived in the real putsch of July 20, 1944, which tragically failed, a proof of his own "grand design,"[4] which however had nothing to do with Clages, Laufer, and their superiors.

The Jewish Agency's Shertok was allowed by the British to interview Brand in Aleppo on June 20 in the presence of a British Intelligence officer, and the British transcript of their talk indeed contained Brand's assertions that Eichmann approached him as a link to an American Jewish organization, the AJDC, and that he was interested in mass Jewish emigration but not to Palestine, due to Arab misgivings.[5] Further, said Brand, "they (the SS) firmly believe that the Jews are a disease, and that they wanted to infect their enemies with it. In Palestine the Jews would form a self-contained force, but what the Germans want is that the Jews should be scattered and act as a corroding element among the nations who are Germany's enemies." This in fact was Hitler's basic philosophy, which had played a role in his forced

---

4 Yehuda Bauer to the present writer.
5 See note 2 in Chapter 28.

emigration policy and which the Western Allies were hardly ready to accept as a good reason for them to allow Jews to enter en masse.

Upon their arrest in Aleppo, Brand and Grosz were sent for interrogation by SIME HQ in Cairo, while Shertok went via Cairo to London. The American WRB representative in Turkey, Ira Hirschmann, who was close to IZL's Bergson–Kook group active in America, was informed about Brand's mission and flew back from the United States to Turkey and then followed Brand to Cairo. The British could not ignore Hirschmann's interest in the case and at first seemed to have reacted favorably while interrogating Grosz and Brand separately. They also held in their custody Samu Springmann, the Hungarian Zionist operative who had created the Zionist "courier service" mentioned earlier. Springmann had asked the Zionist authorities to relieve him of his illegal activity following a painful arrest in Hungary, and he left for Turkey on his way to Palestine; he had been arrested and interned in Cairo before the Nazi invasion of Hungary but had already given the British information on his ties with dubious figures in their eyes.[6]

Shertok, for his part, spent a few hours in Cairo and proceeded on to London via Tripoli, Libya, and Rabat, Morocco, and he arrived in London on June 27. Upon arrival, he gave the British government representatives his "preliminary report" on the Brand–Grosz mission.[7] He described in short Brand's previous rescue efforts in Hungary and gave him high marks as a loyal Zionist and responsible person who had arrived in Istanbul "accompanied by another man" – the dark, sinister figure in the story. "Unfortunately he, too, is a Jew.... He was an agent of the Hungarian police, and was doing odd jobs of work for the Nazis even before Hungary was overrun."

This description of Grosz's activity before the invasion was only partially true, as he served the Zionists in Istanbul loyally and better than their other couriers such as Winninger and the Swiss traitor Gyr. But Shertok wanted to dissociate the Jewish Agency from a Jewish spy in service of the Nazis. Shertok's clever idea was to dissociate Brand's legitimate and maybe pursuable mission from Grosz's hopeless bid for a separate peace by simply denouncing the latter as a "dark and sinister type" with whose mission the Zionists had nothing to do. Yet this could not have worked, as Shertok had no influence over Brand's and Grosz's own behavior under SIME interrogation, in which both admitted that they cooperated among themselves and that Laufer was a principal figure behind their missions, which would finally destroy both.

On June 28, Dr. Chaim Weizmann (the President of the World Zionist Organization), Shertok, and a distinguished delegation of British and "Palestinian" Zionists, Professor Lewis Namier included, met to hear Moshe

---

[6] See Springmann interrogation report.
[7] Hagana Archive, Brand file: copy of British document entitled "Mr. Shertok's Preliminary Report, June 27th, 1944, at 6 p.m. at the Dorchester Hotel, London, W.1."

Shertok's report on a meeting he had with the head of the Refugee Section of the Foreign Office, Alec W. G. Randall, and several other high British officials to discuss Brand's mission. According to what seems to be the British-originated "short minutes" of the ensuing Zionist–British meeting, Shertok started with Brand's wish to return to Hungary.[8] The British could not understand why; he was safe where he was, they said, and when told that he came on a rescue mission and besides left his family behind as hostages, Randall responded by saying that the deportations and killings were continuing with or without Brand. Shertok said that a decision must be made about what Brand should say when he got back. Randall "had agreed that that was important and that there was no objection to Brand's return." "What was the British Government line now? Randall said that what was bothering them was why the Germans were now offering to release Jews. All the time the British had asked them to let the Jews go, for instance, the Zionist veterans, but there had been no response." From this we learn that at a certain stage, probably following the obvious failure of the Refugee Conference in Bermuda in 1943, the British had made a gesture toward the Zionists in this respect; and those "veterans" were among the few who trickled to Palestine from German-allied nations in the Balkans.

The Zionists told Randall that the Nazis "had been prepared to let Jews go [on] a quid pro quo [underlined in original] basis, and in fact an exchange was now pending which included Zionist veteran lists." The British side, obviously trying to avoid becoming a party to deals of that kind with the Germans and eager to limit the numbers and the categories of the immigrants to Palestine, first mentioned Swiss and Swedish offers to take in "some 20,000 children."

The Zionists argued that the Germans should be told that the British were ready to take in the people on the veteran Zionist lists and when that was done further categories, "for instance, the children." Shertok said that it would now be hard to locate the Zionist veterans, scattered all over the Continent, and seeking them would give the Germans the excuse to destroy the large majority; either one should start with a broad category such as children or "go on to say they would accept anyone" whom the Germans would let go. Randall responded by saying "that in such case the Germans might even send undesirable people and spies." Shertok countered by asking what use spies would be if the immigrants were interned at first in neutral countries. Randall seems to have agreed but suggested the children would come first "and the mothers could accompany the children, via the good services of a neutral country such as Spain." Shertok then pressed to the

---

[8] Archival source as above: Hagana Archive, Brand file, Short Minutes of Meeting held at 77, Great Russell Street, London, W.C.1 on Wednesday, the 28th June 1944, Secret. The typewriting and the official categorization of the document as "secret" led me to the conclusion that the minutes of the Zionist meeting were a British official document.

point: a protecting power such as Spain would not do. *There must be an offer to meet the Germans* (my italics). Randall asked who should meet them, and Shertok replied "perhaps it could be a representative of the American Refugee Board, and a British representative." He added that as a government they could only meet the representatives of a government, but there was no reason why they should not appoint agents for this purpose.

Mr. Randall asked "where they would be *if the Germans were to offer to dump a million Jews on them*" (my italics). This infamous phrase, later quoted by Brand as if it was offered to him by Lord Moyne, the British Minister Resident in Cairo, was thus offered to Shertok by the British Refugee Section Chief Randall in London following Shertok's somewhat less explicit plea about "an offer to meet the Germans." About this neither Brand nor the Stern gang, which soon would murder Moyne, knew anything, except that Brand, when he was set free by the British, might have heard it from Shertok himself when he described his efforts in London in Mapai's public meetings upon his return to Palestine. The Israelis would have known nothing about the offer either until the publication of this document here, probably due to Shertok's refusal after the war to admit that he had suggested to "meet the Germans" rather than fight them, as Israel's early ethos was based on the Warsaw ghetto uprising and similar acts of resistance. The Zionists "had replied that if the Germans meant business extraordinary measures would have to be put into operation." Randall then remarked that "even for a few thousand refugees difficulties arose where to put them." His interlocutors swallowed their "Palestinocentric" pride and suggested "camps in North Africa" rather than Palestine. Randall then said that the British could not contemplate meeting the Germans without the Russians knowing about it, as Brand had told them that Eichmann's 10,000 trucks should be used in the Eastern Front only: "It might be regarded as a wedge driven between the Allies." This indeed seemed to have been the Western Allies' primary worry.[9] Shertok said that the Russians indeed should be invited to send an observer. The discussion in fact led to nothing, as the British were busy in the meantime with the interrogation of both Brand and Grosz and inquiring into the background of their missions with the Americans.

According to Ira Hirschmann, the American War Refugee Board (WRB) representative who flew to Cairo and met both Moyne and Brand, the British Minister Resident never met the latter, nor did Brand claim to have met Moyne at that stage but was kept entirely in the custody of British Intelligence.[10] The results of SIME's interrogation seem to have changed Moyne's view. At first, he agreed with Hirschmann to authorize Shertok's idea to cable the Jewish Agency's representative, Barlas, in Istanbul, a sort of positive response to Brand's mission as an interim solution until the final decision could

---

[9] See official correspondence as quoted in Gilbert, *Auschwitz and the Allies*, Chapter 24.
[10] See NA, RG 84, decimal diplomatic files 810.8 1944, General Records Cairo, box 110.

be reached in London. In an addendum to his report to U.S. Ambassador Steinhardt in Ankara,[11] Hirschmann then told him that Brand disclosed a great deal to his SIME interrogators about Laufer, "apparently the leading Gestapo agent in Hungary." Thus, following a cable in this regard from Barlas in Istanbul, the suggested Shertok telegram required more deliberations instead of sending Brand back with some nonbinding offers to negotiate with the Germans further, especially on money rather than goods, in blocked accounts if necessary, as Hirschmann suggested to Moyne at first. Laufer's involvement in both Brand's and Grosz's missions was therefore at least one of the main reasons for British Intelligence's doubts about the whole endeavor, which reached beyond Moyne's own involvement and authority in this case, and for Hirschmann's sudden (for the Zionists), unexpected retreat from the whole affair.

In this connection, we should quote here another OSS X-2 (counterintelligence) memo on the Brand and Grosz missions, which originated in CIC and created a dreadful linkage between the Gestapo/SD agent Laufer, triple agent Grosz, "Dogwood" Schwarz, and the Jewish Agency:[12]

In the event of failure of Brandt [sic] and Gross' [sic] missions in Turkey, the two alternatives proposed are both through the Jews (JOINT in Switzerland and Lisbon – parentheses in original). Why not contact American Intelligence Sources directly, also in Switzerland or Lisbon? The fact that Gross was to keep his mission secret from Brandt [he argued in his SIME interrogation that his, the separate peace feeler, was the main mission, not Brand's – S.A.] in Turkey, that both were to contact separate sources [Brand was supposedly sent to the Zionists on his way to establish contact with the AJDC, and Grosz was supposed to contact "Dogwood," Schwarz, his OSS liaison – S.A.] for the accomplishment of their missions there, is inconsistent with the plan for them to approach identical sources (JOINT) in Switzerland or Lisbon. This highlights the personality of Schwarz, or his importance in German estimation, as the ideal intermediary.

Schwarz – a possible Jewish Agency Agent?
what financial background?
possible deals with Gross and Laufer for personal gain?
How did S. come to OSS?
personal friendship with Laufer began where? When? Contact maintained how?
(First letter from S. to Laufer given Gross by Collek, Istanbul Zionist on 3rd journey March 43 . . .).

This whole show appears primarily to be a Jewish one, with the S.D. in the driver's seat (italics added). Of the Americans [OSS personnel – S.A.] contacted, Lehmann, Kremer and Schwarz ARE CERTAINLY Jews [all bold capital letters in the original; all names are of "Dogwood" Schwarz's associates in OSS station Istanbul– S.A.]. (American) Patriotic considerations may have consciously or sub-consciously received secondary

[11] Ibid.
[12] RG 226, Entry 120, box 20, X-2, letters CIC handwritten on top.

consideration <u>where strong racial sympathy obscured hidden motives of ardent Zionists under</u> <u>S.D. pressure</u> (underlining added). The Jews who already consider themselves a nation, though still without a home or legal status, are probably even now casting about for future allies in the post-war period. That Britain will very likely not be one of these is already apparent. It is possible the Zionists consider the war already won, and are viewing all problems in a post-war light. From the Zionist viewpoint: unity of America and Russia with Great Britain might be less likely to further Zionist aims than would be a disagreement of these powers. Therefore any arrangement with the enemy for the rescue of the remaining Jews in Europe, could hardly be expected to be discriminated against by Zionists on security grounds, especially when the deal implies that the enemy himself believes the jig is up.

<u>For an American Zionist to be anti-British even in a war in which Britain and America are allies is not difficult. This sentiment plays into German hands.</u> (underlining added)

Before Allied suspicions were reaching their unavoidable climax, the Budapest Va'ada continued to cable Istanbul, still waiting for Brand's mission to bear fruit.

On June 6, Budapest informed Istanbul that a meeting between Zionist rescue workers, Laufer (alias "Schroeder"), and the AJDC representative, Dr. Josef Schwartz, in Lisbon required first a conversation with Kasztner and that Istanbul should quickly work for a meeting between the three, "otherwise the matter is in danger." Further, Laufer was mentioned (with a commentary from rescue operative Bader, as "Eichmann's friend") as if he were "ready to go only after the meeting" ("of the returnees to Budapest," i.e., Brand and Grosz). Hansi Brand signed that cable. Istanbul then cabled Budapest on June 7[13] that the "positive use of the responses of the Zionist leadership in Palestine [meaning that such responses were given – S.A.] according to our proposals, required further trips by Brand and Grosz to Palestine – as you envisioned this too. Schroeder should take it into consideration." The rescue mission in Istanbul even forged an alleged "interim agreement" between the Jewish Agency and the Germans, based on Brand's mission, in order to keep it alive. Yet the deportations to Auschwitz continued as before, and Kasztner in Budapest was now trying to save as many Jews as possible by forcing the Allies to follow up on the defunct Brand mission in spite of themselves.

On the Allied side, the "Schroeder"–Laufer–Eichmann triangle was established firmly in this cable as being on the German side, with all the connotations related to Laufer's reputation in Allied eyes. On June 9, Istanbul repeated to Budapest the idea of a meeting with Laufer in Spain, adding that both Brand and Grosz regarded their further trip as imperative. Istanbul

---

[13] Moladti files; see also the detailed description of Istanbul's efforts in Friling, *Arrow in the Dark.*

thus pretended to speak for both emissaries as if they were still free and negotiating with the Allies.

The next cable that we have at our disposal was signed by Kasztner but probably sent by Hansi Brand to Istanbul on July 10, 1944, in which he advised the rescue mission that 1,700 people were in Germany. This was "Kasztner's Train," a group of about 1,700 people allowed by the Gestapo to leave Hungary as a gesture negotiated by Kasztner to prove Eichmann's good will. But they would not be allowed to proceed to Spain until Brand's return to Budapest, or at least until negotiations continued in Spain. Budapest repeated the question of whether the AJDC representative, Dr. Josef Schwartz, was ready to conclude the negotiations in the spirit of "Schroeder's original suggestion" and mentioned that his superiors "were decided to visit him – Dr. Schwartz – next week in Spain [code word]." "These negotiations would be decisive," said Budapest "and please prepare yourselves accordingly." "Kasztner would be present too." Bader was also supposed to join the negotiations "as Joel." Thus, the Germans seemed decided to make the negotiations yield results for them in spite of the fact that Brand and Grosz had already been neutralized by the Allies. Their mission seemed alive, as a German tool in Allied eyes, and thus had to be exposed and killed, as the British publicly did later in July.

Even after the public demise of Brand's mission, a warning was issued by a Major Barry, Chief of the CIC in the American GHQ Middle-East (USAFIME) at Caserta, Italy, on August 7, 1944, formulated in the following terms:[14]

A. There is proof that some representatives of the Jewish Agency *have been used by the German Intelligence Service* (italics added).

B. The greatest mistake made by Allied intelligence and security officials is the presumption that a Jew, any Jew, is perforce Anti-Nazi and Anti-Axis.

C. There is proof that their representatives, to serve the Jewish Agency, and to help Jews in Europe, will and do deal with Nazi party officials and the German Intelligence Service, *sometimes 'selling out' Allied contacts, agencies and operations* (italics added). (Major Barry, AUS, RG 226, Entry 190 – Caserta-SI-OP-48–67, box 172, folder Jewish Agency)

Major Barry thus recommended the "end of our collaboration with them" (i.e., with the Jewish Agency), adding that the Zionists were "completely

---

[14] Signed Major Barry AUS, RG 226, Entry 190 – Caserta-SI-OP-48–67, box 172, folder Jewish Agency; and see table of organization, CIC Middle East, RG 338, AMET, misc. 095 (1945), according to which the Chief of CIC was directly under the Assistant Chief of Staff (ACS), G-2, USAFIME. The main purpose of the organization was security (i.e., maintaining military secrets and preventing the enemy's penetration of same, with the obvious liaison to British ISLD and SIME).

sincere" in their rescue priorities and ready to use all means to serve "their own" – meaning not necessarily Allied – goals:

F. There is a reasonable proof that their representatives buy Nazi support with their own funds and the funds of Allied intelligence agencies if and when they get their hands on any of the latter. (Major Barry, AUS, RG 226, Entry 190 – Caserta-SI-OP-48–67, box 172, folder Jewish Agency)

Thus, Barry strongly recommended against using agents "loyal mainly to them." Barry's recommendations further included a remark by one of his security officers, E. F. Kennedy, arguing at "their favor," and thus "they" agreed that American (i.e., non-Jewish) supervision, loyal without a question, could partially remove the dangers involved in the American–Zionist intelligence cooperation.

Kollek and Überall-Avriel, and their superior Zaslani-Shiloah, the head of the Jewish Agency's Intelligence section, persisted in cooperating with the Americans and drafted a cooperation agreement with OSS late in July.[15] But the American security people, Consul General Pinkerton in Jerusalem, and the American "censor" (a G-2 resident at the Jerusalem Consulate who also controlled American personnel's mail to avoid exclusive British censorship), the former White Russian by the name of Captain Andronovich, were against it.[16]

It remained an ad hoc cooperation, primarily based on Zionist help in interrogating Jewish Balkan refugees.[17] An interrogation of "Zionists who were smuggled out of Hungary through a secret Zionist organization" via Rumania is quite enlightening here. The Hungarian Desk Chief at OSS-USA-FIME in Caserta made the report in cooperation with Arthur F. Giles, the head of the British CID (Home Intelligence, Palestine Police) in Palestine following a visit to the Atlit Interrogation Center. A specific interrogation contained therein vividly described the enormous difficulties for Jews to escape Hungary during the deportations, including from Kasztner's hometown of Cluj via the "Rumanian route," once the Rumanians involved had made enough money from bribes. It told the story of the ghettos in Hungary, the behavior of the anti-Semitic environment, chasing Jewish property during the deportations, and torturing rich Jews to get their money from them.

The final X-2 report, which concluded that "Dogwood" himself was an enemy agent, described the Laufer connection thus:[18]

LAUFER tried again to contact the Americans, this time through Rejo [sic] KASTNER, another Zionist representative in Hungary formerly closely associated with BRAND. According to a traveler-intercept [seems to be censorship

---

[15] July 21, 1944, Caserta file cited in note 14.
[16] See Caserta file in note 14, same folder.
[17] See Caserta file in note 14, same box, folder Hungarian Desk.
[18] See file RG 226, Entry 110, box 35, declassified September 11, 2000.

intercepts – S.A.] of 2 September 1944, KASTNER proposed that a Dr. Schwartz, a leading Zionist in Portugal [Dr. Josef Schwartz, the European representative of the AJDC, stationed in Lisbon, and non-Zionist – S.A.] should meet with a representative of a certain "Dr. SCRHODER' here called a high Gestapo official in Hungary – in all probability our LAUFER. The meeting was to take place in Spain or Portugal, ostensibly for the purpose of negotiating better treatment for the Jews of occupied Europe. It is stated that SCHRODER himself might be present at the negotiations and that he wanted to meet with an American. There is no information on what happened to this plan, but it is probable that this was another attempt on LAUFER's part to reach the Americans through the Zionists, for some purpose controlled by Berlin. (RG 226, Entry 110, box 35)

As such, if related to the rescue of Jews, such an endeavor was anathema. Yet the Laufer connection seemed to the Zionists even later to be of a peculiar interest.

Kasztner's "plan" following the failure of Brand's mission was outlined in a letter sent to Istanbul from Budapest on June 18, 1944, through a courier.[19] In the opening, Kasztner seemed to be beyond despair and yet still business-like, almost imitating the typical Nazi jargon:

Since my last letter 4 weeks elapsed, in which so much happened in the life of the Hung. Jews as never before. Until today 400,000 people were deported and it is made clear without doubt [es wird klipp und klar erklaert] that nothing could prevent the full evacuation of the province.... We are told that about Budapest no decision has yet been made, but we are not bluffing ourselves and getting ready to the worst. In this connection the Germans openly admit that the deported human material is being selected to ... men capable of work, women and girls, and those incapable of work and children. According to the German assertion [der Zusicherung nach] the first two groups are sent to do several works, and the third group will be [wird ... vernichtet] destroyed [underlined in original] in the much fearful Auschwitz. (Document no. 34, Hagana Archive, Moladti file, repository 80/187f/32)

At that stage, Kasztner seemed to believe that not all deportees had been sent to Auschwitz to die.

"These are the naked [underlined in original] facts," continued Kasztner. Having mentioned the basic facts about Brand's mission and the forged "interim agreement" made by the Istanbul Rescue Committee on its own to keep the Brand affair alive, which however led to nothing, he stated that:

Events became in the meantime beyond one's control; [things] that were subject to negotiations are not anymore, and the complete cessation of the deportations is out of the question. We can however negotiate further on the survival of a small number of men incapable of work and children and on the so-called promise [die angebliche

---

[19] See document No. 34, Hagana Archive, Moladti file, Repository 80/187f/32. The letter carried a crossed dateline from Bratislava first, but it remained unsigned. A contemporary or a later reader referred it to Kasztner in Budapest, however. The content and the style are definitely his.

Zusicherung] that nothing will happen to the working.... Jews.... We must live with these miserable assurances [kaergliche Zusicherungen] and use all our power to at least secure the naked existence along this line.... In this connection the following plan was conceived: In Germany [Kasztner used the usual code word here – S.A.] three camps, each for 10,000 people, for the incapable to work categories will be created, which however will be funded and entertained exclusively by us, or by foreign Jews since the disposal [Erledigung] in Auschwitz would cost the Germans nothing except the gas boxes, and spend more they can't and wouldn't. These camps have the goal of becoming transition camps, with the final aim ["Endzweck" – the Nazi jargon was probably repeated verbatim – S.A.] of allowing these people to emigrate to Spain or Portugal, and make it possible to them to continue to Palestine [a code word was used here – S.A.], to Africa or to overseas if the possibility to leave and ships is given. (Document no. 34, Hagana Archive, Moladti File, repository 80/187f/32)

The deal seems clear – the "quid pro quo" is coined in terms of the costs of living of the rescued, and the means should come from abroad, when possible, even if only 30,000 among the "incapable" were now mentioned, rather than the "million Jews" that were the subject matter before Brand's departure.

Kasztner thus defined the next step "as your most important duty, to get an agreement with the Joint [Distribution Committee's representative Dr. Josef Schwartz – S.A.] in Lisbon in this direction through Saly [Mayer in Switzerland – S.A.]...when it is possible to you, it would be therefore paramountly urgent, to intervene with these two governments.... So that the entry visas will be issued immediately [and thus used as "protection papers" for the time being – S.A.]...the Red Cross could also be contacted."

Kasztner grew rather cautious now, following the failure of Brand's mission, when he continued: "Perhaps should one ask for the help of Allied governments, and one could argue that all these people would leave as soon as possible to Palestine because most of them are having [British] entry certificates." The 30,000 "incapable persons" were the target of much effort, although Kasztner was accused later on as if he was given the power by the Nazis to save the few and leave most to their fate. But meanwhile he was trying to strike a financial deal with the Germans and justify it in terms of the actual costs needed to cover the needs of the survivors in those three camps, writing also to the AJDC's representative Dr. Schwartz in Europe on his own.

Kasztner then calculated the needs of the 30,000 in terms of basic costs of living and medication, hinting toward the supply of some more imported goods on top of cash of about 500,000 Swiss Francs per month, which he demanded "briskly" [flott], "which would <u>have</u> [underlined in original] to be supplied by you, when we have the mailing address, you must take care of the medication, vitamins etc.... The matter is extremely urgent, because...the first transports to these camps are getting ready to leave this

week. You should create a special committee for this purpose, it is worth
your effort, [in order] to save children's lives."

Three days earlier, on June 15, 1944, Kasztner had written to either the
Jewish rescue representatives in Geneva or in Istanbul, in which he outlined
the interim tactics chosen by the Va'ada: "In connection with the negotiations
carried out by Joel Brand, we have taken the responsibility ourselves, to
supply certain quantities of merchandise to those authorities who control
the Jewish question."[20] As a quid pro quo, "human lives" [quotation marks
in original] would be offered, i.e. the deportations would be stopped." It
is not clear whether at this stage a general cessation of the deportations
was at all promised or whether such a promise was made by someone other
than Eichmann, such as Becher. The idea was to get supplies "mainly . . . for
the civilian population such as cocoa, medication, men shirts etc. We have
promised . . . to get these things abroad, but immediately started action . . . to
get them in areas under Axis control. This action . . . promises success."[21]

Kasztner concluded by saying that the first transaction was almost ready
and required 8,000,000 Swiss francs, which will allow "certain advantages"
for Jews, and then the rescue of 100,000 Jews was on the agenda. This
means probably that the writer hoped to keep the Jews of Budapest at least
in the city and asked the AJDC for $10,000,000 for that purpose on top
of rescuing thousands among those already deported.[22] He suggested the
following procedure to finance both activities: the money should be loaned,
by the Joint, for example, and covered by the Jewish Community of Budapest,
"whose immovable property alone is worth much more than 50–60 million
dollars," by invoking its own entire means.

Thus, it is clear that when no money or merchandise could be obtained
as yet, other deals had to be conceived by using local Jewish sources, and
the money for such deals would come from Hungarian Jewry itself (i.e.,
from Budapest Jews), who were probably driven hard by the Committee
under Kasztner's leadership to keep the negotiations going while searching
for ways to institutionalize cooperation among them.

In a separate letter to Dr. Schwartz, the AJDC representative, Kasztner
wrote that the names of the camps for the 30,000 incapable of working
would be announced and raised his quest for money, medication, and clothes
for the inmates, as we already know. He added that a special committee
would handle "these actions" under the chairmanship of Baron Phillip von
Freudiger, a leading orthodox figure, and including Kasztner himself, Julius
Link, Joel Brand (as if he were still involved), and a Josef Blum, probably

---

[20] Unsigned copy, same source as in note 19 probably carried to Istanbul by the same courier.
[21] See Moladti file in note 19 and also Braham and Miller, *The Politics of Genocide*, Volume II,
pp. 956–957.
[22] A similar but separate letter probably was sent to the AJDC European representative Josef
Schwartz on June 13 – same Moladti file as in note 19.

also a non-Zionist. In the same letter, Kasztner advised Dr. Schwartz about a group of 380 people who came in from Cluj – his hometown – to Budapest. In Cluj, they were kept in a so-called concentration camp for the "privileged." This and similar camps will be discussed in detail.

We learn from this that the Va'ada and non-Zionists were trying to co-operate in creating lists of privileged Jews who would be allowed to leave Hungary as a gesture of good will made by the Gestapo. This "gesture" was anchored in the Gestapo's initial bid to release several hundred Palestine certificate holders, which Kasztner was trying now to enlarge. He was aiming at much more, as we have seen. But for the time being the list of the privileged who would embark on "Kasztner's Train," sent by Eichmann to Bergen–Belsen exchange camp rather than to Palestine at first, included the anti-Zionist Rabbi Joel Teitelbaum as well as others who paid for their "tickets." The list was drawn as a result of a compromise between all Jewish parties concerned and was not due to Kasztner's decisive influence. He did, however, use his influence to help save members of his own family who were local leading persons anyway, but other members were deported and subsequently murdered by the Nazis, as were the large majority of the Cluj community.

30

Open and Secret War Schemes and Realities

Before and after their direct involvement with rescue problems as they presented themselves upon Brand's arrival, the Jewish Agency's Political Department under Moshe Shertok was involved in other activities related to rescue and the war effort and the old dream of establishing a "Jewish army" in the ranks of Allied forces. A "Jewish Brigade Group," which Churchill finally authorized with Roosevelt's consent, was created not before September 1944, when several Jewish regiments in the British Army – plus more volunteers – were given the much desired status of a separate Jewish fighting unit deployed on the Italian front.[1]

Since late in 1942, the Yishuv had maintained a channel open to British SOE and to the regional A Force under Lieutenant Colonel Tony Simonds, working within the British Army's MI9 organization and not without trouble for him in London.[2] Several members of the Hagana and the Zionist youth movements from Europe were trained as partisans to be dropped into occupied Europe.

Several among them, including women such as Hannah Szenes, a Hungarian-born Labor Zionist poet, were trained by the British for the

---

[1] Later it played an important role in organizing Holocaust survivors to seek haven in Palestine.

[2] See PRO correspondence file in this regard No. WO208/3375, going back to March 1944, dealing with Jewish Agency candidates for SOE operations in the Balkans and at the Swiss border, names included, and the Jewish Agency's intelligence help in the Balkans. Most significant is a letter by Commander Wolfson of MI9 Istanbul (non-Jew) to Tony Simonds, head of A Force in the Middle East, dated June 3, 1944, No. IST/3615. Wolfson argued, "the channels available [to the Balkans] are almost non-existent and the BAT [Jewish Agency or its Intelligence Service – S.A.] one is the only one which provides for any mass displacements of persons both within and outside the Reich." Wolfson went on to identify the source of the trouble in London: "You and I have had direct personal knowledge of the BAT Agency: London only base themselves on secondhand knowledge and, in my opinion, poor and prejudiced knowledge at that." This was a letter of endorsement and support, backing Simonds's own angry letter to Lieutenant Colonel Winterbottom of MI6 and Brigadier Crockatt, the DDMI in London, dated March 25, 1944, same file.

mission not without inner conflicts, as some of them refused to accept British authority. The British themselves finally endorsed the idea, not without a typical remark made by Brigadier Iltyd Clayton, the Chief Political Officer in the British area HQ, that their departure would make these Zionist activists pursue their aims elsewhere rather than in Palestine. The "paratroopers" were dropped as regular British commandos in Yugoslavia and Rumania.[3]

A desperate effort undertaken by the head of the Jewish Agency's own Intelligence Branch, Reuven Zaslani-Shiloah, with OSS Bari after the occupation of Hungary to drop more commandos into that country with American help was declined. The reason was reservations about cooperation with the Jewish Agency emanating from its declared Zionist aims and connections with American personnel devoted to them.[4] The connection was, however, regarded as useful to the extent that OSS could use it in order to receive intelligence from the Jewish Agency without offering anything – especially anything political – in return.[5]

One of those betrayed by the local population upon her arrival in her native country was Hannah Szenes, a Hungarian subject to her Fascist–Hungarian captors in spite of her British woman officer status. She was later

---

[3] I have avoided getting into the different and conflicting internal goals prevailing between the British SOE and MI9 that may have also played a role in limiting the "Jewish commando" operation, nor did I cover the more successful but rather limited Zionist "paratrooper" operation in 1944 in Rumania. Enzo Sereni, dropped by MO9 into northern Italy, was captured and killed by the Germans, thus becoming a Zionist national hero along with Hannah Szenes.

[4] See RG 226, Entry 190, CASERTA-SI-OP-58–67, box 172, folder Jewish Agency, dated March 26, 1945, regarding the end of cooperation between OSS and Teddy Kollek and Zaslani (the Jewish Agency's Intelligence) and George Carpenter, the Jewish Agency's agent in Italy. See the letters of Consul General Pinkerton and G-2 liaison Captain Andronovich (in Jerusalem) against cooperation with the Jewish Agency. "Kolek [sic] and others were not regular Agency officials but were recruited to the special project of saving Jews (Rescue Committee – parentheses in original) rather than to recruit agents to serve Allied interests."

[5] See memo by Stephen B. L. Penrose (now Chief, SI Washington) to 110 (General Donovan), dated February 23, 1945, secret, subject: Relations with the Kantars. Declassified September 5, 2001. The "Kantars" were the Jewish Agency and specifically Zaslani's Intelligence Service. Zaslani has tried to argue that his "people" possessed information about Nazis who might try to create a postwar organization while warning Penrose, whom he knew well when the latter was SI Chief in Cairo, that the sense of revenge among survivors was so intense that they might take the law into their own hands and hinting toward the Jewish Agency as the authority that should be able to control them. In fact, the plans of the "Avengers" who were trying to kill as many Germans as possible became known to Ben-Gurion, who had them cancelled. For his part, Penrose told Donovan that he was aware more than anybody else of the inherent "danger" of dealing with the Jewish Agency, but as he did in Cairo, he told Zaslani that OSS was ready to accept intelligence in return for nothing. Also, the National Archives has recently released the daily reports made to Louis Leary, the OSS Cairo Intelligence operative, by Professor Nelson Glueck, again back in the region. These reports were used by all the parties concerned to convey their views and interests to the Americans during 1945 and reflected the situation on the ground from British, Zionist, and Arab points of view.

executed. Two other members of her group managed to arrive in Budapest and went to see Rezsö Kasztner.[6]

Kasztner was surprised to hear that the paratroopers, one of whom – Peretz Goldstein – was 17, came to organize resistance single-handedly in a country occupied by the German Army and Waffen SS troops, whose pro-Nazi Hungarian and German elements had taken over key positions since the invasion. When asked what exactly they brought from Palestine, says Joel Brand's wife, Hansi, an intimate associate of Kasztner's at the time, one of them, Joel Nussbecher-Palgi, showed the stupefied Kasztner (an old personal friend of his and a fellow Labor Zionist) a few British gold coins.[7]

Rescue operative Pomeranz told us that before the Nazi invasion some $10,000 (U.S.) were transferred from Istanbul by the Yishuv's representatives to Dr. Moshe Schweiger, a Zionist activist in Budapest, who was supposed to organize resistance upon the Nazi march into Hungary. Schweiger's initial reaction to the invasion, which came as a complete surprise to him, was to go back to his hometown in the province, where he was arrested immediately and sent to Mauthausen concentration camp.

Kasztner, the Labor Zionist, stayed in Budapest, ready to try to negotiate with the Germans. On the other hand, several among the Hungarian-oriented leaders and Zionists, Krausz among them, were dead set against any dealings with the Germans and hoped that the Hungarian authorities, who still held several positions of power in Budapest city, with Admiral Horthy as their chief, would help the Jews. They also hoped for aid from neutrals such as the Swiss and the Swedes. However, no tradition of maintaining authority and controlling power in such bodies, including among the Zionists themselves, existed among the various activists, who were politically divided and personally at odds with each other under the conditions of supreme pressure and fateful responsibility.

Then came the deportation en masse from the province, with those interim plans to save some "incapable" ones described earlier. The Yishuv's "paratrooper" mission not only arrived when resistance was technically and politically out of the question but was faced with the old and unsolvable dilemma of the European Jews since the inception of the Holocaust: resistance by what means and with whose support, among the Jews and the non-Jewish population, and for what price, when armed resistance might have sealed the fate of those who were still alive, at least in Budapest city? But the "paratrooper" mission to Hungary became a legend or a myth – a

---

[6] See Report on Sergeant Noah Nussbecher (Micky) of A Force Intelligence Section (MI9), no date, Public Record Office ref. wo208/3405; and see Nussbecher's report to Lieutenant Colonel Simonds dated June 22, 1945, Bari, same reference number. Nussbecher-Palgi, later Director General of El-Al Israel Airlines, published a book on his Hungarian adventures and was grilled by attorney Tamir during the Kasztner Trial in order to make Kasztner seem like a traitor who had Nussbecher extradited to the Germans.

[7] Hansi's interview with the present writer, 1985.

pearl in the crown of Jewish heroism and sacrifice in the ghettos and in the forests – and a link between the Yishuv and the Jews of Europe.

The reality, of course, was much more complicated, cruel, and ugly. Kasztner suggested to Nussbecher-Palgi to meet Eichmann and tell him that he came from Palestine to negotiate on behalf of the Jewish Agency, as if they were a part of the Brand mission. The "paratroopers," however, came to fight and when they tried to contact members of the Zionist youth movements they heard about Brand's mission from them. Nussbecher-Palgi learned about (as he was quoted in the report made by MI9 on his mission) the "special courier [who] had been sent by the Germans to TURKEY to negotiate with the Jewish and Allied authorities regarding the stopping of deportation of Jews (BRAND case – parentheses in original)." Nussbecher-Palgi's opinion was that all this was blackmail and bluff. Soon enough, he found himself watched and isolated in a Nazi-dominated capital. Nussbecher-Palgi and Goldstein probably did not know that Hannah Szenes was already in the custody of the Hungarians. Soon afterward, the Hungarians arrested Nussbecher-Palgi, too; the liaison man who brought them over from Yugoslavia and their radio were captured as well.

Her captors might have tortured Hannah Szenes in order to make her disclose the names and whereabouts of the others. Whether she betrayed them, as Hansi Brand maintained in an interview with the present writer, or the liaison man did we do not know. At any rate, Kasztner's attention was focused on negotiations with the Germans, which he hoped he could bring the Jewish and Zionist organizations abroad to join and possibly also the American War Refugee Board. By now he hoped to mobilize, in addition to the AJDC representative Saly Mayer, the newly appointed WRB representative in Switzerland, the Quaker Roswell McClelland. Hence, our kaleidoscope should focus on the Germans.

An OKW/Chi decrypt dated May 5, 1944, dealt with the appointment of Roswell McClelland (name misspelled in the otherwise meticulous German translations of American names and titles such as that of the Treasury Department to "Schatzamt" and of the WRB to "Kriegsflütlingsaussschuss" and the like) as the WRB's representative in Switzerland, details of his salary, and secret details regarding "an immediate credit from a special Presidential fund" to be used according to his discretion. The credit itself was limited, however, to $10,000 (U.S.) – not a small sum in those days but nothing in comparison to possible Nazi expectations. Another cable signed by Mayer in Bern, dated May 25, 1944, to Elmer Davis, Director of the OWI (Office of War Information) (Gerald Mayer was officially OWI's man in Bern but in fact he was Allen Dulles's cover and right-hand man[8]), and decrypted on June 6, 1944, described the Holocaust in Carpatho-Russia and the Mamaros areas of Hungary on the basis of "reliable sources and even

[8] See Bradsher, "A time to Act," pp. 16–17n.

on the basis of Hungarian newspapers." The process of ghettoization, humiliation, starvation, and dehumanization of the victims by the Hungarian henchmen from April 1944 may explain how the victims were treated in a way that made organized resistance and any previous warnings futile.

On July 11, OKW/Chi decoded (not fully) a cable sent to Shertok in London in which Barlas of the Jewish Agency in Turkey pretended in coordination with Kasztner in Budapest that the Brand mission was still alive, that the negotiations with the Germans were progressing well, and that rescue operative Bader was expected to join them upon Brand's return, about which Shertok was supposed to cable back immediately.

On July 31, 1944, OKW/Chi decoded a cable sent by Dr. Josef Schwartz of the AJDC to his headquarters in New York on July 24 in which he repeated a letter from Joseph Blum of the "Jewish Central Committee" in Budapest, dated June 13, 1944,[9] in which the deportations from the province were described in detail: "400,000 [underlined in decode] Jews were deported, and more transports are organized. Many of those who are capable of work were sent to Waldsee, close to Lugwigshafen, wherefrom thousands of postcards have been received." This "Waldsee" address was a deception behind which Auschwitz was hidden.[10]

Most of the Hungarian province became "judenrein" (note by OKW/Chi: "the last word in original was made in German!").... Till now the Jews of Budapest were not deported." Thus repeating the main points in Kasztner's letter of June 18 to the Rescue Committee in Istanbul just quoted, Blum and others – not just Kasztner – seemed to have believed in June that not all the deportees were sent to immediate death in Auschwitz, and, moreover, Blum repeated the same story about a "concentration camp for 30,000 children, women and the elderly unqualified for work," whose entertainment required an initial $500,000 (U.S.) payment to be deposited by Phillip von Freudiger (the orthodox leader) with Saly Mayer (the AJDC resident representative in Switzerland). Freudiger was described as a "member of the Jewish Central Committee, whose other members were Dr. Reszo Kasztner, Julius Link, Joel Brand [!] and Josef Blum." On top of this, they asked for a monthly budget of $360,000 (U.S.) for the camp.

Josef Schwartz asked New York to at least raise the half million, quoting Blum to the effect that the 30,000 people could be evacuated later to Spain. Schwartz added that he received information from Turkey, including from the papal nuncio in Istanbul (Angelo Giuseppe Roncalli – later Pope John XXIII) that perhaps Jews holding Palestine certificates and children might be allowed to leave under Red Cross protection if a haven for them could be found. Finally, Dr. Schwartz mentioned a group of 1,200 to 1,700 people

9 V.N. No. 2138/7.44 F. Source: RG 457, Entry 1032, box 205.
10 See Bela Vago, "The British Government and the Fate of Hungarian Jewry in 1944," in *Rescue Attempts during the Holocaust* (Jerusalem: Yad Vashem, 1971), pp. 211–212.

"who had already left for Spain" (i.e., "Kasztner's Train"). The meaning of all of this was a desperate effort by the Zionists and non-Zionists in Budapest to remain in business with the Germans, who for their part seemed indeed ready to deal when large sums of money in exchange for a few Jews could serve their foreign currency needs and possibly their political cause (e.g., show to the world that Jews were being saved, for money, while non-Jews were fighting and dying).

OKW/Chi decoded only on August 8 Hirschmann's cable from Ankara in which Horthy's decision to stop the deportations from Hungary was announced plus a repeated hope that the holders of Palestine certificates and children under ten would be allowed to leave Hungary. We may now turn the kaleidoscope around to the British Foreign Office response to the changed situation on the ground and to the so-called "Horthy Offer."

Quoting an OSS-R&A report dated October 19, 1944, on "The Jews in Hungary,":[11]

The Hungarian government, apparently impressed by threats and exhortations and as a result of the subsequent representations of the International Red Cross, now sought to atone for its role in the persecution and deportation of the Jews [in fact, Regent Horthy had to replace his government in order to accomplish that – S.A.]. The story goes back to 21 July 1944 when the International Red Cross Delegation in Washington reported that the Hungarian authorities had given the IRC Committee in Geneva official assurances that transportation of the Jews beyond the Hungarian frontier had ceased [in fact Eichmann had managed to get two more transports sent to Auschwitz afterwards – S.A.]. . . . The Committee was furthermore empowered to cooperate in the evacuation of all Jewish children under ten years of age who are in possession of foreign visas. Of prime importance was the concession that all Jews in Hungary holding entrance visas for Palestine would receive permission to leave for that country." ["S" is mentioned as a source in a footnote, but I could not ascertain its identity except guess that it was the State Department – S.A.].

As a consequence of the above offer by Admiral Horthy the United Kingdom and the United States entered upon a prolonged series of negotiations. The British first suggested that the whole matter be turned over to the Intergovernmental Committee on Refugees. Later they proposed that the formal acceptance of the offer be postponed until the two governments could reach an agreement concerning its implementation [e.g., to prevent too many Jews from reaching Palestine or other territories except U.S. territory proper – S.A.]. The United States discarded both recommendations as 'having a niggardly appearance' and involving considerable delay. (RG 226, Entry 191, box 1, file Jews in Hungary)

Turning our attention to the British at this point, according to an internal Foreign Office memo entitled "Note for the Secretary of State" on the subject of an interview by Mr. Eden "granted to Deputation of National Committee

---

[11] RG 226, Entry 191, box No. 1, file Jews in Hungary.

for Rescue from Nazi Terror at 3.00 p.m. on July 26,"[12] the Foreign Secretary was briefed to tell his interlocutors that:

It has been decided that there should be no negotiations with any enemy government and that no emissary should be sent to Budapest [as asked for by Shertok since Brand's arrival – S.A.] but that any communication which His Majesty's Government may wish to make should be conveyed through the Protecting Power (Switzerland) in the usual way.... The question of the supply of food and clothing through an extension of the parcels system ... is already under consideration.... In view of what appears to be the change in Hungarian policy, the deputation can be told in strict confidence that we have consulted the United States Government and are proposing to consult the Dominions and Latin-American Governments with a view to finding further accommodation. It is difficult to define an exact figure of those likely to be able to leave Hungary, but under present conditions of transport in Europe it is highly probable that even the existing offers to accept Jewish refugees ... would exceed the numbers of those in practice able to leave. (PRO, Ref. no. FO 371/42311)

Having thus expected the Germans to prevent the victims from becoming a flood, Eden was briefed to mention Palestine by referring his audience to the Colonial Office but to reaffirm the old position of "His Majesty's Government not to treat Jews as though they were a separate category but to regard each Jew who possesses a nationality in the first place as a national of the country to which he belongs." Returning to the issue of shipping and transport of refugees, Eden was briefed to maintain that since the Bermuda Conference his government tried to secure neutral shipping for them, but in any event "refugees who were in fact able to leave the Balkans have never been held up through lack of shipping. The reasons, as the Committee are probably aware, have been the refusal of the German and satellite Governments to cooperate" – a distortion at least of the British insistence on maintaining the White Paper quota and regarding Rumanian willingness to allow Jews to go to Palestine. These Jews, however, survived until the final liberation of their country from its alliance with Germany in August. Finally, the Secretary of State was briefed to address himself to a proposal to declare the Jews "an Endangered people":

This proposal is being examined. It should, however, be borne in mind that *it is not the policy of His Majesty's Government to regard Jews as belonging to a separate category. It is felt that discrimination of this kind savours too strongly of the Nazi attitude toward Jews. Further, Allied Governments might dislike the bestowal of a special form of protection on Jews which would not be shared by their non-Jewish nationals, many of whom have suffered in an equal degree with Jews* (italics added). (PRO, Ref. no FO 371/42311)

Behind this remarkable document, formulated in the old Foreign Office lingo when the centrality of the Holocaust in Hitler's war became self-evident,

---

[12] Source: PRO, Ref. No. FO 371/42311.

there was a bitter dispute between the British and the Americans, which ended in a compromise announced on August 17, 1944. On that date, both governments accepted "Horthy's Offer" publicly by offering to "make arrangements for the care of such Jews leaving Hungary who reach neutral or United Nations territory, and also that they will find temporary havens where such people may live in safety."

"The compromise character of this acceptance," so we are told by the anonymous OSS analysts:

... is apparent. The United States had insisted throughout that Great Britain take action to implement the Palestinian phase of the Horthy offer, with few if any strings attached. The United States finally yielded on this point when the British ceased pressing for this country to meet the International Red Cross request (as of 25 July 1944 – parentheses in the original) that "the number of emigrant Jews to be admitted to the United States should be substantially increased and a corresponding number of entry permits accorded." (RG 221, Entry 191, box 1, file Jews in Hungary)

Interestingly enough, when we read an earlier query made by the Nazi Commissioner in Hungary, Edmond Veesenmayer, cabled to Foreign Minister Ribbentrop asking what had become of the idea that Ribbentrop had suggested to Hitler of presenting all the Jews to Roosevelt and Churchill as a gift, as quoted by Bauer,[13] we realize again and again that this "gift" was supposed to be poison – *Gift* in German. In other words, the Germans were toying at that early stage with making the war "Jewish" by using propaganda means in the crude fashion ascribed to Ribbentrop, while later on they were toying with the idea of pushing some remnants of the Jewish population on the United States or in making this option publicly known in order to cause trouble for Roosevelt at home. At least this is how the administration would view it.

At any rate, the OSS-R&A report followed the Horthy Offer further by stating that the Hungarians lapsed then "into relative lethargy" and then "Allied efforts to rescue the Jews of Hungary came to naught for the following reasons:

1. Gestapo agents of the Sondereinsatz Kommando (Eichmann's) in Budapest refused to permit the Jews to emigrate freely from Hungary (source "S" dated August 11).
2. Germany refused, furthermore, to grant transit visas to Spain, Portugal, Sweden, or Switzerland.

---

[13] Quoted by Bauer from IMT-NG 2234, Veesenmayer to Ritter and Ribbentrop, April 3, 1944. Ambassador Ritter was Fritz Kolbe's boss, and his correspondence for and from the Minister was the one given by Kolbe to OSS. I was not able to locate the Veesenmayer letter in Kolbe's Boston Series stored at NARA but was told by Dr. Greg Bradsher, Kolbe's biographer, that Kolbe was not instructed by OSS Bern to seek specifically for Jewish-related materials.

3. The military about-face of Rumania and Bulgaria made it impossible for Jews to depart by that route.
4. The Allied powers temporized and failed to accept completely the Horthy Offer.

Most, but not all, of this was true and reflected a sense of despair as far as the fate of the remaining Budapest Jews were concerned. But the rescue activists, starting with Kasztner, had not given up, as we shall learn in the next chapter.

31

The WRB's Own Reports
OWI's Reservations

The Germans apparently did not read all of the WRB's messages, and in fall 1944 the State Department shifted to code machines and stopped using the previously decoded ciphers.

Thus, in addition to the German decrypts of WRB's activities, let us now examine its own reports by invoking the same "kaleidoscopic" method.

The WRB claimed to have been able to save Jews by intervening with German-allied governments, including the Horthy regime in occupied Hungary. It took steps, as mentioned in a report on the WRB's activities from October 1944, "in cooperation with a private agency," probably the Zionist Rescue Committee in Istanbul, "to establish contact with a mysterious person known only as 'Willy' [Wisliceny – S.A.] who was reported to have been successful in arresting the deportation of Jews from Slovakia."[1] This passage tells us first that those who communicated with "Willy" took him seriously, and thus Kasztner and Brand, who probably stood behind it, indeed believed in the Slovak myth or had to stick to it, having no other option but to try to make it a reality due to changed conditions on the ground. Second, they did reach the WRB in this regard, before Brand was sent to Istanbul, when on April 20 the WRB itself "asked an intermediary in Switzerland [probably Saly Mayer – S.A.] to explore with him [i.e., with Wisliceny] the possibility of arranging for evacuations from Hungary to neutral countries or for holding up deportations or permitting sending relief to those detained. If any such arrangements possible, please indicate amounts you consider would be involved and extent to which such amounts could remain in neutral countries."[2] If the Istanbul Rescue Committee received this seemingly positive indication to negotiate on behalf of an official American agency, this may explain its relative confidence in the Germans, and if the Germans intercepted it, it may explain their interest in Brand's

[1] FDR Library, WRB container 34, folder Hungary No.1.
[2] Ibid.

mission, even if they wanted much more and were ready to give much less in return. If so, the WRB thus created expectations by its very existence and activities that could not, however, meet Jewish hopes nor yield to German machinations.

On May 4, 1944, the WRB was advised by the American Embassy in London that the deportation of Jews from Hungary had begun; on May 11, the American Consulate in Jerusalem was requested by the Board to obtain from the Jewish Agency the names of Hungarian officials responsible for the persecution of Jews, and it tried to make the British and the Soviet governments and the Office of War Information publish warnings and otherwise act in this respect while it approached neutral governments in order to allow Hungarian Jews to seek their protection.[3] All of this was taking place before Brand's arrival in Istanbul, when "the Board also extended its facilities fully for the transmission of applications for the issuance of Palestine immigration certificates – by itself a complicated and troublesome procedure due to British desire 'not to exhaust the existing quota of entry permits within the White Paper's quota' – to the people in Hungary."[4] Later, the WRB tried to induce the Rumanians to open their border to Jews fleeing from Hungary.

The WRB report just quoted then cited the "wide publicity over a period of many months" that was "secured in Hungary, by radio and otherwise, for a series of warnings and appeals to the people of Hungary" in regard to the fate of the Jews, including a statement made by President Roosevelt on March 24 and statements by the members of the Foreign Relations Committees of the Senate and the House. All of this, however, was much less than the initial enthusiasm of the WRB's operatives, whose freedom of action was restricted to verbal activities of that kind and some limited action in neutral countries, in Rumania, Greece, and in Hungary itself – to which we shall return.

The multiple traps are reflected here in the Germans' response to the very creation of the WRB, which might have added to their resolve to annihilate the Hungarian Jewry with lightning speed while pretending to negotiate its fate in order to create the impression that Jews were behind Roosevelt's war and were his primary concern. In fact, Roosevelt's statement prompted reservations at the American Office of War Information(OWI), especially in regard to Jews. OWI Washington cabled "Control Desk NY" that "we should stress the appeals rather than the threats, and should highlight neither his references to the Jewish problem nor his references to the problems of other refugees and sufferers." In an OWI cable from London related to this "persecution of Jews" referred to by the president, instructions were quoted

---

[3] Ibid.
[4] See U.S. Military Liaison Officer (Nicholas Andronovich, who also functioned as American Censor) to the British CIC, Palestine, June 2, 1944, secret, NA, RG 226, Entry 120, box 32.

to the effect that "his denunciation was (not) limited to this subject alone or that it was especially aimed at it."[5] Internally, the WRB itself was told by psychological warfare experts that warnings and threats in regard to the Holocaust were highly problematic:

It would [not] do any good at all to bring home to the German people the German Government's activities in murdering the Jews since the German Government would deny the accuracy of any statements which were made and was in the position to neutralize the effect of any such statements.... The German people would not be particularly concerned about the problem and even if they were somewhat concerned... it would not have any effect, at this stage of the war, on the German Government's position.... Any approach to the German Government would [not] be worthwhile and... any publicity given to any failure of an approach to the German Government would only result in intensification of measures against the Jews. (Memo signed by John Pehle, Executive Director, WRB, FDR Library WRB, container 17, file Memoranda Mr. Pehle, March 14, 1944)

The psychological warfare expert told the WRB, however, that "the only possibility of doing anything... would be to make a deal with some faction in the Nazi party, such as Göring," and he felt it would be very bad policy to make such a deal due to obvious reasons of its exploitation by the alleged Göring faction, which was an integral part of the Nazi regime.[6]

The WRB report of late 1944 quoted earlier then counted American efforts with Sweden, Turkey, and other neutrals to allow entry of holders of American immigration visas and Palestine entry certificates. Around that time – fall 1944 – the Swede Raoul Wallenberg arrived in Budapest and, together with the Swiss Charles Lutz and Moshe Krausz, worked hard to issue Swedish, Swiss, and Palestine immigration or protection papers to Jews.

However, all of these activities did not lead to the departure of Jews from Hungary as:

The Germans denied exit permits and transit visas to substantial groups of Hungarian Jews who had been granted Swedish and Spanish entry visas. At first, the Germans explained [probably to Kasztner – S.A.] that their friendship for the Arabs made it impossible to permit Jews to emigrate unless it was assured that they would not go to Palestine. Then they demanded assurances that all Jews permitted to emigrate would go to Britain and America. (NA, RG 84, American Legation Bern, cable No. 5197, August 11, 1944, secret, from McClelland to WRB via State Department, decimal file 840.1 1944, box 31)

This seems to substantiate our claim that Jewish immigration was perceived by the Nazis, and by the Allies, as a political tool to cause trouble for the

---

[5] NA, RG 208, Refugees – Policy F-359, box 116.
[6] Memo signed by John Pehle, Executive Director, WRB, FDR Library WRB, container 17, file Memoranda Mr. Pehle, March 14, 1944.

fighting Allies at home:

Finally, however, it became clear that the Germans were willing to let the Jews go only in exchange for such articles as trucks, tractors, machine tools, and similar material to support the German war effort. Gestapo agents were reported by our Minister at Bern on September 16 to have demanded $25,000,000 in neutral countries for the purchase of war materials, as well as Allied permission for the export to Germany of the commodities which they might buy. (NA, RG 84, American Legation Bern, cable No. 5197, August 11, 1944, secret, from McClelland to WRB via State Department, decimal file 840.1 1944, box 31)

Allied intervention, especially FDR's open and behind-the-scenes efforts, possibly Allied bombing of Budapest, and the combined efforts of the Swedish king and Pope Pius XII, seem to have driven Admiral Horthy, as we know, "not only into stopping deportation," in the words of WRB representative McClelland following a report from the Zionist Rescue Committee in Budapest, "but also into attempting to make up for the unsavory role he has played already in the persecution and deportation of the Jews by favoring their emigration and relief to them under the supervision of Intercross" (the International Committee of the Red Cross – ICRC).[7] This cable was based on a report made by Kasztner and Komoly that reached the WRB representative directly or indirectly and later quotes Kasztner alone. The report reflects Kasztner's perception of Eichmann and the Gestapo as follows:

In spite of preliminary reassuring news of an agreement between the Hungarian Government and I.C.R.C. to permit Jewish emigration to Palestine and elsewhere, as well as relief of Jews remaining in Hungary, it now appears that ranking Gestapo agents of the so-called "Sondereinsatzkommando" [Eichmann's outfit – S.A.], sent to Budapest especially to direct the deportation of Jews, have no intention of permitting them to emigrate freely, particularly to Palestine, if they can prevent it. After the attack on Hitler [July 20, 1944] and the rapid worsening of the German military situation, the Gestapo in Budapest shifted their interest from the ideological aspect of extermination of the Jews to the purely material benefit in labor, goods and money to be derived therefrom. The essence of their present attitude is contained in a declaration made by the head of the Gestapo to Kasztner to the effect that 'it was his desire to pump out the necessary labor from the Jewry of Hungary and sell the balance of valueless human material against goods with value.' (NA, RG 84, American Legation Bern, cable No. 5197, August 11, 1944, secret, from McClelland to WRB via State Department, decimal file 840.1 1944, box 31)

Thus, one may discern in Kasztner's report a differentiation between the previous SS policy of extermination based on ideological grounds, which therefore could have hardly been stopped even if Brand's mission had succeeded, and recent changes that allowed a deal to save at least those who

---

[7] NA, RG 84, American Legation Bern, cable No. 5197, August 11, 1944, secret, from McClelland to WRB via State Department, decimal file 840.1 1944, box 31.

were "valueless" from the Gestapo's point of view. This seems to be a new variant of the old interim plan regarding the "incapable ones."

Kasztner used arguments that could move the Allies, explaining to them as best he could that Horthy's willingness to help the Jews was not enough; the Germans were the main problem, and they would not allow immigration "unless certain ransom terms are fulfilled."[8] Kasztner informed the WRB that Miklós Krausz, the Jewish Agency's immigration representative in Budapest, had been allowed by the Horthy government to set up an office in the Swiss legation, where the emigration to Palestine of 8,700 families was prepared:

For the first convoy of 2,000 people, Hungarian exit permits and Rumanian transit permits have already been obtained and it is reported that boats are available in the port of Constanza. The German exit permits from Hungary have not (repeat not) been granted and, according to the statements of the Gestapo chief to Kasztner, the permits will not be granted unless certain ransom terms are fulfilled. (NA, RG 84, American Legation Bern, cable No. 5197, August 11, 1944, secret, from McClelland to WRB via State Department, decimal file 840.1 1944, box 31)

A similar opinion was expressed by the Zionist Rescue Mission in Istanbul when they made the following recommendation to the Jewish Agency's Executive on August 26, 1944, following Horthy's offer that "pressure [will be] put to bear on Hungary to implement its obligations" (as made by Horthy), that demands will be made from the Red Cross and the representatives of neutral countries "to keep an alert eye...over the Hungarian situation in order to prevent the resumption of the deportations," and that action will be taken so *"that the proper bodies would come to a modus vivendi with the Germans"*[9] (Italics added).

For the Allies, the very idea of a "modus vivendi with the Germans" to save Jews was totally out of the question, while Hitler, for his part never gave up his intention to get as many Budapest Jews as possible from Horthy.[10]

McClelland turned now, in the same cable, to rescue efforts made by the Zionist "Rescue Committee," with Kasztner as its spokesman to negotiate with the SS, and other Jewish organizations in Hungary and abroad:

When the mission to Istanbul of Joel Brandt [sic]...failed to produce concrete results and he did not return to Hungary but instead proceeded to Jerusalem, Jewish circles in Budapest, in the face of obvious German displeasure, made desperate efforts to keep the negotiations with the Gestapo going by raising goods and valuables from local sources to the value of three million Swiss francs and by stating that a credit of two million Swiss francs would be opened [remark by the side: "by whom?"] to cover the purchase of goods [sheepskins] in Slovakia and tractors in Switzerland...40 tractors.. [were brought by] Sternbuch [the representatives of the ultra-orthodox Agudath-Israel in Switzerland – S.A.] to our attention.... The deal

---

[8] Ibid.
[9] See Hagana Archive, div. 14, file 14/798.
[10] See Braham, *The Politics of Genocide*, Volume II, 766–767.

was negotiated by Link and Freudiger of the Orthodox group in Budapest and relayed to Sternbuch. The Gestapo in Budapest, on the basis of the above offer, refrained from sending to Auschwitz during the initial period of deportations the following groups, totaling 17,290 persons: 1) 1,690 persons; . . . 1,200 Rabbis and prominent Orthodox Jews . . . This group was sent . . . to Strasshof in Austria and later to Bergen-Belsen . . . where they are at the present time. 2) Circa 15,000 persons sent to an unknown destination in Austria, to be kept, as the Gestapo stated, 'on ice'. 3,600 persons in Budapest still. (NA, RG 84, American Legation Bern, cable No. 5197, August 11, 1944, secret, from McClelland to WRB via State Department, decimal file 840.1 1944, box 31)

This was a somewhat confused description of several groups of Jews transferred to Strasshof in Austria for work, as well as "Kasztner's Train" of 1,684, several of whom were dignitaries, some rich people, and some Zionists, including some close to Kasztner who were released by the Gestapo from the ghettos. Their rescue seemed after the war to have been a clear-cut case of Nazi ransoming in blood paid to Kasztner to secure his alleged "collaboration" in regard to the warning and the activation of the hundreds of thousands who were deported at the same time. Kasztner, for his part, claimed that they could have been easily killed as well, and their rescue was the first case in which the Gestapo was brought to make concessions largely thanks to him, and this was in addition to the 18,000 sent to Strasshof labor camp in Austria, most of whom survived. In fact, Kasztner was referring to about 17,000 whose dispatch to Austria was facilitated by the mayor of Vienna, in dire need of slave labor, and authorized by Ernst Kaltenbrunner, himself an Austrian and Eichmann's higher boss.[11]

The Strasshof case is rather unique because among the deportees were very many women, children, and elderly who were not fit to work but who did survive.[12] Kaltenbrunner was aware of this, as indicated in his message to the mayor of Vienna, and promised their liquidation in due course instead of sending them immediately to Auschwitz as Eichmann was regularly doing elsewhere. It is, however, possible that Eichmann, who told Kasztner that these Jews had been "put on ice," was ordered to keep them alive as an advance payment within the framework of the Gestapo Deal (i.e., as a ransom option kept open by the SS). Later, Eichmann told Kasztner that he would use the remnant Jews for slave labor and as a source of "valuables" from abroad as well, as reported by the latter to McClelland. Thus, Kasztner's

---

[11] Peter Black, *Ernst Kaltenbrunner, Vassal Himmlers: Eine SS-Karriere* (Paderborn, München: Ferdinand Schöningh, 1991), pp. 174–175, 288 (German translation). See Kaltenbrunner to Blaschke, IMT XXXIII, pp. 167–169. According to Kaltenbrunner, only about 30% of the Strasshof inmates were capable of work, and hence he told Mayor Blaschke that the rest should be killed later on. Kasztner ascribed the fact that most of them were treated rather well and survived to his own efforts.

[12] See Jozseph Schiler, *The Strasshof Rescue-Operation* (Kibbutz Dalia: Beth Lohamei-Hagetaot Publications, 1999) (Hebrew translation).

strategy did yield results when combined with German needs for working hands, war material, and foreign currency.

In his cable of August 1944, McClelland dwelt at length on the tractor deal and quoted Kasztner again very probably by saying that "before the departure of Brandt [sic], the Gestapo in Budapest had declared that they were willing to trade 1,000 Jews for every ten tractors and even went so far as to give assurance that 'they would destroy the plant' [remark by the side: "What does it mean? Concentration Camp?"] at Auschwitz if delivery of the tractors was seriously begun."

McClelland added to this information his "personal opinion" that the American Joint Distribution Committee's representative in Switzerland, Saly Mayer, "should be allowed to meet agents of the Gestapo (provided that his own government, with whom the matter has been discussed, approves and grants the necessary border permits for the German agents – parentheses in original) in an attempt to draw out negotiations and gain as much time as possible without making any commitments, if possible." The first meeting between Mayer and the SS was made conditional on the release of 500 Jews from Bergen-Belsen upon Kasztner's demand. McClelland, however, wanted the State Department's explicit permission to make commitments in regard to tractors and money in the event that the Mayer negotiations proved to be "impossible to stall."

He reminded the State Department that those whose immigration to Palestine was authorized by Horthy "will not be allowed to leave Hungary unless tractors are obtained." McClelland's "personal opinion" (and he was a devoted, serious, and able rescue worker) was that apart from the maneuver to gain time, it was impossible at this juncture to embark upon a program of buying Jews out of the hands of the Nazis.

Instead, the WRB supported efforts on the spot when the Swede Raoul Wallenberg, officially a secretary in his country's legation in Budapest, and the Swiss Consul, Charles Lutz, in conjunction with Miklós Krausz, would enter the scene and save Jews by issuing protection papers.

PART V

THE END OF THE FINAL SOLUTION: BACK TO HOSTAGE-TAKING TACTICS

32

The Train

Let us now return to the story of "Kasztner's Train" as it actually developed on the ground. The idea of letting 600 Palestine certificate holders leave Hungary originated with the Va'ada upon its earliest meeting with Eichmann's men early in April 1944. The list of 600 grew to 1,684 people thanks to monies paid by Kasztner to the Germans. The Jews were supposed to leave for Portugal or Spain but instead found themselves in the Bergen-Belsen exchange camp. Among the 1,684, there were people from Kasztner's own hometown of Cluj who were allowed to leave the ghetto of Cluj upon Kasztner's request and with Eichmann's consent. For the Germans, the 1,684 could serve as hostages for some kind of exchange deals, as we learn from the following document concerning the Holocaust in Holland and the fate of a few remaining Palestine visa entry holders at Vught and Westerbork camps, from which most of the Dutch Jews were deported to Auschwitz:[1]

In April, 1944 it was stated that: 'The Jewish section VUGHT has been closed down and WESTERBORK is almost empty.... The people with exchange papers for Palestine were sent ... to a special camp ... near Hanover ... [which] appears to be EXCHANGE CAMP BERZEN BILSEN [sic] ..., and as its name suggests, it contains Jews in possession of Palestine certificates and those who own passports ... [of] South American countries. Leaders of Dutch Zionist organizations are in [that] camp, awaiting exchange for Palestine. (NA, RG 59, State Department decimal file 811.111 Visa Division – Refugees 7-2144)

Thus, one can conclude from the Dutch case that the Nazis expected something from keeping a few foreign passport holders and Zionist leaders alive as subjects for "exchange," as we further learn that Bergen-Belsen was

---

[1] NA, RG 59, State Department decimal file 811.111 Visa Division – Refugees 7-2144, British Censorship report, "compiled by special examiners."

indeed used as an "exchange camp."[2] "Kasztner's Train" indeed unloaded its frightened passengers there, not in a neutral country, at first, in anticipation of an Allied "quo."

The use of Jews who possessed a Western (including Palestine) passport for purposes of exchange with German nationals interned in the West had led Eichmann and his aide Otto Hunsche to draft a circular order issued by Ernst Kaltenbrunner, the head of the RSHA, on March 5, 1943, which established later on an "exchange camp" for such nationals at Bergen-Belsen.[3] The German Foreign Office argued that even relatives of foreign passport holders could be exempted from the Final Solution – an issue that proved to be impractical in Eastern Europe because the candidates knew too much and could become the source of "Greuelpropaganda" (e.g., details about the Final Solution), but at any rate the numbers of those exempted were small. Bergen-Belsen was supposed to allow 10,000 foreign passport holders to be exchanged – and yet the camp could be used for other purposes as well, such as extracting goods or money from Hungarian Jews, foreign Jews, or the Allies.

By that time (July 1944), Kasztner had met several times with SS Major Kurt A. Becher, who had been involved in the Manfred Weiss "deal" (i.e., the sale of Hungary's main armament factory to the SS in exchange for the lives of its Jewish owners) and later was described by Kasztner as the one who had informed Himmler about the offers made by the Va'ada that resulted in Brand's mission. In his postwar report, Kasztner referred to Becher as if he – not Fritz Laufer, we should add – was supposed to continue the Brand negotiations in Portugal or in Spain, but he was afraid of being taken hostage by Allied Intelligence and thus suggested a meeting on the French–Spanish border. The fact that Laufer was not mentioned in Kasztner's postwar reports at all is significant in the sense that the connection with him was perceived by Kasztner at that stage as highly sensitive.[4]

Becher seemed to be less fanatical and more businesslike than Eichmann. It is possible that Kasztner had developed the theory that Eichmann was "ideologically" motivated, and thus a hopeless case, and expressed doubts about his previous dealings with him in the following summarized dialogue

---

[2] See Runderlass signed by Dr. Wilhelm Hasrter, Commander of Security Police in Holland, dated May 5, 1943, quoted by Alexandra Wenck, "Der Menschenhandel des Dritten Reiches und die "Endlösung" – das KZ Bergen-Belsen im Spannugsfeld nationalsozialistischer und alliierter Interessen," 1997 dissertation, University of Münster, p. 57 and her Dutch source, *Documents of Persecution of the Dutch Jewry 1940–1945* (Amsterdam: Joods Historisch Amsterdam, 1979), p. 96.

[3] See Wenck, "Der Menschenhandel des Dritten Reiches," especially pp. 55off., and her source *PAAA Inland* IIg, p. 177.

[4] NA, RG 238, Kasztner's Nuremberg interrogation summary No. 2817.

between himself and a "B," a German officer later identified on the document as Becher.[5]

B.: We are in a neutral [i.e., not under Eichmann's control] territory.
Kasztner: I have no neutral territory here; only hostile territory.
B.: You are a cheeky dog (ein frecher Hund).
(Kasztner's personal archive, doc. 4)

Following this opening, the two reviewed the previous talks toward an appeal to "L," which could be "London," and Kasztner repeated Wisliceny's promises, of which none had been fulfilled. "The Auschwitz mill" was immediately put to work and had already killed 300,000 Jews from Hungary. Becher was still expecting some progress following Brand's mission, but Kasztner responded that it was too early to expect far-reaching results, "which would directly or indirectly serve the interest of the German war machine." He added that the Jewish side saw no point in going to "L" unless the deportations would cease, Auschwitz's "mills" was stopped, and something (else) was suggested instead of the trucks (maybe tractors or cash), provided that Hungarian Jews would survive to justify it. The Jewish side then said that it did not inform the outside world about the "violation of the promises," but the truth would come out because "this is the nature of the truth." In fact, as we have seen in the previous section, Kasztner did inform the outside world as best he could.

"B" then said that he wanted to prepare "an exact balance" of what was done by both sides and approach Himmler with it. In this regard, he would talk to the Reichsführer SS about the train of the 1,684, which was held at Bergen-Belsen hostage camp at that stage.

The German further mentioned the departure from Hungary of Kasztner's wife and his mother (in the train). The response was that this was done upon Eichmann's insistence, and then Kasztner added: "We are not motivated by family aspects. I have thought many times whether it would not have been more correct to entice the Zionist youth and organize the people to active resistance instead of the [helpless acceptance] . . . of the [deportations] and the railcars [to Auschwitz]." The German replied that "this would have led to nothing," and Kasztner retorted "Maybe, but our honor would have been saved. Our people went to the railcars like cattle, because we were sure about the success of the negotiations and missed the chance to warn them and tell them about their terrible, forthcoming fate."

This would become the main accusation against Kasztner after the war, including in the scholarly literature on the Hungarian Holocaust. Hence, let

[5] The meeting took place on July 17, 1944, source: Kasztner personal archive, doc. 4; see also doc. 16, a letter in Hungarian written shortly after the war. Both documents were made available to the present writer courtesy of Mr. Dov Dinur, Kasztner's biographer.

us examine the option mentioned by Kasztner, to "entice the Zionist youth" to resist the deportations from the province, which in fact was a "nonstarter" from the beginning and a bluff used to push Becher.

While the Va'ada was waiting in vain for some response to the Gestapo Deal, Zionist activists from various youth movements tried, with growing difficulties, to smuggle their own people and others over the border to Rumania. The free movement of Jews at that time across Hungary was forbidden, their assets and cash were frozen or confiscated, and they were robbed or pursued by the local authorities, while the Germans and Hungarians sought their lives. One must emphasize here the already mentioned role of the Wehrmacht in the deportation of the Jews from the province and the attempt to empty Budapest city's ghetto, too, quoted as a security problem in the OKW War Diaries, which has not been resolved properly.[6]

The very structure of the German occupation in Hungary seems to have been rather overlapping, while the role of the Hungarians in instigating the quick deportations under terrible conditions is sometimes underestimated due to our focus on Eichmann and his death squad, whose role was central but not exclusive during the deportations from the Hungarian province.

In a recent research publication, Christian Gerlach and Götz Aly emphasized the role of the Hungarians in the "last chapter" of the Holocaust[7] and also pointed out the role of the German plenipotentiary Edmund Veesenmayer in the German occupation regime. They also called our attention to the possible roles of Otto Winkelmann, the Higher SS and Police Leader in Hungary, of the BdS, the regional SS–Police–SD commander, Hans Geschke, and also the periodization of the occupation time: Germany was still confident about winning the war in March 1944, but during the high summer its military situation deteriorated dramatically. Hence, one could assume that on the one hand the deportations were to be continued during the whole period and explain thereby the limits of rescue efforts abroad. But the authors are also right when they tell us that a large number of deportees were sent for work, even to Auschwitz and from there elsewhere, when Germany desperately needed working hands. Many among them, however, were killed on the spot in the last phases of the war.

At any rate, during the deportations, few were able to flee to the borders, including Jewish members of communities close to the Rumanian boundary. In all, about 7,000 people were able to escape until August 23, when Rumania sued for peace with the Allies and the border became a front line. Until then, the Zionist youth movements were busy with that form of rescue on their own on the rather small scale of which they were capable due to their own inadequate organization, Hungarian–German countermeasures, and the total helplessness of the beleaguered Jews, many of them women

---

[6] *Kriegstagebuch des Oberkommandos des Wehrmacht*, Teilb. 1 – Band 4, 827–853.
[7] See Gerlach and Aly, *Das Letzte Kapitel*.

and children, since the men were taken by the Hungarians to serve in labor battalions in the face of the coming Soviet onslaught. The Va'ada helped finance this effort; however, already in June the deportations, conducted on an enormous scale, "pushed the Zionist underground to the verge of events,"[8] when they realized that they had no real impact on the situation. By now, they had diverted their members to Budapest city, which was still under a degree of autonomous Hungarian, Horthy-supported control, and tried to get false identity papers and arrange for other rescue options.

The Jews of Budapest itself seemed now to be the next and the last Nazi target. In mid-June, Jewish residences were marked. The Allies and the Jewish leadership abroad seemed unable to at least push Admiral Horthy, still the Regent of Hungary and with some power in his own capital, to intervene in favor of the Budapest Jews. But, by the end of June, foreign pressures on Horthy, including strong intervention by Franklin Roosevelt, combined with the initial success of "Overlord" to make Horthy soon overthrow the pro-Nazi cabinet imposed on him by the Germans and protect the 100,000 Jews of Budapest plus many more who had found refuge in the capital. The developments since late June, Horthy's final decision to appoint more and more anti-German or loyal ministers, his lengthy negotiations with the German plenipotentiary Edmond Veesenmayer, and the role of the anti-Semitic Hungarians and the Hungarian head of the gendarmerie, László Ferenczy (the most important instrument of deportations from the province, "without which Eichmann would have been helpless") are thoroughly discussed in Randolph Braham's second volume[9] and help us to realize that Eichmann was not the only actor in this tragedy.

The story also includes Hitler's willingness to allow a limited number of Budapest Jews to leave the country should Horthy be willing to deport the rest.[10] It is clear here that the Germans were not free to act in the capital without Hungarian consent, especially Horthy's. In this sense, Kasztner's caution in regard to armed resistance, which might have prompted utmost measures to be undertaken against all Hungarian Jewry, including those of Budapest, while the Germans were still intact in that part of Europe could be justified ex post facto.

But Kasztner did not know much about the diplomatic activity abroad and certainly not on the date of "Overlord." When the landing took place, its initial success did not achieve a breakthrough from the beachhead as yet. Thus, most of June was spent on the interim plans mentioned in Chapter 29

[8] Asher Cohen, *The Halutz Resistance in Hungary 1942–1944* (Haifa: Hakibbutz Hameuchad Publishing House, Institute of Research of the Holocaust Period, University of Haifa, 1984), p. 131.

[9] Braham, *The Politics of Genocide*, Volume II, pp. 766–795.

[10] Miklós Krausz ascribed this offer to himself and to FDR's personal intervention in my interview with Krausz of May 8, 1985; see also Bauer, *Jews for Sale?*, pp. 286–287.

and on enlarging the list of names for Kasztner's Train until the number was almost tripled to 1,684 men, women, and children, divided after the war by Kasztner himself into ten subgroups. They included Zionists, who were given this opportunity (guaranteed by nothing more than Eichmann's word) on the basis of partisan affiliations, and included Jabotinsky's followers and youth movement activists but not Kasztner himself or all of the members of his family, nor all members of the Zionist "Rescue Committee." Kasztner's own discretion in naming these people was rather limited, and the decisions were made by chairman Otto Komoly and others, such as orthodox leader Phillip Freudiger, who resented Kasztner's effort to dominate the scene. Freudiger had his separate channel to the Germans, but finally it seems that all the Jewish parties agreed on the list and the required payments in cash and treasure to Becher, which he promised to return after the war.[11] But as a liaison to Eichmann, Kasztner made the impression of being the chief person and had to pretend to be the same in order to be taken seriously by the Germans.

The second group consisted of dignitaries from all spheres of Hungarian Jewish life, including people from Cluj, Kasztner's Transylvanian hometown and where he had personal influence on the listing. Many others were also involved in this, including Freudiger, who, with Kasztner's consent, picked up Jewish Rabbis, scholars, writers, and other real dignitaries, including the Rabbi of Szatmar, Joel Teitelbaum, a devoted anti-Zionist. The third group was smaller but bought its tickets for more money. This was one of the sources of the financing of the whole transport.

The rest of the story was told in Kasztner's own report discussed earlier, which reached Roswell McClelland of the WRB. The transport was held in a separate compound in Bergen-Belsen, used at the time as a German internment camp for hostages. It was divided into two, and a few hundred of the transportees were allowed to go to Switzerland in August 1944. At that point in time, Rumania defected from the Nazi camp, and Himmler ordered the cessation of the deportations from Hungary to avoid trouble with Horthy at a time when Germany's military situation in the Balkans required such caution.[12] The rest of the transportees waited in agony at Bergen-Belsen until the end of the year, when Kasztner managed to make Becher convince Himmler that their release would bring an Allied "quo." These Jews also crossed the Swiss border. The scholar who recently interviewed some survivors from

[11] Regarding Becher's promise to return the money, see his letter of May 30, 1948, to Dr. Chaim Posner, Director of the Palestine Office (Jewish Agency's Branch) in Geneva, Central Zionist Archive (CZA) file L 17/170. For Hungarian Jewish resentment of Kasztner's assumed role as central figure toward the Germans, see the testimony of Zionist activist Szilagyi in Cohen, *The Halutz Resistance in Hungary*, p. 133.

[12] See Braham, vol. 11, pp. 796–797.

the second group still sensed hatred, rage, and repression of facts, directed mainly against Kasztner.[13]

Why he, the Jew who among others saved them, became the target or directed against himself the incredible emotions accumulated among these people while waiting in Bergen-Belsen for months is a question that goes beyond his person and behavior.

Thus, Miklós Moshe Krausz, the member of a religious Zionist party and the Jewish Agency's immigration officer in Budapest, who always cultivated high hopes in the Hungarian help and in the Hungarian regent Horthy, not only found himself right when Horthy intervened late in June and later stopped the deportations but ascribed it to his own intervention with the American ambassador in Turkey, Laurence Steinhardt – an allegation that has no roots in reality. Steinhardt allegedly met afterward with Roosevelt and convinced the U.S. president to bring pressure to bear on the Hungarian admiral. In an interview with the present writer in 1985, Krausz went on to say that once Horthy agreed to Jewish immigration from Budapest abroad – and made Hitler agree as well – the much larger number of immigrants allowed to go free, now about 40,000, allegedly annoyed Kasztner no end because he had bought the lives of only 1,684 for an enormous sum of money. Therefore, Kasztner went so far as to torpedo the larger "Horthy deal."

Based on Veesenmayer's exchange of messages with the Nazi Foreign Office, quoted by Bauer,[14] we know that in fact the Germans were ready to let some Jews go free in order to kill most of them. Furthermore, OKW/Chi within five days had decrypted Krausz's message regarding the alleged German offer to allow 2,000 Palestine certificate holders to go to Portugal, as it had a clear picture of names, affiliations, and functions of all the rescue operatives assembled in Turkey, plus ambassador Steinhardt's complaint to Washington that there were by then too many of them there and they were interfering with each other. Finally, the Germans could register Ira Hirschmann's urgent request to be allowed to return to the United States because nothing much could be done from Ankara to save the Hungarian Jews.[15]

---

[13] I experienced this bitterness personally when I suggested to the Habima National Theater in Tel-Aviv the idea of doing a docudrama on Kasztner. The Chairman of the Theater Board, Mr. Moshe Zanbar, who was on Kasztner's Train and was probably released to Switzerland in the second echelon, refused even to hear the name mentioned in his vicinity. The outcome was that someone else picked up the idea and produced a docudrama on Kasztner for another Israeli theater.

[14] Bauer, *Jews for Sale?*, pp. 213–215.

[15] See OKW/Chi V.N. 246/11.44 (USA) F. 30.10.44 (taf-wex), received November 1, 1944, decrypted November 5, 1944, regarding Krausz's 2,000 certificates, source: RG 457, Entry 1032, box 213; see also OKW/Chi V.N. 8569/9/44 F. of September 16, received September 20, decoded September 22, in which WRB Bern informed the State Department that the Germans

The WRB, however, reported Eichmann's refusal to let the Hungarian Jews go "unless tractors are obtained in trade for them" and that Kasztner was very much concerned about getting the tractors or at least money instead that could buy goods in neutral Switzerland. Hence, the rescue efforts concentrated now in that country, or were supposed to. Thus, Kasztner used his ties with AJDC's Saly Mayer and the WRB's representative in Switzerland, Roswell McClelland, and a series of meetings took place between them and Kurt Becher and his aides on the Swiss border to discuss rescue in fall and winter 1944–1945 that finally brought about the release of the second Bergen-Belsen group into Switzerland.

A Jewish Agency document, carrying a separate letterhead in Hebrew, that was recently declassified and should be read in this connection is an unsigned memo (probably written by Kollek or Zaslani) dated November 12, 1944.[16] Entitled "Switzerland as a Base for Operations," the writer or writers approached the OSS higher echelon, however without indicating the name of the addressee. Connecting their intention to exploit the experience and ties gained so far in Istanbul with the liberation of the Balkan countries and the shifting of the battle front to the Austrian frontier, they argued that in Switzerland the "close connection" with "important Axis personalities," which allegedly proved so valuable in Turkey, could be maintained and developed:[17]

> The visit of Kastner [sic], a leading Hungarian Jewish personality in Switzerland, at the beginning of November, 1944 [related to the Becher–Mayer negotiations–S.A.] proves that the contacts with top ranking Nazis are still existing, at the time Joel Brand left on his mission. The fact that the Nazis attempt again and again to approach Jewish, neutral or Allied relief organisations enable us to be in contact with important German circles, which fact should be exploited for the Allied cause. People like KRUMEY, LAUFER, KLAGES, who are regarded as leaders of the Nazi Underground after Germany's defeat, are the sponsors of those negotiations (underlines added).

I have underlined this sentence, written in November 1944, when Clages was dead after having participated in the kidnapping of Horthy's son, because of

---

refused to allow the Jews of Hungary to leave or to be transported through German territory to other countries, and finally Hirschmann's urgent message to WRB's Director, John Pehle, dated September 19, 1944, in which he asked to be allowed to return to the United States since nothing could be done from Ankara to save Hungarian Jews – OKW/Chi V.N. No. 1/1689, received on September 21, 1944, decoded September 24, 1944. Source: RG 457, Entry 1032, box 206.

[16] RG 226, Entry 210, box 101699, folder 10F3, declassified September 11, 2000 but released in February 2002.

[17] At that late time, Himmler's masseur, Felix Kersten, and SD-Aussland Chief Schellenberg were trying to forge contacts with the Allies, mainly in Stockholm. I do not attach too much importance to them, as the decision remained in Himmler's and mainly Hitler's hands, but I will deal with specific cases.

its dual meaning. All of them – Laufer finally included – were described as Nazis who might play their own game. But as "Nazi Underground leaders," who were also interested in the Jewish connection, they became again an intelligence object that might entail the rescue of Jews. For that reason, the Jewish Agency asked for cooperation with OSS to deal with them in Switzerland while "under the cover of such negotiations on questions of relief and exchange of Jews, important information may be obtained, of particular value to Allied Security Organizations. It is also not unlikely that we may succeed in luring into Switzerland, under the pretext of negotiations, Germans whom Allied Security Organizations are interested in getting hold of." How would this activity be compatible with rescue? The old trap situation was working here again when in fact the Jewish Agency wanted to establish its own base in Switzerland, the closest neutral country to a collapsing Germany with its Jewish survivors in labor and concentration camps, as argued further in the same memo, on top of the existing efforts undertaken by Nathan Schwalb and the few other Zionist operatives in that country, and tried its best in making its plans compatible with those of OSS without any real chance of either getting its approval or Swiss approval.[18] At the same time, the WRB persisted in its appeals to the administration to at least bomb the railroads leading to Auschwitz, the bridges over them, and the gas chambers – a plea suggested before and rejected by both the British and the Americans.

---

[18] See in this connection Friling, *Arrow in the Dark*, Vol. II, pp. 860–873, on the Zionist–AJDC cooperation regarding financing of rescue and immigration to Palestine. According to Friling, the AJDC decided upon a full-fledged cooperation with the Zionists once they realized that the WRB was a rather weak creature.

33

The Bombing Controversy – Speer and Zuckerman

The Allies received rather exact information in real time about the final stages of the Holocaust, which had not always been the case earlier. The destination was now known, the routes known, the railroads marked, and bridges pinpointed by the Allied intelligence agencies for the purposes of the 15th U.S. Air Force, based in Italy and capable of bombing the railroads leading to Auschwitz and the gas chambers. Several overtures were made by Jewish organizations, including the Yishuv's leadership, to the Allies to bomb the railroads and the gas chambers and stop the factory of death, but they allegedly were not made rigorously enough. Sometimes, as Dina Porat tells us, the Jewish Agency's officials were in doubt among themselves whether such approaches would have any effect on the Allies or even be of any help to the inmates.[1] In other words, the Zionists allegedly succumbed to the catastrophe rather than rising to meet it.

I have asked Albert Speer what would have been the result of an effective bombing run that would have destroyed the gas chambers in Auschwitz. He replied:

Hitler would have hit the roof. . . . He would have ordered the return to mass shooting. And immediately, as a matter of top priority – which it wasn't beforehand – in terms of military personnel, of allocating equipment, and the like. Instead of shipping those people to Auschwitz within months, they should have been shot on the spot within two weeks. About the Hungarian Jews, the question is – to be sought in the Militärarchiv at Freiburg, whether he had the power – in terms of available German forces in Hungary, to do it. (Speer interview with the author, Heidelberg, July 11–14, 1972, and ensuring correspondence)

The "catch" in this could be divided in two. One is the legacy of the alleged success of the bombing campaign against Germany, which in fact was not decisive at least until late in 1944, according to Speer in the same

---

[1] Porat, *An Entangled Leadership*, pp. 392–404.

interview. But the campaign was at first a substitute for the opening of a second front on the Continent, a rather successful long-range, if very costly, endeavor, and also a very successful public relations campaign, which in turn encouraged people to believe that the bombing might destroy Auschwitz and thus stop the Holocaust.

At the same time, the shorter-range problematic bombing campaign only fed Nazi fire against the remaining Jews. A typical argument in this respect was made by Kurt Becher, Kasztner's SS partner in negotiating a deal to save the Hungarian Jews, when he brought the Holocaust into the context of the Allied bombing offensive. According to Kasztner's postwar report,[2] Becher accused the Allies of killing "millions of German mothers and women" by aerial bombing; here the image of "the inhumane Jew" was combined with actual military operations conducted by air marshals who would resist any attempt to "divert" their bombers from the German cities and other "war winning" objectives.

For his part, Albert Speer said in his interview with me that Jewish responsibility for the air raids was mentioned in Hitler's immediate company as a matter of accepted routine, related to the "British–Jewish war against Germany."

Solly Zuckerman, a brilliant Jewish anatomist of South African origin (and a son-in-law of Lord Reading), had examined earlier the damage done to human victims by aerial bombing in England, realizing that their effect was rather limited and could be considerably reduced by adopting rather simple means of civil defense. He further studied the limited damage caused by "carpet bombing," including Allied attacks of that kind in North Africa and in Sicily, and as a result he interfered with the strategy of Sir Arthur Harris, C in C of British Bomber Command, to bomb German cities and thus win the war from the air. Nonetheless, put into the uniform of an RAF Group Captain and appointed Chief Target Planning Officer of SHAEF (Supreme Headquarters, Allied Expeditionary Force), he convinced General Eisenhower's deputy, Sir Arthur Tedder, that railway targets could be successfully attacked at a relatively close distance, such as from northern France, if enough repeated heavy bombing could hit vital communication and control systems. The precondition was a sustained attack, in large numbers, which in terms of the timetable coincided with the German occupation of Hungary since mid-March 1944 and culminated when "Overlord" was approaching in June of the same year. It was at this time that the tide of the deportation from Hungary to Auschwitz was reaching a peak. General Eisenhower, as Supreme Allied

---

[2] See the report submitted by Kasztner to the Zionist Congress in 1946, which was republished by the "Association for the Commemoration of Dr. Israel Kasztner," translated by Benyamin Gat-Rimon, under the title "Kasztner's Truth," without date or place of publication, p. 144. This report will be referred to as "Hebrew Bericht" (translation of original German term for "report").

Commander, endorsed Tedder's (his deputy in charge of air operations) request for the heavy bombers and forced a decision by the Combined Chiefs of Staff to that effect.[3] Eisenhower repeatedly used the heavy bombers to break out from the Normandy bridgehead in the summer – when the Jewish Agency's pleas to bomb Auschwitz and the railroads and bridges leading to it first reached Churchill – while the "air barons" were impatiently waiting to get them back in order to resume their "strategic bombing" of Germany and territories under its control. On the face of it, the Americans had a whole Air Force, the 15th, which was relatively free to pursue such operations even during the peak months of the land war in France. Yet the 15th was supposed to support land operations in Italy proper and only then bomb other targets. The 15th did attack, including targets in Budapest, synthetic oil targets in Auschwitz, and railway junctions at Debrecen, but not the gas chambers. The explicit refusal to do this could be related to several issues: one was strategic and bureaucratic, the other possibly political.

The air war in Europe, both related and unrelated to the landing in France, was indeed a chapter by itself, and the study of the Jewish effort regarding the bombing of Auschwitz requires some knowledge of Allied decisions, starting with a JCS directive issued in January 1944[4] not to divert the bombing effort toward "civilian" matters at that specific time, and some knowledge about the Hungarian situation itself.

By late June, the Allies had won the invasion battle in Normandy but were worried about the shallow depth of their bridgehead in France and were still unable to achieve a breakthrough in the bloody battles around Caen and in the French "bocage." They prepared to use the heavy bomber force for that purpose; they were worried about German reserves remaining unused against them in Normandy for a relatively long time due to the sustained German belief that the main Allied landing would take place in the Pas de Calais, leading straight to the heart of Germany.[5] The strategic bombing of Germany itself stopped almost completely thanks also to Solly Zuckerman's "transportation plan" in France; then came the repeated bombings aimed at piercing the German defenses in Normandy, accompanied by the heavy bombing of the V-1 missile sites before and following the rather alarming use of the cruise missiles by the Germans against London, which kept the British and U.S. bombers busy. The ballistic missiles A-4, known later as V-2, came next, and the Messerschmidt Me 262, the formidable jet fighter,

---

3 See Weinberg, *A World at Arms*, pp. 683–684.

4 See Weinberg, *A World at Arms*, pp. 574–580, on strategic bombing in general, and see also David S. Wyman, "Why Auschwitz Was Never Bombed," *Commentary* 65, No. 5 (May 1978), 405–406, and Michael J. Neufeld and Michael Berenbaum (eds.), *The Bombing of Auschwitz: Should the Allies Have Attempted It?* (New York: St. Martin's Press, in association with the United States Holocaust Memorial Museum, 2000).

5 See Percy Ernst Schramm, *Aus dem Kriegstagebuch des Oberkommandos der Wehrmacht, die Invasion 1944* (München, DTV, 1963), pp. 100–101.

was looming on the horizon with the new XX series submarines. Thus, bombing priorities were indeed a "hot potato" at that juncture in direct relationship to the ground war. Bombing by the relatively less burdened U.S. 15th Air Force, by the 8th Air Force, when released, and by British Bomber Command was supposed to concentrate in the early summer on "(a) Aircraft industry, (b) Oil, (c) ball bearing, (d) Vehicular production."[6] Thus, Adolf Eichmann's truck demand in exchange for "million Jews," made in mid-May 1944, touched upon an extremely important war target. The Allied air crews were expected to die trying to knock off truck factories; on the other hand, the Allies were supposed to deliver the same products to the Nazis in order to save Jews. No one was completely sure whether the Germans were developing an atomic bomb until fall 1944.[7] Still, the last major German war production effort required more hands, as they were quickly losing their occupied territories, and this might have been one of the reasons for the German decision to send a certain number of Hungarian Jews to work in Austria and in Germany once the majority were already dead.

The Allies had their own worries and methods of doing things. As described by Solly Zuckerman,[8] those involved bombing priorities and similar decisions: "most of the people with whom I was now dealing seem to prefer a priori belief to disciplined observations"; Churchill was able, in several crucial cases, to intervene and impose his will upon the bureaucrats and the empire builders, including the mobilization of the RAF to launch several sorties in an effort to help the Polish uprising in Warsaw in summer 1944, but bombing Auschwitz was not one of the issues he was able to decide, nor did the RAF Warsaw effort help the Poles in any substantial way. The U.S. 15th Air Force bombed targets in Budapest and in Auschwitz itself, railroads in other parts of Hungary to facilitate Soviet strategic moves, but not the railroads leading to Auschwitz or the gas chambers. This required a sustained effort, but according to Solly Zuckerman, the real intelligence, which showed hard and convincing evidence as to the havoc brought upon the Germans by concentrated bombing of transportation targets, was hardly used by the Allied air "barons": "Despite the hard evidence provided [by captured German records in – S.A.] in Paris and Brussels . . . the intelligence

---

[6] See David Eisenhower *Eisenhower at War: 1943–1945* (New York: Random House, 1987), p. 348.

[7] For the rather ineffective early and dedicated American intelligence effort to discover the extent of German progress toward atomic bomb development and the activities of the "Alsos" team created by General Groves later in 1943, which became operational in practical terms in August 1944 but gathered its decisive evidence on the non-existent German bomb in autumn 1944, see Richard Rhodes, *The Making of the Atomic Bomb* (New York: Simon and Schuster, 1986), pp. 605–610, 612–613.

[8] See Solly Zuckerman, *From Apes to Warlords* (London: Hamish Hamilton, 1978), pp. 236–237, and see Lord Zuckerman, "The Doctrine of Destruction," *New York Review of Books*, March 19, 1990.

agencies and planners had become prisoners of an antirailway [bombing] prejudice." However, and this was one of the ironies of the actual bombing policy, in Budapest, U.S. 15th Air Force bombing of industrial and oil targets, once adopted by the air "barons" and the planners rather than concentrating further on transportation targets, might have helped Admiral Horthy to at least regain control over the capital and stop the deportations of the Jews in early July 1944 – which by itself made any Western "deals" with the Germans seem unnecessary – and maybe also to stop the bombing or make the Jewish mass presence in Budapest a factor limiting the air offensive (in Horthy's view of alleged Jewish power in the West). Of course, they had no such power, but the Jews of Budapest at last seemed to have escaped. For a short while in fall 1944, a pro-Nazi rebellion toppled Horthy altogether, and the deportations, and on-the-spot killings by local Fascists, were resumed in Budapest as well as in Theresienstadt and the remaining ghettos in Poland. At that juncture, Jewish pleas to bomb Auschwitz reached the American authorities when the Germans were able to stabilize the situation again in Holland, having avoided a complete disaster at the Falaise pocket, in the Metz area in France, and along their own boundaries, allowing the return to the previous air strategy by both Bomber Command and the USAF.

The preceding description may at least explain why the railroads leading to Auschwitz were not attacked earlier in 1944 when much closer French targets, whose bombing might have made the difference between "Overlord's" success and its failure, were forced upon the "air barons" by the Joint Chiefs, as Speer told us. Zuckerman, who was behind that decision, agreed with him, saying:[9] "(i) In my view, Speer was right when he said that the bombing of Auschwitz would have been a very problematic matter before early 1944. I would put the date even later." Regarding the bombing itself, Zuckerman wrote:

What exactly do you yourself think would have happened if, with bombing accuracy as poor as it was, the American bombers had dropped their loads on the Auschwitz camp itself? Hitting the railway lines to the camp wouldn't have made much difference. Where I believe the transportation plan might have affected the camp is in cutting off supplies to them, such as they were, as well as hindering the transport of further victims to the death chambers. (Letters to the author, January 19 and March 20, 1987)

However, the best way to do it was to concentrate a major effort against the embarkation stations. But this did not promise success by itself and could have meant that the victims could be killed by shooting in their own areas or be led short distances to improvised killing centers instead of being shipped by railway elsewhere – and the responsibility for the German decision to do so might have been laid at Allied doors. It is very hard to prove whether

[9] Letters of January 19 and March 20, 1987, to the present writer.

the same political logic might explain the American refusal to try to attack the gas chambers, even when these structures could not be repaired as easily as railroads and did not require a meaningful "diversion" of bombers to achieve the desired goal, especially when General Ira Eaker's 15th Air Force bombed industrial targets at Auschwitz.

But according to Speer in his interview just cited, Hitler indeed would have accelerated his killing of Jews – and thus in Speer's view Auschwitz was not the precondition for Hitler to execute Jews wherever he had the power to do so one way or another. The order of the battle of the Germans in Hungary between March 1944 and February 1945, when greater Budapest was finally occupied by the Soviets, reflects various levels of German military presence, army and Waffen SS. Eastern Hungary was made "Operationsgebiet" upon the invasion in March 1944, and Western Hungary was made a military operation area later during the summer,[10] explaining thereby the initial German drive to deport the Jews of the Carpathians as soon as possible from Eastern Hungary and then from other parts of the Hungarian province in early July. Yet Hungarian involvement and input in this regard also played a very important role. Hungarians carried out the deportations and the related maltreatment of the deportees. Thus, they (plus some German units available or improvised) could use shooting or even create local killing centers when we remember that most of the killing centers in Poland – except Auschwitz – were simple makeshift factories of death using submarine engines. Later, regent Horthy intervened to prevent the deportations from Budapest proper. However, in fall of 1944, Hungarian Nazis deposed Horthy, and the Final Solution was resumed under the conditions of that period of time, which included the need for working hands. By then, enough Germans had become experts in killing Jews, making them march by foot – and die – on their way from Hungary to Austria. The logic of avoiding military service at the front by remaining loyal to the supreme ideological cause – that of completing the Final Solution – must be added here.[11]

When Horthy stopped the deportations in July 1944, the bombing of Auschwitz was not necessary as far as the Hungarian Jews were concerned (a fact known to the Allies), but it could have been badly needed to save the lives of the remnants of Polish, Slovak, and Theresienstadt Jews who were gassed in Auschwitz during the summer and the fall. But these people,

---

[10] See Schramm, *Kriegstagebuch des Oberkommandos der Wehrmacht 1944–1945*, Teilband 1, eine Dokumentation, Band 4, 3. Abschnitt, Der Fall "Margarethe" (Besetzung Ungarns) durchgeführt ab 19. März bis 31 März 1944, S. 179–254, and 7 Abschnitt, Die Ereignisse in Ungarn von Anfang April bis zum Schlacht um Budapest und zur endgültigen Legaliesierung des politischen Umschwungs (5. November 1944), pp. 827–853.

[11] See Gerhard L. Weinberg, "The Allies and the Holocaust," in Michael Berenbaum and Abraham J. Peck (ed.), *The Holocaust and History: The Known, the Unknown, the Disputed, and the Reexamined* (Washington, DC), and Bloomington, IN: Indiana University Press, 1998), pp. 480–491.

brought over while the actual situation in the various battle fronts changed in such a way that the German war machine recovered from time to time from the blows inflicted on it, could be perceived as if they could be killed by mass shooting as Hitler had done in Russia before. Revenge was not just an important dimension of Hitler's character but an official, legitimate element in Nazism as such – a politicized aspect of German aggression and their sense of victimization, bordering now on desperation and with the personal benefit derived from "serving the cause" but not at the front. Members of the Western elites could have and did view it as a sort of fact of life, or death, which did not seem to have been their problem in practical terms but was a source of trouble to themselves and to their own cause, possibly also due to their own experience at the time with "Vergeltungswaffen" such as the V-1 and V-2.

One could also add the psychological effect of aerial bombing, when one studies the wartime propaganda pictures and movies in this regard, as having given the Allied nations a kind of immediate sense of revenge against German crimes. Germany seemed to have been punished already – and maybe it would get rid of Hitler immediately – and thus no immediate action might have seemed necessary to work for the cause of the Jews, while Hitler made the Jews specifically responsible for the bombing. At least until later in 1944, this had not yet decisively impaired his war machine but at first generated very alarming SD reports about the impact of the bombing. Only later, while the German population was depressed and gloomy over the bombing, "they were also extraordinarily angry at their tormentors and were demanding retaliation . . . ," which drove Hitler and his cronies to believe that the bombing would even encourage German fanaticism[12] while many Germans felt that they were caught anyway in the web of Nazi crimes.

The whole issue of civilians (non-Allied citizens in Hitler's hands) was a "nonissue" legally and raised questions of German reprisals against Allied POWs if Hitler were pushed beyond a certain point, and one could further fear the use of chemical (especially poison gas) weapons by the Nazis if revenge plus the approaching defeat provoked them that far. The Allies could take measures to protect their POWs, as they had had more than enough German ones in their hands since late in 1943, and poison gas was theoretically a double-edged sword, which Churchill considered using as a response to the German missile attacks against London, when commenced at the peak of the Hungarian Holocaust – an idea that the Chiefs of Staff categorically rejected against Churchill's repeated approaches.[13] The Jews had none of these weapons and no way of pushing huge military machines

---

[12] See Murray Williamson, *Luftwaffe* (Baltimore: Easton Press edition, 1985), pp. 283–284.
[13] See Martin Gilbert, *Winston S. Churchill: Volume VII, The Road to Victory, 1941–1945* (Boston: Houghton Mifflin, 1986), pp. 840–843 and 864–865; see also Weinberg, *The World at Arms*, pp. 691, 784, on the development of the poison gas Tabun.

beyond the point to which Winston Churchill himself failed to push them, while Churchill's attention was now concentrated on various measures to be taken in the face of the new V-weapon threat to London, one of them a mass evacuation of the city. Later, he and the British and American "air barons" had other priorities.

The legacy of the Allied failure to bomb Auschwitz became, however, one of the most common sources of popular criticism of the Jewish leadership. This had its roots with the original demand by Rabbi Weissmandel (the rescue operative in Slovakia) to undertake the bombing. At least, it is argued, they could have made Churchill and Roosevelt do it, but they failed to do so, period. The trap aspect of the bombing story, as the contributions of Speer and Zuckerman to it help us understand it, could now be summed up as follows: the image, or myth, spread by the British and the Americans, about the alleged success of aerial bombing against Germany in 1943 and until mid-1944, which was partially politically motivated and was partially a bureaucratic phenomenon, and which in terms of long-range rather than immediate results was correct, created expectations among Jews that bombing, especially of Auschwitz and the railroads leading to it, could stop the Holocaust. Yet the bombing strategy itself was extremely costly and largely ineffective in achieving its immediate goals, especially with regard to such targets and at such distances. Its accumulated effect was very probably considerable when we calculate the attrition rate that Allied air forces had imposed on the Luftwaffe since the "big week" of February 1944 (in which long-range fighters joined the American bomber streams for the first time and the Allies concentrated on various sensitive targets such as synthetic oil plants) and add to this the diversion of huge German resources for home defense. The bombing offensive, however, fed Hitler's wrath, in a direct connection with his concept of the "Jew's war" against him, and helped unite his nation behind him and justify further Nazi atrocities against the remaining Jews.

34

The "Great Season"

While the realities in Europe proved to be complicated enough, Menachem Begin proclaimed an open "rebellion" against "Nazo–British" rule in Palestine in defiance of the Jewish Agency's policy in January 1944. This was another form of terrorism – following the peculiar kind of Sternist activities that were "stamped out" by the Yishuv and the British in 1942. Thus, so we were told previously by our Agency source, "Resolutions against terrorism were adopted by all Jewish public bodies. *The public was taught to understand the great harm caused by these terrorist activities* (italics added), both from the human point of view as well as from the Zionist political point of view."[1] The role of the Labor elite in its own eyes as the "teacher of the public" or as a mobilizing elite becomes clear here. The Labor elite pursued a degree of control over the Yishuv, which in retrospect seems to have required almost antidemocratic regimentation. Indeed Ben-Gurion and his Mapai associates, such as Berl Katzenelson (who died later in 1944), tried to influence the Hebrew media and had a variety of media at their disposal, but they never succeeded completely due to the rather heterogeneous character of the Yishuv. Nor would Ben-Gurion go beyond certain democratic practices. He was aiming at this stage at the unified Labor base, and later at a direct public campaign – general elections to the Palestine Jewish National Committee – which in fact had not taken place in the Yishuv proper since the 1930s. Lord Moyne's assassination at the hands of the Sternists in November 1944 gave Ben-Gurion, following two decisive election victories earlier in 1944, the opportunity he wanted to fight both the Sternists and the Beginites across the board in the framework of the "Great Season": the extradition of IZL

---

[1] See note 1 in Chapter 21. The deliberations within the Jewish Agency's executive in this regard, which took place between February and April 1944, were neither simple nor made without opposition within the Agency's ranks; Yitzhak Gruenbaum, the chairman of the "Rescue Committee," even resigned from the Executive Council because of this. For details, see Bauer, *Diplomacy and Underground in Zionism*, pp. 273–274.

members and Sternists to the British. However, even beforehand, according to the Jewish Agency's memo, actions were taken to warn the British in regard to various attempts on the lives of high officials, against CID centers, a German detainees camp, British colonial officials abroad in charge of the Arab League idea, exposed arms stores, and the like. Yet the "volunteers" in charge of the continued "Small Season" were unable to prevent Lord Moyne's assassination in Cairo on November 6, 1944. This murder, however, prompted the "Great Season," described in the 1945 Jewish Agency memo as "many hundred arrests... affected through the cooperation with the Jewish public." Moreover, the memo added – and this becomes known here for the first time:

After the murder... a Jewish volunteer was sent, with the consent of the Palestine Authorities, to Egypt to disclose any contacts of the terrorists in that country and to take preventive measures against possible further... activities.... Another envoy was sent to Syria.... Two special envoys went to Baghdad... [when] it became known that members of the Iraqi cabinet had received threatening letters, allegedly from Jewish terrorists... but fortunately it was ascertained that the matter was not serious. (memo "Jewish Terrorist Gangs in Palestine," RG 226, Entry 190, box 73, CAIRO-SI-OP-4-7)

The author then complained about British ingratitude toward the "volunteers," including arrests made among them because of illegal arms possession. These people were sentenced to long periods in prison, later to be remitted in half by the British military commander.

The Jewish Agency estimated the membership of the Stern group as about 300–400 members, mostly "deserters from the Polish Army who arrived in Palestine 2–3 years ago and belonged in Poland to the extremist faction of the N.M.O." The strength of the NMO/IZL itself was estimated "at present at 1,500–2,000 members.... The present uncontested commander of the N.M.O. is Menachem Begin, who regards himself as Jabotinsky's successor." Begin was described in the report as a "personal friend" of Nathan Friedman, the Stern group commander – an unfounded allegation.[2] Other details were true – Menachem Begin came to Palestine (in mid-1942) as a member of the Polish Army under General Wladyslaw Anders, which was recruited among Polish exiles in the Soviet Union and permitted to leave Russia at that time.[3]

---

[2] See for the most recent biography Sasson Sofer, *Begin – An Anatomy of Leadership* (London: Basil Blackwell, 1988), especially pp. 54–60.

[3] Anders's army trained on its way to the Western Front in Palestine, and Begin, according to the report, "worked in the office of the Polish Town major in Jerusalem, but was subsequently released." It seems that the Jewish Agency informed OSS about the Polish connection of the Revisionists and Begin due to Polish activities in the United States at the time aimed at enhancing their own cause, possibly with Jewish revisionist support.

As the Agency's report described Begin's goals, the NMO/IZL:

... hope to establish the nucleus of an underground resistance movement which will, at a given moment, lead a general insurrection of the Jewish population.... They assume that successful terrorist activities [even if they are opposed to Stern's indiscriminate tactics of terror directed against individuals – S.A.] will harm the British prestige in the Middle East and weaken the British grip on the Arabs. This will compel Great Britain to give in and enter into negotiations with the Jews. The Americans who are interested in weakening the British position in the Middle East will sympathize with any force which works to that end. (memo "Jewish Terrorist Gangs in Palestine")

Besides, the United States would do its utmost to keep the peace in that vital land bridge between the European fronts and the Asian fronts. "Disturbances in Palestine will impress public opinion in the United States, and Great Britain will subsequently be requested to change her policy in favor of the Jews." This political plank was indeed typical of Begin's own view of the "revolt,"[4] and seemingly it did materialize after the war when the U.S. intervened, also due to public pressure in favor of the Jews, against British interests. The reasons were, however, the fate of the survivors in European DP camps, some of whom were saved thanks to Kasztner, the postwar awareness of the Holocaust among American Jews under the leadership of Rabbi Abba Hillel Silver, and the adoption of a rather moderate partition plan by Ben-Gurion and his associates against Begin's and the Sternists' ideals (which included not only the quest for Western Palestine as a whole but also for Trans-Jordan based not only on ideological grounds but on the hope that millions of Jews would inhabit both – millions who by now were dead), and British and Arab uncompromising stances. At the time under review here, Jews were not a high priority on anybody's agenda, even if the British Cabinet was engaged at the time in its secret deliberations regarding the partition of Palestine, which meant Jewish independence in one part (about which Begin knew nothing) but prohibited terror actions against the British, on top of the continued efforts to induce the British government to do more for rescue and allow commando operations in Nazi-occupied territories. In other words, Jewish terrorism would become a weapon in the hands of the British and induce the Americans to ignore the Zionists as a whole and even damage rescue endeavors.

The attempt on Moyne's life was justified by the Sternists in terms of his previous support of the White Paper policy as Secretary of State for the Colonies, due to an anti-Zionist speech he made in the House of Lords two years before, and British – not exclusively German – responsibility for the fate of the Jewish people since the inception of the White Paper policy. The

---

[4] See minutes of Sne–Begin meeting on September 10, 1944, Hagana Archive, Division 80/15316. Moshe Sne was at the time the nominal political Chief of the Territorial Staff of the Hagana.

Sternists attributed to Lord Moyne a major role in regard to the fate of the
S.S. "Struma," a refugee ship turned back and later sunk in the Black Sea,
and in the diversion of Palestine-bound Jewish refugees to Mauritius. Ex
post facto they also alleged that Moyne played a decisive role in turning
down the "deal" to save the Jews of Hungary. In fact, they knew nothing of
his involvement in the British cabinet deliberations since late 1943 in favor
of Jewish independence, at least in a partitioned Palestine, nor had they any
idea of Moyne's personal, very close ties with Churchill.[5] Finally, they did
not realize, or did not attach any importance to, the opening of Palestine to
Jews who arrived now in Turkey, mainly from Rumania, and proceeded to
Palestine with explicit British permission – when within the White Paper's
quota. True, this was a trickle, but typically for Labor Zionists, even a trickle
was an actual gain under the circumstances, which should have been carefully
developed into a stream. They also prohibited a terror campaign against the
British because they later agreed to deploy a Jewish Brigade Group within
the ranks of the British Army in Europe and because of the inherent danger
in terrorism to the Yishuv itself.

The Yishuv leadership's response to Moyne's murder, which one may
attribute mainly to Ben-Gurion (i.e., the rounding up and the extradition
of Sternists and Begin's followers to the British authorities in Palestine) either directly or by information given by the Hagana to the British CID,[6]
might have helped calm down Churchill's anger and facilitated Ben-Gurion's
Balkan trip later in 1944 aimed explicitly at organizing Jewish immigration
to Palestine. On top of this, the British deployed the newly formed Palestine–
Jewish Brigade Group in Europe, which stayed there for a while after the
war and played an important role in mobilizing the survivors for the Zionist
cause, having gathered experience and training toward a possible war with
the Arabs. Yet one could argue that the British moved because the Sternists
and Begin's IZL started forcibly to push them to do so – an "activist" approach that seemed more and more attractive to the passionate Jewish youth
and made both the Sternists and the IZL a sort of threatening alternative to
the Social Democratic leadership of the Yishuv.

Ben-Gurion's own demand for full and immediate independence, next to
Begin's terror acts and the "Great Season" aimed at stopping them, threats of
noncooperation with the mandatory government if the White Paper policy
was not soon completely abandoned, and his implied threats of the use of

[5] For their motives in selecting Moyne as a symbolic target, see Heller, *LEHI*, Volume I, pp. 209–
210.
[6] See "H.G.S." information in the CID files in the Hagana Archive, Tel-Aviv, which meant
information received from the Hagana, leading to the questioning or the arrest and, in some
cases, to the transfer of the person in question to British-held territories in Africa, where the
questioning continued, in some cases by Palestine Police agents. The British CID files found
their way to and were released by the Israeli Home Intelligence, known as the General Security
Service, to the Hagana Archive, Division 47.

force when necessary (an exaggerated perception of the military power of the Hagana and its state of preparedness radiated from him)[7] made him no less an "activist" in the eyes of the youth without shedding one drop of British blood.

In retrospect, Ben-Gurion's tactics seem to have been "activist" enough to seize the initiative from the hands of the Sternists and Begin's IZL without accepting their various planks or their analysis of world and regional affairs, counterproductive as they were.

But Ben-Gurion's "activism," largely political and verbal, could have supplied General George Strong, the G-2 director, as we have seen in Chapter 15, with ammunition with the Army Chief himself, General George C. Marshall, to plead against the Zionists.[8] Weizmann's focus, which calculated such damages and was by nature much more restrained, and that of Shertok-Sharett after him, was almost solely directed toward the great powers and if possible toward some agreement with the Arabs. Ben-Gurion's focus, and that was his advantage over both Weizmann and Shertok-Sharett, was directed toward outside powers provided that he was able to gain enough support at home and among the Jewish people first, remembering that only the "home front" could carry the ensuing struggle with Arabs. Therefore, when Menachem Begin arrived in Palestine and was elected IZL commander, and soon enough proclaimed – in direct competition with the Sternists – his own "revolt" against the British, Ben-Gurion was able to neutralize their influence to a degree by his own "activist" posture, along with enhanced efforts to bring in Jewish immigrants – from Arab countries as well when possible. But, as reflected in a G-2 or CIC report from spring 1944,[9] Ben-Gurion's posture could be interpreted as if it "continues to approach the intransigent nationalism [underlined in original] advocated by the Revisionists," when in fact Ben-Gurion was talking on March 27, 1944, against the mandatory government's reconstruction plan, its proposed new taxation, and the White Paper, and he was further reported to have said that when the present war ended, the Jewish war would begin [underlined in original], which the U.S. Army Intelligence brought together with Begin's and the Sternists' actual "revolt" against the British during the war against Fascism.

The "Great Season," which culminated in the transfer of the extradited IZL/NMO members to prison camps in British territories in Africa, where young Shmuel Tamir would soon join them, neutralized the Sternists and IZL for a while and might have prompted several British "quos" such as the deployment of a Jewish Brigade Group within the ranks of the British Army

---

[7] OSS and CIC reports about this reflected true and inflated estimates; see, for example, RG 165 files.

[8] See discussion in Chapter 15.

[9] See source: GSI Main HQ Ninth Army Weekly Military Newsletter No. 58, April 20, 1944.

in the European Theater and Ben-Gurion's authorized trip to the Balkans late in 1944. For the Jewish leadership, the "Great Season" would be linked, at least in the eyes of several of the exiled, to Moyne's alleged refusal to save Holocaust victims and make the Yishuv's leadership perfect "collaborators" with the British, just as Kasztner was portrayed as a collaborator with the Nazis.

35

Becher, Mayer, and the Death Marches

Kasztner was not the only Jewish personality who had approached the Germans hoping to "deal" with them, but the ultra-orthodox Sternbuch brothers, representing an orthodox rabbinical group in America and situated in Montreux, Switzerland, also tried to deal with them. We are told by Randolph Braham that the ultra-orthodox Rescue Committee, headed by the Sternbuch brothers, worked on a giant rescue effort that was supposed to allow 750,000 Jews to leave Europe;[1] this effort with Himmler, in which the Sternbuchs acted through the former Swiss Federal President, Jean-Marie Musy, was supported by a variety of personalities, such as the right-wing Zionist businessman Dr. Ruben Hecht.

In the meantime, on December 1, 1944, the second "Kasztner Train" from Bergen-Belsen, carrying about 1,328 Jews who had left Budapest five months before, was allowed to cross the border to Switzerland in connection with money payments made by Hungarian Jewry itself, of which Kasztner remained in debt of about $65,000 (U.S.), according to his 1945 report.[2] This was done in the framework of the "Becher–Kasztner" line, stressing a certain economic quid pro quo but one that required more sums and goods to be supplied by the Allies.

[1] See Randolph L. Braham, *The Politics of Genocide: The Holocaust in Hungary*, Volume II (New York: Columbia University Press, 1981), p. 967.

[2] Kasztner's Hebrew "Bericht," pp. 163–164. For the ensuing trouble in this regard related to the search for the "Becher Deposit," see CZA file L17/170, "Becher Deposit." Becher allegedly gave the monies and a large number of valuables in full to the Zionist leader Dr. Moshe Schweiger in Bad Ischl, Austria. It was then handed over by the latter to an American CIC unit, but it seemed to have partially vanished due to Becher's own or American efforts. The file cited also includes the calculation of cash paid by Kasztner to Becher's aide Kettlitz and other cash payments deposited in Switzerland to buy tractors and Becher's correspondence in this regard with the Jewish Agency's Geneva representative Dr. Posner, most of which goes beyond the scope of this book.

In the January meeting between Musy and Himmler, so we are told by Schellenberg, the following decisions were arrived at thanks to Himmler's "active intervention":[3] First, every fortnight one train with about 1,200 Jews would leave for Switzerland, travel conditions, food, and so on. "to be as good as possible." Second, "the Jewish organizations, with which . . . Musy worked, should actively support the settlement of the Jewish Problem permitted by Himmler, with the object of initiating a fundamental change in world anti-German propaganda."

This paragraph of the "agreement" reminds us of the language used by Laufer and Clages upon sending Grosz on his separate peace mission. Now that we can argue with a higher degree of confidence that SD Ausland Chief Schellenberg himself was behind Grosz's mission, and that his target then was to split the Allies, we can further argue that he repeated the same tactics here, as he and Himmler were ready to allow limited numbers of Jews to escape while most others did not. At this stage, Himmler seems to have returned to a limited hostage-taking strategy, but he learned enough from the Becher negotiations that a few Jews should be allowed to escape from the decimated ghetto in Theresienstadt in order to give such a tactic a chance. Most inmates had already been deported either to Auschwitz or to work in Germany.

At this stage, Charles Dwork's one-man "Jewish Desk" at OSS R&A was receiving copies of many messages pertaining to Jews, including from the State Department. We thus find a copy of a message by Sir Herbert Emerson, the IGCR Director, dated March 20, 1945, to the State Department and the WRB, according to which Saly Mayer described the Musy train affair as follows:

Musy, a retired federal councilor, was attacked in the press on account of the high prices he had paid for obtaining the release of a few political and Jewish internees. In order to exonerate himself and at the suggestion of the Vatican and Dr. Steinbuch [Sternbuch]-Montreux of American Orthodox Rabbi Federation, he negotiated release of the Theresienstadt group, stating, without authorization, that [Sally] Mayer would show gratitude in cash. . . . Mayer of course refused to make any payment and the arrival of further group seems unlikely. (NA, RG 200, Duker/Dwork Papers, box 29, folder 362)[4]

Adding that Jews have been exterminated in Theresienstadt itself, which was not the case except for those who died of illness and maltreatment, Emerson was right when he stated that the camp population had now dwindled from 35,000–40,000 to 8,000–12,000. At any rate, Emerson's main concern about the 1,200 liberated Jews, among them deportees from Holland, was that they

---

[3] See the newly declassified Schellenberg papers, RG 226, Entry 123, box 11, Bern-SI-Int-71–75.
[4] NA, RG 200, Duker/Dwork Papers, box 29, folder 362.

should be able to return to their home countries rather than go to Palestine.[5] Indeed, a process of Zionization did take root among many survivors at that stage, and Theresienstadt allowed some degree of communal Zionist activities. Regardless of Emerson's worries, his messages may tell us that both rescue operations depended on ransom and that the main ransoming party was supposed to be the American Joint Distribution Committee and its Swiss resident Saly Mayer, who was forbidden to do exactly that.

Schellenberg and Himmler might have hoped that the blurring of the truth in regard to the Final Solution by saving a few Jews at this stage would help Nazi Germany to deal with the West (fearing Moscow's enormous gains, while most Jews were dead anyway) with Jewish aid, as the Sternbuchs, with whom Musy worked, would go to any length to save their brethren. It could at least help Schellenberg and Himmler – living in their world of fantasy – to separate themselves from Hitler's known uncompromising attitude toward Jews if Hitler could be persuaded that he had already achieved his basic goal regarding the Jews and to use the rest for political purposes.

The political purpose could again be a wedge driven between the Western Allies and Stalin. A rift between his enemies was indeed one of Hitler's hopes and the Allies' main concern. How the Sternbuchs believed that a large number of Jews could be saved in this connection we do not know, and neither did Himmler. But he agreed, on the face of it, that there should no longer be any monetary payment made but a definite sum per train should be held in trust by Musy "of which we should later have free use." Himmler then returned to using this money for "tractors, cars, medical supplies and similar things," bearing in mind that these were the only arguments that could convince Hitler, as I interpret this, but Schellenberg maintained that he convinced Himmler that the money should be handed over to the International Red Cross. The reason for that might have been Schellenberg's awareness of "Operation Safehaven" invoked by the Western Allies, which was supposed to keep track of money transfers and other transactions that might have been used by the Nazis to keep their cause alive after the war, hide and support Nazis in neutral countries, and especially revive and expand their activities in due course.[6] Thus, direct ransoming of Jews remained out of the question for the Allies, especially when it involved foreign currency, and Jews who were ready to deal with Germans directly by using foreign currency could be tainted as serving the postwar Nazi cause. The strategic reason for this could also be Western caution about dealing with the Germans in any such form, behind Soviet backs, especially in the face of Stalin's misgivings

---

[5] Cable via U.S. Embassy London, copy to Strategic Service Unit, War Department, Duker/Dwork papers, box 10.

[6] See Petersen, *From Hitler's Doorstep*, p. 492, on OSS Bern and the Safehaven program as one of the main concerns of Allen Dulles's organization in the last weeks of the war and after V-E Day, including a related document.

toward the "Sunrise" negotiations[7] aimed at German capitulation in northern Italy. Even when Nazi Germany was doomed, Japan still held millions of soldiers in China, facing a weak and internally focused Chiang Kai-Shek. Japan might have even continued the war from the mainland now that no one knew whether the atomic bomb would work or not, and Soviet participation in the Far East war, promised by Stalin following V-E Day only, was imperative to save many American and British lives. An ongoing trouble was caused, in Allied minds, by the fear for the lives of British and American POWs – whether the desperate Nazis would use them as hostages or even kill them en masse.[8]

However, in the meantime, according to Schellenberg, "Hitler forbade any German, under threat of death, to help not only one Jew, but interestingly enough also any American or English POW, to cross the frontier. Each attempt was to be reported to him personally." According to Schellenberg, Hitler was shown a deciphered report from "a de Gaulle agency in Spain in which it was asserted that Himmler, through his deputy Schellenberg, had made a deal with . . . Musy to obtain right of asylum for 250 Nazi leaders" in Switzerland. On the other hand, Dwork received a copy of an analysis of the Musy train affair, cabled to OSS–HQ, in which the release of the few was understood as if those who remained behind were treated as hostages, and hence this alleged hostage-taking maneuver of the Nazi side was described as a plan instigated by Hermann Göring to use Musy not just for dealing with Jews but to warn the Allies that unless prominent Nazis were given asylum in Switzerland, prominent others now held in Nazi hands, such as Leon Blum, Edouard Daladier, Paul Reynoud, and even Marshal Petain, the King of the Belgians, would have to share the fate of the Nazis in their reduit in the Alps.[9] The fear of such a reduit played a role in SHAEF's planning indeed when General Eisenhower's troops were ordered south rather than to the northeast and allowed the much debated conquest of Berlin by the Soviets alone.

In mid-March 1945, Himmler might have been closer to his departure point from Hitler. Himmler's masseur, Felix Kersten, who had already moved to the safety of neutral Sweden, was kept informed by Schellenberg through the Musy negotiations, and thus a meeting was arranged between Himmler and an official Jewish personality, on German soil, parallel to the Kasztner–Becher effort, which continued further and to which we shall soon return.

[7] For "Sunrise" and the Soviets' use of it, once they were refused permission to participate in the talks, see Bradley F. Smith, *The Shadow Warriors*, pp. 286–287.

[8] See PRO, CAB 65/50, WM 43 (45) War Cabinet, 12 April, 1945, in which the issue of the POWs was mentioned as one of the problems with regard to the American-inspired war crimes trials. For the British War Cabinet capitulation in regard to the trials, see CAB 57 (45), May 3, 1945. See also NA, RG 226, Entry 146, General Counsel, containing various reports on war crimes, box 37, cables, fear of retaliation against Allied prisoners.

[9] Duker/Dwork papers, box 29, folder 36.

Finally, Himmler's own last-minute efforts with the Western Allies led later to his dismissal and declaration by Hitler to be a traitor to the Nazi cause.

Turning our attention to the other channel of negotiations with Himmler on the fate of the remaining Jews, we learn from the scholarly literature that once Saly Mayer, the Swiss representative of an American-based international Jewish organization such as the Joint Distribution Committee (AJDC), entered into negotiations, Kurt Becher was able to get Himmler's permission – probably with Hitler's consent – to allow the first group of the Kasztner Train to cross the border; but no real quid pro quo could be obtained by Becher from Saly Mayer, who had no power to make offers of that kind. In fact, he was bound by WRB instructions, sympathetic as they were, and the State Department's approval thereof, which excluded any real "deal."[10] The ensuing negotiations, in which Becher, Mayer, and Kasztner were involved along with several other Jewish representatives and Roswell McClelland of the WRB, were a frustrating, agonizing process, which Mayer stalled, asking for German concessions first, and with Kasztner bluffing that Allied monies were released but not delivered due to "misunderstandings." When the negotiations commenced, the German side, Becher included, returned to the 10,000 trucks in exchange for "a million Jews."[11]

Saly Meyer responded that he could not be party to any deal that involved the delivery of war materiel, which could be used against Allied troops. The Germans retorted that the proposition of 10,000 trucks was not theirs but had originated with Jewish circles in Budapest "and had been made by Kasztner." Instead, they asked for Allied permission to allow neutrals such as Switzerland to supply them with products such as machine tools. Mayer remained doubtful about that but soon transformed the matter to cash to the end without paying it as the only quid pro quo and managed to keep the promised money hanging in the air. Yet the German description of the "truck deal," which had originated in 1943 and could have been offered by the German agent Laufer first, could be correct in the sense that Brand had adopted it.

In the meantime, the Fascist Hungarians overthrew the Horthy regime, and Eichmann, who had to leave Budapest upon Horthy's decision to protect the Jews in the capital, returned to Budapest and was prepared to march several thousand Jews out of town to the Austrian border unless Kasztner and friends supplied trucks to transport them, as he reported later,[12] while Becher was negotiating. Both activities could be supplementary, with the truck issue

---

[10] Braham *The Politics of Genocide*, Volume II, p. 963.

[11] McClelland to State Department, Bern cable 5588, August 26, 1944, FDR Library WRB, container 56, file Jews in Hungary (Aug. 44, 840.1).

[12] See Kasztner's Nuremberg interrogation summary No. 2817 and his "Hebrew Bericht," p. 142.

looming always in the background as an important strategic good, probably of political significance, in order to make the Allies negotiate. Roswell McClelland and Saly Mayer, with Kasztner in the background, supplied some "quo" late in October as the U.S. Government was ready to allow the AJDC to transfer five million U.S. dollars – more than twenty million Swiss francs – to Switzerland to be used by the WRB for rescue purposes. In the cable authorizing the transfer, signed by Secretary Hull and which Mayer showed Becher, nothing was said about buying goods, let alone strategic ones, with this money; but according to Kasztner, Becher was impressed and hoped that he had managed to open some kind of channel or back door to FDR's "special representative" in Europe, hoping for some "latent political gains," as Kasztner put it, as well as a personal alibi.[13] Yet soon he, let alone Eichmann, would want to get the money, cash on the nail, with no empty promises.

Becher took Kasztner to Vienna, arguing in favor of Himmler's personal "friendliness" and explaining his own problems with his SS rivals, who accused him of "believing the lies of the international Jewry." Kasztner was impressed by being allowed to "look into their intimate kitchen," and differentiated between the "high ranking, decorated Waffen-S.S. officer and the professional murderers," such as Eichmann,[14] who put Becher's own life supposedly at stake. Kasztner thought that Becher was the stronger and yet the vulnerable party; his own role was to get from him "with tact and care" whatever it was possible to get:

On these little things it depended whether it would be possible to get something for the Jewish cause or not. Following this conversation – in which some little things were agreed such as the return of the train ransom as it seems to me, after the war – Becher said that following the above-mentioned meeting with McClelland, he "would recommend to Himmler to stop the annihilation of the Jews." (Kasztner's Bericht)

Eichmann and the Fascist Hungarians, Veesenmayer, and Ribbentrop proceeded with Hitler's original idea of deporting most Jews up to the last moment. The ups and downs in regard to the fate of the Budapest Jews (first Eichmann marched thousands for work to the Austrian border but left the aged and the young alone, and later he tried to get more) took place during several weeks from October until November 26. At that point, Becher advised Kasztner that "he has won across the whole board" and that the Final Solution was terminated. The Auschwitz "mills" would be stopped and destroyed, Jewish lives would be honored, and Jewish forced laborers in Germany would be treated like others "from the East."[15] This was supposed to happen late in November; however, in October 1944, the

[13] Kasztner, "Hebrew Bericht," p. 145.
[14] Ibid., 148.
[15] Ibid., 159.

first Musy–Himmler–Schellenberg meeting described earlier took place, and according to Kasztner he himself advised Becher, without authorization from anyone, that Mayer was "working day and night" to release the promised five million dollars on November 20. In fact, Kasztner pushed the tired Mayer relentlessly to continue the talks when the latter almost gave up.[16] It looks like Musy's and Becher's "lines" combined here, even if Himmler was very cautious and still tried to operate within a scheme acceptable to Hitler. The gassing in Auschwitz was indeed stopped in November, but the reason for this might have been Germany's dire need for working hands, which Himmler might have hoped to disguise as a general order to stop the Final Solution. Thus we cannot but maintain that the high-ranking Nazis, Hitler on top, did not give up or fully internalize the upcoming defeat before February 1945. Once they did, Hitler pursued his annihilation campaign against the one enemy against whom he could claim victory. Himmler, for his part, still had some hopes of dealing with the remnants of the Jews, along with the preparations for the Ardennes offensive in order to split the Allies, just as the rescuers hoped to deal with him.

At last, by fall 1944, when Allied armies were approaching Germany's heart from all directions, a wedge seemed to have been driven between SS "hardliners" and possibly Hitler himself and the so-called SS "pragmatists" such as Becher, who wanted an alibi for himself but still hoped to serve Himmler's own interests as well in terms of using Jews to approach the West. But this meant for Becher sparing their lives as far as possible. As Kasztner formulated it after the war:[17]

I escaped the fate of the other Jewish leaders because the complete liquidation of the Hungarian Jews was a failure and also because SS Standartenfuehrer Becher took me under his wings *in order to establish an eventual alibi to himself* [underlining in original]. He was anxious to demonstrate after the fall of 1944 that he disapproved the deportations and exterminations and endeavored consistently to furnish me with evidence that he tried to save the Jews." (NA, RG 200, Duker/Dwork Papers, box 3)

The same was the case with Dieter Wisliceny, who was mobilized to stop the deportation of the remnants of the Slovak Jews to Auschwitz, without much success.[18] Thanks to this, at last Kasztner was able to save a few Jews who

---

[16] Ibid., 156.
[17] See Kasztner's report: "SS Personalities Connected with the Extermination of Hungarian Jews," NA, RG 200, Duker/Dwork Papers, box 3. Kasztner gave a similar statement to IMT prosecutors in London later during summer 1945: IMT Trial doc. No. 2605 PS (USA 242), NA, RG 238.
[18] See Testimony of Dieter Wisliceny, taken at Nuremberg, Germany, November 14, 1945, by Lieutenant Colonel Smith W. Brookhart, Jr., OUSCC, in Mendelsohn, *The "Final Solution" in the Extermination Camps and the Aftermath*, pp. 6–51.

took refuge in Bratislava, Rabbi Weissmandel included, while Eichmann's deputy, Alois Brunner, deported most of them to death.[19]

Eichmann operated according to "Hitler's line," at least in mobilizing Budapest's Jews to work according to Kasztner's Bericht:[20] On November 21, he ordered the march of more Jews from Budapest, which was stopped for a short while "due to false impressions of 'some gentlemen,'" meaning SS General Hans Jüttner and the former Auschwitz commander Rudolf Höss, who happened to be under way from Vienna to Budapest and saw that those being marched were unable to work. Eichmann resumed the marches and told Kasztner that he of course did not want to jeopardize the Becher talks but needed more Budapest Jews, about 65,000–70,000, for work on the Austrian border. True, the Reich committed itself not to move more Jews, "but elderly and young Germans were digging fortifications, and where was the quo"? "The Americans want only to gain time, toward the anticipated victory." These comments by Eichmann of course, were true, and he was no fool. His strategy was based on some kind of belief in victory, as he told Kasztner that "Germany's crisis was over and Germany would win . . . [due to] new weapons. . . . Budapest would be lost, but not Vienna." If this was the reason, Jews working to save Vienna were important; only those who would lose the last hope of victory would be ready to use Jews for other purposes such as saving their own neck or capitulating to the Western Allies. Kasztner believed that the latter were now in charge and that the Final Solution was in principle over.

---

[19] See Yehuda Bauer, Yeshaiahu Yelinek, Livia Rothkirchen, John S. Conway, and others, *Leadership in Time of Distress: The "Working Group" in Slovakia 1942–1944*, (Kibbutz Dalia: Sifriat Poalim Publishing House, Foundation of Former Czechoslovak Citizens, 2001), pp. 95–97 (in Herbrew).

[20] Kasztner, "Bericht," pp. 156–157.

36

The "End" of the Final Solution – Budapest

The evidence that we can add to the existing literature in regard to Himmler's order to stop the Final Solution late in 1944 (as seemed to Kasztner at the time to have been the case thanks to Becher's "complete victory" described earlier) is a message sent by McClelland to the WRB and State Department on January 20, 1945, which first quoted "German press denials of any intention to exterminate inmates" of Auschwitz and Birkenau, following a strongly worded warning to Himmler personally, signed by Secretary of State Cordell Hull.[1] McClelland added to this that he was unable to confirm reports "originated in Polish circles in London" that the SS was instructed to kill all inmates of Jewish camps "who could not be evacuated in face of Allied advance." However, McClelland continued:

based on a great deal of fragmentary information collected during past several months regarding course of Nazi policy toward Jewish deportees in camps, and more particularly on very recent statements of two intelligent Jewish women who reached Switzerland during late December having spent three months in Auschwitz August through October 1944 ... I think it can be reliably stated that Nazis have abandoned extermination of Jews as a general policy, and certainly of those capable of working. On other hand they show tendency continue doing away on small scale with elderly people and children. (FDR Library WRB container 56, file Jewish refugees, Jan–June 1945, cable no. 416)

According to the same testimony, Jewish women from Warsaw, Radom, and Lodz were sent to Auschwitz and thence to Germany proper. The Warsaw part of this testimony could relate to women who had been sent to labor camps in Poland from the Warsaw ghetto before it was totally destroyed in 1943. Others, including Slovak and Hungarian women, were sent from Auschwitz to work in Germany, while in Auschwitz itself "there was little wanton brutality, no 'selection' of ill for extermination, and even some

[1] FDR Library WRB container 56, file Jewish refugees, Jan–June 1945, cable no. 416.

slight effort on part of camp authorities allow the ill to recover." This concurs with Himmler's later argument in his meeting with Norbert Masur, the representative of the World Jewish Congress in April 1945, in which he denied the Holocaust altogether. Hostage-taking and denial could be supplementary, and the policy in this regard might have been pursued by Himmler late in 1944 in the exchanges cited earlier between Becher and Kasztner and then between Musy, Schellenberg, and Himmler himself. The fact that the "Musy Train" carried 1,200 Jews from Theresienstadt, the ghetto in which "bevorzügte Juden" ("preferential Jews") were interned, when earlier most had been sent to Auschwitz to be killed instantly, and where the Jews had a sort of camp autonomy, indicates that Himmler did hope that some game of denial could be tried, which would have been impossible with inmates of any other camp.

However, the "end" of the Final Solution entailed various dimensions, many of them tragic. Jews marched from Auschwitz all the way to Germany for work, those who were Hungarian marched to Austria and Germany, out of whom many died under way or were rounded up by local Nazis and shot in the last months of the war, and those who were sent for work in south German camps and industrial complexes require a thorough study. In Bergen-Belsen, which since summer 1944 had become an enormous complex for inmates brought over from evacuated camps abroad and in Germany itself, as described by Alexandra Wenck, Camp Commander Joseph Krämer lost control over the horrible conditions in which even he was unable to function.[2]

Those Hungarians who were marched toward the Austrian border were mostly women and youngsters (many among the fit had been ordered to serve in Hungarian labor battalions) so that the marches brought about incredible suffering and many deaths without any value for the Germans. Thus, they were ordered stopped by Himmler upon the advice of SS officers such as former Auschwitz Commander Rudolf Höss and SS General Hans Jüttner, who happened to watch the marched on their way from Vienna to Budapest.

Another reason for Himmler's interest in the Budapest Jews may be reflected in the OKW/Chi intercept of a "Marton/Kasztner Plan."[3] According to this message, Dr. Ernst Marton, a Transylvanian Jewish leader who had served in the Rumanian Parliament and was then a refugee in Rumania, and Dr. Rezsö Kasztner, the "representative of the Jewish Agency

---

[2] See Wenck, "Der Menschenhandel des Dritten Reiches," pp. 250ff. See also Alexandra Wenck, *Zwischen Menschenhandel und "Endlösung": Das Konzentrationslager Bergen–Belsn* (Paderborn and München: Ferdinand Schöningh Verlag, 2000).

[3] OKW/Chi V.N. 1485/11.44 (USA) F., received November 22, 1944, decrypted November 27, from Katzki in Ankara via State Department to Pohle [sic] WRB, source: RG 457, Entry 1032, box 206.

in Budapest," suggested to the Rumanian government to exchange the surviving Jews in Hungary with the Germans who were left behind in Rumania
when it switched sides and joined the Allies in August. Thus, according to
Dr. Marton, the Jewish survivors would be given POW status, while Kasztner
added the Red Cross as an instrument for conducting the exchange and
added to this that the Germans were ready to consider it, provided that
the Rumanians would agree. As he understood the situation, the exchange
would depend also upon all of the Allies, the Soviets included. Kasztner indeed mentioned this plan in his postwar report[4] as if it was in fact limited to
Germans in north Transylvania, already occupied by the Soviets and incorporated back into Rumania, which the Rumanians made public and about
which he mobilized Kurt Becher and the ICRC representative in Budapest,
Friedrich Born, to discuss with higher German authorities. A similar idea
originated among the Hungarians, so far as I could trace it,[5] who were now
worried that the Rumanians and Soviets would occupy Transylvania, including the 200,000 Saxon (Transylvanian Germans) inhabitants in the region,
whose fate might have been coupled with that of the Budapest Jews. Having
thus acquired real trump cards, or so Kasztner thought, Becher advised him
on November 26 that Himmler ordered the end of the Final Solution. He further agreed to the exchange of Germans in Rumanian hands with Budapest
Jews, and Kasztner was supposed to discuss this with the Red Army's commanders in one of the front sectors close to Budapest held by the Waffen
SS.[6] The key to this promising endeavor seems to have been dependent on
the Soviets, who soon enough took over the Rumanian scene. More research
in former Soviet archives is required here to ascertain Stalin's stance (e.g.,
whether he cared at all about the Jews of Budapest). Possibly the Germans
did to the extent that many of the Budapest Jews became prey of the local
Hungarian Fascists in circumstances that allowed the Germans only limited
control over the beleaguered city.

Kurt Becher was advised that the Saly Mayer negotiations were hopelessly
stalled, upon which the whole deal with Himmler was supposed to depend. It
was indeed expected that the WRB would not deliver anything to Himmler,
but the timing, as Kasztner formulated it, was very bad and required his own
departure to the Swiss border. The Rumanian scheme was thus abandoned
(if it had entailed any promise at all) in favor of the priority given to the
stalled negotiations in Switzerland.

By now, the AJDC European representative, Dr. Josef Schwartz, and
Roswell McClelland, the WRB envoy, agreed on a "new line" of offering
the Germans five million dollars (U.S) through the Red Cross for "board

---

[4] Kasztner, "Bericht," pp. 130–131.
[5] Translation of Otto Komoly's Diary. See also the relevant quote in Bela Vago, "The Budapest
Jewry in Summer 1944," *Yad-Vashem Studies* 8 (1971), 87.
[6] Kasztner, "Bericht," p. 132.

and lodging" for Jews under German control. In fact, this was Kasztner's own proposal to save 30,000 Jews "incapable to work" to be interned in three German camps, which he had transmitted to Dr. Schwartz, among others, in June 1944, as we have seen.

As before, the administration in Washington authorized the pledge "solely in order that Saly Mayer may have something tangible with which to hold open the negotiations."

We have at our disposal a number of apprehended German messages that reached the Americans in December 1944 in which Swiss–German economic talks were reported in detail.[7] By themselves, these messages are interesting because they show Swiss dependence on German exports, German deals with other neutrals such as Sweden, and the growing Allied pressure felt keenly by the Swiss with regard to German transactions. Becher's negotiations were taking place amid serious problems that Germany was facing in Switzerland and could easily have been seen by the Allies as a Nazi way of breaking their economic blockade in its sensitive Swiss hole. Besides, they might have known about such deals from the intercepted or otherwise apprehended German traffic.

By now, the Russians were closing in on Budapest city, while the Hungarian Fascists were roaming the streets and killing Jews. This was the time when Raoul Wallenberg, Miklós Krausz, and Swiss diplomats protected and saved many Jews while the Soviet siege was completed and the city became a battlefield. The remaining Budapest Jews were liberated in February 1945.

By now, Becher was fully collaborating with Kasztner, as were Hermann Krumey and Dieter Wisliceny, Eichmann's aides, while Eichmann maneuvered between Hitler's uncompromising position and Himmler's experiments with Musy and Becher. Becher finally understood that there would be no Allied "quo" for the German "quid" with regard to Jews, while Himmler was ready to accept the sparing of Jewish lives without economic preconditions not before February 1945, but only later was he ready to act completely on his own. During fall 1944 and winter 1945, Schellenberg and Becher were operating parallel to each other.

In regard to Budapest city, where about 120,000 Jews were pushed into a ghetto, living under Arrow Cross (i.e., Hungarian Fascist) control and subjected to their atrocities, Becher was not operating alone, nor was even Eichmann. Hungary was indeed a sort of "dual kingdom" in which Foreign Minister Ribbentrop was represented through Edmund Veesenmayer, the so-called German diplomatic envoy, who worked closely with the Fascist Hungarians (he was also an SS General "honoris causa"). Ribbentrop also had his deciphering service, as we know, while at that stage the Americans

---

7 RG 226, Entry 123, box 2, Bern-SI-INT-14-26, folder Switzerland.

were able to read German diplomatic messages sent to him from Budapest and elsewhere thanks to Fritz Kolbe.[8]

Here we have an "Ultra" message of some importance.[9] This message, without date but probably from January 1945, tells us that the Swedish "Legationsskeretaer Wallenberg sich unter deutschem Schutz (Waffen SS – parentheses in original) gestellt habe"; that is, Wallenberg received the protection of the Waffen SS, and this may imply that his efforts to save Jews were included in that protection. The story remains unclear, because the commander of the Wehrmacht's 13th Panzer Division, General Gerhard Schmiedhuber, who was credited with the rescue of the Ghetto by some historians died during an abortive effort to break out of the besieged city. The city commander, SS Obergruppenführer Karl Pfeffer-Wildenbruch, survived, fell into Russian hands and claimed the credit to himself upon his release from a Russian POW camp in a private correspondence with Charles Lutz, the former Swiss Consul in Budapest.[10] Pfeffer, a professional police officer and later a Waffen SS General, never disclosed any further details, until his death in a car accident later on. His motives could have been varied between his pure military duties, which required full Hungarian mobilization rather than killing children, in face of the Soviet onslaught all the way to his fear of Russian revenge if made responsible to the massacre. Kaszroer, however, would have wanted Becher, nominally a Waffen SS Lieutenant Colonel by now, to bring about. Pfeffer-Wildenbruch's intervention, as he claimed after the war and was quoted by Bauer to this effect.[11]

Kasztner stuck now to Becher, who left Budapest for Vienna, dragging along with him a large booty of Hungarian state treasures and a small group of Jews, something like personal hostages, who were supposed to prepare lists of the monies given to him since his involvement in Hungary.

The changes in Himmler's attitude since autumn 1944 signified only a desire to spare Jewish lives for forced labor and as trump cards for economic

---

[8] See, for example, RG 226, Entry 123, box 2, Bern-SI-INT-14-26, in which is contained a whole collection of American diplomatic cables in regard to Hungary beginning in 1943 that were deciphered by the Germans and redeciphered or apprehended by the Americans late in 1944. Some OSS cables were deciphered as well, when sent via Harrison in Bern, as one can compare those in this "collection" to the originals in other OSS files.

[9] NA, RG 226, Entry 123, Bern-SI-INT-29-33, box 3, folder Hungary. The reading was either done in Bern or supplied by Fritz Kolbe to Allen Dulles in Bern or at the "Special Branch" of G-2 in Washington. It includes the original handwritten translation or otherwise received German version plus an English translation and a typed version thereof.

[10] Nachlass Pfeffer-Wildenbruch, Bundesarchiv, Militararchiv Freiburg/BN 370/1–11.

[11] This is how Bauer interprets a stage in Becher's interrogation by Kasztner at Nuremberg when Kasztner suddenly stopped the stenographer and discussed some matter in private with Becher (who did not seem to remember any intervention on his part as a "Waffen–SS" liaison to the local fighting units, as suggested by Kasztner). Regarding this and Bauer's description of Becher's role in regard to the fate of Budapest's Jews, see Bauer, *Jews for Sale?*, pp. 236–237.

and political purposes, by itself a legitimate option in Hitler's eyes. But when the end was approaching, the Führer hardly needed trump cards but just wanted to kill all the Jews if he could.

The final break between Himmler and Hitler occurred, according to Kasztner, early in April, several weeks before the latter was reported dead, but even then the story was complicated.[12] The complications need not be repeated here, but the general picture is that of the concentration camps being partially evacuated to other camps, of camps being handed over to the Allies in spite of Hitler's orders due to local conditions, Becher's (and possibly Schellenberg's) intervention, and Himmler's orders. There is no way to ascertain finally who was right when we read the contradictory ex post facto reports made by Schellenberg, Becher, and even Kasztner about this stage, which culminated with the meeting between Norbert Masur, the representative of the World Jewish Congress, and Heinrich Himmler.

Masur quoted Himmler as if the Reichsführer SS gave him a review of the "historical development of anti-Semitism in Europe and particularly the efforts of his party to remove the Jewish problem from the Reich."[13] That Reich was already divided into three large occupied areas and approaching its final doomsday. "He reminded Masur that he himself [Himmler] had pressed the policy of removing Jews from Germany without violence and that he in 1935 had formed an organization to foster the migration of Jews out of Germany." Himmler, of course, was talking about Hitler's forced emigration policy, blurring dates and facts when he vaguely remembered Eichmann's "Zentralestelle für jüdische Auswanderung" (i.e., the Gestapo's Central Office for Jewish Emigration), whose origins were in the latter's activity in Vienna after the Anschluss in 1938 rather than 1935. The line of thought, however, was to make the Allies partly responsible for the later fate of the Jews because they refused to go along with Hitler's forced emigration policy. This brought Himmler to his next point, the denial of the Holocaust itself, while speaking "with considerable length and bitterness of the extent to which the Allies had propagandized German atrocities. He mentioned specifically Poland and Russia. With respect to Poland, Himmler stated that atrocity stories were vicious propaganda since the crematoria were the only means … (to) cope with [a] rapidly spreading typhus epidemic." But Himmler had something specific in mind regarding Becher's recent appointment to save the inmates of the concentration camps in Germany itself. In defiance of the truth about the death camps outside Germany, he referred to something real when "he was particularly bitter concerning Allied propaganda during the past few days on the concentration camps at Bergen Belsen and Buchenwald."

---

[12] Kasztner, "Bericht," pp. 192–194.
[13] See report 1547 cabled by Herschel Johnson, U.S. Minister in Stockholm, to Secretary of State, April 25, 1945, in FDR Library WRB, container 70, document LFG-1441.

At least in the case of Bergen-Belsen, it does seem that Himmler ordered this camp, originally a "hostage camp," to be surrendered to the Allies without any further evacuations. Thus, Becher, Kasztner, and Krumey proceeded on April 10 to Berlin, and first the SS officers went to Eichmann's office to make sure that he would not interfere with their effort to save Bergen-Belsen.[14] They proceeded to the camp and helped surrender its inmates to the British without fighting. The place was crowded with thousands of Jews marched from the East, many ill and dying of hunger; there were several thousand "bevorzügte," but the scene was horrible – no food, no sanitary conditions. Even the ruthless camp commandant (Joseph Krämer) was unable to keep the inmates alive when he was ordered to; but he was, however, persuaded to leave the camp and all its surviving inmates to the approaching British intact, even if Himmler was careful enough to order Becher the next day to stay away from the act of surrender and leave it to the Wehrmacht authorities.[15]

Then the Kasztner–Becher mission left for Neuengamme concentration camp near Hamburg, which was subject to negotiations between Himmler and the Swedish Red Cross Chief, Count Bernadotte, through Schellenberg and later evacuated. Thus, the group returned to Berlin, where Becher learned that Buchenwald had fallen to the Americans, but many inmates had been evacuated to other camps such as Flössenburg and Dachau. The Becher–Kasztner group then split. Becher took upon himself Mauthausen and Flössenburg, while Kasztner, Krumey, Hunsche, and Wisliceny as well, all of them Eichmann's aides, proceeded to Theresienstadt, where they arrived on April 16. There they met Rolf Günther, Eichmann's closest deputy, and handed over to him Himmler's surrender order. On April 19, the Kasztner group returned to the Swiss border, waiting for Becher, before meeting McClelland, Mayer, and Schwalb. The latter were not interested, as Becher had nothing more to offer. This was the story, according to Kasztner, when Himmler met Masur on April 20, as described previously.

According to Masur's report, Himmler pointed out that Bergen-Belsen and Buchenwald and their inmates had been left intact for the Allies at his own command and that "all he was getting in return was Allied horror stories." Those "horror stories," some of which were filmed by Allied newsreel teams and shocked the world when hills of corpses were bulldozed aside to be buried by the British, were tragic–ironic in the sense that Bergen-Belsen had indeed once been a sort of a special camp for hostages, next to its "regular" functions, and both Bergen-Belsen and Buchenwald were used to absorb the marching columns of Jews who were being brought to Germany since late 1944. Many died at the hands of the SS guards on their way or were

[14] Kasztner, "Hebrew Bericht," 195.
[15] Ibid., 197.

treated brutally in the camp. The SS guards were not told anything about the return to the old hostage-trading tactics by Himmler. Shortly afterward, when the Allies were cutting Germany into pieces – when transportation collapsed thanks to better aerial bombing capabilities and the concentration on transportation targets – many among the poor "hostages" at Bergen-Belsen died of starvation, mistreatment, ill health, and cold. Some died of overeating, in their condition, when the Allies suddenly distributed food; they were literally the victims of victory.

In southern Germany, especially in the camps that had been built to create underground works for German aircraft production, such as the satellite camps of Dachau (Käufering and Mühldorf) into which Jews (mainly from Hungary) were brought back to Germany for the first time since the "Altreich" became "judenrein," conditions were horrible from the beginning.[16] The sick were shipped to Auschwitz to be gassed, at least until October 1944, and in April 1945, according to Edith Raim's sources, RSHA chief Ernst Kaltenbrunner ordered the liquidation of the Jewish inmates of Dachau and mainly of its satellite by aerial bombing or other methods, following Hitler's orders.[17] The resulting marching and transporting of the Jews from those camps toward Tyrol and other places in south Germany itself, which Raim ascribed to Kaltenbrunner's changed attitude, continued until the end of the war. Many died as a result of American warplane action, which strafed German railroads as a matter of routine.

Late in April 1945, Himmler and Schellenberg gave Masur information about the camps still held by the Nazis. Himmler then "gave only half a promise that there would be no further evacuation of Jews from camp to camp," probably because he had lost control anyway or wanted to maintain his bargaining power in this regard, but he did promise "free access to camps" by the Red Cross for delivery of food and medical supplies and that "no Jews would be shot." He however "emphasized in the strongest possible terms that no publicity should be given to the conference (with Masur) and that absolute secrecy must surround his liberation of any Jews." This seems to justify our arguments that he had broken with Hitler now, even if in his own way, but hardly beforehand. "He referred to them all as 'Poles' apparently mindful of his promise to Hitler that he would not release any more Jews."

Becher now outranked Eichmann and seemingly had the power to intervene with the commandants of the concentration camps to prevent the liquidation of Jewish inmates in the last moment of Hitler's Reich agony. Still, Hitler intervened and issued an order forbidding any release of Jews.

---

[16] See Edith Raim, "Die Dachauer KZ-Aussenkommandos Käufering und Mühldorf, Rüstungsbauten und Zwangsarbeit im letzten Kriegsjahr 1944/5," dissertation, University of Munich, 1991.

[17] Raim, "Die Dachauer KZ-Aussenkommandos," pp. 271 ff.

According to Rudolf Höss, the former Auschwitz commandant and by then deputy head of the concentration camp system, Hitler issued the order due to reports that the liberated Buchenwald inmates were plundering Weimar.[18] I doubt it, as his reasons remained "political" as usual – he would leave behind the legacy of the one who "fought" the Jews to the end.

When Schellenberg tried to push him again and again to openly break with Hitler, Himmler exploded and said, "Hitler has been furious for days that Buchenwald and Bergen Belsen were not evacuated a hundred percent." Schellenberg allegedly tried to free an American Air Force General named Vanamann, a POW, and have him fly to meet Roosevelt via Switzerland just before FDR died, combining an offer to treat U.S. POWs better and an offer by Himmler to negotiate with the Western powers. This crazy idea of course led to nothing, but now, on April 22, Himmler declared himself ready to meet Count Bernadotte of the Swedish Red Cross and request from him officially to carry the declaration of capitulation "in his name" – Himmler's – to the Western powers. The Count declined by saying that Himmler could write directly to General Eisenhower. Schellenberg responded that it would be impossible "should Hitler still be alive." He thus requested yet another meeting between Himmler and Bernadotte. The meeting took place in the Swedish Consulate at Lübeck by candlelight, thanks to an air attack, on April 23. Himmler said: "We Germans must declare ourselves as beaten by the Western Allies. That is what I request you, through the Swedish Government, to convey to General Eisenhower. . . . To the Russians it is impossible . . . to capitulate. We will continue to fight there until the Western Allied front has, so to speak, relieved the fighting German front [i.e., taken over from the Germans]." This idea to transform Germany's war into an West–East war was of course Himmler's last hope, with himself as Hitler's heir and a sort of ally of the Western Allies. Bernadotte agreed to pass the message and, as expected, Schellenberg received a negative response from the Allies on April 26 through the Swedish government. Himmler's very last hope was to use occupied Denmark and Norway, and whatever else he could master in Germany proper, as Hitler's official successor, but on May 1 he learned that the dying Führer made Admiral Karl Dönitz his heir. Schellenberg does not tell us about Himmler's removal by Hitler from all his offices and his declaration to be a traitor of the cause, but with this the Himmler drama practically ended but not necessarily the tragedy of Jewish inmates in southern Germany. The very large number of camps in and around Dachau, now hosting marched Jews from the north and others who were kept in labor camps around it, were supposed to be bombed by the Luftwaffe before the arrival of the Allies, but in fact many of these Jews were idly marched around

[18] IMT, Volume XI, p. 407.

or shipped by railcars toward Tyrol, shot by SS guards, and strafed by low-flying Allied fighter-bombers. Many died at this final stage.[19]

As far as Kasztner was concerned, he and Becher were supposed to reunite on April 20 to meet McClelland, Mayer, and Schwalb, but as we know the latter were no longer interested. On his way, driven in Becher's car, Kasztner sometimes even spoke to a group of bewildered Jews, in the middle of the dying Nazi Reich, descending from Becher's SS Mercedes in his high boots, about the glorious future waiting for them in Zion.

[19] See Raim, "Die Dachauer KZ-Aussenkommandos," and see also Georg Tessin (ed.), *Verbände und Truppen der deutschen Wehrmacht und Waffen-SS im Zweiten Weltkrieg 1939–1945* (Osnabrück: Biblio Verlag, 1996); Sechzenter Band, Christian Zweng (ed.), *Verzeichnis der Friedensgarnisonen 1932–1939 und Stationierungen im Kriege 1939–1945*, p. 3. Waffen SS; SS/Polizei, Teil 2 Wehrkreis vii–xiii, regarding the large numbers of "AL" (Arbeitslager für Juden) as "Aussenstellen" of Dachau Concentration Camp in late 1944–1945.

Epilogue

Self-Traps: The OSS and Kasztner at Nuremberg

The tragic irony of the Holocaust, that Jews were victims of politicized conspiracy theories, is to be sought in the politicization of the Holocaust itself among the victims and among their various kinsmen. One of the rescuers, Rezsö Kasztner, was actively involved in the Nuremberg War Crimes Trials, and this brought about his assassination. The OSS, too, at least in the person of Charles Dwork, tried to make the "Jewish case" therein a separate subject, but the prevalent refusal to allow the Jews a specific standing among Hitler's victims limited his role considerably. Kasztner trapped himself and was trapped by others of his own people as a part of the "rescue debate" that had already started during his rescue activities and became perhaps the best-known case afterward in relationship to the politicization of the debate by the Zionist Right, Left, and the ultraorthodox.

In fact, it was not just Kasztner who was trapped – and assassinated – due to his rescue efforts as compared to the enormous dimensions of the Holocaust in Hungary. In fact, a number of self-traps had been set by rescue activists for themselves, for the Zionists, and for the Allies ever since the Europa Plan negotiations by creating the impression that the Germans (or at least Heinrich Himmler) were ready to deal, and thus important rescue options may have been lost. Hence, the onus of the blame for failing to deal would fall on Labor Zionists who did not push the Allies to do so and on Allied shoulders. Yet, as discussed in the text, Himmler was not dealing but killing, except for some cases dictated to him by local conditions and the benefit expected from saving the lives of those very few whose lives served political purposes, labor needs, or economic gains, until almost the very end of the war.

Another self-trap was set by Fritz Laufer (perhaps one of the most important double agents of World War II, who might have even survived it to serve the Americans against the Russians, or vice versa) when as early as 1943 he suggested to rescue operative Samu Springmann, and later to Joel Brand, the "truck deal" to save Jews. Brand accepted it and brought it to the Allies and to the Zionists as "Eichmann's offer." In fact, it was Brand's own offer, agreed upon with Laufer, about which he had serious doubts from the beginning. Yet Brand argued then and later that his failure to return to Budapest with some Allied "quo" prompted the speed and the magnitude of the Holocaust in Hungary, nothing of which had anything to do with German intentions and Hungarian ferocity on the ground.

To this the "Dogwood" saga must be added, which combined a Jewish–Zionist grand design to topple Hitler, end the war, or at least detach Hungary from the Axis by collaborating with anti-Nazis such as Count von Moltke, with Abwehr and Gestapo/SD operatives, and double agents such as Laufer and agents such as Bandi Grosz. Another option was to deal with the enemy over Jewish lives, which seemed to have been endorsed by the Germans, leading to the Brand–Grosz mission. The "mission" became a cause célèbre of Jewish–Zionist collaboration with the Nazis in Allied eyes for years after its failure, while for his part Brand made it a cause célèbre of Zionist and Allied failure to save Jews in large numbers. As such, the case was politicized (i.e., it became a "conspiracy" related to the alleged power and control priorities of the Labor Zionists as described by their enemies until this very day, especially those who "rebelled" against the British under Menachem Begin's leadership or followed "Yair" Stern's legacy while the British were still fighting the Nazis in the first place), and the Nazis – not the British – murdered the European Jews and/or prevented their departure en masse from Europe. Hence, David Ben-Gurion, the Labor leader and Chairman of the Jewish Agency, neutralized the rebels during the "Great Season" of 1944. Shmuel Tamir, the attorney in Kasztner's trial in Israel, grew up on IZL/Stern myths.

The enormous damage inflicted on the Zionist cause due to the terror acts of Begin's IZL and the Stern gang during World War II, until the "Great Season" at least, accepted as common wisdom among most Zionists at the time, started to fade away when a Labor Zionist active in occupied Hungary, Reszo Kasztner, trapped himself during a court proceeding in Israel. He fell victim to a vendetta of one of the "Great Season's" victims, attorney Shmuel Tamir, powered by orthodox functionary Miklós Krausz's vendetta. After that, the IZL/Stern legacies, in spite of the historical differences between them, gained enormous ground among Zionists and non- Zionists and became a part of the legacy of the Holocaust, right or rather badly wrong.

Kasztner referred to Kurt Becher in various testimonies given to the Allies immediately after the war in a restrained and balanced fashion, but he gave him yet another affidavit in August 1947, while at Nuremberg as an aide to the American prosecution team, in which he declared him to have done "everything within the realm of his possibilities and position to save innocent human lives from the blind fury of killing of the Nazi leaders." Next to the legal battle at Nuremberg, in which he wanted to portray "Becher's option" as a valid alternative to the behavior of the Nazi defendants, Kasztner was

obviously interested in gathering as much credit as he could for Becher –
and hence for himself – for rescuing as many Jews as possible, including
those interned in Budapest's ghetto. Kasztner further wrote that "even if the
form and the basis of our negotiations may be highly objectionable, I did not
doubt for one moment the good intentions of Kurt Becher and in my opinion
he is deserving, when his case is judged by Allied or German authorities, of
the fullest possible consideration."[1] Kasztner went so far as to make "this
statement not only in my name, but also on behalf of the Jewish Agency and
the Jewish World Congress," without any authorization by them to do so,
and signed as if he were an official of the Jewish Agency in Geneva (which
he was not) and "Former Chairman of the Zionist Organization in Hungary
1943–1945" (which he was not but rather Otto Komoly's deputy). Becher
used these titles to inquire into the fate of the monies deposited in Switzerland
by one of his aides during the 1944–1945 negotiations in a letter sent by him
to a Zionist representative in Switzerland, which remained unanswered, as
this official was smart enough not to deal with an ex-SS colonel.[2]

For his part, Kasztner informed the Jewish Agency that the money was
supposed to be kept by Becher as a deposit and that he intervened to have
Becher released (on top of the affidavit that he had initially given about him
in May 1945). In fact, Becher gave the deposit – all of it or parts of it –
shortly after V-E day to the Hungarian Zionist leader Dr. Moshe Schweiger,
who was released by Becher from Mauthausen concentration camp thanks
to Kasztner's intervention on his behalf.[3] Schweiger was afraid to keep the
deposit in the hostile environment in which he found himself even after
liberation, and he handed the deposit over to American Intelligence unit
CIC 215. The records of CIC 215 were never released by the U.S. Army
and possibly were destroyed after the war. The deposit finally landed in a
blocked account in a Salzburg bank. Jewish Agency representatives recovered
the bank deposit later on, having gained the impression that they recovered
only a small part of the original deposit and that Becher – who later became
a very successful grain merchant in West Germany – had kept the rest.[4]

In the meantime, Kasztner settled in Israel, and after a visit to Nuremberg
as an American prosecution team member during which he tried to recover
the rest of the Becher deposit and issued the above-mentioned affidavit and

[1] Source in Braham 2, *The Politics of Genocide*, Volume II, p. 1019n.
[2] See Central Zionist Archive (CZA) file L 17/176, Becher Deposit, correspondence between
    Becher, following Kasztner's intervention, and Dr. Chaim Posner, Head of Jewish Agency
    Office in Geneva, through July 1948.
[3] Schweiger's affidavit in German, Geneva, October 21, 1945, Hagana Archive, Division 14,
    copies to: Shertok, Gruenbaum, Schind for Ben-Gurion; (Pinchas "Pino") Ginzburg was an
    immigration operative.
[4] See Arian report, CZA, file L17/70. The previous Prussian Police official Dr. Dagobert David
    Arian, now in Palestine, was empowered by the Jewish Agency to retrieve the deposit as if it
    represented the Hungarian Jews on Kasztner's behalf.

more of the same in Becher's and Krumey's favor, he started a political career in Israel. He was regarded as a prominent Hungarian Jewish leader, which he was not (he was a Transylvanian), was a candidate in the general elections to the Knesset, and finally assumed a relatively high position in a Labor-controlled Ministry.

In the early 1950s, Malkiel Gruenwald, a dubious Jerusalem figure of Hungarian background, started to spread rumors against Kasztner. This hotelier and former gossip and sex magazine reporter was an ardent member of Miklós Krausz's orthodox political party, and he inflated and spread Krausz's vendettas against Kasztner by means of mimeographed leaflets among the party's other members. The state, which was Kasztner's employer, decided to bring a libel suit against Gruenwald. The letter about Kasztner's effort in Becher's favor was found in the prosecution files given to Gruenwald's defense, thus prompting a disastrous cross examination about the Becher connection during Gruenwald's trial in which Kasztner denied that he had intervened in Becher's favor.

Caught red-handed as having perjured himself, the case was then transformed into "Kasztner's trial." The libel suit became the most important event in Israel's political life in the early 1950s and the source of the ongoing "rescue debate" among Jews and non-Jews of all colors elsewhere. Kasztner was declared by Benjamin Halevi, the sole District Court judge presiding, as the one "who sold his soul to the devil" by accepting the lives of the 1,684 Jews in the train group while allowing the rest of the Hungarian Jews to perish in Auschwitz without warning them and allowing them their choice to resist or flee, especially in the case of his hometown of Cluj, where he was given several hundred lives by Eichmann while the others were deported to Auschwitz. The Israeli Supreme Court finally overturned most of the verdict, arguing that Judge Halevi had accepted attorney Tamir's false argument that Kasztner and Eichmann were equal partners negotiating on equal footings, not including the affidavits given by Kasztner in Becher's favor. Yet right-wing extremists assassinated Kasztner before then. Ever since the verdict of Judge Halevi, the statement that Kasztner "sold his soul to the devil" remained in the memory of most people, who did not bother to read the long, learned exoneration passed by the majority of the Supreme Court as formulated by Chief Justice Shimon Agranat.[5]

However, at Nuremberg, Kasztner could have expected the Allies to leave Colonel Becher alone anyway because Becher's position and rank would hardly make him a worthy defendant, as the Allies indicted the few, not the many, at Nuremberg, unless he – Kasztner – had made him a major war criminal such as Edmund Veesenmayer, the Nazi High Commissioner in occupied Hungary and SS General, and others who prepared for or carried out the

---

[5] See a recent discussion in Pnina Lahav, *Judgment In Jerusalem: Chief Justice Simon Agranat and the Zionist Century* (Berkeley: University of California Press, 1997), pp. 121–144.

Holocaust in Hungary with the same zeal as Eichmann had done.[6] Becher maneuvered here as best he could and thus justified Kasztner's own strategy of trying to drive a wedge between him and Adolf Eichmann and Eichmann's superior, RSHA Chief Ernst Kaltenbrunner. The latter was hanged following the IMT proceedings thanks to Kasztner's own affidavit and Becher's and Wisliceny's testimonies. Moreover, giving Becher his due at Nuremberg was a part of the rescue strategy itself. Those who saved Jews should have been acknowledged; otherwise, one could not have expected them to have done it to begin with.

In Israel of the early 1950s and among the American readers of Ben Hecht's *Perfidy*, it could be argued that Kasztner saved a full SS colonel, Becher (who had been promoted to this rank to outrank Eichmann) from Allied gallows. In fact, even Edmund Veesenmayer, the Nazi High Commissioner in Hungary, who justified the "removal" of the Hungarian Jews due to security reasons even in his Nuremberg trial, escaped the gallows and received a prison term, which was commuted by the Clemency Board of the American Occupation authorities in 1951. Veesenmayer lived for twenty years after Kasztner's assassination. Kasztner's conduct in a foreign country during the hell of the Holocaust could not be explained within the rules of a libel suit when cross examined by a counsel who was one of the victims of the legacy of the "Great Season" and had sworn to get his head and blemish the Mapai Party.

Having discussed elsewhere[7] Kasztner's contribution to the first phase of the Nuremberg process, the Trials of the Major War Criminals at the International Military Tribunal (IMT), I shall broaden it to an extent in order to discuss in short the OSS's role at the IMT, especially that of its "Jewish Desk," as performed by Dr. Charles Irving Dwork as best he could, also using information received from Kasztner and other sources such as the huge collection of Gestapo records from Bucharest. Overshadowed as his role was by the prosecution's Court's charter and other considerations, this left Dwork bitter and disappointed,[8] as if the multiple trap had closed on him when the Holocaust was over.[9]

---

[6] See the Veesenmayer court proceedings, including Kasztner's testimony in the Nuremberg Trials Ministries Case, Court 4, Case 11, Nuremberg, 1949, pp. 2702–2750, 3617–3659, 7143–7158, 13062–13460.

[7] See my "Preparations for the Nuremberg Trials: The O.S.S., Charles Dwork, and the Holocaust, *Holocaust and Genocide Studies* 12, No. 2 (fall 1998), 257–281.

[8] For the description in the text of the preparations for the IMT, see in addition to my "Preparations for the Nuremberg Trials," my article "Israel Kasztner, O.S.S. and the 'Spearhead Theory' at Nuremberg," in Daniel Gutwein and Menachem Mautner (eds.), *Justice and History* (Jerusalem: Zalman Shazar Center for Israeli History, 1999), pp. 305–338 (in Hebrew).

[9] For a recent study of the road to the IMT, see Arieh J. Kochavi, *Prelude to Nuremberg: Allied War Crimes Policy and the Question of Punishment* (Chapel Hill and London: University of North Carolina Press, 1998).

Dwork's job since sometime in 1943 had been to collect evidence on Nazi war crimes toward the rather unclear target of bringing the Nazis to justice.

The internal American deliberations brought about a final decision, sponsored by Henry L. Stimson, the Secretary of War, to work toward an international military tribunal, fair as could be, in order to avoid other options such as British ideas of executing a small number of major war criminals without due trial. The number here was of great importance to the British, as one could hardly put 12 million members of the Nazi Party or even thousands of SS killers on trial effectively in their view, nor grant to the few who would be tried the privilege of a fair trial, which would be viewed by the Germans anyway as a "victor's trial." Thus, some kind of procedure to shortcut the regular proceedings was supported by Henry Morgenthau, Jr., the Jewish Secretary of the Treasury, combined as it was with his "plan" to transform Germany into an agrarian land. Stimson adopted the concept of a fair procedure for the war criminals as a part of his whole legal thinking while sharply rejecting the collective punishment against 70 million Germans. Meanwhile, in his department several officials were working on the legal base of the forthcoming trials. The most important among them in my view was Colonel Murray C. Barneys, who developed the concept of a "conspiracy" in order to prove that the Nazis had conspired since Hitler's ascendance to commit their future crimes, the Holocaust included. Hence, the accused in the ensuing international proceedings would have to be prosecuted for the regime's crimes since its inception. This ancient, essential legal concept may have been endorsed, knowingly or not, by the "intentionalist" school among the Holocaust historians following the IMT, which was after all the first and finally a rather impressive dealing with the Nazi war crimes even if the prosecution did not endorse Colonel Barneys's conspiracy concept fully. In fact, the "conspiracy" – due to Soviet reservations – was limited to the war itself and to related war crimes.

In April 1945, the U.S. Supreme Court Associate Justice Robert H. Jackson made a public speech in favor of international proceedings to try the Nazi criminals and was offered the job of Chief of Counsel, believing at first that he would represent the Allies as a whole, but he was ready then to represent the United States only. In May 1945, Jackson was appointed U.S. Chief of Counsel and immediately started to create the political and legal base among the Allies for the international military proceedings. Internally, he agreed with General William J. Donovan, the OSS Director, on cooperation between his staff, the Army's Judge Advocate General, and OSS.[10] Thus, Jackson's own staff was comprised of lawyers known to him plus Colonel Murray C. Barneys, appointed Executive Officer, and Lieutenant Colonel Benjamin Kaplan, a New York lawyer who during the war had been

[10] See NA, RG 226, Entry 190, box 720, folder 1360 – WASH-DIR-OFF-OP-266, War Crimes.

working on military procurement under Assistant Secretary of War John J. McCloy and others, and a Prosecution Review Board under Colonel Robert G. Storey, also an old acquaintance of Justice Jackson.[11] OSS R&A was entrusted with various articles of the draft indictment under R&A's head, William Langer, and his aide Carl Schorske. The analysis of the evidence was entrusted to Franz Neumann, the neo-Marxist author of the "spearhead theory" of the Holocaust and the Frankfurt School economist, who was soon to be joined by other members of R&A's Central European Section such as Otto Kirchheimer, Herbert Marcuse, and Dwork, too. While OSS was preparing for the trial, Dr. Jacob Robinson, a noted legal expert and historian representing the American Jewish Conference and the World Jewish Congress, met with Justice Jackson early in June 1945 in New York to discuss the "Jewish clause" in the indictment. Robinson tried his best to not only introduce a specific Jewish clause into the indictment but to anchor it to the conspiracy concept itself.[12] Robinson then placed Hitler on top of a pyramid that included Alfred Rosenberg, Joseph Goebbels, the Gauleiter, the Reich government, the high military staff, and the members of all the other agencies entrusted with the Holocaust. He added that "while they did not aim for immediate destruction of the Jews who were beyond their control, they directed their propaganda to poison the relationships between Jews and non-Jews so as to make their living together impossible." Thus, the leading officials of the German radio network and news agency were also added to Robinson's list. Justice Jackson "was interested to know how the statistical data of Jewish casualties were obtained." Robinson explained and was asked to submit the information later on to Justice Jackson's office. He added that the Jews were keen not to overstate their losses nor to seek revenge. Conscious of accusations that the Jews were avengers and used to overstating their cause, Robinson proceeded to supply evidence for the Nazi conspiracy by arguing that Nazi anti-Semitism was aimed at destroying not only the Jews but democracy itself, thus "universalizing" the Holocaust within its particular Jewish context: "We believe that a specific indictment for the crimes committed against our people will clear the atmosphere in Europe and make it easier for the survivors to reestablish themselves there." Yet the postwar logic of the multiple trap prevented a "specific Jewish indictment" precisely because it was supposed to be specific. If the Nazis were so successful in their

---

[11] Storey, whose initials PS ("Paris Storey" for his Review Board location in the French capital) became the common marking for the captured German records submitted to the IMT, was a Texas lawyer who served during the war as Colonel in the U.S. Army Air Corps doing legal and intelligence work. See Telford Taylor, *The Anatomy of the Nuremberg Trials: A Personal Memoir* (Boston: Little Brown, 1992). Taylor, who joined Jackson's staff in London in summer 1945, became Chief of Counsel in the subsequent trials. He did not think highly of Storey and of other lawyers in the "Jackson Group," except Benjamin Kaplan; see Taylor, *The Anatomy of the Nuremberg Trials*, p. 48.

[12] Duker/Dwork Papers, RG 200, box 9, folder 88.

anti-Semitic campaign, the Jewish case would be blurred among many other atrocities committed by the Nazis and *not* be given separate representation. Indeed, only "crimes against humanity," not "crimes against the Jews," were invoked at the IMT by the prosecution, as Justice Jackson explained already in this early stage of the preparations, also responding to Robinson's request for a specific Jewish representation by invoking the Roman term of "amicus curiae"[13] to legalize Jewish solidarity in the prosecution. With regard to a separate Jewish representation at the IMT, Jackson "indicated that the international military tribunal might not be well disposed towards such an idea. Furthermore, other groups might also ask for the same consideration, which would complicate matters." Also here the singling out of Jews, as they were singled out by the Nazis, did not contribute to their cause but had an adverse influence due to Nazi atrocities against others who were not singled out to the same extent. From Dwork's private papers, we learn that shortly after the Jackson–Robinson meeting Colonel Benjamin Kaplan and Franz Neumann left for London as members of an advance prosecution group while Kaplan maintained direct contact with Dwork for further information and substantiation of the indictment.[14] For his part, Dwork suggested to Kaplan to use the good services of Dr. Jacob Robinson as the head of the prosecution office in charge of translation and interpretation of the documentation to be submitted to the IMT in the four official languages to be used therein.[15] Obviously, Dwork wanted the "Jewish cause" to be represented in the prosecution team next to Franz Neumann, without success.

On August 17, Dwork wrote to Kaplan that he had received the Richter documentation from Bucharest – indeed to this day the only Gestapo operation outside Germany that fell into Allied hands intact at that stage. From a quick study of the 25,000 records (many were newspaper clips and the like), Dwork was convinced that he could prove that the responsibility for the deportation and murder of the Jews rested with a hierarchy on top of which stood Hitler and descended down to Himmler, further down to Gestapo chief Müller, and from him to Eichmann. Apart from some confusion about Müller's exact position, we can find here Kasztner's fingerprints as well due to his testimony given to WRB's representative Herbert Katzki in Switzerland in May 1945, which was forwarded to Dwork in full and included Kasztner's

---

[13] Representation through a recognized friend or relative in the court.

[14] Dwork personal papers, Dwork to Kaplan, August 17, mailed from room 4E869 in the Pentagon, secret.

[15] Robinson became deputy counsel and historical adviser ahead of and during Eichmann's trial in Jerusalem and later published a learned legal and historical response to Hannah Arendt's *Eichmann in Jerusalem*, in which he counted numerous legal and factual errors in her book. See Jacob Robinson, *And the Crooked Shall Be Made Straight: The Jews of Europe in the Face of the Holocaust in the Light of Historical Truth and the Eichmann Trial in Jerusalem and of the International Law* (Jerusalem: Bialik Foundation, 1963) (translated into the Hebrew, edited by the author).

views of the Final Solution and its perpetrators.[16] Dwork refrained from adopting Kasztner's argument that Eichmann's initiative was decisive in the execution of the Final Solution, a position that was later adopted by various historians as if the Holocaust was perpetrated to a large extent from the "bottom" and endorsed by Hitler from "above," but did repeat in his letter to Colonel Kaplan that "by the way, Eichmann was Himmler's brother-in-law" (a myth). Kasztner further elaborated on Eichmann's main guilt in his view, arguing that those deported to the death camps were killed by gas only upon Eichmann's written orders and that the camps' commanders did not have their own authority to put them to death. Kasztner further argued that the initial decision was made by Hitler simultaneously with or shortly following his decision to attack the Soviet Union. Kasztner added to Hitler two other personalities – the Grand Mufti of Jerusalem and Eichmann (in order of importance). He indeed was exposed through Eichmann himself to the Mufti's unsavory role in preventing rescue when he intervened to prevent the departure of a few Jews from Bialistok and Hungary to Palestine or anywhere else, while serving the Nazi cause by spreading anti-Western, Muslim propaganda and by raising Muslim volunteers for the Waffen SS, but here he introduced his political–Zionist motives in a historical report, adding that the initiative to murder the Jews came from Eichmann and ascended all the way up to Hitler via Müller, whose exact position he confused and also confused Dwork. Kasztner went on to describe the initial phases of the Holocaust. Until the end of 1942, as he was quoted, all the Jews were indiscriminately gassed in the various killing centers, including "Tremblinka" [sic]. However, at that time it was allegedly "decided" to allow the Jews capable of work to survive "as long as they could be supported."

The first statement was wrong, and the other one was obviously devised by Kasztner to justify his strategy of making the third parties ransom Jews as best he could, which developed into the Becher–Mayer negotiations, while he in fact tried also to make them support those who were incapable of work. Kasztner's free handling of the facts was very much a part of his character as an ambitious, activist Zionist politician, which gave him the power to face Eichmann but also contributed to his doom in his beloved Zion.

Having used Kasztner's testimony as best he could, Charles Dwork promised to send Colonel Kaplan copies of all of the key documents in the Gestapo office in Bucharest before suggesting any interpretation or comments on his part since missing technical support seriously hampered his work. On August 23, 1945, Dwork wrote a very polite letter to Franz Neumann in London advising him on the Gestapo files from Bucharest and emphasizing the Gestapo's role in the Final Solution, especially that of Eichmann and Müller, following Kasztner. Dwork asked for Neumann's opinion on this and previous reports written by him, including "the

---

[16] See note 17 in Chapter 35.

unavoidable criticism" of the senior neo-Marxist scholar,[17] but Neumann's response, if any, is not documented. Yet on September 7, 1945, Dwork commented (the document remaining unsigned) rather bitterly on an indictment draft pertaining to the Holocaust as formulated by "Washington" – very probably by Neumann's "Frankfurt School" colleagues at OSS R&A.[18] Dwork quoted the draft formulation to wit that "Jews constituted their school of experience" and added that this formulation was "basically wrong." In fact, he was dealing here with Neumann's "spearhead theory" in its postwar form.[19] Dwork invoked historical facts, among them the argument that the Nazis had started their campaign against their political adversaries, not against the Jews as a whole. He further differentiated between the concentration camps, whose inmates were political prisoners and others, and the death camps, whose victims were Jews and Gypsies. Dwork's fingerprints here are clearly discernable when the misspelled name of the death camp at "Tremblinka" (Treblinka) is repeated here following Kasztner's early testimony quoted earlier and the remark "see our file on Eichmann." Accordingly, Dwork rejected the argument that the death camps were subordinated to the Nazi occupation authorities in Poland but maintained that they were subordinated to the Gestapo and Eichmann in Berlin as evidence for the supreme and exclusive interest of the Third Reich in destroying the Jews. By itself this argument was factually wrong, and yet in essence it was correct by placing the Holocaust as a central particular result of Nazi ideology and politics. Dwork, however, did not seem to believe that he had a chance against Neumann and his colleagues and refused to join him in London. He preferred to stay in Washington, offering Neumann and Kaplan help in producing a "complete and detailed" indictment pertaining to the Holocaust, but London did not respond to this offer nor did it ask for the Rumanian documentation.

At that stage, the prosecution team was ready at least to indict RSHA chief Ernst Kaltenbrunner, one among the two (the other was the anti-Semitic publisher Julius Streicher) selected among the two dozen defendants to stand trial at Nuremberg in direct connection with the Holocaust. On September 13, Kaplan asked Dwork for information on Kaltenbrunner, believing that the man was of "supreme importance" and participated in the "meeting in which the decision was made to exterminate all the Jews of Europe,"

---

[17] Dwork personal papers.

[18] Comments on the Washington Draft, War Crimes, Duker/Dwork Papers, NA, RG 200, box 10, No. 99.

[19] In addition to the above-mentioned literature pertaining to the "Spearhead Theory," see Barry M. Katz's previous publications *Foreign Intelligence: Research and Analysis in the Office of Strategic Services, 1942–1945* (Cambridge, MA, and London: Harvard University Press, 1989) and "The Criticism of Arms: The Frankfurt School Goes to War," *Journal of Modern History* 59 (1989), 439–478. See also Marquardt-Bigman, "Amerikanische Geheimdienstanalysen des nationalsozialistischen Deutschlands."

and he was the one who suggested the use of gas to murder them.[20] The "Wannsee Protocol," obviously and wrongly referred to by Kaplan, was only later found in the files of the German Foreign Ministry by the American prosecutor, Dr. Robert Kempner. Although Dwork had only some press story on it, having received a relevant letter in the meantime from a Jewish friend in London, he added that the investigation of the senior SS and Gestapo officers and the other leaders of the Third Reich now in the hands of the Americans has not "properly" exposed the crimes committed. He thus referred Colonel Kaplan to one of his own main sources on the Holocaust: "More information on Kaltenbrunner could be obtained from Dr. Joel [Rezsö] Kasztner" (Dwork obviously confused his name with Joel Brand's), who among other things was an intermediary between the Gestapo and the Allies in "barter deals" aimed at rescuing the "Jews of the Balkans."

On October 1, 1945, Colonel Kaplan wrote to Dr. Dwork [21] that "Dr. Joel [Rezsö] Kasztner was in London several weeks ago and he gave us a complete statement of his activities in Hungary and his dealings with the Gestapo in his attempts to save Hungarian Jewry from extinction." Dwork, however, seemed to have expected the IMT to be a rather disappointing affair from the point of view of Jewish rights and Jewish interest as the only victim singled out for murder. Soon enough, he resigned and returned to civilian life, keeping with him a variety of records pertaining to his time at OSS. Colonel Barneys, too, was pushed aside by more powerful and practical people among Justice Jackson's prosecution team. But also Franz Neumann and the whole OSS group left Nuremberg before the IMT even started. The reasons could have been methodological since General Donovan was interested in oral testimonies while Jackson wanted to support the indictment by using captured documents.[22] Yet the main reason may have been a personal and political clash between two strong-willed leaders, a reality that existed all the way through World War II at various levels of the giant machines that ran it, and thus my interest in them seems to be justified next to, and sometimes even on top of, the political level dealt with by other scholars. According to William Casey, at the time a young OSS-SI officer, the political aspect of Donovan's behavior may have been related to the whole purpose of the Nuremberg trials and the future of Germany, inspired by early "cold warriors." Hence William Casey, a future CIA Director and an early cold

---

[20] Kaplan to Dwork, September 13, 1945, NA, RG 226, Entry 191, box 1, No. 12.

[21] NA, RG 226, Entry 191, box 1, No. 12.

[22] See Whitney R. Harris, "Justice Jackson at Nuremberg," *The International Lawyer* 20, No. 3 (1986), 867–896, and see also Whitney R. Harris, *Tyranny on Trial: The Evidence at Nuremberg* (Dallas: Southern Methodist University Press, 1954, fourth printing, 1970) and also my interview with Mr. Harris, who was Jackson's aide at Nuremberg, Los Angeles, May 30, 1987.

warrior, described Donovan's attitude toward his own role at Nuremberg thus:[23]

I remember vividly having dinner one evening at Claridge's with General Donovan, Justice Jackson, Ed Pauley, who had just been appointed Reparations Commissioner, and Isidor Lubin, Chief of the Bureau of Statistics, who had signed on as Pauley's deputy. Lubin [an early Jewish New Dealer – S.A.] spoke at great length and with considerable vehemence about why it was important to convict the Hitler Jugend and other organizations en masse so that Russian demands for reparations could be satisfied by German slave labor. Both Donovan and I were appalled by this acceptance of the concept of collective guilt. Donovan was soon disillusioned with the Nuremberg trials and quit." (William Casey, *The Secret War Against Hitler*, p. 218)

Indeed the concept of convicting Nazi organizations such as the Nazi party, the SS, and the Gestapo, so that their members would have to prove that they were not guilty, had already been accepted by Justice Jackson in his conversation with Dr. Robinson in Washington, yet in reality the prosecution had to actively prove their particular guilt at Nuremberg. Also the issue of Jewish vengeance – here linked to Soviet vengeance – created various early McCarthyan episodes that go beyond the scope of this book, such as the removal of Colonel William Bernstein – the officer in charge of looted Nazi assets – from his position in occupied Germany. His papers, stored at the Harry S. Truman Library in Independence, Missouri, wait for an interested historian.

At any rate, the final outcome at Nuremberg was more balanced than expected by Dwork and Robinson. Not only did Robert Jackson refer to the "Jewish people" as such in his opening address (elsewhere he called them a "race"), but the Holocaust imposed itself on the proceedings in a way that silenced Hermann Göring himself after a successful abuse of the freedom of speech allowed him by the presiding judge, Lord Lawrence.[24]

Moreover, the American prosecution, perhaps against William Casey's and British advice, proceeded to the so-called "subsequent trials" at Nuremberg – a lengthy, difficult, and finally disappointing series of trials against various leading members of the Nazi economy, armed forces, government, and several SS agencies. The British, who refused to allow the judiciary a prolonged role in what they believed was basically the political problem of the future of a democratic Germany, summarily executed some Nazi criminals in their occupation zone and turned to other matters.

[23] See William Casey, *The Secret War against Hitler* (Washington, DC: Regnery Gateway, 1988), p. 218.
[24] See Harris, "Justice Jackson at Nuremberg," pp. 886–889.

Malkiel Gruenwald as CID Informant

As described previously, Kasztner's activities at Nuremberg, and their complexity, could not be fully nor accurately described during the State of Israel's initial libel suit against Malkiel Gruenwald, which was in fact transformed by Shmuel Tamir, a politically inspired attorney, with the support of some media,[25] into "Kasztner's trial," resulting in Kasztner's violent death. Gruenwald became a hero, at least to Hollywood's screenwriter Ben Hecht and to many American Jews who grew up reading his book, entitled *Perfidy*. The initial verdict, coined in such easy-to-remember terms as if Kasztner "sold his soul to the devil" by negotiating the lives of 1,684 Jewish survivors, overshadowed the long and complicated verdict of the majority of the Israeli Supreme Court, which exonerated Kasztner posthumously.

Years later, the Israeli Home Intelligence released Gruenwald's personal file dating back to his activities in British Palestine.[26] According to the file, Gruenwald had behind him a long criminal career in Hungary and in independent Austria, which assumed political color later on when he denounced and threatened orthodox Jewish leaders who generated his wrath, and then he denounced Labor Zionist activists to the Austrian Fascist government. Later, he was involved in misleading refugees to count on his support, in exchange for their money, on their way to Palestine.

Finally, when he escaped to British Palestine in the late 1930s, he became a sort of informant of British Police Intelligence (CID), denouncing Hitler's refugees who were desperately trying to reach Palestine by ship (S.S. "Patria") during the war as "Nazi spies." As a loyal British subject, Gruenwald asked the mandatory authorities to refuse the "Patria" passengers entry because their voyage was organized by the Jewish Agency, whose office in Vienna was supposedly serving the Nazis. Indeed, one of the British arguments in blocking Jewish immigration to the only Jewish "National Home" at the time was that the Gestapo might use the refugees as Nazi spies. Another ship, the S.S. "Struma," was not allowed to proceed to Palestine due to the spy argument, with the net result, as Kushner concluded, the sad, and at the time much publicized, story that the vessel sank in the Black Sea, leaving only one survivor.

---

[25] See Weitz, *The Man Who Was Murdered Twice*, mainly pp. 101–104, about the role of journalist Uri Avneri in exploiting the Kasztner case for political purposes, and further in his text about the role of Ma'ariv, a daily mass-circulated paper, edited at the time by veteran NZO/IZL members or sympathizers.

[26] The file was compiled by the so-called Shai, the Hagana's (the Zionist mainstream underground army) counterintelligence organ, Division 112, Hagana Archive. Most of the file's contents were published in 1985 by Isser Harel, the former Head of the Israeli Security Services, in his *The Truth about the Kaesztner Murder* (Jerusalem: Edanim Publishers, Yediot Aharonot Edition, 1985) (in Hebrew), yet Harel did not disclose his sources.

Notes on Sources

I primarily aimed at intelligence records in which I searched for Nazi documents hereto unknown (Gestapo/SD being not just the machine of destruction but agencies gathering intelligence on the victims, the Allies, and rescue efforts undertaken to get in touch with and even to save the victims). My assumption was that intelligence (divided into information gathering and security of one's own intelligence and otherwise vital interest) was, and still is, the least-researched aspect of World War II and the prewar years, while the diplomatic and the related internal deliberations of the British Foreign Office and the War Cabinet or the American State Department records were studied by other scholars.

Intelligence gathered by the Nazis and by both Western Allies, whose cooperation in this regard pertained not just to rescue during the Holocaust, had to be undertaken in secret and thus became obviously a target for intelligence agencies among the Germans and the Allies. Intelligence, and mainly decrypts of German radio traffic, could tell us more on the Holocaust itself, as for example was the case in Italy after the fall of Mussolini, where we can follow the role of the highest SS echelons in Berlin to enforce the deportation of Jews amid a chaotic situation in Italy at first and then all the way to Auschwitz using decrypted SS radio traffic intercepted by the British and given to the Americans. Other British decrypts of SS radio traffic could tell us more on the Holocaust in other countries, as they are being released now into the custody of the Public Record Office (PRO) at Kew, Surrey.

BBC 4, whose researcher David List, working for producer Detlef Siebert, had conducted a thorough study in the Public Record Office toward a documentary entitled *Hitler and Himmler* (of which I was one of the consultants), generously provided me with the copies of the British Intelligence records pertaining to rescue endeavors of Jews allegedly authorized by Heinrich Himmler and the related investigations by the relevant British Intelligence agencies, including those pertaining to Zionist rescue activities.

The above-mentioned British decrypts were known as ISOS – Intelligence Service Oliver Strachey – in honor of the Section head of the code-breaking unit at Bletchley Park (which was responsible to the head of SIS, also known as MI6) and since December 1940 had included the Abwehr's hand cipher, but later on also SD (Himmler's Sicherheitsdienst) messages contained in a subseries entitled ISOSICLE. The British in addition to the Rome decrypts gave more ISOSICLE to OSS, but their handling may have been related to the so-called "security-service type" of these decrypts and hence they were not part of the diplomatic and military exchange between the two countries, as National Security Agency (NSA) historian Robert Hanyok kindly explained to me. Also the U.S./U.K. intelligence exchange agreement of July 1943 was not retroactive. Stored at the U.S. National Archives, the Rome ISOSICLE that did reach the Americans and a few others were discussed earlier in connection with the rescue endeavors in the Balkans.

On the other hand, some information had been available previously about German intercepts of Allied radio traffic. But when we study those decrypts captured by the Americans after the war, stored as they are at the U.S. National Archives, we need first to consult the related American postwar study on them available at the National Cryptologic Museum at Fort Meade, Maryland.

This nine-volume study of "European Axis Intelligence" as revealed by TICOM, the so-called "Target Intelligence Committee," which was formed in October 1944 and acted under the authority and on behalf of the Chairman, London SIGINT (Signal Intelligence) Board (British), the Chief of Staff, European Theater, U.S. Army, and the Commander-in-Chief, United States Fleet, was prepared under the direction of the chief of the Army Security Agency submitted on May 1, 1946, and declassified rather recently thanks to the efforts of historian David Alvarez. This material shows that the Germans had broken the American high-grade diplomatic cipher known as the strip system 02 sometime in 1943 (having broken the low-grade code systems "gray" and "brown" previously). Thus, we have at our disposal decrypted messages from Washington to Moscow and vice versa, Ankara to Washington, Bern to Washington, and others, including intercepts up until late 1944 dealing with or directly sent by the American agency created by President Roosevelt in January 1944 to save Jews. Then the State Department shifted over to cipher machines, as Professor Alvarez told me.

The evaluation offered by the TICOM study of the value that the Germans derived from these decrypts, albeit formulated as "not accurately known," tended to minimize it by arguing that the strip systems were read too late in the war to be of any great value. Yet according to the same report, which was based also on interviews with the German personnel of the Supreme Command code-breaking section (OKW/Chi), its decrypts reached Hitler via the Chief of Operations (Jodl) and the Chief of the OKW, the Supreme

Command of the German Armed Forces (Keitel), and he did read some. Moreover, from studying the original German OKW/ Chi decrypts at the U.S. National Archives, it seems that many were read almost in real time. This was true with regard to the War Refugee Board's traffic, so the Germans knew what was intended by the Agency's officials concerning rescue in general and specifically in Rumania and Hungary, who personally was involved in this, what were the connections between the field workers and Jewish organizations in America, plus information pertaining to rescue gathered by the Germans from other sources, from censorship, from couriers, and other means used by the rescuers during both the planning and implementation of rescue efforts. Other intelligence reports made by Allied agencies reflect at least views and even actions taken or recommended by such bureaucracies concerning Jews, rescue of Jews, and Palestine. It should be noted that the Americans had basically two intelligence organizations – to make a very complicated story simpler, the Army's and Navy's – under their commanding officers and assistants in charge of intelligence, and OSS, which was under the Joint Chief's supervision.

According to the official *History of U.S. Communications Intelligence during World War II: Policy and Administration*, authored by Robert Louis Benson (Center for Cryptologic History, Series IV, World War II, Vol. 8, National Security Agency, Central Security Service, Washington, D.C., 1997), and David Alvarez's *Secret Messages, Codebreaking and American Diplomacy 1930–1945* (University of Kansas Press, Lawrence, 2000), the American Signal Intelligence Service (SIS – later SSS and still later SSA), born in early 1929, was expanded rapidly before Pearl Harbor and especially afterward. Having solved the high-grade Japanese diplomatic code, the expanded operation moved to Arlington Hall station later on. American SIS-SSS code breakers remained highly successful with regard to Japanese ciphers, and thanks to a growing cooperation with British MI6, formalized in May 1943, G-2's "Special Branch" had access to British decrypts of high-grade German military and diplomatic messages on top of previously agreed cooperation between MI6 and U.S. Army Intelligence. "Special Branch" created out of the raw decrypts known as "Ultra" the so-called "Magic Diplomatic Summary," which made it more user-friendly, and distributed it within and outside the War Department. Hence, we could follow "Ultra" decrypts in addition to reports made by British Intelligence agencies as the source of G-2 reports and activities beginning in late 1943 at least and British-originated decrypts sent by "Special Branch" all the way to the White House as part of the so-called "Collection of Multinational Diplomatic Translations of White House Interest," which at least could give us an idea of what seemed to be of interest to people in the White House at a given point in time. OSS, on the other hand, was supposed to be barred by G-2 from receiving any decrypts at all due to a personal and bureaucratic rivalry between Generals Donovan and Strong, the respective service chiefs. But OSS succeeded in circumventing this rule and did receive Abwehr, SD, and German Police decrypts from the British, some of which were cited earlier. Thus, a special relationship emerged between British MI6 and OSS-X-2 (counterintelligence) that culminated in the inquiries about the rescue endeavor referred to by the Americans as the "Gestapo Deal."

A story by itself is source "Boston," or the German diplomatic service employee Fritz Kolbe, who started to supply OSS with first-rate intelligence from Nazi Foreign Office sources and their contacts abroad by August 1943. In fact, it took quite some time until Colonel McCormack of G-2's "Special Branch" was ready to accept Kolbe's messages as bona fide intelligence, and the procedure of translating and disseminating them, according to NARA's historian and archivist, Dr. Greg Bradsher, was long and complicated. Yet within the period covered by my research cited earlier, they were regarded as reliable information of immediate practical ramifications pertaining to Jews and rescue, even if Kolbe was never told to concentrate on Jewish matters. Finally, Kolbe's reports were incorporated into "Ultra," so we may find them in different record groups (RG) stored in the U.S. National Archives. Known to historians for several years, Kolbe's complete "Boston series" plus location aids are now available at the National Archives, and I used them as a source for the Americans to corroborate Holocaust and rescue-related information on the German side.

Thus, the bulk of my documentation came from the U.S. National Archives, abbreviated NARA (National Archives and Records Administration). The reader may be advised to use the most recent finding aid *Holocaust-Era Assets* by Dr. Greg Bradsher (NARA, Washington, D.C., 1999), to get acquainted with the record groups and some detailed contents thereof. I have used captured German records, Allied intelligence on the Holocaust and on Palestine, related American agency records, and inner and inter-Allied deliberations on Jews and the Holocaust in addition to my work at the FDR Presidential Archive, which was thoroughly combed by other historians as well.

My primary source collection from the U.S. National Archives is divided into the following main groups: Record Group (RG) 226 and RG 200, Office of Strategic Services (OSS), and the Duker/Dwork collection. Dr. Charles Dwork was in charge of collecting data on war crimes against Jews beginning in 1943 and later served also as Jewish Affairs Desk Officer at OSS R&A. Dr. Abraham Duker, who served as Polish Desk Officer at OSS FNB (Foreign Nationalities Bureau) and later also assisted Dwork in preparing the indictment pertaining to Jews in the Nuremberg International War Crimes Trial for a short while, received official documents taken by Dwork upon his release from active service and kept them in his custody until the late 1980s. He donated them to Tel-Aviv University, but finally they were returned and are now open to research with the other sources mentioned at the U.S. National Archives located in College Park, Maryland.

During his service, Dwork had access to the records of Gustav Richter, the Gestapo representative in Bucharest, the only complete series of such SS documents. Dwork intended to use them at the Trial of the Major War Criminals at Nuremberg. Other NARA records, specifically microfilmed German records of the Reichsfuehrer SS and the Chief of the German Police, put under the title T-175, into which the Richter documentation was incorporated, were used in addition to the intelligence records. On top of this, the late Dr. Dwork kept some OSS and other related records in his Manhattan home. His widow, Mrs. Shirley Dwork, kindly made them available to me, and they were used under the title Dwork/ P.

Much of RG 226 has been opened to research since 1985, but more, including hereto withdrawn files or parts withdrawn from within a larger document, is being released under the Nazi War Crimes Disclosure Act passed by Congress and implemented during President Bill Clinton's second term. Several important records released in 1999, 2000, 2001, and early 2002 were used here thanks to this Act. Several "waves" of declassification of OSS records, including British-originated ones, helped me a great deal, but I must let the interested reader know that not all of the OSS records had been released when I finished writing this book.

Finally, I have used NARA's Record Group 457, Records of the National Security Agency (or rather of its predecessors), which contains a number of important sections. One of these is known as the Historic Cryptographic Collection (HCC), pre–World War I through World War II. Here we may find in Entry 1032, HCC, folder 1019, "German Decrypts of U.S Diplomatic Messages," or OKW/Chi and a "Collection of Multinational Diplomatic Translations of White House Interest."

Primary Zionist sources such as relevant files surveyed at the Central Zionist Archive in Jerusalem, mainly those collected in Record Group S/25, which for the most part have been available for several decades, were used or quoted by using other scholars who worked primarily on Zionist archives. To this were added documents pertaining to the Holocaust in Hungary, mainly correspondence with the Zionist Rescue Committee in Hungary, plus British Intelligence reports on the Yishuv and its various organizations, the Hagana's own reports on the activities of the British and of the Revisionist movement (the "Irgun," or IZL, and the "Stern Gang," or LEHI) in the Hagana Archive, Tel-Aviv, heretofore almost completely new to scholarship and taken from Record Divisions or Record Groups 14, 47, 80, and 112 in the Hagana Archive.

British sources held at the Public Record Office were quoted in their specific context or indirectly by using other scholars' works. Among the British sources, I have used Record Group 47, CID, at the Hagana Archive in Tel-Aviv. The Criminal Investigation Department of the Palestine Police under Arthur F. Giles was probably the "most effective intelligence organization" in British Palestine during World War II, as described by British and Israeli scholars. I have further used British Intelligence records drawn by their Middle East Center in Cairo during World War II, such as SIME (Security Intelligence, Middle East), under Brigadier Raymond Maunsell, and PICME (Political Intelligence, ME), under Brigadiers Clayton and Quilliam, drawn from the PRO and NARA, in addition to Foreign Office (FO) records.

I was also assisted by the Bundesarchiv-Militärarchiv, Freiburg in Breisgau, regarding the German order of the battle in Hungary and used other German primary sources such as the recently published series *Hitler: Reden, Schriften, Anordnungen*, published and annotated by Clemens Vollnhals, München, New York, London, Paris, 1992–1994 (so far seventeen volumes), and the *Kriegstagebuch des Oberkommandos der Wehrmacht*, (nine volumes), published by Percy Ernst Schramm, Bonn, no publication date. Schramm was the official historian of the German Army, and he created an editorial board, adding comments and timetables attached to it.

Hitler's *Monologe im Führerhauptquartier*, 1980 edition, Hamburg, and the previous English translations of Hitler's so-called "Table Talks" were also used when necessary. Finally, I have used the most extensive German study edited by the Militärgeschitliches Forschungsamt at Potsdam, entitled *Germany and the Second World War*, especially volume IV, *The Attack on the Soviet Union*, in English translation, Clarendon Press, Oxford, 1998.

Archives Used

Berlin Document Center (also copies in NARA)
Budesarchiv, Koblenz
Bundesarchiv-Miltarärchiv, Freiburg, Breisgau
Central Zionist Archive, Jerusalem
Edward R. Stettinius Papers, University of Virginia
Eichmann Trial, Jerusalem, Prosecution Collection T/37, vol. II
Franklin Delano Roosevelt Memorial Library, Hyde Park, New York
Hagana Archive, Tel-Aviv
Israel Kasztner's Personal Archive, courtesy of Mr. Dov Dinur, Haifa
Jabotinsky Archive, Tel-Aviv
Library of Congress, Washington, D.C.
Dr. Charles I. Dwork, personal papers, courtesy of Mrs. Shirley Dwork
Public Record Office, Kew, Surrey
U.S. National Archives, College Park, Maryland

Interviews and Correspondence

Bar-Yosef, Prof. Rivka
Berman, Yitzhak
Best, Dr. Werner
Brand, Mrs. Hansi

Dallek, Prof. Robert
Duker, Dr. Abraham
Dwork, Mrs. Shirley
Elath (Epstein), Eliahu
Glidden, Harold
Goldberg, Arthur J.
Hadari, Prof. Ze'ev "Venia"
Harris, Whitney R.
Hurewitz, Prof. J. C.
Kempner, Dr. Robert M. W.
Krausz, Moshe
Rivlin, Gershon
Schorske, Prof. Carl
Schwalb, Nathan
Speer, Albert
Springmann, Samuel (Samu)
Zuckerman, Lord Solly

Selected Bibliography

The relative advantage, and disadvantage, of this research compared to others is the use of new primary sources in various languages and of research published before in Hebrew. The non-Hebrew reader may gain herewith an idea of what is available in Hebrew and at least be informed which title is available in Hebrew or used by me in Hebrew translation. Not all titles mentioned in the Bibliography were cited in the text, but they appear here for the benefit of those who wish to use them for further research.

Published Records Collections and Related Guides

A Consolidated File of Interrogations of Hermann Göring, Washington, DC: U.S. Library of Congress, John Toland Papers. Container 12, # ED 100/288, no date.

Akten zur deutschen auswärtigen Politik, 1918–1945, Aus dem Archiv des deutschen Auswärtigen Amtes, Serie D, 1937–1941, 13 volumes. Baden Baden: Imprimerie Nationale, 1950–1964.

Akten zur deutschen auswärtigen Politik, 1918–1945, Aus dem Archiv des deutschen Auswärtigen Amtes, Serie E, 1942–1945, eight volumes. Göttingen: Vandenhoeck & Ruprecht, 1969–1979.

Ancel, Jan (ed.). *Documents Concerning the Fate of Romanian Jewry during the Holocaust*, 12 volumes. New York: Beate Klarsfeld Foundation, 1987.

Bradsher, Greg (ed.). *Holocaust Era Assets*. College Park, MD: United States National Archives and Records Administration, 1996.

Documents on German Foreign Policy, 1918–1945, Series D (1937–1945), vols. 8–13. Washington, DC: U.S. Government Printing Office, 1949–1953.

Domarus, Max (ed.) *Hitler: Reden und Proklamationen 1932–1945*, vols. I–II. Würzburg: Edition Schmidt, 1962–1963.

Edward R. Stettinius Papers, University of Virginia.

European Axis Intelligence, nine volumes, as revealed by TICOM (Target Intelligence Committee), prepared under the direction of the Chief of the Army Security Agency, May 1, 1946, available at the NSA's Decrypts Museum, Fort Meade, MD.

Field, Henry. *"M" Project for F.D.R. – Studies on Migration and Settlement*. Ann Arbor, MI: Edwards Brothers, 1962 (lithograph).

Foreign Relations of the United States, volumes covering years 1939–1945. Washington, DC: U.S. Government Printing Office, 1955–1970.

Guides to German Records Microfilmed at Alexandria, VA, No. 81: Records of the Reich Leader of the SS and Chief of the German Police, Part IV. Washington, DC: National Archives and Records Service, General Services Administration, 1982.

Heiber, Helmut, and David M. Glantz (eds.). *Hitler and His Generals, Military Conferences 1942–1945*. New York: Enigma Books, 2003.

Hillgruber, Andreas (ed.). *Staatsmänner und Diplomaten bei Hitler, vertrauliche Aufzeichnungen über Unterredungen mit Vertretern des Auslands*, two volumes. Frankfurt: Bernard und Graefe Verlag, 1967.

Hitler: Reden, Schriften, Anordnungen, 17 volumes. München, New York, London, Paris: Clemens Vollnhals, Institut für Zeitgeschichte, 1992–2003.

Hitler's Secret Conversations, 1941–1944. New York: Farrar, Straus and Young, 1953.

Jochmann, Werner (ed.). *Hitler: Monologe im Führerhauptquartier, 1941–1944. Die Aufzeichnungen Heinrich Heims*. Hamburg: Albrecht Knaus, 1980.

Jabotinsky, Zeev. *In the Storm: Collected articles 1925–1939*. Jerusalem: Eri Jabotinsky, private publication, 1953. In Hebrew.

Jacobsen, Hans Adolf, and Werner Jochmann (eds.). *Ausgewählte Dokumente zur Geschichte des Nationalsozialismus 1933–1945*, vol. I. Bielefeld: Arbeitsblätter für politische und soziale Bildung, 1961.

Kriegstagebuch des Oberkommandos der Wehrmacht, nine volumes. Bonn: Percy Ernst Schramm, no date.

Mendelsohn, John (ed.). *The Holocaust, Selected Documents in Eighteen Volumes*. New York and London: Garland Publishers Inc., 1982. See especially vol. 12, *The "Final Solution" in the Extermination Camps and the Aftermath*, vol. 15, *Relief in Hungary and the Failure of the Joel Brand Mission*, and vol. 16, *Rescue to Switzerland, the Musy and the Saly Mayer Affairs*, with an introduction by Sybil Milton.

Nicholas, H. G. (ed.). *Washington Dispatches 1941–1945: Weekly Political Reports from the British Embassy*. Chicago: University of Chicago Press, 1981.

Nuremberg Military Tribunals under Control Council Law No. 10, 15 volumes. Washington, DC: U.S. Government Printing Office, 1949–1953. Documents in English translation.

Schramm, Percy Ernst. *Aus dem Kriegstagebuch des Oberkommandos der Wehrmacht, die Invasion 1944*. München: Deutscher Taschenbuch Verlag (DTV), 1963.

Smith, Bradley F., and Agnes Peterson (eds.). *Heinrich Himmler: Geheimreden 1933 bis 1945*. Berlin: Propyläen Verlag, 1974.

Tessin, Georg (ed.). *Verbände und Truppen der deutschen Wehrmacht und Waffen- SS im Zweiten Weltkrieg 1939–1945*. Osnabrück: Biblio Verlag, 1996. Based on records of the German Federal Archive. Sechzenter Band, *Verzeichnis der Friedensgarnisonen 1932–1939 und Stationierungen im Kriege 1939–1945*, edited by Christian Zweng 3. *Waffen SS; SS/Polizei, Teil 2, Wehrkreis vii–xiii.*

Trials of Major War Criminals before the International Military Tribunal. Official text, vols. XXV–XLII. Nuremberg: International Military Tribunal, 1947–1949.

Vichy-Auschwitz: Die Zusammenarbeit zwischen der Deutschen und Französischen Behörden bei der Endlösung der Judenfrage. Reinbeck bei Hamburg: Serge Klarsfeld, 1989.

Watts, Franklin (ed.). *Voices of History 1942–1943*. New York: Gramercy Publishing, 1943.

Wildt, Michael. *Die Judenpolitik des SD 1935 bis 1938, eine Dokumentation*. Stuttgart: Schriftenreihe für Zeitgeschichte, Deutsche Verlags-Anstalt, 1995.

Published Works: Official Histories and Scholarly Works

World War II

Blumenson, Martin. *Kasserine Pass*, paperback edition. New York: Cooper Square Press, 2000.

van Creveld, Martin. *Hitler's Strategy 1940–1941: The Balkan Clue*. Cambridge: Cambridge University Press, 1973.

Cruickshank, Charles. *The Fourth Arm: Psychological Warfare 1938–1945*. London: Davis-Pointer Publishers, 1977.

Förster, Jürgen. "Hitler's Decision in Favor of War against the Soviet Union." In *Germany and the Second World War: The Attack on the Soviet Union*, Part I of Vol. IV, edited by the Militärgeschichtliches Forschungsamt, Potsdam, Germany. Oxford: Clarendon Press, 1998.

Garland, Lieutenant Colonel Albert N., and Howard McGaw Smyth, assisted by Martin Blumenson. *United States Army in World War Two: The Mediterranean Theater of Operations, Sicily and the Surrender of Italy*. Norwalk, CT: Easton Press edition, 1995.

Hastings, Max. *Bomber Command, Churchill's Epic Campaign: The Inside Story of the RAF's Valiant Attempt to End the War*. New York: Simon and Schuster, 1989, paper edition.

Hildebrand, Klaus. *Deutsche Aussenpolitik 1933–1945*. Stuttgart: W. Kohlhamer Verlag, 1971.

Hillgruber, Andreas. *Hitler's Strategie: Politik und Kriegsführung, 1940–1941*. Frankfurt: Benard und Graefe Verlag, 1965, and later editions.

Kloss, Erhard. *Der Luftkrieg über Deutschland 1939–1945: Deutsche Berichte und Pressestimmen des neutralen Auslands*. München: Deutscher Taschenbuch Verlag, 1964.

Laurie, Clayton D. *The Propaganda Warriors: America's Crusade against Nazi Germany*. Lawrence: University of Kansas Press, 1996.

Lukacs, John. *Five Days in London, May 1940*. New Haven and London: Yale University Press, 2000.

Medlicott, W.N. *The Economic Blockade*, vol. II. London: Kraus International Publications, revised edition, 1978.

Müller, Rolf-Dieter. "From Economic Alliance to a War of Colonial Exploitation." In Militärgeschichtliches Forschungsamt Potsdam, *Germany and the Second World War: The Attack on the Soviet Union*. Oxford: Clarendon Press, 1998.

Seaton, Jean and Ben Pimlott (eds.). *The Media in British Politics*. Aldershot: Hants, 1987.

Sherry, Michael S. *The Rise of American Air Power: The Creation of Armageddon*. New Haven and London: Yale University Press, 1987.

Stoller, Mark A. *Allies and Adversaries: The Joint Chiefs of Staffs, Grand Alliance and U.S. Strategy in WW II*. Chapel Hill: University of North Carolina Press, 2000.

Weinberg, Gerhard L. *A World at Arms: A Global History of WW II*. Cambridge: Cambridge University Press, 1994.

Williamson, Murray. *Luftwaffe*. Baltimore: Easton Press edition, 1985.

Winkler, Allan M. *The Politics of Propaganda: The Office of War Information 1942–1945*. New Haven, CT: Yale University Press, 1990.

Zuckerman, Solly, *From Apes to Warlords*. London: Hamish Hamilton, 1978.

The Holocaust – Nazism and Anti-Semitism

Adam, Uwe D. *Judenpolitik im Dritten Reich*. Düsseldorf: Droste Verlag, 1979.

Aly, Götz. *"Endlösung": Völkerverschiebung und der Mord an den Juden*. Frankfurt: S. Fischer Verlag, 1995.

Arendt, Hannah. *Eichmann in Jerusalem: Ein Bericht von der Banalität des Bösen*. München: Piper, 1964. German translation.

Aronson, Shlomo. *Reinhard Heydrich und die Frühgeschichte von Gestapo und SD*. Stuttgart: Deutsche Verlags-Anstalt, 1972.

Bauer, Yehuda. *American Jewry and the Holocaust: A History of the American Jewish Joint Distribution Committee, 1939–1945*. Detroit: Wayne State University Press, 1981.

Bauer, Yehuda. *Jews for Sale?* New Haven: Yale University Press, 1994.

Bauer, Yehuda, Yeshaiahu Yelinek, Livia Rothkirchen, John S. Conway, et al. *Leadership in Time of Distress: The "Working Group" in Slovakia 1942–1944*. Kibbutz Dalia: Sifriat Poalim Publishing House, Foundation of former Czechoslovak Citizens, 2001. In Hebrew.

Bender, Sara. *Facing Death: The Jews in Bialistok 1939–1943*. Tel-Aviv: Am-Oved Publishing House, 1997. In Hebrew.

Bendersky, Joseph W. *The "Jewish Threat": Anti-Semitic Politics of the U.S. Army*. New York: Basic Books, 2000.

Berenbaum, Michael, and Abraham J. Peck (eds.). *The Holocaust and History: The Known, the Unknown, the Disputed, and the Reexamined*. Washington, DC, and Bloomington, IN: Indiana University Press, 1998.

Breitman, Richard. *Official Secrets: What the Nazis Planned, What Western Governments Knew*. New York and London: Hill and Wang, 1998.

Breitman, Richard, and Alan M. Kraut. *American Refugee Policy and European Jewry 1933–1945*. Bloomington and Indianapolis: Indiana University Press, 1987.

Browning, Christopher R. *The Final Solution and the German Foreign Office*. New York: Holmes & Meier, 1978.

Browning, Christopher R. *The Path to Genocide: Essays on Launching the Final Solution*. Cambridge: Cambridge University Press, 1992.

Browning, Christopher R. *Initiating the Final Solution: The Fateful Months of September–October 1941*. Washington, DC: United States Holocaust Memorial Museum, Center for Advanced Holocaust Studies, 2003.

Burrin, Phillip. *Hitler and the Jews: The Genesis of the Holocaust*. London: Edward Arnold, 1989.

Dawidowicz, Lucy C. *The War against the Jews 1933–1945*. Tel-Aviv: Zmora-Bitan Publishers, 1975. Hebrew translation.

Dinnerstein, Leonard. *Anti-Semitism in America*. New York and Oxford: Oxford University Press, 1994.

Feingold, Henry L. *The Politics of Rescue: The Roosevelt Administration and the Holocaust 1938–1945.* New Brunswick, NJ: Rutgers University Press, 1970.

Fleming, Gerald. *Hitler and the Final Solution.* Oxford: Oxford University Press, 1986.

Friedlander, Henry. *The Origins of Nazi Genocide, from Euthanasia to the Final Solution.* Chapel Hill: University of North Carolina Press, 1995.

Friedlander, Saul (ed.). *Probing the Limits of Representation: Nazism and the "Final Solution."* Cambridge, MA and London: Harvard University Press, 1992.

Fuller, J. F. C. *A Military History of the Western World,* vol. three. New York: Funk and Wagnalls, 1956.

Gellately, Robert. *Backing Hitler: Consent and Coercion in Nazi Germany.* New York and Oxford: Oxford University Press, 2001.

Gilbert, Martin. *Auschwitz and the Allies: A Devastating Account of How the Allies Responded to the News of Hitler's Mass Murder.* Tel-Aviv: Am-Oved, 1988. Hebrew translation.

Gilman, Peter and Leni. *Collar and Lot! How Britain Interned and Expelled Its Wartime Refugees.* London: Quartet Books, 1980.

Harris, Whitney H. *Tyranny on Trial: The Evidence at Nuremberg.* Dallas, TX: Southern Methodist University Press, 1954; fourth printing, 1970.

Hartog, L. J. *Der Befehl zum Judenmord: Hitler, Amerika, und die Juden.* Bodenheim: Syndikat Buchgesellschaft, 1977.

Hausner, Gideon. *Justice in Jerusalem.* New York: Harper and Row, 1966.

Herbert, Ulrich (publisher). *Nationalsozialistische Vernichtungspolitik 1939–1945, Neue Forschungen und Kontroversen/National Socialist Extermination Policies: Contemporary Perspectives and Controversies – Volume Two, War and Genocide,* edited by Omer Bartov. New York and Oxford: Berghahn Books, 2000. English translation.

Hilberg, Raul. *The Destruction of the European Jews.* London: W. E. Ellen, 1961, and later editions.

Jaher, Frederic Copel. *A Scapegoat in the New Wilderness: The Origins and Rise of Anti-Semitism in America.* Cambridge, MA: Harvard University Press, 1994.

Johnson, Eric A. *Nazi Terror: The Gestapo, Jews, and Ordinary Germans.* New York: Basic Books, 2000.

Kempner, Robert M. W. *SS im Kreuzverhör.* München: Rütten+Loening Verlag, 1965.

Kochavi, Arieh J. *Prelude to Nuremberg: Allied War Crimes Policy and the Question of Punishment.* Chapel Hill and London: University of North Carolina Press, 1998.

Kushner, Tony. *The Persistence of Prejudice: Antisemitism in British Society during the Second World War.* Manchester and New York: Manchester University Press, 1989.

Kushner, Tony. *The Holocaust and the Liberal Imagination.* Oxford: Blackwell, 1994.

Laqueur, Walter. *The Terrible Secret: The Suppression of the Truth about Hitler's "Final Solution."* Jerusalem and Tel-Aviv: Schocken Publishing House, 1981. Hebrew translation.

Laqueur, Walter, and Richard Breitman. *Breaking the Silence.* New York: Simon and Schuster, 1986.

Lazowik, Ya'akov. *Hitler's Bureaucrats: The Nazi Security Police and the Banality of Evil.* Jerusalem: Hebrew University, Magnes Press, 2001. In Hebrew.

Longerich, Peter. *Policy of Destruction: Nazi Anti-Jewish Policy and the Genesis of the 'Final Solution.'* Washington, DC: United States Holocaust Memorial Museum, Center for Advanced Holocaust Studies, 1999.

Marrus, Michael R. *The Holocaust in History.* Hanover and London: University Press of New England, 1987.

Marrus, Michael R. *The Nuremberg War Crimes Trials 1945–6: A Documentary History.* Boston and New York: Bedford Books, 1997.

Neufeld, Michael J., and Michael Berenbaum (eds.). *The Bombing of Auschwitz: Should the Allies Have Attempted It?* New York: St. Martin's Press, in association with the United States Holocaust Memorial Museum, 2000.

Neumann, Franz. *Behemoth.* Tel-Aviv: Sifriat Poalim, 1943. Hebrew translation.

Robinson, Jacob. *And the Crooked shall Be Made Straight: The Jews of Europe in the Face of the Holocaust, in the Light of Historical Truth and the Eichmann Trial in Jerusalem, and of the International Law.* Jerusalem: Bialik Foundation, 1963. Translated into the Hebrew, edited by the author.

Schiler, Joseph. *The Strasshof Rescue-Operation.* Kibbutz Dalia: Beth Lohamei-Hagetaot Publications, 1999. Hebrew translation.

Schlesinger, Arthur M., Jr. *Robert Kennedy and His Times.* Boston: Houghton Mifflin, 1978.

Schleuness, Karl E. *The Twisted Road to Auschwitz: Nazi Policy Toward German Jews 1933–1939.* Urbana: University of Illinois Press, 1970.

Shaw, Stanford J. *Turkey and the Holocaust: Turkey's Role in Rescuing Turkish and European Jewry from Nazi Persecution, 1933–1945.* New York: New York University Press, 1993.

Sjöberg, Tommie. *The Powers and the Persecuted: The Refugee Problem and the Intergovernmental Committee on Refugees.* Lund: Lund University Press, 1991.

Wasserstein, Bernard. *Britain and the Jews of Europe 1939–1945.* London and Oxford: Institute of Jewish Affairs and Clarendon Press, 1979.

Wells, Herbert George. *The Outlook for Homo Sapiens.* London: Readers Union, 1942, quoted in Brian Cheyette, *Construction of 'the Jew' in English literature and society, racial representations, 1875–1945.* Cambridge: Cambridge University Press, 1993.

Wenck, Alexandra. *Zwischen Menschenhandel und "Endlösung": Das Konzentrationslager Bergen-Belsen.* Paderborn and München: Ferdinand Schöningh Verlag, 2000.

Wistrich, Robert S. (ed.). *Demonizing the Other: Antisemitism, Racism and Xenophobia.* Amsterdam: Harwood Academic Publishers, 1999.

Wyman, David S. *The Abandonment of the Jews: America and the Holocaust 1941–1945.* New York: Pantheon Press, 1984.

Intelligence, Including Official Histories

Alvarez, David. *Secret Messages: Codebreaking and American Diplomacy 1930–1945.* Lawrence: University of Kansas Press, 2000.

Andrew, Christopher. *Her Majesty's Secret Service: The Making of the British Intelligence Community.* New York: Viking, 1986.

Benson, Robert Lewis. *History of U.S. Communications Intelligence during World War II: Policy and Administration,* Series IV, World War II, vol. 8. Fort Meade,

MD: Center for Cryptologic History, National Security Agency, Central Security Service, 1997.

Budiansky, Stephen. *Battle of Wits: The Complete Story of Code Breaking in World War II*. New York: The Free Press, 2000.

Casey, William. *The Secret War against Hitler*. Washington, DC: Regnery Gateway, 1988.

Clark, Ronald. *The Man Who Broke Purple: The Life of William F. Friedman, Who Deciphered the Japanese Code in World War II*. Boston: Little Brown, 1977.

Curry, John. *The Security Service 1908–1945, The Official History*. Kew, Surrey: Public Record Office, 1999.

Heideking, Juergen, and Christof Mauch. *American Intelligence and the German Resistance to Hitler: A Documentary History*. Boulder, CO: Westview Press, 1996.

Hinsley, H. F. et al. *British Intelligence in the Second World War: Volume 1, 1939–Summer 1941*. London: Her Majesty's Stationery Office, 1979.

Hinsley, Sir Harry F., and C. A. G. Simkins. *British Intelligence in the Second World War: Volume 4, Security and Counter-Intelligence*. London: Her Majesty's Stationery Office, 1990.

Howard, Michael. *British Intelligence in the Second World War: Volume 5, Strategic Deception*. New York: Cambridge University Press, 1990.

Kahn, David. *Hitler's Spies: German Military Intelligence in World War II*. New York: DA-APO Press, 2000.

Katz, Barry M. *Foreign Intelligence: Research and Analysis in the Office of Strategic Services, 1942–1945*. Cambridge, MA: Harvard University Press, 1989.

Lefen, Asa. *The Roots of the Israeli Intelligence Community*. Tel-Aviv: Ministry of Defense Publishing House, 1997. In Hebrew.

Mayer, Wilfried. *Unternehmen Sieben*. Frankfurt: Filo Verlag, 1993.

Perisco, Joseph. *Roosevelt's Secret War: FDR and World War Two Espionage*. New York: Random House, 2001.

Petersen, Neal H. (editor and annotator). *From Hitler's Doorstep: The Wartime Intelligence Reports of Allen Dulles, 1942–1945*. University Park: The Pennsylvania State University Press, 1996.

Porter, Bernard. *Plots and Paranoia: A History of Political Espionage in Britain 1790–1988*. London and New York: Routledge, 1992.

Rubin, Barry. *Istanbul Intrigues: A True Life Casablanca*. New York: McGraw-Hill, 1989.

Sayer, Ian, and Douglas Botting. *America's Secret Army: The Untold Story of the Counter Intelligence Corps*. London: Grafton Books, 1989.

Smith, Bradley F. *The Shadow Warriors: O.S.S. and the Origins of the C.I.A.* New York: Basic Books, 1983.

Smith, Michael. *Foley, The Spy Who Saved 10,000 Jews*. London: Coronet Books, Hodder and Stoughton, 1999.

Smith, Michael, and Ralph Erskine (eds.). *Action This Day: Bletchley Park from the Breaking of the Enigma Code to the Birth of the Modern Computer*. London and New York: Bantam Press, 2001.

Stafford, David. *Churchill & Secret Service*. London: Abacus, 2000.

West, Nigel. *MI6*. London: Widenfeld and Nicolson, 1983.

Palestine and Zionism

Almog, Shmuel. *Zionism and History*. Jerusalem: Magnes Press, 1982. In Hebrew.

Almog, Shmuel. *The Jewish Point: Jews as Seen by Themselves and by Others*. Tel-Aviv: Sifriat Poalim, 2002. In Hebrew.

Antonius, George. *The Arab Awakening*. London: Hamish Hamilton, 1938.

Avineri, Shlomo. *Varieties of Zionist Thought*. Tel-Aviv: Am-Oved, 1980. In Hebrew.

Avizohar, Meir. *National and Social Ideals as Reflected in Mapai – The Israeli Labour Party 1930–1942*. Tel-Aviv: Am-Oved, 1990. In Hebrew.

Barlas, Haim. *Rescue during the Holocaust*. Kibbutz Lohamei-Hagetaot: Lohamei-Hagetaot Publishing House, 1975. In Hebrew.

Bauer, Yehuda. *From Diplomacy to Resistance: A History of Jewish Palestine 1939–1945*. New York: Atheneum, 1970.

Bauer, Yehuda. *Diplomacy and Underground in Zionism 1939–1945*, second edition. Jerusalem: Sifriat Poalim, 1966. In Hebrew.

Baumel Tydor, Judith. *Between Ideology and Propaganda: The "Irgun" Delegation and the Origins of American-Jewish Right-Wing Militancy*. Jerusalem: Magnes Press, 1999. In Hebrew.

Cohen, Asher. *The Halutz Resistance in Hungary 1942–1944*. Tel-Aviv: Hakibbutz Hameuchad Publishing House, Institute of Research of the Holocaust Period, University of Haifa, 1984. In Hebrew.

Dotan, Shmuel. *The Partition Controversy during the Mandate Period*. Jerusalem: Yad Izhak Ben-Zvi Publications, 1980. In Hebrew.

Dotan, Shmuel. *Reds: About Domestic Communist Rejections of Different Kinds of Zionism during the 30's, 40's, and 50's*. Kefar Sava: Shevna Hasofer Publications, 1993. In Hebrew.

Eshkoli (Wagman), Hava. *Silence: Mapai and the Holocaust – 1939–1942*. Jerusalem: Yad Izhak Ben Zvi, 1994.

Eyal, Yigal. *The First Intifada: The Suppression of the Arab Revolt by the British Army 1936–1939*. Tel-Aviv: Ma'archot Publishing House, 1998. In Hebrew.

Friedman, Isaiah. *The Question of Palestine 1914–1918: British–Jewish–Arab Relations*. New York: Schocken Books, 1973.

Friedman, Isaiah. *Germany, Turkey and Zionism, 1897–1918*. Jerusalem: Bialik Foundation, 1996. Hebrew translation.

Friling, Tuvia. *Arrow in the Dark: David Ben-Gurion, The Yishuv's Leadership, and Rescue Efforts during the Holocaust*. Sede Boker, Jerusalem, and Tel-Aviv: Hamerkaz Lemoreshet Ben-Gurion and Institute for Contemporary Jewry, Hebrew University, 1998. In Hebrew.

Gelber, Yoav. *The Standard Bearers: The Mission of the Volunteers for the Jewish People – Volume III, History of Voluntary Mobilization*. Jerusalem: Yad Izhak Ben-Zvi, 1983. In Hebrew.

Gorny, Yosef. *The Arab Question and the Jewish Problem: Ideological-Political Trends in Zionism in their Attitude toward the Arab Entity in Palestine 1882–1948*. Tel-Aviv: Am-Oved, 1985. In Hebrew.

Gorny, Yosef. *Policy and Fantasy: Federal Plans in the Zionist Political Thought 1917–1948*. Jerusalem: Yad Izhak Ben-Zvi, 1993. In Hebrew.

Gorny, Yosef. *Achdut-Ha'av'oda 1919–1930: The Intellectual Sources and the Political System*. Tel-Aviv: Hakibbutz Hameuchad, 1993. In Hebrew.

Hacohen, Devora Z. *The Million Plan.* Tel-Aviv: Ministry of Defense, 1995. In Hebrew.

Hecht, Ben. *Perfidy.* Tel-Aviv: Israel Printing House, 1970. Hebrew translation.

Heller, Yosef. *LEHI: Ideology and Politics 1940–1949,* vols. I and II. Jerusalem: Zalman Shazar Center and Ketter Publications, 1989. In Hebrew.

Horowitz, Dan, and Moshe Lissak. *The Origins of Israeli Polity.* Tel-Aviv: Am-Oved, 1977. In Hebrew.

Ilan, Amitzur. *America, Britain and Palestine, 1939–1945: The Inception and the Development of American Involvement in the British Palestine Policy.* Jerusalem: Yad Izhak Ben-Zvi, 1979. In Hebrew.

Kanari, Baruch. *To Carry Their People: The Realization, the Mission and Self Image of the United Kibbutz.* Tel-Aviv: Hakibbutz Hameuchad, 1989. In Hebrew.

Katzburg, Nathaniel. *The Palestine Problem in British Policy 1940–1945.* Jerusalem: Yad Izhak Ben-Zvi, 1977. In Hebrew.

Lahav, Pnina. *Judgment in Jerusalem: Chief Justice Simon Agranat and the Zionist Century.* Berkeley: University of California Press, 1997.

Lewis, Bernard. *Semites and Anti-Semites: An Inquiry into Conflict and Prejudice.* New York: W. W. Norton, 1986.

Lissak, Moshe, Anita Shapiro, and Gavriel Cohen (eds.). *The History of the Jewish Yishuv in Palestine since the First Alya: The British Mandate Period,* vol. II. Jerusalem: The Israel Academy of Sciences and Humanities, 1995. In Hebrew.

Margalit, Elkana. *The Gordonia Youth Movement: Idea and a Way of Life.* Tel-Aviv: Publisher, 1986. In Hebrew.

Medding, Peter Y. *Mapai in Israel: Political Organization and Government in a New Society.* Cambridge: Cambridge University Press, 1972.

Ofer, Dalia. *Illegal Immigration during the Holocaust.* Jerusalem: Yad Izhak Ben-Zvi, 1988. In Hebrew.

Ofer, Dalia. *Escaping the Holocaust: Illegal Immigration to the Land of Israel, 1939–1944.* New York: Oxford, 1990. English version of the preceding work.

Porat, Dina. *An Entangled Leadership: The Yishuv and the Holocaust 1942–1945.* Tel-Aviv: Am Oved, 1986. In Hebrew.

Porat, Dina. *The Blue and the Yellow Star of David.* Cambridge, MA: Harvard University Press, 1990. English version of the preceding work.

Porath, Yehoshua. *The Palestinian-Arab National Movement, 1918–1929.* London: Frank Cass, 1974, and vol. II, *The Palestinian-Arab National Movement, 1929–1939: From Riots to Rebellion.* London: Frank Cass, 1977.

Porath, Yehoshua. *In the Test of Political Reality: Palestine, Arab Unity and British Policy 1930–1945.* Jerusalem: Yad Itzhak Ben-Zvi, 1985. In Hebrew.

Porath, Yehoshua. *A Pen Carrying Sword: The Life Story of Uriel Shelach (Jonathan Ratosh).* Tel-Aviv: Machbarot Lesifrut Publishers, 1989. In Hebrew.

Reinharz, Jehuda, Gideon Shimoni, and Yosef Salmon. *Jewish Nationalism and Politics: New Perspectives.* Jerusalem and Boston: Zalman Shazar Center for Jewish History, and the Tauber Institute, Brandeis University, 1996. In Hebrew.

Shapiro, David H. *From Philanthropy to Activism: The Political Transformation of American Zionism in the Holocaust Years 1933–1945.* Jerusalem: Bialik Foundation, 2001. In Hebrew.

Shavit, Ya'akov. *The Myths of the Right.* Zofit: Beit Berl and Moshe Sharett Institute, 1986. In Hebrew.

Shavit, Ya'akov. *From a Hebrew to a Canaanite: Aspects in the History, Ideology and Utopia of the 'Hebrew Renaissance' – from Radical Zionism to Anti-Zionism.* Jerusalem: Domino Press, 1984. In Hebrew.

Shimoni, Gideon. *The Zionist Ideology.* Hanover and London: Brandeis University Press, University Press of New England, 1995.

Stanislavski, Michael. *Zionism and the Fin de Siècle: Cosmopolitanism and Nationalism from Nordau to Jabotinsky.* Berkeley: University of California Press, 2001.

Sternhell, Zeev. *Nation-Building or a New Society? The Zionist Labor Movement (1904– 1940) and the Origins of Israel.* Tel-Aviv: Am-Oved, 1995. In Hebrew.

Sykes, Christopher. *Cross Roads to Israel: Palestine from Balfour to Bevin.* Tel-Aviv: Ma'arachot Publishing House, 1966. Hebrew translation.

Tzahor, Zeev. *Vision and Reckoning, Ben-Gurion: Ideology and Politics.* Tel-Aviv: Sifriat Poalim, 1994. In Hebrew.

Vital, David. *The Origins of Zionism: Volume I, The Beginning of the Movement.* Tel-Aviv: Am-Oved, 1978. Hebrew translation.

Weinbaum, Laurence. *A Marriage of Convenience: The New Zionist Organization and the Polish Government 1936–1939.* New York and Boulder: East European Monographs, 1993.

Weitz, Yechiam. *Aware but Helpless: Mapai and the Holocaust – 1943–1945.* Jerusalem: Yad Izhak Ben-Zvi, 1994.

Zeira, Moti. *Rural Collective Settlement and Jewish Culture in Eretz Israel during the 20s.* Jerusalem: Yad Izhak Ben-Zvi, 2002. In Hebrew.

Zweig, Ronald W. *Britain and Palestine during the Second World War.* Woodbridge, Suffolk: The Boydell Press for the Royal Historical Society, 1986.

Hungary and Rumania

Braham, Randolph L. *The Politics of Genocide: The Holocaust in Hungary,* vols. I and II. New York: Columbia University Press, 1981.

Braham, Randolph L., with Scott Miller (eds.). *The Nazis' Last Victims: The Holocaust in Hungary.* Detroit: Wayne State University Press, 1998.

Gerlach, Christian, and Götz Aly. *Das Letzte Kapitel, Der Mord an den ungarischen Juden.* Stuttgart and München: Deutsche Verlags-Anstalt, 2002.

Heinen, Armin. *Die Legion 'Erzengel Michael' in Rumänien: Soziale Bewegung und politische Organisation.* München: Oldenbourg Verlag, 1986.

Hillgruber, Andreas. *Hitler, König Carol, und Marschall Antonescu: Die deutsch-rumänischen Beziehungen 1938–1944.* Wiesbaden: Steiner Verlag, 1954.

Macartney, Carlyle A. *October Fifteenth: A History of Modern Hungary 1929–1945.* Edinburgh: Edinburgh University Press, 1956.

Szöllösi-Janze, Margit. *Die Pfeilkreuzlerbewegung in Ungarn: Historischer Kontext, Entwicklung und Herrschaft.* München: Oldenbourg Verlag, 1989.

Ungravy, Krisztian. *Die Schlacht um Budapest: Stalingrad an der Donau, 1944–1945.* Munchen: Herbig Verlag, 1999.

Biographies

Amichal Yevin, Ada. *Sambation, Ideology in Permanent Test: A biography of Dr. Israel Eldad.* Beith-El: Sifriat Beith-El, 1995. In Hebrew.

Aronson, Shlomo. *David Ben-Gurion: The Renaissance Leader that Waned*. Sede Boker: Ben-Gurion University Press, 1999. In Hebrew.

Beschloss, Michael. *The Conquerors: Roosevelt, Truman and the Destruction of Nazi Germany 1941–1945*. Waterville, MA: Thorndike Press, 2002.

Black, Peter. *Ernst Kaltenbrunner, Vassal Himmlers: Eine SS-Karriere*. München: Ferdinand Schöningh, 1991. German translation.

Breitman, Richard. *The Architect of Genocide: Himmler and the Final Solution*. New York: Alfred A. Knopf, 1991.

Dallek, Robert. *Franklin D. Roosevelt and American Foreign Policy, 1932–1945*. New York: Oxford University Press, 1979.

Davis, Kenneth S. *FDR: The War President, 1940–1943*. New York: Random House, 2000.

Eisenhower, David. *Eisenhower at War 1943–1945*. New York: Random House, 1987.

D'Este, Carlo. *Patton: A Genius for War*. New York: HarperCollins, 1995.

Elpeleg, Zvi. *Grand Mufti*. Tel-Aviv: Ministry of Defense, 1989. In Hebrew.

Ford, Corey. *Donovan of OSS*. Boston, Toronto: Little Brown, 1970.

Gilbert, Martin. *Winston S. Churchill: Volume VII: The Road to Victory, 1941–1945*. Boston: Houghton Mifflin, 1986.

Herbert, Ulrich. *Best: Biographische Studien über Radikalismus, Weltanschauung und Vernunft 1903–1989*. Bonn: Verlag J. H. W. Dietz Nachfolger, 1996.

Hirsch, H. N. *The Enigma of Felix Frankfurter*. New York: Basic Books, 1981.

Howarth, Patrick. *Intelligence Chief Extraordinary: The Life of the Ninth Duke of Portland*. London: Vintage/Elbury, 1986.

Isaacson, Walter, and Evan Thomas. *The Wise Men: Six Friends and the World They Made*. New York: Simon and Schuster, 1986.

Jäckel, Eberhard. *Hitlers Weltanschauung, Entwurf einer Herrschaft*. Stuttgart: Deutsche Verlags-Anstalt, 1986.

James, Robert Rhodes. *Churchill, A Study in Failure 1900–1939*. London: Weidenfeld and Nicholson, 1990.

Jenkins, Roy. *Churchill, a Biography*. New York: Farrar, Straus and Giroux, 2001.

Jones, R. V. *Most Secret War*. Tel-Aviv: Ma'arachot, 1984. Hebrew translation.

Katz, Shmuel. *Lone Wolf: A Biography of Vladimir (Ze'ev) Jabotinsky*. New York: Barricade Books, 1996.

Kershow, Ian. *Hitler 1936–1945: Nemesis*. New York: W. W. Norton, 2001. Paperback edition.

Larrabee, Eric. *Commander in Chief: Franklin Delano Roosevelt, His Lieutenants and Their War*. New York: Harper and Row, 1987.

Leuchtenberg, William E. *The FDR Years*. New York: Columbia University Press, 1995.

Rock, William R. *Chamberlain and Roosevelt: British Foreign Policy and the United States, 1937–1940*. Columbus: Ohio State University Press, 1988.

Rose, Norman A. *Chaim Weizmann: A Biography*. New York: Viking, 1986.

Shapiro, Anita. *Berl*, vol. II. Tel-Aviv: Am-Oved, 1980. In Hebrew.

Sheffer, Gabriel. *Moshe Sharett: Biography of a Political Moderate*. Oxford: Oxford University Press, 1996.

Sofer, Sasson. *Begin – An Anatomy of Leadership*. Oxford: Oxford University Press, 1988.

Steel, Ronald. *Walter Lippmann and the American Century.* New York: Vintage Books, Random House, 1981.

Teveth, Shabtai. *David's Zeal: The Life of David Ben-Gurion,* vol. II. Tel-Aviv and Jerusalem: Schocken, 1980. In Hebrew.

Teveth, Shabtai. *Ben-Gurion and the Arabs of Palestine: From Peace to War.* Tel-Aviv and Jerusalem: Schocken, 1985. In Hebrew.

Teveth, Shabtai. *Ben-Gurion and the Holocaust.* New York: Harcourt Brace, 1996.

Teveth, Shabtai. *The Vanished Years and the Black Hole.* Tel-Aviv: Dvir Publishing House, 1999. In Hebrew.

Weitz, Yechiam. *The Man Who Was Murdered Twice: The Life, the Trial and the Death of Dr. Israel Kasztner.* Jerusalem: Ketter Publications, 1995. In Hebrew.

Diaries and Memorabilia

Ascher, Haim. *Two Rivers and the Great Sea.* Tel Aviv: private publication, 1996. In Hebrew.

Bader, Menachem. *Sad Missions,* revised edition. Tel-Aviv: Sifriat Poalim, 1958. In Hebrew.

Ben-Gurion, David. *Left Behind (Post-Mortem) Memoirs: Volume VI, January–August 1939,* edited and annotated by Meir Avizohar. Tel-Aviv: Am-Oved, 1987. In Hebrew.

Berman, Yitzhak. *Stormy Days.* Tel-Aviv: Ministry of Defense, 1993. In Hebrew.

Biss, Andreas. *Der Stopp der Endlösung.* Stuttgart: Seewald, 1976.

Brand, Joel. *In the Mission of the Sentenced to Death.* Tel-Aviv: Ayanot Publishers, 1956. In Hebrew.

Brand, Joel, and Hansi Brand. *The Devil and the Soul.* Tel-Aviv: Ledori Publishers, 1957. In Hebrew.

Churchill, Winston S. *The Second World War.* six volumes. Tel-Aviv: Am-Hasefer Publishers, 1957. Hebrew translation.

Elpeleg, Zvi. *In the Eyes of the Mufti: The Diaries of Hajj Amin.* Translated and Annotated. Tel-Aviv: Tel-Aviv University Press and Hakibbutz Hameuchad, 1995. In Hebrew.

Engel, Gerhard. *Heeresadjutant bei Hitler 1938–1943: Aufzeichnungen des Major Engel,* Hildegard von Kotze, publisher and commentator. Stuttgart: Deutsche Verlags-Anstalt, Schriftenreihe der Vierteljahreshefte für Zeitgeschichte, 1975.

Freedman, Max (annatator). *Roosevelt and Frankfurter: Their Correspondence 1928–1945.* Boston: Little Brown, 1967.

Goebbels, Joseph. *Die Tagebücher von Joseph Goebbels: Sämtliche Fragmente. Teil I, Aufzeichnungen 1924–1941, Band 4, 1.1.1940–8.7.1941,* edited by Elke Fröhlich. München: Saur Verlag, 1987; *Teil II. Diktate 1941–1945,* edited by Elke Fröhlich. 15 volumes. München: Saur, 1993–1996.

Hadari, Zeev Venia. *Against All Odds: Istanbul 1942–1945.* Tel-Aviv: Ministry of Defense, 1992. In Hebrew.

Halder, Generaloberst Franz. *Kriegstagebuch,* edited by Hans-Adolf Jacobsen. Three volumes. Stuttgart: W. Kohlhamer, 1962–1964.

Harel, Isser. *The Truth about the Kaesztner Murder: Jewish Terrorism in Israel.* Jerusalem: Edanim Publishers, Yediot Aharonot edition, 1985. In Hebrew.

Hitler, Adolf. *Mein Kampf.* München: Eher Verlag, 1934 edition.

Kasztner, Dr. Rezsö. *Der Bericht des jüdischen Rettungskomitees aus Budapest 1942–1945*, (no further publishing data) – quoted in text as "Bericht," 1946.

Kasztner, Dr. Rezsö. "Hebrew Bericht," report submitted by Dr. Rezsö Kasztner to the Zionist Congress in 1946, published by the Association for the Commemoration of Dr. Israel Kasztner, translated by Binyamin Gat-Rimon under the title "Kasztner's Truth," without date or place of publication.

Rauschning, Hermann. *Hitler Speaks*. London: T. Butterworth, 1939.

Rommel, Erwin. *The Rommel Papers*, edited by B. H. Liddle Hart. Norwalk, CT: Easton Press edition, 1988.

Schwarz, Alfred. *Der Mensch im Widerstreit mit sich Selbst, Der Schock der Besinnung*. Vienna: Verlag für Wissenscaft und Kunst, 1981.

Schellenberg, Walter. *Memoiren*. Köln: Verlag für Politik und Wirtschaft, 1956.

Speer, Albert. *Erinnerungen*. Berlin: Propyläen Verlag, 1970.

Stimson, Henry Louis. *Stimson's Diaries*, microfilmed in the Library of Congress, Volumes 46/52–55.

Tamir, Shmuel. *Son of this Land*, vols. I and II. Tel-Aviv: Zmora Bitan Publishers, 2002. In Hebrew.

Taylor, Telford. *The Anatomy of the Nuremberg Trials: A Personal Memoir*. Boston: Little Brown, 1992.

Weissberg, Alex. *Advocate for the Dead – The Story of Joel Brand*. London: A. Deutsch, 1958.

Weissmandel, Michael Dov-Ber. *Under Duress*. New York: Emuna Publishers, 1960.

Historical Background

Bower, Tom. *Blind Eye to Murder: Britain, America and the Purging of Nazi Germany – A Pledge Betrayed*. London: Paladin/Granda, 1983.

Cannadine, David. *The Decline and Fall of the British Aristocracy*. New York: Vintage Books, Random House, 1999.

Dahrendorf, Ralph. *Gesellschaft und Demokratie in Deutschland*. München: R. Piper Verlag, 1964.

Fromkin, David. *A Peace to End All Peace: The Fall of the Ottoman Empire and the Creation of the Modern Middle East*. New York: Owl Paperback, 1989.

Garraty, John A. *The Great Depression: An Inquiry into the Causes, Course, and Consequences of the Worldwide Depression of the Nineteen Thirties, as Seen by Contemporaries and in the Light of History*. San Diego and New York: Harcourt Brace Jovanovich, 1986.

Glanz, David M. *Stumbling Colossus: The Red Army on the Eve of World War II*. Lawrence: University of Kansas Press, 1998.

Herzstein, Robert E. *Roosevelt and Hitler: Prelude to War*. New York: Paragon House, 1989.

Luebbert, Gregory M. *Liberalism, Fascism, or Social Democracy: Social Classes and the Political Origins of Regimes in Interwar Europe*. New York: Oxford University Press, 1991.

Martel, Gordon (ed.). *The 'Times' and Appeasement: The Journals of A. L. Kennedy 1932–39*. Cambridge: Cambridge University Press, 2001.

Milward, Alan S. *The German War Economy 1939–1945*. Stuttgart: Deutsche Verlags-Anstalt, 1966. German translation by Schriftenreihe der Vierteljahrschefte für Zeitgeschichte.

Mosse, George L. *The Crisis of German Ideology: Intellectual Origins of the Third Reich*. New York: Schocken Books, 1988 edition.

Rhodes, Richard. *The Making of the Atomic Bomb*. New York: Simon and Schuster, 1986.

Sontheimer, Kurt. *Anti-Demokratisches Denken in der Weimarer Republik: Die politischen Ideen des deutschen Nationalismus zwischen 1918 und 1933*. München: Nympherburger Verlagshandlung, 1968.

Jews and Judaism

Arendt, Hannah. *The Origins of Totalitarianism*. San Diego and New York: Harcourt, Brace Jovanovich, 1958.

Cheyette, Brian. *Construction of 'the Jew' in English Literature and Society: Racial Representations, 1875–1945*. Cambridge: Cambridge University Press, 1993.

Erikson, Erik H. *Childhood and Society*. Tel-Aviv: Sifriat Poalim, 1963. Hebrew translation.

Fishberg, Maurice. *The Jews: A Study of Race and Environment*. New York and Melbourne: Arno Press, 1911.

Katz, Jacob. *Jewish Nationalism: Essays and Studies*. Jerusalem: The Zionist Library, 1979. In Hebrew.

Ne'eman Arad, Gulie. *America, Its Jews and the Rise of Nazism*. Bloomington and Indianapolis: Indiana University Press, 2000.

Schiff, Ofer. *Assimilation in Pride: Antisemitism, Holocaust, and Zionism as Challenges to Universalistic American Jewish Ideology*. Tel-Aviv: Am-Oved, 2001. In Hebrew.

Scholem, Gershom. *Explications and Implications: Writings on Jewish Heritage and Renaissance*. Tel-Aviv: Am-Oved, 1975. In Hebrew.

Stember, Charles E. *Jews in the Mind of America*. New York, London: Basic Books, 1966.

Urbach, Ephraim E. *On Zionism and Judaism: Essays*. Jerusalem: The Zionist Library, 1985. In Hebrew.

Unpublished Sources

Friling, Tuvia. "David Ben Gurion and the Catastrophe of European Jewry 1939–1945." Ph.D. thesis, Hebrew University, Jerusalem, 1990. In Hebrew.

Haruvi, Eldad. "British Intelligence and Secret Cooperation with the Yishuv during WWII." Master's Thesis, Haifa University, 1999. In Hebrew.

Haruvi, Eldad. "The Criminal Investigation Department of the Palestine Police Force, 1920–1948." Ph. D. dissertation, Haifa University, 2002. In Hebrew.

Kulka, Otto D. "The Jewish Question in the Third Reich, Its Significance in National Socialist Ideology and Politics." Volume II. Jerusalem: Hebrew University, 1975. In Hebrew.

Raim, Edith. "Die Dachauer KZ-Aussenkommandos Käufering und Mühldorf, Rüstungsbauten und Zwangsarbeit im letzten Kriegsjahr 1944/5." Dissertation, University of Munich, 1991.

Wenck, Alexandra. "Der Menschenhandel des Dritten Reiches, und die 'Endlösung' – das KZ Bergen-Belsen im Spannugsfeld nationalsozialistischer und aliierter Interssen." Dissertation, University of Münster, 1997.

Articles

Abitbul, Michel. "North Africa and the Rescue of Jewish Refugees in the Second World War: The Failure of the Fadala Plan." In *Contemporary Jewry: Studies in Honor of Moshe Davis*, edited by Geoffrey Wigoder. Jerusalem: Institute of Contemporary Jewry, Hebrew University, 1984, pp. 115–124.

Ancel, Jean. "Plans for Deportation of Rumanian Jews and Their Discontinuation in Light of Documentary Evidence (July–October 1942)." *Yad Vashem Studies*, 16 (1981): 299–332. In Hebrew.

Aronson, Shlomo. "Die Dreifache Falle, Hitler, die Alliierten und die Juden." *Vierteljahreshefte für Zeitgeschichte* No. 1 (1984): 29–65.

Aronson, Shlomo. "Preparations for the Nuremberg Trial: The O.S.S., Charles Dwork, and the Holocaust." *Holocaust and Genocide Studies* 12, No. 2 (Fall 1998): 257–281.

Aronson, Shlomo. "Israel Kasztner, OSS and the 'Spearhead Theory' at Nuremberg." In *Justice and History*, edited by Daniel Gutwein and Menachem Mautner. Jerusalem: Zalman Shazar Center for Israeli History, 1999, pp. 305–338. In Hebrew.

Aronson, Shlomo, and Peter Longerich. "The Final Solution: Preparations and Implementation." In *The Encyclopedia of the Holocaust*, edited by Walter Laqueur. New Haven and London: Yale University Press, 2001, pp.184–187.

Avizohar, Meir. "Fighting Zionism." Introduction to the academic publication of David Ben-Gurion, *Left Behind (Post-Mortem) Memoirs: Volume VI, January–August 1939*, edited and annotated by Meir Avizohar. Tel-Aviv: Am-Oved, 1987, pp. 18–21. In Hebrew.

Bajohr, Frank. "Karl Kaufmann – Gauleiter in Hamburg," *Vierteljahreshefte für Zeitgeschchte* 2 (1995): 267–296.

Bankier, David. "Signaling the Final Solution to the German People," *Dapim, Studies on the Shoah* 17 (2002): 7–26. In Hebrew.

Bauer, Yehuda. "The Goldberg Report." *Midstream* (February, 1985): 25–26.

Ben-Gurion, David. "The Menace of Hitlerism and the Dread of War." Reprinted in *The State of Israel and Eretz-Israel*, edited by Adam Doron. Zofit: Beit Berl, 1988, pp. 411–412. In Hebrew.

Ben-Israel, Hedva. "National Identity of the Scholar and the Study of Nationalism." *Academia* 11 (2002): 13–17. In Hebrew.

Bradsher, Greg. "A Time to Act: The Beginning of the Fritz Kolbe Story, 1900–1943." *Prologue, Quarterly of the National Archives and Records Administration*, 34, No. 1 (Spring 2002): 7–24.

Breitman, Richard, and Shlomo Aronson. "The End of the 'Final Solution'? Nazi Plans to Ransom Jews in 1944." *Central European History* 25, No. 2 (1993): 177–203.

Bush, Jonathan A. "The Supreme Crime" and Its Origins: The Lost Legislative History of the Crime of Aggressive War." *Columbia Law Review* 102, No. 8 (December 2002): 224–243.

Cecil, Robert. "Five of Six at War: Section V of MI6." *Intelligence and National Security* 9, No. 2 (April 1994): 345–353.

Charters, David A. "British Intelligence in the Palestine Campaign, 1945–47." *Intelligence and National Security* No. 1 (January 1991): 115–140.

Cohen, Gavriel. "Churchill and the Genesis of the Cabinet Committee on Palestine (April–June 1943)." *Hazionuth, Studies in the History of the Zionist Movement and the Jewish Community in Palestine* 4 (1976). In Hebrew.

Cohen, Michael J. "The British White Paper on Palestine, May 1939, Part 2: The Testing of a Policy, 1942–1945." *Historical Journal* 19 (1976): 727–758.

Dovey, H. O. "The Middle East Intelligence Center." *Intelligence and National Security* 4 (October 1989): 800–812.

Dovey, H. O. "Security in Syria, 1941–1945." *Intelligence and National Security* 6, No. 2 (April 1991): 418–446.

Dreisziger, Nador F. (ed.). *Hungary and the Second World War.* Special issue, *Hungarian Studies Review* 10, 1983.

Fox, John P. "German and Austrian Jews in Britain's Armed Forces and British and German Citizenship Policies 1939–1945." *Yearbook of the Leo Baeck Institute* 37 (1992): 415–459.

Friling, Tuvia. "Istanbul 1942–1945: The Kollek–Avriel Network and the Berman–Offner Networks." In *Intelligence and the Holocaust*, edited by David Bankier. Forthcoming.

Gelber, Yoav. "Zionist Policy and the Fate of European Jewry, 1943–1944." *Studies in Zionism, A Journal of Israel Studies* No. 7 (Spring 1983): 133–167.

Gerlach, Christian, "Wirtschaftsinteressen, Besetzungspolitik und der Mord an den Juden." In *Nationalsozialistische Vernichtungspolitik 1939–1945, Neue Forschungen und Kontroversen.* Frankfurt: Ulrich Herbert, 1998, pp. 263–291.

Gerlach, Christian. "The Ghettoization in Hungary, 1944, and the Jewish Response." Paper delivered at the 25th German Studies Association Conference, Washington, DC, October 25, 2001.

Gorny, Yosef. "Review of Zeev Sternhell's *Nation-Building or a New Society? The Zionist Labor Movement (1904–1940) and the Origins of Israel.* Tel-Aviv: Am-Oved, 1995." In Hebrew. *Katedra, Quarterly for the History of Eretz-Yisrael and its Development* 79 (March 1996): 182–191. In Hebrew.

Harris, Whitney R. "Justice Jackson at Nuremberg." *The International Lawyer* 20, No. 3 (1986): 867–896.

Heideking, Jürgen, and Christoph Mauch. "Das Herman-Dossier, Helmuth James Graf von Moltke, die Deutsche Emigration in Istanbul und der Amerikanische Geheimdienst Office of Strategic Services (O.S.S)," *Vierteljahreshefte für Zeitgeschichte* 4 (1992): 567–623.

Horn, Wolfgang. "Ein unbekannter Aufsatz Hitlers aus dem Frühjahr 1924." *Vierteljahreshefte für Zeitgeschichte* 16 (1968): 280–294.

Karpy, Daniel. "The Mufti of Jerusalem, Amin el Husseini, and his Political Activities during WWII (October 1941–July 1943)." *Hazionut (Zionism)* 9 (1971): 285–316. In Hebrew.

Karpy, Daniel. "The Mufti's Plan to Poison the Waters of Tel-Aviv." *HA-UMMA Quarterly, A Forum for National Thought*, No. 152 (Summer 2003): 37–41. In Hebrew.

Katz, Barry M. "The Criticism of Arms: The Frankfurt School Goes to War." *Journal of Modern History* 59 (1989): 439–478.

Katz, Barry M. "American Intelligence and the Holocaust: An Ambiguous Record." In *New Records – New Perspectives*, edited by Shlomo Aronson. Sede Boker: Ben-Gurion Research Center, 2002, pp. 54–64.

Kaufman, Menachem. "George Antonius and the United States: The Offspring of Palestinian Arab Relations with the United States." In *Contemporary Jewry, Studies in Honor of Moshe Davis*, edited by Geoffrey Wigoder. Jerusalem: The Institute of Contemporary Jewry, Hebrew University, 1984, pp. 21–51. In Hebrew.

Kaufman, William W. "Two American Ambassadors: Bullitt and Kennedy." In *The Diplomats 1919–1939*, edited by Gordon Craig and Felix Gilbert. Princeton, NJ: Princeton University Press, 1953, pp. 649–681.

Lanchester, John. "Bond in Torment." *London Review of Books*, September 5, 2002.

Marquardt-Bigman, Petra. "Amerikanische Geheimdienstanalysen des national-sozialistischen Deutschlands." *Tel-Aviver Jahrbuch für Deutsche Geschichte: Nationalsozialismus aus heutiger Perspektive* 23 (1994): 325–344.

Nicosia, Francis R. "Ein nützlicher Feind. Zionismus im nationalsozialistischen Deutschland 1933–1939." *Vierteljahreshefte für Zeitgeschichte* 37 (1989): 367–400.

Nicosia, Francis R. "The End of Emancipation and the Illusion of Preferential Treatment: German Zionism, 1933–1938." *Yearbook of the Leo Baeck Institute* 36 (1991): 243–265.

Oz-Salzberger, Fania. "Jewish Sources of the Modern Republic." *Tcheleth, A Periodical for Israeli Thought* 13 (2002): 89–130. In Hebrew.

Quazzaz, Ayad al. "The Iraqi-British War of 1941: A Review Article." *International Journal of Middle East Studies* 7 (October 1976): 591–596.

Reinharz, Jehuda. "Jewish Refugees from Germany in Palestine: The First Years (1932–1939)." In *National Jewish Solidarity in the Modern Period*, edited by Benjamin Pinkus and Ilan Troen. Sede Boker: Ben-Gurion University Press, 1988, pp. 173–194. In Hebrew.

Rotenstreich, Nathan. "Toynbee, Arnold Joseph" In *Encyclopedia Hebraica*, vol. 15. Jerusalem: Encyclopedia Publishing Company, 1966, pp. 408–413. In Hebrew.

Shapiro, David H. "The Haifa Office of Interrogation of Refugees from Enemy Territories." *Yad-Vashem Studies*. Forthcoming.

Stegemann, Bernd. "Hitler's Ziele im ersten Kriegsjahr 1939/1940." *Militärgeschichtliche Mitteilungen* 1 (1980): 92–103.

Terry, Nicholas. "Conflicting Signals: British Intelligence on the 'Final Solution' Through Radio Intercepts and Other Sources, 1941–1942." *Yad-Vashem Studies* 32 (Spring 2004).

Troen, Ilan. "Organizing the Rescue of Jews in the Modern Period." In *National Jewish Solidarity in the Modern Period*, edited by Benjamin Pinkus and Ilan Troen. Sede Boker: Ben-Gurion University Press, 1988, pp. 3–18. In Hebrew.

Vago, Bela. "The Budapest Jewry in Summer 1944." *Yad-Vashem Studies* 8 (1970): 81–105. In Hebrew.

Vago, Bela. "The British Government and the Fate of Hungarian Jewry in 1944." *Yad-Vashem Studies* (1971): 168–182. In Hebrew.

Weinberg, Gerhard L. "Hitler's Image of the United States." *The American Historical Review* 69 (July 1964): 1006–1021.

Weinberg, Gerhard L. "Hitler and England, 1933–1945: Pretence and Reality." *German Studies Review* 8 (May 1985): 299–309.

Weinberg, Gerhard L. "The Allies and the Holocaust." In *The Holocaust and History: The Known, the Unknown, the Disputed, and the Reexamined*, edited by Michael Berenbaum and Abraham J. Peck. Washington, DC and Bloomington, IN: Indiana University Press, 1998, pp. 480–491.

Wildt, Michael. "The SD and Palestine: New Evidence from Captured German Documents in Moscow." In *New Records – New Perspectives*, edited by Shlomo Aronson. Sede Boker: Ben-Gurion Research Institute, 2002, pp. 64–77.

Wilhelm, Hans-Heinrich. "Wie geheim war die 'Endlösung'?" In *Miscellanea: Festschrift für Helmut Krausnick*, edited by Wolfgang Benz. Stuttgart: Deutsche Verlags-Anstalt, 1980, pp. 131–148.

Witte, Peter, and Stephen Tyas. "A New Document on the Deportation and Murder of Jews during 'Einsatz Reinhardt' 1942." *Journal of Holocaust and Genocide Studies* 15, No. 3 (2001): 468–486.

Worman, Kurt. "German Jews in Israel: The Cultural Situation." *Leo Baeck Institute Yearbook* 15 (1970): 73–103.

Wyman, David S. "Why Auschwitz Was Never Bombed." *Commentary* 65, No. 5 (May 1978): 405–406.

Zuckerman, Lord. "The Doctrine of Destruction." *New York Review of Books*, March 19, 1990.

Zweig, Ronald W. "The Political Use of Military Intelligence: Evaluating the Threat of a Jewish Revolt against Britain during the Second World War." In *Diplomacy and Intelligence During the Second World War: Essays in Honor of H. F. Hinsley.* Cambridge: Cambridge University Press, 1985, pp. 109–125, 286–293.

Zweig, Ronald W. "Feeding the Camps: Allied Blockade Policy and the Relief of Concentration Camps in Germany, 1944–1945." *Historical Journal* 41, 3 (1998): 825–851.

Index